The Principalship

A Theory of Professional Learning and Practice

The Principalship

A Theory of Professional Learning and Practice

Ann Weaver Hart
University of Utah

Paul V. Bredeson
University of Wisconsin

McGraw-Hill, Inc.

New York   St. Louis   San Francisco   Auckland   Bogotá   Caracas   Lisbon
London   Madrid   Mexico City   Milan   Montreal   New Delhi
San Juan   Singapore   Sydney   Tokyo   Toronto

This book was developed by Lane Akers, Inc.

This book was set in Palatino by ComCom, Inc.
The editor was Lane Akers;
the production supervisor was Paula Keller.
The cover was designed by Yael Dresdner.
Project supervision was done by Tage Publishing Service, Inc.
Quebecor Printing/Fairfield was printer and binder.

THE PRINCIPALSHIP
A Theory of Professional Learning and Practice

This book is printed on acid-free paper.

1 2 3 4 5 6 7 8 9 0   FGR   FGR   9 0 9 8 7 6 5

ISBN 0-07-026913-0

Library of Congress Cataloging-in-Publication Data

Hart, Ann Weaver, (1948).
    The principalship: a theory of professional learning and practice / Ann Weaver
Hart, Paul V. Bredeson.
        p.   cm.
    Includes bibliographical references and index.
    ISBN 0-07-026913-0
    1. School principals—United States.   2. Educational leadership—
United States.   I. Bredeson, Paul V.   II. Title.
LB2831.92.H365   1996
371.2'012'0973—dc20   95-16628

BK
6785

About the Authors

ANN WEAVER HART is Dean of the Graduate School and Professor of Educational Administration at the University of Utah. Before her appointment as dean, she served as Associate Dean of the Graduate School of Education. Dr. Hart has been on the faculty of the University of Utah since 1984. Prior to beginning her academic career, she worked as a junior high school principal and a junior, middle, and senior high school teacher.

Dr. Hart's research and scholarship focus on two issues in educational organizations: (1) leadership and leader succession and (2) work design. In both her areas of scholarship, Dr. Hart brings an interactive, organizational theoretical perspective to her work, exploring the dynamics of relationships and change.

Dr. Hart is married to Randy Bret Hart, an attorney in Salt Lake City, and has four daughters, Kimberly, Liza, Emily, and Allyson. She enjoys hiking and camping in the Wasatch Mountains of Utah and backpacking in the West with her family. Her favorite leisure activity is reading fiction, history, and the history of science.

PAUL V. BREDESON is Professor of Educational Administration at the University of Wisconsin-Madison. Over the past 12 years, Dr. Bredeson's research has been centered on alternative conceptions of leadership, especially in regard to school principals. His research and scholarship are grounded in professional work experiences as a high school Spanish teacher, high school principal, federal project director for bilingual administrator training program, and as an executive director of a university school consortium. Dr. Bredeson has also been an active member of the National Policy Board for Educational Administration and has served as president of two national associations—the National Council of Professors of Educational Administration and the University Council for Educational Administration.

Dr. Bredeson is married to Mary Colleen Bredeson, a reading specialist in Stoughton, Wisconsin. They have two children, Erica and Christian. Dr. Bredeson is an avid gardener and enjoys long walks and biking through the rolling hills of southern Wisconsin.

Contents in Brief

Contents

Foreword

This book began in 1988 at the University Council for Educational Administration conference in Cincinnati, Ohio, although we did not know it at the time. Our colleagues, Richard A. Rossmiller and Diana Pounder, joined with us in a symposium organized by Pounder and Bredeson. We came together to discuss the discomfort we and many of our colleagues who had worked as both professors and school administrators felt with the level of distrust and disrespect we perceived between scholars who studied school administration and practitioners who "did" administration.

In Cincinnati, we talked about the attitudes and feelings of our professorial and practitioner colleagues. We also began to explore what we saw as a refusal to acknowledge the legitimacy and rigor of each other's activities by some members of the two groups. We believed then and believe even more strongly now that the activities, goals, and values that sustain rigorous scholarship and those that sustain the successful practice of school leadership are not only compatible but mutually supportive. This book represents our attempt to embody that belief in a method of preparing for and practicing school leadership. The book provides a method for applying rigorous applied scholarship to the practice of school leadership, observing the effects of that application (evaluation), and adjusting and reassessing as a result of that observation. We see this as the scholarship of practice—rigorously applying the knowledge of the profession to unique educational problems, observing outcomes, and adjusting and developing new actions appropriate to the situation.

Our work as teachers of administration also contributed to this book. We observed that many of our students were able to master successfully the content of leadership and principalship courses and seminars, but they treated this content knowledge as separate from and only vaguely related to their work as educators.

Cases, even when written by the students, seemed forced efforts to tie practice and theory together. Their formal study of leadership and organizational theory, represented by papers, essays, and test scores, provided no relief from their complaints about the too "theoretical" coursework and its lack of practical applicability to their work in schools. Admittedly, many of our students were working as teachers during their studies and had no opportunity to experience the phenomenon they studied, but this seemed to inflame rather than alleviate their discontent. Responses to essay assignments asking students to apply this content knowledge to an educational problem more often than not reverted to compendiums of conventional wisdom, assertions of belief, and personal stories.

The languages of scholarship and practice also limited our ability to communicate with students. One of us was once advised by a student to "buy a dictionary of common usage and use it." The other author learned from a student on a course evaluation that "at least my vocabulary has improved." Language embodies the norms, practices, beliefs, and values of those who use it, and the chasm between practice and scholarship we experienced was in part a linguistic one.

Finally, we found that different purposes separate inquiry by scholars from inquiry and action by professionals. The similarities and linkages that make these two forms of inquiry symbiotic appear to us to be poorly articulated in education. The easiest solution to this imprecision for most professors and administrators is to dismiss the relevance, usefulness, rigor, or importance of the knowledge-gathering and analysis activities of the other group.

As we already have said, this book represents our attempt to provide a method of preparing for and practicing school leadership that capitalizes on the strengths of inquiry in practice and scholarship. We begin with an introduction to the principalship and the process that inducts new administrators and teacher leaders into the profession of educational leadership in Chapter 1. Three forms of knowledge—experiential, empirical, and theoretical—form the basis of this discussion. These forms of knowledge provide a framework that principals can learn to systematically apply to the unique challenges each will face in her or his work.

Action is a fundamental difference between scholarship and professional practice. In Chapter 2, we introduce ways in which educational professionals can connect knowledge and action in their work. The professions share the features of expert thinking and the exercise of expertise we explore in this chapter. Expert thinking provides a way in which principals can apply their knowledge to the unique situations of practice they encounter. Patterns, types of problems, variables, and factors repeat but never in exactly the same combinations. Chapter 2 also reviews the development of and the current state of the professional knowledge base for school administration accepted by many in their field. In a scholarly environment in which concepts of social science, norms of inquiry, and standards for validating new knowledge are changing and in a rapidly changing practice environment, school leaders need help enhancing their ability to adapt and integrate new knowledge from many sources within their school contexts. In this chapter we visit shifting definitions of professional expertise and professional practice, from technical skills and competencies acquisition to theory application. We draw on Schon's concept of a "researcher in the practice context" to illustrate the processes of professional inquiry we develop through the rest of the book. Finally, we survey the most common problem-solving errors to which professionals are vulnerable. We return later in the book to methods school leaders can use to mitigate and avoid these errors.

Chapter 3 expands this discussion into leaders' social contexts. It introduces the social system of formal and informal relationships in schools and the dynamics emerging when a new formal leader (principal) is assigned. The chapter explores the features and patterns of interaction that develop between principals as members, albeit important members, of the social and technical systems of schools and the others who study and work there. Here the debate about the right and proper role of schools in society merges with debates about principals' roles, the role of teacher leadership, and students' roles and outcomes. Consequently, the chapter includes a discussion of social structure, technology broadly defined as the ways work is done, the people who populate schools and their conventional roles, and school environments. We sample studies of teachers', principals', students', and communities' and parents' concepts of their roles in schools.

The part principals play in this complex social environment forms the subject of Chapter 4. Here we emphasize repeatedly our conviction, borne out through research and experience, that principals exercise or fail to exercise leadership within a specific context. The interaction dynamics occurring when a new principal assumes the role of formal leader of a school structure the relationships that affect this leadership. Chapter 4 addresses leaderships' interdependence features—organization and leader. It introduces the reader to the school as the source of principal influence, ways in which the power of context can be tapped, and the mix of people, leaders, and events that shape the outcomes of this interaction. Relying on organizational socialization as the theoretical framework, the chapter provides for principals a perspective from which they can assess and plan their own taking-charge experiences.

In Chapter 5, we turn to principals' work, its characteristic features and tasks. While we avoid the job surveys and descriptions available in other texts, this chapter guides the reader through the transitions occurring when an educator moves from principal teacher to principal. It reviews the historic roots of the modern principalship from management, organization, educational administration theory to empirical research on principals and their work.

Unlike political leaders and informal leaders emerging from social movements, principals serve as formally appointed leaders in established social organizations. Chapter 6 specifically addresses the unique features of this reality—principals as formal leaders in schools. The chapter relies on several useful theoretical perspectives on this specific relationship: social role theory and power; traditional leadership studies on traits, the situation, leaders' behavior, and contingency, context, and culture; and frameworks for leadership based on skills, processes and responsibilities of effective leaders, principals as managers, and the formal leadership duality of tasks and people. It also explores the power of analogies for communicating leaderships' characteristics to others. These analogies include leader as developer of learning organizations; designer; teacher of teachers; steward; and symbol, potter, poet, actor, and healer. The chapter provides for each reader a view of the principal each would be were he or she to fill each of these views of the principal as the formal leaders in a school.

All leaders must at some point take charge. Leader succession is the transition of power from one formally appointed leader to another. Chapter 7 provides a look at the features of leadership during and resulting from leader succession. This appointment and taking-charge process is unavoidable for formal organizational leaders. Few principals ever establish new, entrepreneurial schools; most are appointed to lead existing organizations. This chapter confronts each principal's desire to be a leader and make a positive difference in one school. It surveys research reports of positive, negative, and neutral effects from leader succession in education and in other kinds of organizations. Elaborating on explanations for these observed differences, the chapter confronts the context, predecessor, personal and behavioral, and leader succession stages that influence the outcomes of leader succession.

The succession perspective of Chapter 7 expands in Chapter 8 to a social-symbolic look at leadership. This chapter presents principals' leadership as interaction with the professionals and students who work in a school. It explores motivation, interaction and structure; school culture; and processes of interaction.

The purpose of principals' leadership remains always to influence student and school outcomes. Chapter 9 addresses this outcome goal directly. It addresses guiding assumptions about principal influence on student learning, relationships between principals' instructional leadership behavior and school and student outcomes, direct and indirect impacts on student outcomes, and levels of impact (student, school, district, and beyond). In the process, this chapter explores the challenges and dilemmas principals face when choosing instructional leadership actions. Educational productivity factors used to assess outcomes: student ability, development, and motivation; instructional amount and quality; and psychological environments played out as the "curriculum of the home," morale or climate of the classroom social group, peer group outside of school, and minimum leisure-time television viewing are introduced and discussed. Principals' influence over these factors shape the final discussion and conclusions.

In Chapter 10, we turn to the process people experience when becoming a principal. The effects of social role (illustrated through theory in fiction and scholarship) are played out through role taking and role making. New and prospective principals observe, people experience transitions from teacher to principal, and educators are socialized as principals and as principals in a particular educational context. This chapter illuminates the social dynamics that attend each of these salient experiences in the professional lives of educational leaders. The chapter also provides data about principals—their education, experience, gender, ethnicity, and age profiles. However, we continue to emphasize in this view of the "becoming a principal" process that social forces influence role learning and shape the action choices all formal leaders, including principals, make in enacting their roles. We introduce principals in this chapter to disparate views of socialization to the principal's role—from students', teachers', and new principals' perspectives. In this chapter we confront the pressures, advantages, and disadvantages of on-the-job training experienced by new principals in the first year. The challenge to "make a role" or "make a mark" plays a major role in this experience.

In Chapter 11, we turn to the building blocks of expert thinking and leadership on which principals can draw to maximize their positive effects in schools. Drawing on the discussions in previous chapters, we elaborate leadership values and beliefs, professional knowledge and expertise, and processes and behaviors that emerge from the three forms of professional knowledge introduced in Chapter 1. These building blocks form the foundation for the theory of professional visualization we then introduce in Chapter 12.

Professional visualization makes professional learning and expert practice consistent with knowledge, values, and intentions. Chapter 12 is devoted to laying a professional development foundation for readers that will carry them through the early leadership experience and on to continuous professional growth. Professional visualization, then, is a means for creating deliberate structures, theories, or maps for taking action. In this chapter, we pull together the experiential, empirical, and theoretical knowledge discussed and applied through exercises in previous chapters. In this chapter, the reader explores a plan of action, a structure that will nurture and facilitate a lifetime of actions that maximize professional knowledge into action.

The intellectual journey that brought us to this book is unfinished. We each continue to work as scholars and practitioners of educational administration, experiencing each day the pressures for action with incomplete knowledge. However, we find the framework provided by professional visualization continually enhances the possibility for success in complex social organizations. The adventure is exciting; the goal is worthy. We hope our readers agree.

Preface

Most principalship texts are eclectic overviews of best current practice and their supporting theories and research. A few texts explore the principalship using specific points of view like reflective practice or instructional leadership. Whatever their approach, most of them fail to provide a clear organizing framework for school leadership, one that will enable principals to repeatedly adapt themselves to new and unique settings. They also fail to provide systematic ways in which novices can structure a professional self-concept that is keyed to school and student performance.

This text views the principalship as a social role in a complex social organization. Leadership involves far more than simply certifying oneself in easily defined skills and tasks. It is a complex social process in which authority must be socially and morally earned. Consequently, social role theory and social learning theory not only frame our book but guide its choice of topics and its instructional perspective. Examples of topics that are unique to this book include:

- Making transitions to formal leadership roles.
- Role taking and role making in the principalship.
- Mechanisms for accomplishing work in complex social systems.
- Leadership responsibilities and roles in self-managing work groups.
- Processes of leadership validation and influence (how to exert leadership).

This approach to the principalship is most timely since today's principals must face new, innovative school configurations, redesigned teacher roles, site-based governance, and school choice. Dealing with such problems requires that principals have a rich a flexible repertoire of professional skills. Otherwise, their education becomes too conventional and setting specific. Consequently, this book frames leadership in the social-psychology principals of formal work groups. Such principles are not role-bound or tradition-specific. Following is a list of the most important and unique features of our text.

1. *Social-Interaction Perspective*—We focus on leadership as a process of social interaction rather than a unidirectional form of influence. This view helps students adapt to both their initial and subsequent leadership experiences.
2. *Work Group Focus*—Work groups at various levels (school, department, classroom) are used as the basic unit of analysis and are examined during periods of change as well as stability.
3. *Ongoing Focus on Instructional Leadership*—Rather than treating instructional leadership as a discrete topic to be dealt with in one or two chapters, we treat it as an ongoing theme throughout the text.
4. *Diagnostic Focus*—We offer specific methods for diagnosing the social and cultural context of schools, so that principals will be able to understand the unique characteristics of each school they are assigned to lead.
5. *Reflective Approach*—Since nearly all administration students are experienced teachers, our text legitimizes their experience by repeatedly asking them to reflect on the information presented.

ACKNOWLEDGMENTS

Few text authors can sculpt their ideas into polished form without help from colleagues and students. We would like begin our acknowledgements by expressing our appreciation to our many graduate students whose critical views and penetrating questions have forced us back to the drawing board on many occasions. We also wish to express our thanks to the many reviewers whose insightful comments and suggestions have helped us through the seemingly endless process of drafting and redrafting the manuscript. These include Bruce Barnett, University of Northern Colorado; Fred Carver, University of Georgia; Sharon Conley, University of Maryland; John Greer, Georgia State University; Cecil Miskel, University of Michigan; Karen Osterman, Hofstra University; and Kent Peterson, University of Wisconsin.

Without the ongoing emotional and intellectual support that our families and partners provided this project would have been impossible. Heartfelt thanks to Randy Hart and Mary Bredson. Finally, our editor, Lane Akers, provided invaluable guidance in getting the project off the ground and much needed encouragement whenever our energy faltered.

Ann Weaver Hart

Paul V. Bredeson

Introduction to the Principalship:

Induction to Professional Knowledge

Sitting at a bare desk in my new office I found myself staring at the name plate on the door—**PRINCIPAL'S OFFICE.** I remembered my first day in the classroom ten years earlier when similar feelings of excitement, anxiety, and bewilderment created an almost paralyzing spell that quickly evaporated when the eight o'clock bell rang and 25 well-tanned and wildly energetic freshmen came into the room for their first class of introductory Spanish. I snapped into high instructional gear and soon wondered how I'd get my final grades turned in by June 2.

As I thought about beginning my job as a principal, I realized that I could wait for someone to come into my office or for the telephone to ring. No doubt there would be plenty of people and events competing for my time and helping to shape what I was supposed to do as the high school principal. It wasn't that I hadn't thought about the principalship and what I would do if I were "in charge." After all, I had worked in schools for a decade, completed an advanced degree in educational administration, obtained a professional license certifying my preparation, and convinced the district selection team that I was the best candidate to fill the job. I wanted, however, to be proactive, not reactive, in how I came to understand and carry out my work as a school principal. My eyes returned to the name plate on my door—**PRINCIPAL'S OFFICE.**

As a reader and aspiring administrator, you may be surprised that someone sitting in the principal's office might still have lingering questions about the job. Our purpose in presenting this scenario is to emphasize the need for you to take an active part in constructing your own role and work as a principal. What is it you need to know? What are the sources of knowledge on which you should draw? How can you come to understand more completely the principal's role, its demands and its possibilities? How can you learn to apply your knowledge to your professional work within this role?

Professional work is a continuous process of learning and application, questioning and development—in part because the knowledge bases of professions grow continuously, and the settings in which this knowledge is applied change. Quality school leadership requires an eclectic array of knowledge, skills, and talents from educators, along with flexibility and a sense of humor. A good principal must teach, learn, and lead simultaneously. She acquires and uses the specialized knowledge of teaching to help young people learn while continuing to learn herself. Curriculum, instructional theory and innovations, technology, law, and the rules and regulations of her district and state require constant learning and updating. A principal uses knowledge about children, youth, and adults working and learning together to lead. Charisma offers another source of authority. If these fail, and the principal relies only on the power of position, no authority other than hierarchy stands behind her (French & Raven, 1959; Yukl, 1989).

At the same time, the complex social environment of the school demands that the principal master the norms, expectations, and assumptions shaping the beliefs and behavior of teachers, students, and the community. Schools are the only complex work organizations in which work processes and outcomes for children and youth are intimately tied to adults' work processes and outcomes. All this takes place in a "fishbowl" of public interest, concern, and criticism.

In this book, we depart from most traditional examinations of the principalship. Rather than introducing you, the aspiring principal, to the technical tasks, responsibilities, or skills included in principals' job descriptions, we rely on other authors' work and on your own experience as educators for these technical introductions. Drawing on these materials and on examples from practice as references, we introduce social processes and analytical techniques that will enhance your ability to apply this knowledge to the actions you take as an educational leader. These techniques will allow you to draw on the combined professional resources of those who work in schools and to promote improved learning cycles that include your own experiences throughout your professional career. We hope that this book will provide you with a framework to which you can return repeatedly as you grow and develop.

Our commitment to this approach began at a professional conference at which we confronted our own and our colleagues' ambivalence about knowledge, practice, research, and the profession of educational administration. We each experienced disjunction and angst during our careers as we moved from school administration to the professorship and then worked to connect our scholarship and teaching with our profession. We also felt dismay at the contempt with which our former colleagues in administration viewed our "retreat" to the "ivory tower" of scholarship and the lack of respect many of our new colleagues demonstrated for the practice of school administration. These mutual feelings of distrust and disrespect are more than a difference in the nature of daily activities; they represent a fundamental refusal to acknowledge the legitimacy of each other's activities, goals, and values. They create a context of competition and conflict that not only reflects the differences between theory and practice but glorifies them.

Having worked in both professions—school administrator and university professor—and remained proud of our achievements, we were painfully aware of our failures and shortcomings, and personally informed of the challenges facing administrators and professors. In many ways, we started over in a new career when we left K–12 administration, but we had not expected the depth and breadth of this change to be as great as they were. After all, we were simply teaching and writing about what we formerly did, or at least we thought so at the beginning.

Our work as teachers of administration has contributed to the perspective taken in this book. We observed that many of our students were able to conquer the content of leadership and principalship courses and seminars, but that they treated this content knowledge as separate from, and only vaguely related to, their work as educators. Cases, even when written by them, seemed forced efforts to tie practice and theory together. Formal tests in leadership and organizational theory seminars resulted in a bevy of A's and B's for our students but led to no reduction in their complaints about the "theoretical" course work and its lack of practical applicability to work in schools. Responses to essay questions asking them to apply their knowledge to an educational problem more often than not resulted in treatises of conventional wisdom, stories, and beliefs.

The languages of scholarship and practice also limit our ability to communicate to students. One of us was advised by a student on a course evaluation form to "buy a dictionary of common usage and use it." The other received a similar comment: "This course has certainly increased my vocabulary." Language embodies the norms, practices, beliefs, and values of those who use it, and the chasm between practice and scholarship we have experienced is in part a vocabulary, syntax, and argot gap.

Finally, we have observed that the differences between the purposes of inquiry by professional practitioners and the purposes of inquiry by scholars are poorly articulated, by professors as well as by practitioners. The easiest solution to this lack of clarity is, for most professors and administration students, to simply dismiss the relevance, usefulness, rigor, or importance of each other's knowledge-gathering activities. In one interview study, our practitioner colleagues described rigorous, refereed journal articles as "cute." One of our professor colleagues said in reference to administrator preparation programs, "I'm not interested in practice." The result of this mutual dismissal is the reinforcement of the ticket-punching mentality by some students of educational administration (If I have to have your degree to get my certificate or license, then I'll just have to get your degree, but let's both be clear about it—you have nothing of value to offer me.) and support for professors' allegations that their students lack analytical and problem-solving skills and are sloppy thinkers.

No growth and development in the educational leadership profession will result from professionals who demonstrate a systematic contempt for knowledge and learning and professors who demonstrate contempt for practice. This is, after all, a professional field that exists because a profession exists, and that profession benefits from the presence of educated and analytical practitioners. We have tested the techniques presented in the chapters that follow in our own professional work prior to becoming professors, and also as university administrators since we became professors, and we have found them useful and enlightening. We also have discovered that we sometimes can find little or no application for some of the discipline-based content that creeps into formal educational administration study under the rubric of the knowledge base. This is a bitter pill to swallow, especially when it includes some of the content we teach in our own seminars and courses, but it provides an important test. The basic disciplines contribute a necessary conceptual foundation for our work as educational administrators, and we must be able to consciously draw the conceptual and applied connections between these disciplines and educational practice. We believe that professors should not rely on the assertion that any particular content is important to justify their curriculum, pedagogy, or philosophical orientation. At the same time, we believe that educational administration students who reject the insights of systematic scholarship because they personally have not experienced the phenomena or outcomes reported represent the worst possible future for education and a guarantee that the future will recreate the past, unmodified by new ideas, growth, and development. As you read, we hope you will become increasingly comfortable with both the complexity and indeterminacy of practice and the usefulness of professional knowledge to practitioners seeking to maximize their success in the complex contexts of educational leadership.

PROFESSIONAL TRANSITIONS

As you pursue your studies in school leadership and choose to become school leaders, you will confront a major adult learning experience—induction into the profession of administration and into a new set of adult relationships. This induction process requires that you learn not only regulations, laws, budgeting and planning principles, conflict management, group decision-making processes, and a plethora of other formal skills and knowledge but also new cultural and social knowledge imbedded in the profession of administration (Duke, 1987). You will take on formal social leadership, a role carrying the expectation that you can and will simultaneously lead groups of highly educated and independent professionals and that you will grow and develop personally.

Leadership in schools requires far more than simple competence in discrete skills and tasks. Certainly, a high school principal must build a master schedule; an elementary school principal must be able to plan and orchestrate back-to-school night. But leadership—influence on people's beliefs, values, aspirations, and behavior, and encouragement and support toward the achievement of shared goals—is more than the exercising of formal authority in the role of principal. It is a complex social process requiring validation by the group in a reciprocal relationship of mutual and interactive effects (Dornbusch & Scott, 1975; Hart, 1993). In schools, teachers form the core work group of adults whom principals aspire to lead. Expert professional knowledge used by the best school leaders comes from their own and their peers' discrete and concrete experiences, from research on a broad range of subjects related to learning and educational organizations, and from concepts and theories related to students' learning and to schools.

This book approaches school leadership from a social interaction perspective, asserting that teachers, parents, students, and others intimately involved in schools form the powerful human resource that principals must marshal toward the accomplishment of shared goals—students' learning and well-being. We draw on knowledge in many forms to examine the interaction dynamics that make school leaders more successful in their work, but we make no claim that the illustrations we provide include even a substantial proportion of the knowledge on which you will draw as a school leader. The acquisition of leadership skills, competencies, tasks, and roles dominates the perspective of many books on the principalship. Other texts focus on formal roles and job description categories like personnel administration, budgeting, planning, teacher supervision, and public relations. We believe that the acquisition of concrete skills and the mastery of set roles are important parts of, but only the first steps in, developing expert professional knowledge about school leadership. This knowledge, once acquired, must be constantly adjusted, applied, and transferred to new situations and to the facilitation and empowerment of others (Reitzug, 1994). New knowledge must be added, and its impact on old beliefs and practices evaluated, if a professional is to grow and develop appropriately.

In contrast to perspectives that view preparation for the principalship as the acquisition of competencies and skills, we examine transitions to the principal's formal leadership role as a process through which one person seeks to affect others by the force of socially validated authority and legitimation using knowledge in many forms. The successful practitioner of this kind of leadership constantly connects the resources and talents of all aspects of a school's instructional system to help forge an effective and productive professional effort (Dwyer, Lee, Rowan & Bossert, 1983). Certainly, knowledge, skill, and competence are the foundation of this process, but they are only the beginning. The process is dynamic, and change and creative leadership by principals often require that they take and make new roles, marshal social influence to get the work done in schools, and exert influence on self-managing professional groups (groups of teachers).

We define leadership as reciprocal influence, interaction, and connection among talented, educated, and dedicated professionals—a process of validation by teachers (primarily) of their principals. We examine examples from the literature on leadership and schools that support this definition. Through reciprocal influence, teachers grant principals the authority to act on their behalf and on the behalf of the school. Without this legitimate, socially validated professional authority, principals are left with little more than formal rules and regulations that they constantly must enforce. We believe that socially validated authority is the core of leadership in professional organizations, and decades of research on leadership in social groups affirm this belief. Simply put, mutual trust guides the relationship, and this trust does *not* require that people always agree.

Principals, as school leaders and members of a profession, possess a body of professional knowledge. They hold this knowledge in concert as a group rather than as individuals. Some principals understand and use computer management systems to monitor student progress with facility; other principals excel in instructional leadership and professional development activities; still others shine when marshaling community resources to achieve a reduction in dropout rates or an increase in education and community collaboration of social services. All of these achievements fill central needs in schools, and the mastery of the necessary skills has a place in the core knowledge of the school administration profession. Not all professional school administrators possess these skills and knowledge equally. In this sense, school administration is like other professions. Although a body of professional knowledge exists, it vests in the group of professionals as a whole rather than in individual practitioners of the profession who accept and use it with varying talent and facility (Connell & Peck, 1993). Research reports, collected writings, differences in philosophical approaches, varying techniques, and personal experience and orientation all affect how individuals function within the profession. The combination of all these writings, practices, and points of view makes up the profession at large. Dominant perspectives and approaches may evolve and change, but the *profession* includes them all—peripheral, central, dominant, developing.

This accumulated group knowledge is not static. As a profession grows and develops, practitioners acquire and apply new knowledge and skills drawn from a variety of sources. Individual professionals, too, grow and develop. Consequently, professional knowledge (unlike knowledge in an academic field such as chemistry or sociology) changes with the experiences of practitioners as well as with the outcomes of research. Practice, research, and theory in professional fields shape the knowledge base. A major disease outbreak such as Legionnaires' disease or AIDS, for example, drives research and practice in health care as powerfully as do new discoveries in gene theory, microbiology, or biochemistry. A literacy crisis among young people in our large urban centers sparks reading research more energetically than advances in cognitive psychology and schema theory. The professions thus span the boundaries between experiential, empirical, and theoretical knowledge.

Professionals must be able to span these boundaries in order to draw simultaneously on the best new knowledge and the most salient experiences. As research and development provide information useful to them, and as theories help them make sense of the problems they encounter in practice, professionals develop a working consensus about the knowledge base of their profession and about its use in daily work. This developmental feature of knowledge in the professions means that knowledge comes in a variety of forms and from different sources—experience, research, and theory (Garrison, 1986). No hierarchy dictates which source of knowledge is superior. Professionals are accountable for their actions based on the combined sources of knowledge. Professionals exercise expert judgment as they deal with problems of practice. Ultimately, professionals are highly pragmatic. They attempt to resolve problems, not to reify one form of knowledge.

Educators face their own unique set of challenges as they seek to apply experiential, research, and theoretical knowledge to the professional decisions they make. They must concentrate their professional efforts on a complex combination of personal, social, organizational, and process factors that affect learning outcomes for children and youth while, at the same time, working to create and preserve work environments that are accepted by parents and their communities and that appeal to effective adult teachers who shape students' learning and lives. For example, a first grader may face the morning with no breakfast, walk to school through a neighborhood where shootings occur regularly, attend a school where the schedule conflicts with her parents' work schedules, and face instruction tailored to a learning style different from her own. While principals seek to address various students' learning problems, they must also find training and development opportunities for teachers, strive for compensation and work structures that appeal to teachers, respond to parents' concerns about the school schedule (that may conflict with teachers' needs and desires), and coordinate a myriad of additional organizational and personal factors. Students must be able to feel hopeful about their futures and fundamentally affirmed in their studies. Effective teachers must find the school workplace supportive and fulfilling or they will leave for greener pastures. Numerous studies report that the best and brightest teachers find the current school work environment less appealing than do their less able peers, and that they leave the education profession in much higher numbers (National Governors' Association, 1986; Carnegie Forum on Education and the Economy, 1986).

Educational administration is concerned with all these factors. Consequently, educational administrators face problems, dynamics, and challenges different from those addressed by other educational professionals. At the individual level, principals must attend to the use of resources and the best new knowledge about learning to help each child learn. This may require the use of specific research from cognitive psychology or even neuroscience. At the classroom level, principals are responsible for supervising the instruction and the learning environment of each child and of groups of children. This may require the use of knowledge from sociology, psychology, social psychology, and anthropology. At the school level, principals also are responsible for organizing and leading an adult workplace, which requires an understanding of adult developmental psychology, industrial and personnel social psychology, and work design principles. They consider instruction and curriculum, child and adolescent development and psychological health, and social growth for youth and children. When working alongside teachers, principals apply their knowledge of facilitation, support, and critique to stimulate the talents and resources of the faculty toward the achievement of their goals. In addition to the disciplines just mentioned, principals may need to be familiar with history, marketing, philosophy, and applied ethics.

All these tasks and responsibilities require complex professional knowledge. We began this chapter by asserting that principals teach, learn, and lead. In fact, principals accomplish their most important professional work by becoming voracious learners about teaching, learning, and professional organization, thus influencing and shaping the motivation, commitment, and action of other professionals. When they are successful, principals lead groups of adult professionals in united efforts to improve the learning of individual young people and enhance overall school effectiveness. Their success depends on their ability to influence the actions of groups of people toward the accomplishment of common goals. Educational administration thus stands as a field of professional practice within education—the practice of educational leadership (Duke, 1987).

Throughout the following pages, we examine the knowledge and social forces shaping the professional practice of people in one of the most important major roles filled by educational administrators—that of the school principal. We begin our examination of the school principal by introducing the current state of professional experiences with the knowledge, values, and skills related to the principalship, ways in which principals and other professionals acquire the knowledge of practice, and the application of that knowledge to the problems of practice in professional work groups. After exploring the experiential knowledge of school leaders and the work of the principal in the school, we move to research revealing important empirical knowledge about schools and leaders. Last, we explore theories about schools, organizations, and adult workplaces that both frame and challenge top-down beliefs and practices about leadership in schools. We discuss the social transition to leadership and the visualization and professional theorizing that will help you apply your growing knowledge to the practice of your chosen profession. This final section ends with a chapter designed to help you develop a personal framework for visualizing leadership and a plan for theorizing in a practice context directed toward action.

We rely throughout this text on three primary sources of knowledge—experience, research, and theory. The distinctions among these are not as clear as this discussion implies, however. Learning is an interactive process through which people use their experiences along with other sources of knowledge to alter their frameworks (theories) for making sense of knowledge and making action decisions (Boud, Keogh & Walker, 1985). We strive to emphasize throughout the book that this iterative process lasts a lifetime and involves reflection on knowledge from many sources. Growth and development require that learning affect beliefs and actions, and sources of knowledge exist along a continuum from the totally concrete and experiential to the totally abstract and theoretical. We are committed to the belief that a profession's progress depends on an iterative process in which knowledge and action are interactive and mutually influential. Thus, we often ask you to reflect on your own professional learning and action.

In this first chapter, we introduce steps critical to your success, as many of our readers seek to become school leaders and grow and develop in that leadership role. These steps are not exclusive to school leadership, but our discussion will focus on examples and implications from school leadership. First, we examine the induction to principals' knowledge, values, and skills on which many of you are embarking. This dynamic experience includes the introduction of knowledge through professional socialization processes. For each new principal, professional socialization is complemented and adjusted by induction to a particular school—its culture, beliefs, needs, and environments. Socialization is universal in its processes but unique in its content for each new principal in each school setting. Consequently, organizational socialization also plays an important part.

Next, we introduce the forms of knowledge that guide and organize the remainder of the book—experiential, research based or empirical, and theoretical. We discuss the continuum of abstraction these forms of knowledge represent. The contributions of each to an expert professional's development and practice structure the substance of this discussion. The usefulness of these different forms of knowledge depends on a professional's ability to reflect on knowledge and personalize and internalize it so that knowledge becomes a regular input into the decision-making process. Schon (1983) calls this professional process reflection-in-action and reflection-on-action. Reflection-in-action and reflection-on-action repeatedly figure in our discussion of the processes through which beginning professionals learn to connect their knowledge with their decisions and actions in subsequent chapters (Schon, 1983, 1987). Finally, we lay out a specific process we call professional visualization that will help you develop as a school leader and apply new knowledge to the practice of your profession on an ongoing basis.

INDUCTION TO PRINCIPALS' KNOWLEDGE, VALUES, AND SKILLS

The concrete details of work for principals differ from school to school, yet principals share similar social experiences and global goals (Bredeson, 1985, 1991b). This similarity within differences characterizes administrative leadership, although each organization includes very different people with various goals and requires carefully planned and unique actions. The processes through which these elements are brought together are much the same from site to site (Schein, 1985).

Administrative work is also diverse, fragmented, fast-paced, and immediate, making it difficult for new principals to take control over their own time. Classic studies of managerial work describe it as diverse, fragmented, short-term, verbal, and action-oriented (Mintzberg, 1973). Similar studies of elementary and high school principals affirm that the school work environment often pressures principals into a fire-fighting mentality. Brief (three minutes or less) verbal interactions dominate many principals' days and make reflection, thoughtfulness, or strategic planning an elusive goal (Kmetz & Willower, 1982; Martin & Willower, 1981).

In addition to a fragmented work environment pressuring them to react rather than act on a regular basis, new principals must carefully diagnose and analyze dilemmas and problematic situations that arise in order to act effectively. Yet many find themselves having difficulty seizing control over their activities and time. Because the work is unfamiliar and nonroutine, it at first requires deliberate thought even to complete ubiquitous organizational and administrative tasks. Equally vexing is the problem of determining what is immediate versus what is important. As principals gain experience and learn from it, they find many of these complex tasks less distracting because they are routine and require little conscious attention. Research on the induction and professional socialization of principals repeatedly emphasizes the pervasive sense of overload experienced by new principals. Careful forethought and planning can help aspiring principals prepare for this induction period.

Professional Induction and Socialization

The first-time ascent to school leadership carries with it a unique set of experiences; they will never be repeated. This assignment involves many firsts: first formal leadership in a school, first professional membership in the particular school or, if an insider, first leadership role in the school, first induction experience into leadership, first socialization into the role of leader. Depending on the mix of experiences and context, a new leader may be facing additional firsts.

These first experiences shape the future. Induction and socialization to a new profession have such profound and long-lasting effects that a body of theory and research in the social and administrative sciences focuses exclusively on this unique and critical time in adult careers. Duke asserted that induction to the profession of educational administration teaches aspiring professionals "the importance of specialized knowledge (expertise), as well as the values and ethics that guide the use of this knowledge" (1987, p. 262). Greenfield (1985a; 1991) emphasized the power of newly learned values, ethics, and expectations during the "moral socialization" of new principals. Greenfield's argument highlights the important part played by professional character-building experiences for new principals.

While professional socialization has dramatic impacts on the future for principals as well as other professionals, it is not a clearly defined and discrete period of time in an educator's work life. Although principals often mark the end of their professional socialization with the end of their first year in the principalship, this landmark may result as much from the school calendar as it does from the real and personal experiences of any single principal (Duke, Isaacson, Sagor & Schmuck, 1984; Hart, 1988; Oliver, forthcoming). Actually, induction to the principalship begins when one is a teacher, because almost all school principals are teachers first. Their early, salient, and vivid experiences as educators occur in classrooms with children and youth. If you are currently in the throes of induction, having made the decision to explore educational administration as a career direction, this book is designed to help you form a plan to shape that experience. We also hope that it will provide a framework with which you can structure your developing career and personal growth as a school leader.

Induction experiences vary markedly in different settings. As we pointed out earlier, professional socialization to educational administration begins with your socialization as a teacher and continues through the anticipation of an administration career, preservice formal training, the first years of the principalship, and ongoing professional growth. Educational leadership, however, is not reserved to principals (Wasley, 1991). Leadership and teacher socialization often meld in schools where people acknowledge the critical contribution professionals possessing varied knowledge and experience bring to the definition and solution of educational problems. Changes in teacher leadership and mentor roles also affect leadership opportunities in education (Bird & Little, 1983).

We therefore affirm the leadership experiences of many educators. These precede their interest in educational administration, and we hope that you will draw on similar experiences as you work through this book. Your individual experiences are fundamental to preliminary socialization and development processes that contribute to your preparation for formal school leadership positions. Teacher leadership growth in schools contributes to the mix of talent and energy devoted to solving educational problems. This mix may lead you to a formal leadership position as a principal, or it may reinforce your desire to be an educational leader while remaining in your current role. Our focus in this book is on the former, but we believe that the knowledge-to-action techniques that you learn will serve you well whatever your decision.

When educators choose to expand their formal preparation for leadership by seeking professional education in school administration, they declare to their colleagues their intention to seek leadership opportunities. Candidacy (or preparation) for administrative positions leads to the development of an administrative perspective through interpersonal and social processes and as a result of the immediate context (Greenfield, 1977a, 1977b). It often requires that people gradually divest themselves of their identities as teachers or largely reshape their professional self-concepts (Hart, 1993). New principals learn an unfamiliar body of knowledge related directly to expanded organizational and community perspectives and then learn ways to adapt, thrive, and prosper in their new roles as they help others achieve their educational goals.

This expanded or altered perspective may place stress on your individual self-concept as a professional educator, on your relationship with your colleagues, and on your beliefs about the generally prescribed organizational role to which you aspire. Professional socialization thus performs a critical part in the development of professional expertise among principals. Greenfield (1985a) argued that two main purposes drive the professional socialization of principals—moral socialization and technical socialization. Moral socialization endows aspiring and new principals with the values, beliefs, and attitudes shared by the existing members of the group. It makes new members sensitive to and accepting of the norms of practice. Technical socialization provides aspiring and new principals with the knowledge, skills, and techniques (the technology of school leaders by Scott's [1987] definition) needed to perform well. Patience and perseverance with this developmental process can provide you with a solid foundation on which to build a satisfying and productive career. Knowledge about the process will help you overcome less-than-ideal circumstances and capitalize on good experiences.

The new principal should not, however, expect to acquire *all* the technical knowledge and skills that will make him an excellent leader in multiple settings for the rest of his career. You will discover many wonderful sources of technical knowledge—from conflict management to site-based decision making, to technological innovations. Technical socialization refers to the *fundamental* technical knowledge needed to perform at a basic, competent level. The framework of this book relies on the assumption that professional school principals continually acquire new technical and moral knowledge and that technical and moral socialization simply begin that process.

A number of important studies shape knowledge about this critical period for new principals (Duke et al., 1984; Greenfield, 1985a). Duke and his colleagues (1984) asked successful veteran principals and currently working novices to reflect on their first years in the principalship. From these new school leaders' reflections, they constructed a model of principals' professional socialization that included four features. These four features were: (1) duration of the socialization period; (2) mechanisms of socialization; (3) relationships between early expectations and the realities of the job encountered; and (4) the formal and informal preparation new leaders received for a career in school administration.[1] The sample of veteran principals said that their experiences as teachers were an important part of their overall socialization to educational leadership. Consequently, the researchers argued that anticipatory socialization—a time period emphasized by a number of other scholars of socialization (Van Maanen, 1976)—must be included in any framework for understanding induction to the principalship. Your professional thinking and behavior as a principal have already been partially shaped by your experiences as a teacher.

Socialization research findings support the argument that anticipation of leadership plays a part in shaping school leaders' beliefs about themselves and about school leaders in general. Duke and his colleagues envisioned a set of experiences for each new school leader that would help the new professional move from anticipation through entry into the principalship. From their research, they saw these experiences ending with a period of intense development or *metamorphosis* (using Van Maanen's term) in the first formal leadership assignment. In other words, when a new principal takes on the role of designated and official leader in a school, these first-time experiences shape forever her beliefs and skills as an educator.

Although most newly appointed principals work for some time in university degree programs, in internships, and in other positions in schools that provide them with leadership experiences (such as assistant principal), veteran principals argue that professional socialization extends well into the first year of the principalship and, for some, beyond the first year (Parkay, Currie & Rhodes, 1992). Even during the period of formal university study, informal interactions with faculty, school administrators, and other students shape principals' development perhaps more than formal course work.

The experiences veteran principals have shared about their own evolving and gradual development as leaders should be seen as an affirmation of human development rather than as a limitation and a discouraging factor in professional growth. Feelings of newness and vulnerability many principals describe are not unique, nor should they be accompanied by the apprehension that they presage inadequacy or failure. Each major milestone in professional and personal development brings with it uncertainty and self-doubt. Ascension to leadership in schools should not be an exception to this rule, if only because it carries with it responsibility for adult teachers' satisfaction and growth and—*most important*—responsibility for the learning and future of young people.

---

[1]Others examine the stages of principal professional socialization (Daresh, 1986; Roberts & Wright, 1989; Parkay, Currie & Rhodes, 1992). We return to this body of research in greater detail in later chapters as we discuss the research on professional socialization and the theories that illuminate patterns in the socialization experience.

Socialization can be formal and informal, but few new principals benefit from the support available through formal socialization experiences. More commonly, urban and suburban school districts have administrator mentor programs. However, even when such formal socialization processes are not present, aspiring principals can draw on what they have learned about leadership in other formal and informal roles. Many new principals merely receive written job descriptions which often are vague and offer little guidance about specific expectations held by the district. Others receive a summary of rules and regulations or a school year calendar of expected activities. The lack of formal processes for inducting and socializing new principals reflects a historical belief that educators "know" what they need to do. In the current and complex reality in which schools operate, this trusting belief is misplaced. For example, the National Policy Board for Educational Administration recently endorsed an initiative by the Chief State School Officers to develop national standards for school principals. The vagueness of induction components and specified professional knowledge makes principal evaluation problematic as well. Few generally accepted and clear criteria exist in the profession on which school leaders can rely when evaluating principals.

Induction and socialization to school leadership thus are spotty for many beginning principals. They seldom have structured, formal opportunities to meet regularly with other new principals to talk about shared experiences or with groups of experienced principals the district might want them to see as models for exemplary practice. They seldom talk openly about changes the superintendent or school board would like to see in a particular school, in the district at large, or in systemic priorities and goals. The meetings they do attend often include all principals and focus on short-term problems, thus providing little in the way of activities uniquely designed for new members of the group (Greenfield, 1985a, 1991).

Instead of formal socialization, Duke and his colleagues found that principals learn about the expectations held for them and about valued norms of conduct and belief from principals with whom they work, from predecessors, secretaries, and teachers in the school to which they are assigned, and from central office administrators to whom they are accountable. The prevalence of this reliance on informal socialization was labeled by Duke and his colleagues a "sink or swim" strategy. If the secretaries want a new principal to succeed and are open with information and willing to help, success is likely. If staff are hostile or peers are unfriendly and information is withheld, problems are more likely to develop (Hart, 1993).

Numerous instances of these situations probably come to mind out of your own experience. For example, a secretary may be a good sounding board as a new principal tries to understand local school traditions. The principal can benefit from reminders about ordering ceremonial supplies for school graduation. As a first-year high school principal, one of the authors remembers vividly approaching baccalaureate and graduation ceremonies without tassels for students' mortar boards. The credits had been earned, the faculty were ready, and the graduation processionals had been rehearsed, but no one ever told me I was supposed to order the tassels!

The prevalence of the sink or swim strategy may also account for the power of surprise to shape the professional socialization of new principals. Most new principals begin with a set of expectations that contrast sharply with the realities of the job (Duke et al., 1984). No matter how many years an educator spends as a teacher, the entry into a formal leadership role (even in the same school or district), with new expectations and reshaped personal relationships carries with it "surprise and sensemaking" (Louis, 1980). This surprise can be debilitating or exhilarating, but new principals, indeed all professionals beginning work in a new setting, should definitely expect to experience and deal with it. The surprise is certain; successful sensemaking depends on the person's response.

From this description of the induction period, one can see that other people exert tremendous influence over most new principals' induction and professional socialization. New principals say the teachers in the school to which they are first assigned as principals exert the most important influence on their early development as school leaders. This influence is followed by that of assistant principals and students. "Consistent with the general literature on socialization, first-year principals seem to be very concerned about their acceptance by others and gratified when it occurs" (Duke et al., 1984, p. 23).

New principals must be aware, however, that sources of influence and sources of satisfaction and support differ. In research on new principals, teachers are named the primary sources of both satisfaction and dissatisfaction by new principals (Greenfield, 1985a). Social science research affirms that salient groups affect our sense of well-being in positive and negative ways. Consequently, your spouse or partner will have a great deal more influence over your beliefs, attitudes, and interpretations of self than do friends or casual acquaintances. You care what they think (Monane, 1967). Teachers' impacts on principals emanate in part from their expectations and beliefs about what principals are and do. Teachers' beliefs about the longevity of a principal's effects also influence principals' initial socialization. This may be the result of an attitude commonly expressed by teachers that "principals come and principals go, but we'll still be here" (Cosgrove, 1986). Given the common career patterns of school principals, as a new principal you need to be aware of your own plans and the influence of others' expectations on those plans.

Studies of attempts by school districts to change principals' beliefs and actions after socialization has taken place illustrate the resilience of the habits and values established by this process. Leithwood, Steinback, and Begley (in press), for example, studied an attempt to link preservice and early career experiences with instructional leadership activities by principals. Their results were discouraging. Following an extensive training program, preservice and inservice principals were able and eager to voice instructional leadership values and praised their socialization experiences. They valued opportunities to learn through socialization when learning related directly to their work and occurred in schools. The disappointment came when instructional leadership effects were measured independent of principals' reports of their experiences. The researchers surveyed principals who had worked with the instructional leadership development project. They found that formal experiences with instructional leadership socialization had no effect on the comparative value and importance principals placed on instructional leadership tasks in their work as opposed to technical, managerial, or oversight tasks. In other words, deeply imbedded valuing of managerial tasks, budget, scheduling, and other traditional oversight tasks overshadowed instructional leadership in the daily work lives of principals. One might well conclude from this outcome that the values and beliefs established early in an education career and the immediate demands of daily work have strong effects on principals despite their newness to a leadership assignment. One also might conclude that educational organizations cannot expect instructional leadership from their principals until they evaluate principals on their instructional leadership with weight equal to budgeting, public relations, scheduling, and other managerial tasks. No one with any sense commits career suicide. The criteria to which evaluations are tied cannot be separated from principals' work.

Many scholars and practitioners interested in improving the outcomes of the induction process for school leaders work to change formal courses in educational administration programs in universities. They also seek carefully articulated and planned internships and field experiences designed to shape new principals' beliefs and values as well as their discrete skills. Peer Assisted Leadership (PAL), developed by a group of colleagues at the Far West Laboratory for Educational Research in San Francisco, California, is one such effort. PAL provides well-trained peer coaches who shadow and question each other and provide informed feedback and the opportunity to reflect deliberately on one's own administrative practice (Barnett, 1985). Other efforts to increase the influence of trained mentors on the quality of school leadership internships are rapidly growing across the country. Daresh and Playko (1989) focus their work particularly on mentor principals' development and on the responsibility of the profession to design and use systematically planned and executed means for improving the practice of school leadership.

Many groups across the United States, the United Kingdom, the Netherlands, and other countries also are seizing the opportunity that this renewed interest in systematic learning through experience guided by mentors represents. For example, the Utah Educational Leadership Consortium, developed as a partnership among the universities preparing administrators, the Utah Principals Academy, the Utah School Boards Association, the Utah Association of Elementary School Principals, the Utah Association of Secondary School Principals, and the Utah School Superintendents Association, has developed to unite and improve the overall preparation of school leaders. Other states also are developing strong mentorship programs. The Wisconsin Administrator Leadership Academy is one example.

These groups commit resources and time to mentor principals' training and to planning and developing statewide commitments to improving the preparation of school leaders. Similar consortia are developing in many states in the United States and in many other countries as educational professionals become increasingly committed to improving the learning connections between formal classroom study and experience in the field for school leaders.

Formal opportunities to participate in cycles of deliberate professional learning during induction and professional socialization lay a foundation for growth and learning throughout a career. These cycles combine systematic rational processes, emotional reactions to highly salient experiences, contact with research reports, and deeply personal experiences. This combination of rational and nonrational (*not* irrational) aspects of experiences creates committed, intensely involved educational leaders.[2]

By understanding the acquisition of knowledge by other professionals, you can vicariously use your experiences, the research you examine, and powerful theories in the social and behavioral sciences, ethics, and history to enhance and expand your professional careers. Scientific (or positivist) research and theory are part of this process in the rational model. But values and beliefs also shape education. These traditions are not "rational" in the traditional Western sense, but neither are they irrational in that sense. We do not wish to overemphasize this point, but you must be prepared to face dilemmas of professional practice that border on conundrums and defy rational decision-making models, as well as failed administrative strategies proffered at workshops that dominate much of the management literature (although perhaps not management practice). In subsequent chapters of this book, we return to this theme to examine and outline means through which new principals can shape a lifelong plan for professional growth and learning.

Research and development work on the professional socialization of principals has its critics—not necessarily because of its quality or value, but because it may oversimplify the complex interaction of new principals with the school they are assigned to lead. MacPherson (1984) asserted that any study of anticipatory, preservice socialization will yield incomplete knowledge at best, because the socialization takes place within a given context, under specific conditions, and it is shaped by unique personal relationships. In Chapters 11 and 12 we address this issue directly by introducing you to the building blocks of expert thinking and a theory of professional visualization. School factors shape professional socialization; task-specific learning; the practical, routine tasks principals must master; feelings of isolation and inadequacy; the need for technical assistance; and the influence of peers, assistants, and office staff (Alvey, 1983; DuBose, 1986; Marrion, 1983). The professional socialization literature also emphasizes how important it is that a principal have a highly salient and socially imbedded professional socialization experience (Greenfield, 1985a).

The Organizational Socialization of New Principals

As the preceding sections of this chapter foreshadow, a new principal's power to affect a school comes only in part from the formal and legitimate authority

---

[2]The difference between nonrational and irrational experiences is subtle but critical. A nonrational experience involves observations and events that touch the deeply human, affective, cultural, political, valuational, and ethical aspects of school leadership. They are intensely real and engage a school leader in the examination of professional issues that defy the linear reasoning of scientific methods, management decision-making charts, or other highly rational models. They are not irrational, because they do not violate a chain of logic applying scientific rational logic while pretending to adhere to these values. The nonrational in school leadership emanates from imbedded values and ethical conflicts that defy both the methods and assumptions of our currently dominant rational models of decision making.

of the role. How much authority does a principal really have to secure compliance from teachers and pupils with any edict, regardless of its source, value, or the power of district and state behind it? Practicing school principals often say they feel less powerful than they did as teachers to shape actual behaviors and outcomes.

The precept that formal authority alone will get a principal only a few feet down a miles-long journey toward effectiveness stands so firmly in organizational theory and draws so ubiquitously from research on schools that it hardly needs to be stated (Scott, 1987). To test the assertion, think about your role as a classroom teacher or other professional educator. On a daily basis how much direct authority does your principal have over your professional work? How effectively is your principal's formal authority influencing your motivation and commitment to teaching and learning or to the service of children and youth? At the individual level, reliance on formal authority poses a problem for every new principal.

> We cannot force others to give us their approval, regardless of how much power we have over them, because coercing them to express their admiration or praise would make these expressions worthless. . . . There are fundamental differences between the dynamics of power in a collective situation and the power of one individual over another. The weakness of the isolated subordinate limits the significance of his approval or disapproval of the superior. The agreement that emerges in a collectivity of subordinates concerning their judgment of the superior, on the other hand, has far-reaching implications for developments in the social structure (Blau, 1964, pp. 17, 23).

The impacts of schools on new principals as they move from anticipation and formal induction into school-level experiences emerge from an understanding of the power of context. Yes, the principal is "in charge"; no, the principal cannot force others to act professionally, responsibly, or uniformly. Studies of principals' earliest experiences highlight the importance of context, and each principal should plan and prepare for strong, school-based influence over her newly emerging professional actions and developing self-concept.

Schools exert this influence by creating a context that isolates a new principal and provides him with an accessible group of peers providing the most salient and immediate source of support and information. Schools provide a context for the principal's socialization by placing before him a set of unique instructional needs, community values and beliefs, student characteristics, and a faculty.

Finally, a principal experiences her socialization in close contact with, or in the absence of, role models. She will feel more or less pressure to divest herself of the emerging professional self-concept shaped by early formal experiences and years as a teacher, or she may find her early values and professional self-image affirmed and supported (Jones, 1986; Van Maanen & Schein, 1979). In each school, in each community, these forces combine in a unique mix that a principal who aspires to success must be prepared to assess and meet while remaining true to her own central professional values. This is no trivial challenge.

We find strong evidence in the literature on school administration that these context-laden factors deserve the attention of principals undergoing the transition to leadership in schools. In a review of the leader succession and organizational socialization research, Hart (1993) found evidence that a more powerful and complete understanding of this complex process of becoming a leader in an organization like a school emerges when a principal pays careful attention to his interaction with the school context. Leadership is a social experience. We return to this theme throughout the book. In the following sections of this chapter, we expand the concepts of knowledge as experience, research, and theory that shape much of the following discussion of the principalship.

FORMS OF PROFESSIONAL KNOWLEDGE: EXPERIENTIAL, RESEARCH BASED (EMPIRICAL), AND THEORETICAL

Training for school administration occurs in institutions and takes on a formality that makes transition to practice in which action is required problematic. While formal training provides knowledge and skills, these important sources of professional expertise are decoupled from the actual settings in which they must be applied unless direct effort places students in real settings with real consequences tied to their actions. The high costs of providing professional preparation for principals full time and at the work site (schools) and conventions of certification and degree programs which we have come to expect from formal courses at colleges and universities make it difficult to put to use what we know about learning processes that link knowledge to action in professional education. In the introduction to this chapter, we described three sources of knowledge—experiential, empirical, and theoretical—which provide a systematic method for enhancing the impact of knowledge from these sources on world views, professional socialization, beliefs, and actions. Although these are not pure types, they provide useful distinctions that can help individual principals and those preparing for leadership roles in schools frame their own professional learning and growth experiences. By continually returning to all three sources of knowledge, we believe principals seeking to enhance their own learning can address the ancient Greeks' dilemma posed again by Dewey (1933, p. 128):

> How is learning (or inquiry) possible? For either we know already what we are after, and then we do not learn or inquire; or we do not know, and then we cannot inquire, for we do not know what to look for.

In this book, we hope to block the refrain that we do not know what we do not know. We hope our readers will learn to discover what they do not know while shaping their own inquiry, their professional ways of knowing, and their personal theorizing.

Experiential Knowledge

Professionals of educational leadership face a complex challenge if they hope to tie knowledge to action. Principals say that, under the press of daily work, they rely more on experience than on the content of formal courses or inservice training to guide their actions (Hart, 1990a). Even as they described the usefulness of their formal coursework, respondents to Duke and his colleagues (1984) said that the socialization benefits of their university preparation outweighed the content of their studies in preparing them for their work as principals. Schon (1987, pp. 309, 310) pointed out the difficulties of relying on the formal knowledge of university work when seeking to improve the practice of school professionals: "It is extremely difficult in a university setting to achieve focused, long-term continuity of attention and commitment to work on the institutional and intellectual problems of a school." The weight of evidence thus suggests that school leaders, like other professionals, find it difficult to tie "knowledge" to their beliefs, values, and behaviors in leadership roles.

People label the knowledge gleaned from experience in a number of ways that carry with them both positive and negative connotations—conventional wisdom, tacit knowledge, experiential learning, common sense. Here we intend a specific and positive meaning for the knowledge acquired through professional experience. Experiential knowledge is gained directly from the outcomes of actions taken personally in similar circumstances and indirectly by talking with others like ourselves who have had similar experiences. Personal experience provides the most vivid experiential knowledge, and vicarious experience provides a sample of the vivid experiences of others. The exactness of fit when experiential knowledge is applied affects its value and appropriateness, as do its accuracy and richness of detail, and the learner's ability to use experience to examine existing beliefs frankly and openly.

Experience provides a constant and recurring source of knowledge in everyday life. In professional preparation for the principalship, opportunities to get experience and learn from it may be limited; however, one's ability to learn from experience is invaluable. Experiential learning is a respected focus of inquiry. The effects of experience on beliefs and behaviors is a well-developed line of research, and it has garnered devoted adherents who systematize and study these effects (Boud, Keogh & Walker, 1985). Schon (1983, 1987) asserted that professionals apply two formats to structure learning from experience—reflection-in-action, a form of simultaneous application of knowledge and learning while adjusting behavior in the midst of action, and reflection-on-action, returning to an experience carefully and thoughtfully after it is over to see what can be learned from the outcome. These formats provide a twofold source of rich information about their work for school leaders. First, principals must act. Often their decisions occur in an abbreviated time frame that borders on an emergency. Reflection-in-action gives principals a framework for tying their actions to basic knowledge and past experience. Second, school leaders learn by reflecting on the positive and negative outcomes of their actions. Reflection-on-action frames the sense-making process through which principals assess the salutary outcomes of their decisions.

Examples of reflection-in-action and reflection-on-action occur in school administration. Principals often find themselves deluged by dozens of incidents requiring action as they walk around the school at the beginning of the school day. Watching an expert principal deal effectively with a student who forgot his lunch money, a teacher who needs to leave early for an appointment, a custodian's concerns about graffiti in the girls' bathroom, while high-fiving and welcoming students walking down the halls is watching professional poetry in action. It may even look effortless, as Michael Jordan's one-hand fade-away jump shots often appear effortless. Reflection-in-action and reflection-on-action are part of this principal's professional knowledge base. Decisions about how to spend her time, the utility of management by walking around, and the effects of her behaviors and decisions on the creation of a positive learning environment in the school are informed by her daily experiences and her reflections on them. Within this apparently simple scenario, a principal would have to assess the relative time-relevant importance of each pressing event, plan her movements through the school, assess the reactions and responses to her decisions, and store information about effective and less effective responses she observes for the future.

Systematic models of reflection-on-action help illustrate its usefulness to principals and other professionals. Boud, Keogh, and Walter (1985) offered a three-stage model of experiential learning: (1) returning to the experience; (2) attending to feelings; and (3) reevaluating the experience. By completing each of these stages, learners benefit more appropriately and completely from their own and others' experiences. First, the learner can concentrate on what happened, tell the experience to others, and try to remain free of premature judgments by systematically noting or telling about the essential features of an experience (returning to the experience). Second, by deliberately attending to their feelings, learners help to prevent vicarious or projected emotions from becoming barriers to learning (attending to feelings). Mood and affect influence the quality of school administrators' problem solving as well as their ability to learn from their experiences (Leithwood & Hallinger, 1993). Third, learners can protect themselves from too quickly reaching conclusions that obscure important issues by deliberately reevaluating the circumstances of an experience or problem. Premature closure, often characterized by shooting from the hip, poses a major obstacle to high-quality problem solving or experiential learning and particularly plagues novices (Barrows, 1988). Just because a principal has an experience does not guarantee that he will notice critical aspects of that same experience, aspects that make the difference between the skilled application of knowledge to the new situation and a stab in the dark.

> It is easy to jump from the initial experience to evaluation, and judgments are often a part of the original experience. [By doing this we] can potentially lose a great deal of value. We may find ourselves operating on false assumptions or reflecting on information which we have not comprehended sufficiently (Boud, Keogh & Walker, 1985, p. 30).

Simon (1993) noted that expert chess players take no more trials and consider no more alternatives when making decisions about moves on the chess board than do novices. They do, however, notice patterns that reoccur and make better choices as a result of this pattern recognition. Noticing seems to be a central component of the development of expertise. Patterns (theories if you accept a more formal perspective) thus shape the good decisions of experts emanating from experience. Similarly, an effective principal recognizes patterns of failure among selected groups of students. Based on this, she acts to examine school structures, processes, and resources to ameliorate the conditions contributing to failure.

These findings about relationships between expert knowledge and the recognition of patterns have important implications for professional knowledge in educational administration. Carefully structured and examined professional experiences contribute to the growth and development of a principal in three important ways. First, as experiences and learning accumulate and inappropriate inferences and judgments are reduced, knowledge (and pattern recognition) improves. Second, as knowledge increases and the principal learns to draw associations between past problems and features of new situations, the ability to draw appropriate inferences improves. Especially difficult problems accelerate learning when successfully dealt with, because they force a person to confront relevant deviations from the expected and habitual, establishing a powerful connection between action and memory (Bower, Black & Turner, 1979; Pearson, Hansen & Gordon, 1979; Nickolson & Imlack, 1981). Difficult problems and surprises (a critical feature of professional socialization identified by veteran and novice principals) that challenge existing preconceptions bring with them hidden benefits. The surprise of having to place an express order for student graduation tassels provided an important lesson in planning as well as a better understanding of the sometimes hidden role expectations held by teachers for the principal.

> When the phenomenon at hand eludes the ordinary categories of knowledge-in-practice, presenting itself as unique or unstable, the practitioner may surface and criticize his initial understanding of the phenomenon, construct a new description of it, and test the new description by an on-the-spot experiment (Schon, 1983, pp. 62–63).

When this test of experience is mounted, it takes on new meaning and worth. Each new experience and set of outcomes adds to accumulated knowledge and results in adjustments to professional assumptions and beliefs. The more careful and systematic this reflective process is, the more productive learning from experience is.

All people learn from experience to some degree. Differences exist, however, in the thoughtfulness with which we challenge our existing beliefs about reality as a result of these experiences. A novice principal attending to the details of his experience learns much more than one who "goes with the flow." When undertaken deliberately by the novice principal, experiential learning results in increased awareness and sensitivity to one's own thinking and values and makes improved thinking and action more likely. It facilitates additive learning that builds systematically—experience with research and theory. New principals can learn to observe their own practice, their experiences, responses, and adjustment in behavior, knowledge, and understanding—especially with the help of skilled veterans (Hart, 1992).

Leadership training programs often exhort principals and other educational leaders to serve as mentors or coaches to new professionals. Educational administrators face unique challenges when they attempt to function as coaches in the process of experiential learning, however. Schon (1987) asserted that expert professionals sometimes become so adept at using experience as a source of knowledge that they have difficulty retracing their own thinking processes to explain their reasoning to novices. Their skills become so automatic that they cannot describe to others the process by which they arrive at outcomes. They may even come to see their expertise as innate or tacit rather than knowledge based as it becomes more automatic and the speed of the cycle of action, observation, pattern recognition, choice, and action increases.

This cycle through which systematic knowledge becomes tacit for an individual while it remains knowledge based for the profession is poorly understood. Research and theory provide guidelines for understanding how a particular principal's actions might reasonably be understood, yet each situation is unique in content and outcome. In the remainder of this chapter, we examine two other sources of knowledge that inform the professional practice of school principals—research (empirical) and theoretical.

Empirical Knowledge

The formal knowledge that students encounter in university study often comes from systematic experimentation, observation, and analysis. In the strictest terms, this process yields empirical knowledge. In a professional field like educational administration, empirical knowledge is based on evidence systematically collected and analyzed. This evidence can come either from controlled experimentation or from actual field practice, but it must be gathered and assessed using the rigorous standards generally accepted for the methods employed and appropriate to the nature of the professional problem (Drew, Hardman, & Hart, in press). Empiricism demands evidence confirming or disconfirming goodness of fit to a given situation and can be accumulated in many ways. Highly controlled experiments in laboratories have high reliability and internal validity but are poorly generalized to complex, uncontrolled settings. Even committed experimentalists recognize these limitations. As Jerome Kagan (1978) pointed out, controlled experiments have revealed how children respond to stress under artificial circumstances while isolated from their normal support and guidance systems in the family; observations of children in the real world reveal how these same children behave under stress in their normal environments. School administrators never work under carefully controlled experimental conditions; they must know how major variables interact in natural settings.

Field experiments in real schools consequently provide a second source of empirical knowledge. Although this knowledge is more generalizable, it also may be less reliable according to the principles of careful experimental design. By relinquishing the control of the laboratory, the researcher sacrifices some confidence that the outcomes observed are trustworthy and dependable—reflecting what would have happened had all circumstances been within the control of the researcher (Drew, Hardman & Hart, in press). Careful experimental research provides guidance about important relationships among the five commonplaces of school (Haller & Knapp, 1985) to which educators should attend; rigorous field research yields context-based information about how these patterns emerge in real-life settings.

A third source of empirical knowledge—actuarial data sets such as statewide scores of student performance on standardized tests—allows the inquirer to see large, sweeping patterns occurring in groups of people or types of schools. All the richness and idiosyncrasy of people and events are lost in the bigger picture. For example, the actuarial studies of principals' effects on school performance yielded evidence that principals make a difference, but failed to indicate exactly *how* they make a difference (Bossert, Dwyer, Rowan & Lee, 1982; Ogawa & Hart, 1985). These classic "black box" studies allow us to evaluate outcomes on a large but not an individual scale. They cannot be used to predict the outcome of any single event or set of events for a specific group of people in a particular school. Principals can use this kind of knowledge to improve the likelihood that a desired outcome will occur in a given set of circumstances.

A final source of empirical knowledge comes from case studies of highly individualized experiences, providing vivid, unique details, and relevance. Case studies are often called phenomenological research; anthropologists and other social scientists less concerned with generalizability than with the representation of reality choose this form of inquiry. Comparability and pattern recognition come from multiple case studies of similar settings (Yin, 1985). Empirical knowledge varies in form, content, and use from experiential knowledge but presents a continuum from the personalized and unique to the patterned and general professional behaviors. This same continuum describes the levels of administrative action from specific behavior to general principles of administrative behavior. Dewey (1933, p. 97) spoke persuasively of the uses of empirical knowledge as "we discriminate between beliefs that rest upon tested evidence and those that do not," cautioning that we should be on guard to establish the "kind and degree of assent or belief that is justified" depending on the form of knowledge.

The usefulness of empirical knowledge to administrators depends on its quality, its fit in the given circumstances, and the depth of understanding provided by the analysis. Like detailed but inaccurate features on a map, inappropriately applied empirical knowledge is worse than useless. When practitioners attempt to chart a course on the basis of such data, they can become hopelessly misled and lost.

Theoretical Knowledge

Theoretical knowledge often receives vigorous criticism from principals working in the trenches every day in schools. Absent specific models for using theory, principals find it distant, inaccessible, and abstruse. Abstract and removed from the salience and immediacy of experience, theory seems only remotely useful when taken alone. When appropriately used, theory provides explanatory, descriptive, heuristic, and, at times, predictive frameworks for our knowledge of practice that provide general patterns useful for identification, comparison, and generalization. It includes the general or abstract principles of a body of facts, science, or art. Theory can serve as the basis from which practitioners and scholars organize the search for new facts, establish their relationships to existing knowledge, and explain generally observed phenomena.

The utility of theories for the practice of administration rests with the ability of people to use them as broad, organizing principles, like maps, for defining types or patterns of problems and choices in the administration of the social world of schools. Administrators might see a set of circumstances as indicative of role stress—the ambiguity, conflict, and overload people experience in a given work role—and draw on role theory or organizational behavior research to seek potential interventions or solutions (Bacharach, Bamberger & Mitchell, 1990).

A map metaphor helps illustrate the uses of theory for administrative practice and the relationship of theoretical knowledge to empirical and experiential knowledge. The U.S. Geological Survey prepares maps of the United States that render important physical features of the landscape. These maps render this physical reality in the form of elevations, topography, and vegetation. Anyone can purchase one of these maps in a local sporting goods store or county office. They depict sections of the American landscape, including roads and trails, rivers, mountains, ravines, and ridges as they were measured in the latest surveys or satellite photographs. The colors of these maps are dull (green and tan with black details) and the features of the maps bear no visual resemblance to the magnificent geological and geographical features they depict. Nevertheless, people who have never set foot in a mountain range for which they possess a U.S. Geological Survey map can find their way and have a magnificent experience.

Maps help users only when they provide a good fit between the symbolic rendition on paper and the physical reality. The more accurate the map, the more authentic the adventurer's experience. Like maps, theories should be continually challenged and assessed for their representative and explanatory value, and improved as new or more accurate information is gathered. Hikers may take shortcuts and gradually change a trail over the years; the map maker may miss an important detail, misread an altitude, or take measurements with poorly calibrated instruments. Measurement and instrumentation may be improved, making more accurate measurements possible, or satellites may give the map maker a new view, but the "proof of the pudding" for each trip lies in the success of the adventurer guided by the map. The same proof of theory for educational leaders lies in explanations useful in their individual experiences.

Individual experience matters. Anyone who has spent a night or two lost in the mountains develops a deep appreciation for the interpretation and understanding of maps. Each of the authors has been lost in the "real world," hoping that time, streams, and boulders would reveal her or his location.

Like theories, maps never approximate the beauty and detail of the world they represent.

> Although they can help us find our way, they cannot walk us to our destination. Theories project an interpretable and useful image, but they are no substitute for the reality they represent in symbol and allegory. Other forms of knowledge . . . add important details (Hart, 1990a, p. 158).

One of the authors over years of backpacking in the Wind River Mountains of Wyoming has come to appreciate how this relationship between the theory (map), the empirical reality (the physical mountain range), and the experience (a trip to the mountains) works. In 1980, my husband and I headed into a poorly mapped section of the Wind River Mountains with few trails, seeking Europe Canyon. Europe Canyon lies above the timberline at the continental divide north of the famous South Pass over which pioneers traveled along the Oregon Trail in the nineteenth century. The U.S. Geological Survey map we carried accurately represented satellite features of ridge and mountain, but empirical data about the human and animal traffic creating trails were out of date. We had difficulty finding any trails, cairns were scarce, and we made our way up by following game trails and finding an occasional cairn marking human traffic. One frightening, lightning-filled, and sleepless night, we established camp on a steep slope 11,200 feet above a pristine mountain lake free of algae or fish and still sporting ice floes in July. Clearly, we had failed to find Europe Canyon. The next day, emboldened by sunshine and wind, we climbed over a nearby ridge and descended on Europe Canyon and some of the best fishing of our lives.

For years, we believed we had camped at Shoestring Lake—matching our map (theory) with the physical characteristics of the lake and the surroundings (context) of the lake with its name in a mountain guidebook. Yet a careful reading of maps and the accounts of other hikers led us to doubt earlier conclusions. Several years ago, we approached Europe Canyon with our family on another trip from the south instead of the northwest. Our beliefs about Shoestring Lake failed to jibe with new information. Another trip confirmed growing suspicions. From this new perspective, and with increased experience, we discovered that our exciting night in 1980 was spent above Long Lake. In 1993, standing above the real Shoestring Lake on the summit of Halls Peak with hearts filled with awe and reverence, we expanded our knowledge. The new panorama revealed that Long Lake lay four or five miles to the north, nestled above Europe Canyon. Shoestring Lake and Halls Lake lay at our feet. It took a combination of knowledge, experience, maps, time, and emotion to develop our current "understanding" of this section of the Wind River range. In 1994, we returned to Halls Lake and hiked the section of the range between Halls Lake and Europe Canyon, further increasing our understanding of the topography of this magnificent mountain range. More learning lies ahead.

Empirical knowledge is the source of some learning. The research of biologists, botanists, geologists, and meteorologists—accumulated by backpack, horseback, and satellite—contributes rich and helpful information about the mountains rendered passable to a stranger because of a map. Experience offers still more information, and to the pilgrim passing through the mountains, the richest and most memorable source of knowledge. A journey on foot has no parallel and remains forever vivid and personal for those who take it. Each pass, each river, teaches something new. Each thunderstorm remains forever in the memory.

CONCLUSION

Principals become formal leaders by virtue of their positions and roles, but it remains to each principal to exert leadership and become an exemplar of professional leaders in schools. The complexity of the principal's role in modern schools increases at the same time that the knowledge base on which principals draw becomes more and more advanced. In this environment of knowledge-based and social complexity, increasing diversity, and exploding demands on schools, principals must master not only the knowledge base current at the time of their professional preservice education but the skills necessary to develop professional habits of learning and of tying their constantly expanding knowledge to their professional actions. Relevant professional knowledge can be gleaned from experience, research, and theory.

The induction period during which professional socialization takes place sets the stage for the development of the habits and skills of professional reflection-in-action and reflection-on-action and begins the developmental process through which principals learn the moral and technical skills of their new profession. Additional influence emanates from the particular school in which a principal takes on his or her first formal leadership position. Learning and development, however, require ongoing problem solving and decision making by principals, and problem-solving errors plague novices, in particular, as they seek to establish and recognize patterns of professional practice. The need for lifelong patterns of problem solving and professional growth accompanies a career of leadership in schools.

In Chapter 2, we examine the development of a knowledge-to-action link for students of the principalship. We discuss ways in which professionals connect the three forms of knowledge to professional action while applying knowledge to the unique problems of practice and avoiding the problem-solving errors. We turn to the uses of knowledge by professionals, particularly school principals and other educational leaders. The problem-solving errors to which professionals fall victim are identified by researchers and the impacts of these errors on the efforts of, and outcomes for, education professionals are introduced.

SUGGESTED ACTIVITIES

1. Interview three new principals. What surprised them the most about their first job? Ask each to describe his or her career path and professional preparation. What were the primary reasons each chose to become a principal? If the principal was beginning his or her professional career again, what changes, if any, would he or she make?
2. We have described three primary sources of professional knowledge: experiential, empirical, and theoretical. As these principals carry out their professional responsibilities, what knowledge from each informs their practice?
3. Find out what formal induction processes your school district has in place for new principals and assistant principals? What are its main features such as duration, content, format, participants, and so forth?
4. What suggestions do these principals have for enhancing the socialization processes for the principalship?

Connecting Knowledge and Action:

Leadership Is More Than Knowing

A major concern in improving the quality of principals for the twenty-first century lies in finding more effective ways to transfer knowledge into school practice. Simply knowing how things should be alone is insufficient; principals must become proficient in applying knowledge in ways that enhance the development of every person in the school.

(National Association of Elementary and Secondary School
Principals, *Principals for the 21st Century*, 1990, p. 38).

In the previous chapter we described three primary forms of knowledge—experiential, empirical, and theoretical. We described how professionals develop knowledge-in-action. We will argue throughout this text that these three ways of knowing become integrated into the knowledge base that informs the professional practice of school principals. In this chapter we examine how professional knowledge is defined and how principals connect this body of expert knowledge to unique problems of practice in schools. First, we provide a brief historical overview of the search for a professional knowledge base in educational administration and the limitations of various descriptive and theoretical frameworks. Next, using the three forms of knowledge—experiential, empirical, and theoretical described in Chapter 1—we examine the relationships among definitions of professional expertise, knowledge, and practice. Finally, we describe five common problem-solving errors often committed by beginning principals.

A BRIEF HISTORY OF THE SEARCH FOR A PROFESSIONAL KNOWLEDGE BASE

Since the release of *A Nation at Risk* in 1983, reform rhetoric and countless initiatives to improve educational outcomes for students have filled legislative dockets, professional meeting agendas, scholarly journals, local newspaper articles, and blue-ribbon commission reports. The recommendations and strategies designed to bring about improvements in education have been focused on the quality and rigor of curricula, the preparation and quality of teachers, organizational and structural dimensions for educational delivery, effective school practices, financial-political support and control, and articulation of K–12 education with the world of work, to name just a few. Regardless of the foci of particular reform initiatives, the importance of leadership, especially that of the school principal, is reasserted either explicitly or implicitly throughout long lists of recommendations to improve the overall quality of education.

Given the importance of school leadership by principals cited in all these reports, the National Commission on Excellence in Educational Administration, the National Commission for the Principalship, and the National Policy Board for Educational Administration have outlined in major publications how universities, professional organizations, and state credentialling agencies can work together to recruit, prepare, and sustain the professional development of school principals.[1]

In the current educational reform environment, there is general agreement that the old management frameworks, both theoretical and practical, are no longer appropriate to the challenges of principals in today's schools. Yet, traditional "principalship paradigms," developed, researched, and used to train aspiring administrators throughout this century, have been remarkably durable. The durability of these frameworks has led many scholars and practitioners to argue that given contemporary school and social realities, administrative theory and practice have become increasingly disparate. Thus, educators share a renewed interest in assessing the efficacy of the professional knowledge base needed to prepare, support, and guide school principals in their daily professional work.

Since the nineteenth century, Americans have looked to their schools for solutions to help ameliorate pressing social, economic, political, and educational problems brought about by rapidly changing social conditions. As a result, the knowledge base for educators has been dynamic and responsive to changing social conditions and demands. As the current fervor for reform suggests, the professional knowledge base for school leadership continues to be shaped.

Reconsideration of the professional knowledge base for educational administration is not a new phenomenon in educational administration. Jack A. Culbertson (1988) provides an excellent historical assessment of the relationship of the professional knowledge base in educational administration to changing concepts of social science, norms of inquiry, and standards for validation of new knowledge. He describes how definitions of administration and priorities within those definitions have changed and been legitimated over the past 100 years. As concepts of social science changed, as belief systems in schol-

---

[1]For greater detail of these educational reform initiatives and for specific issues related to leadership in schools, you may want to review *Principals for the 21st Century* (1990), *Leaders for America's Schools* (1987), *Principals for our Changing Schools* (1990), and *NPBEA Report* (1989, 1993).

arly communities changed, as societal issues emerged and subsided, and as the needs of practitioners shifted, concomitant changes in the definition of administration occurred.

> Classroom management was highlighted in the 1875–1900 period. From 1901–1925, the concept of administration as a general function came to the fore. In the second quarter of the twentieth century, specialized functions of administration became focuses for inquiry. In the 1951–1966 era, the concept of administration qua administration, the notion that there were general principles of administration which could be applied across organizational types with little regard for the purposes of that organization or its situational uniqueness, guided inquiry and theory development. More recently, diverse definitions of administration have prevailed as scholars have pursued pluralistic approaches to inquiry" (p. 22).

Each of these fundamental shifts in basic understandings of what educational administration was had important implications for the preparation of administrators and for how professionals put their knowledge into action.

TYPOLOGY IS A TYPOLOGY IS A TYPOLOGY

Countless social problems affecting schools, dramatic changes in student populations, and shifts in the priorities of the mission of education in this country present significant challenges for school leaders and contribute to the current press to reassess the knowledge base for school principals. Various attempts to reformulate the knowledge base for school administrators provide a plethora of understandings, images, and vocabularies to capture, refocus, and codify professional knowledge. The publications mentioned previously are examples of recent efforts to redefine the professional knowledge base for principals in the twenty-first century. A review of books on the school principalship and general educational administration textbooks offers ample evidence that there is no shortage of verbiage when it comes to describing what, how, and why principals do what they do. Students, professors, and practitioners in educational administration have become all too familiar with facile typologies and profile assessment instruments renaming the major organizational, structural, social, and process factors used to describe schools and the people who work and learn in them. Table 2.1 contains selected knowledge-base organizers currently used by other authors to describe, prescribe, and define leadership behaviors for principals.

These frameworks represent particular views of school administration, some theoretical, some descriptive, grounded in empirical findings, in professional experience, and in legitimated social science norms of disciplined inquiry and knowledge validation. These frameworks also reflect changing attitudes about the knowledge base for principals. The organizers used to frame the professional knowledge base in school administration point to the fundamental belief that it is possible to codify a body of hierarchically organized knowledge that defines professional expertise through scientific inquiry

TABLE 2.1. Selected Knowledge-Base Organizers for Principals

Principalship Leadership as a Set of Forces (Sergiovanni, 1991)
  Technical
  Human
  Educational
  Symbolic
  Cultural

Leadership as the Application of Technical Knowledge in Specified Task Areas within Integrative Systems (Kimbrough, R. B. & Burkett, C. W., 1990)
  Instruction and Curriculum
  Community and School Relations
  Staff Personnel
  Organization and Structure of the School
  School Plant Facilities

Instructional Managers as High Performing Principals (Drake, T. L. & Roe, W. H., 1986)
  Twelve Basic Competencies
  Commitment to School Mission and Concern for Its Image
  Proactive Leadership Orientation
  Decisiveness
  Interpersonal and Organizational Sensitivity
  Information Search, Analysis, Concept Formation
  Intellectual Flexibility
  Persuasiveness and Managing Interaction
  Tactical Adaptability
  Motivational and Developmental Concern
  Control and Evaluation
  Organizational Ability and Delegation
  Communication

Moral and Visionary Craftsmanship (Blumberg, A. & Greenfield, W., 1986)
  Sense of Vision
  Proactive—Initiates Action
  Resourcefulness
  Goal Oriented
  Personally Secure
  Tolerance for Ambiguity
  Testers of Limits
  Sensitivity to Power Dynamics
  Analytical
  Take Charge Personalities
  People Oriented

Social System Role Incumbent (Lipham, J. M., Rankin, R. F. & Hoeh, J. A. Jr., 1985)
  Goal Setter
  Values Clarifier
  System Manager
  Decisionmaker
  Change Agent
  Instructional Leader
  Personnel Manager
  Evaluator

Social System Role Incumbent *(continued)*
  Inservice Coordinator
  Budget/Resource Manager
  School-Community Liaison
Leader-Manager of Functional Tasks (Hughes, L. W. & Ubben, G. C., 1989)
  Organizer/Delegator/Coordinator/Evaluator of:
    Curriculum Development
    Instructional Improvement
    Pupil Services
    Financial/Facility Management
    Community Relations
Functional Leader in Four Domains (National Commission for the Principalship, 1990)
  Functional Domain
    Leadership
    Information Collection
    Problem Analysis
    Judgment
    Organizational Oversight
    Implementation
    Delegation
  Programmatic Domain
    Instructional Program
    Curriculum Design
    Student Guidance and Development
    Staff Development
    Measurement and Evaluation
    Resource Allocation
  Interpersonal Domain
    Motivating Others
    Sensitivity
    Oral Expression
    Written Expression
  Contextual Domain
    Philosophical and Cultural Values
    Legal and Regulatory
    Policy and Political Influences
    Public and Media Relationships

by scholars. The body of knowledge thus developed is then used to specify the preservice curriculum for future practitioners and to inform the professional practice of school principals.

We commend these frameworks to you as useful references on the principalship. Each perspective contains large volumes of detailed information that you as a principal can access, much the same as a student uses encyclopedias, an attorney searches in reference books for legal codes and case law, and a physician consults general medical reference books. As useful as these reference sources are, they remain conceptually inadequate for the preparation of school principals. With the exception of the Blumberg and Greenfield list, the taxonomies are context neutral and thus provide little to help you as an aspiring principal to see the critical linkage among factors in each taxonomy, administrative behavior, and the situations of practice in which knowledge, beliefs, values, and professional practice come together. Another major weakness of these taxonomies is that they fail to recognize the complexity of professional expertise by looking to facile lists of discrete administrative tasks and skills rather than to expertise grounded in experiential, empirical, theoretical, and reflective sources, which we believe are critical to understanding and to professional practice.

Schon (1983) describes the perennial search for a professional knowledge base as a quest for "technical rationality" which defines and guides professional practice. Most attempts to reconceptualize the professional knowledge base have been based on a specific world view that represents professional practice as instrumental problem solving made rigorous by the application of scientific theory. Real knowledge, typically generated by empirical science and then codified in theory, flows downward from a hierarchy of formal ways of knowing to lower levels and less formal ways of knowing to school principals. Principals then transform theoretical truths of their profession into actions in order to deal with problems of practice in their daily work lives.

All of the efforts put into work on the knowledge base are not simply esoteric, ivory-tower activities to keep professors and other scholars employed. Successful leadership in schools requires professional expertise in many areas and scholars and educators have legitimately and seriously sought to identify these areas. The degree to which various sources of professional knowledge are codified systematically to better inform administrative practice is dependent upon four essential knowledge-base properties. Typically, professional knowledge is described as an acquired body of technical knowledge that is specialized, standardized, scientific, and firmly bounded. In the area of school leadership, identifiable administrative practices and behaviors exist that are both situationally appropriate and effective. Specific legal parameters and processes guide practice. Effective and efficient strategies are used to allocate resources. Standard operating procedures, process skills, and administrative behaviors contribute to successful leadership in schools. Thus, types of professional knowledge can and have been defined, measured, and made verifiable within accepted norms of social science research and within standard professional practice in schools. When educators look at the multiple roles of school principals, however, they assert persuasively that many of the tasks and problems principals deal with on a daily basis are not amenable to the application of silver-bullet bits of specialized technical knowledge.

Schon (1983) notes that situations of practice for many professionals tend to be characterized by *complexity, uncertainty, instability,* and *uniqueness.* Thus, teaching and administrative practice within the field of education have been viewed by some scholars as minor professions similar to nursing and public administration. Our own belief is that a knowledge base for principals defined solely as technical expertise is a narrow definition of professionalism and not sufficient for effective leadership in schools.

Within situations of professional practice, principals must deal with fluid and somewhat ambiguous ends within unstable institutional and social environments. Such conditions of professional practice do not make the professional knowledge base for teachers and principals any less rigorous than that of an engineer or of a dentist; they simply mean that each action requires a principal to use knowledge in a contextually appropriate way to deal effectively with a specific problem. Though situational uniqueness is important to recognize, we do not mean to suggest that every situation a principal confronts is idiosyncratic. However, even with comparable cases principals must recognize complexity and contextual nuances that require differential application of technical knowledge. Next we turn to three sources of professional knowledge that inform principals' practice as effective educational leaders.

SOURCES OF PROFESSIONAL KNOWLEDGE

In Chapter 1, we discussed three sources of professional knowledge: *empirical knowledge, theoretical knowledge,* and *experiential knowledge,* and a process for integrating them through *knowledge-in-action.* For purposes of explication, we discuss each of them separately in this book. However, as useful as this is for presentation in this text, we do not believe that these sources of professional knowledge are so easily or discreetly separable. The order in which each is presented and described in no way is meant to suggest any notion of linearity in terms of how such knowledge is acquired, nor to imply any priority or hierarchy in these sources of professional knowledge. In fact, we argue throughout this text that professional expertise in the school principalship is a way of knowing that is a synergistic product of multiple sources and perspectives combined, accessed, and put into practice in purposeful ways. Our purpose in elaborating on these sources of knowledge is to illustrate how various sources of knowledge are related and how you as an aspiring principal can think about developing your own understanding of professional leadership expertise to influence teaching and learning activities in your schools.

Instructional Leadership Knowledge: Empirical

The improvement of learning outcomes for students in schools is the clearest and least contestable of goals stated for educational reform across the nation. Principals are central players in bringing about improvement in educational outcomes for all learners in their schools. What do principals need to know to work toward this goal? And, what specifically do principals do to realize this desired outcome? One source of knowledge needed to respond to these queries is empirical knowledge, supported by empirical research.

Empirical knowledge postulates that "real knowledge" is that which is acquired from systematic, disciplined inquiry of the "real world." In the field of educational administration, empirical studies and knowledge resulting from those works have been the product of the dominant epistemology, *positivism.* Positivism is a philosophical view which holds that only propositions that are analytically or empirically testable have meaning. All other propositions are speculative and devalued. Within this epistemology, empiricism is real-world evidence, reliant on, or derived from, observation of and experimentation with phenomena of interest, used to confirm or refute scientific propositions.

Herbert J. Walberg (1990) provides an especially timely and comprehensive analysis of empirical research in education related to educational outcomes. Meta-analysis of 2,575 empirical studies resulted in a framework highlighting nine generalizable factors demonstrably influential on students' cognitive, affective, and behavioral learning outcomes. The factors are organized into three categories: student aptitude, instruction, and psychological environments. *Student aptitude* includes (1) ability or prior achievement, measured by standard tests; (2) development, indicated by chronological age or maturation stage; and (3) motivation, indicated by a measure of self-concept or a measure of the student's willingness to persevere intensively on learning tasks. *Instruction* includes (4) amount of time students spend engaged in learning and (5) quality of instructional experiences (method and content aspects). The third group, *psychological environments,* includes (6) curriculum of the home; (7) morale or climate of the classroom social group; (8) peer group influence outside school; and (9) television viewing time.

Walberg concluded, "Collectively the various studies suggest that the three groups of previously defined nine factors are powerful and consistent in influencing learning. . . . The first five essential factors appear to substitute, compensate, or trade off for one another at diminishing rates of return. Immense quantities of time, for example, may be required for a moderate amount of learning if motivation, ability, or instructional quality is minimal. Thus, no single essential factor overwhelms the others; all appear important" (p. 284–285).

These findings provide a useful empirical framework for principals to use as they examine factors that significantly influence student learning. In addition, these findings identify factors that are under the direct control of educators' zones of professional practice and those that are outside the direct influence of teachers and principals. Further analysis by Walberg (1990) revealed that within the category of *instruction,* for example, the quality of instruction through particular professional activities and teaching strategies showed differential effect sizes in terms of student learning outcomes. *Effect size* (ES) is a statistic calculated as a measure of "the magnitude of a difference or relationship in a sample or population" (Borg & Gall, 1989, p. 358). Effect size helps researchers and practitioners interpret practical significance when statistically significant findings are reported. "The meaning of ES is dependent on the measures used, the absolute difference between group means, the shape of the score distribution, and the subjects in the sample" (p. 364). Walberg reported large effect sizes for: reinforcement/reward for correct performance by the student (1.17); acceleration programs and other advanced learning opportunities for students (1.00); reading training that coaches learners to adjust reading speed and techniques to purposes (.97); instructional cues and corrective feedback (.97); cooperative programs (.76); personalized instruction (.57), and adaptive instruction (.45). Small effect sizes and negative effect sizes were reported for class size (−.09); programmed instruction (−.03); homogeneous groups (.10);

and inquiry biology (.16). What exactly do these effect size statistics tell you as an instructional leader?

For purposes of illustration let's assume that the effect size of 1.17 is the result of a comparison between experimental conditions in which students were given particular rewards and positive reinforcements with positive learning outcomes. The control groups were given no rewards and minimal if any positive reinforcement for their learning outcomes. If the posttest mean score of the experimental group was 80 and the corresponding posttest mean score for the control group was 70, there is a mean difference of 10 points. To determine if this statistical difference has any practical significance, we would need to determine the standard deviation of posttest scores for the control group and divide the mean difference score between the two groups by the standard deviation. If the standard deviation is 8.547, the effect size is $10/8.547 = 1.17$. This indicates that the average experimental posttest score of 80 places a student at approximately the 87th percentile of the control group distribution. An effect size of 1.17 for reinforcement in this sample, then, is an impressive influence on learning outcomes. Given the sheer number of studies included in Walberg's analysis of these studies, the findings summarized and conclusions posited are powerful empirical sources of professional knowledge for principals as they plan and carry out instructional leadership responsibilities in instructional supervision, staff and program evaluation, and professional development programs in schools. We have referred to one major review of empirical research to illustrate our point. Findings in effective schools literature, in the *Handbook of Research on Teaching* (Wittrock, 1986), and in a rich variety of scholarly and practitioner journals suggest the depth of this source of professional knowledge. With reference to the findings briefly described above, the next section is an overview of a number of theoretical frameworks that illustrate theoretical knowledge and its contribution to instructional leadership expertise and its application.

Instructional Leadership Knowledge: Theoretical

Theory is explanation. This is probably the most parsimonious definition that can be given. Borg and Gall (1989) define theory as a "system for explaining a set of phenomena by specifying constructs and laws that relate these constructs to each other" (p. 171). Irvin contends that theory "is only a model, and it has no more reality than its creator endows upon it" (in Brass, *Design for Decision,* 1953). Theory helps us organize what we know about particular phenomena of interest; for example, the ways in which individuals acquire knowledge (cognitive theory), why students and faculty behave in certain ways (motivation theory), anxieties about a new job in an organization (role transition theory), restructured professional work in schools (job/work redesign theory), appropriateness of learning tasks for groups of children (developmental theory), and competing interest group demands for particular programs in schools (exchange theory). Each of these theoretical frameworks helps us to: (1) define, classify, and organize the relevancy of particular facts; (2) explain phenomena of interest at levels of abstraction that summarize and include many facts and human events so that our explanations move beyond idiosyncratic descriptions of singular, unrelated events; (3) at times, predict likely outcomes based on a particular set of facts and relationships; and (4) suggest directions for further research.

At this point let's examine some familiar theories that have implications for teaching and learning environments in schools and for principals as instructional leaders. The theories are illustrative of theoretical knowledge for instructional leadership. As you read through the brief descriptions of these educational theories, think about ways in which the theory informs principals' instructional leadership knowledge and behaviors.

Piaget's Stage Theory of Cognitive Development

Volumes have been written on the work of Jean Piaget; the stage theory of cognitive development describes how developmental changes in individuals' intellectual, social, and moral capacities are linked to identifiable stages of physical maturation beginning in infancy and traced to adulthood. Four general stages are identified—sensimotor, preoperational, concrete operations, and formal operations. Each is further articulated and described in terms of stages of cognitive development. Stage theory postulates that as individuals develop, with obvious variance based on differences in maturation and in environmental factors, they move from reflexive-instinctive patterns of behaviors for making sense of their world to increasingly complex levels of abstraction with increased capacity for symbolic thinking and reasoning. Principals working with teachers to examine the efficacy of preprimary curriculum and assessment strategies, might use Piaget's stages of development as a useful organizer to formulate questions, gather information, and facilitate changes to meet individual student needs.

Need Hierarchy Theory

Why do people do what they do? The search for an answer to this basic question about human behavior is greatly informed by theories of motivation. Maslow's need hierarchy theory is a content theory of motivation predicated on the notion that individuals have five levels of need (physiological, safety and security, belonging-love, esteem, and self-actualization) and that attempts to satisfy these needs are the salient factors that explain motivation to behave in particular ways. Though these needs are interrelated, there is a hierarchy of prepotency in that lower-level needs must be satisfied before higher-level needs have any likelihood of affecting behavior. In crime-ridden, ill-disciplined school settings, basic survival and safety needs must be satisfied for teachers and for students before professional development programs and enrichment activities will have much impact on what motivates teacher and student behavior. The effective schools literature emphasizes the importance of safe, disciplined, and supportive learning environments as necessary conditions for positive learning outcomes (Purkey, S. & Smith, M., 1983).

Theory of Meaningful Verbal Learning: Advance Organizers

The theory of meaningful verbal learning posits that new and more highly differentiated learning material is assimilated into previously learned material. Ausubel (1977) contends that cognitive structures are the most important variables that influence learning. Therefore, one needs to consider the cognitive structures of the learner and the material to be learned to devise strategies to link new learning to already existing knowledge structures. One information-processing strategy is the use of advance organizers. Ausubel describes two types of advance organizers: *expository organizers,* used when the material to be learned is completely new to learners, and *comparative organizers,* used when the ideas or concepts to be learned are familiar or relatable to previously learned ideas. According to Ausubel, "advance organizers (AO) are ideational scaffolds presented at higher levels of abstraction, generality, and inclusiveness than the material to be learned, they serve to provide specifically relevant anchoring ideas for more differentiated and detailed material that is subsequently presented" (Ausubel, 1977, p. 167). Having an understanding of the theory of advance organizers supported by the empirical evidence cited in the Walberg review, a principal's supervisory activities carried out in feedback sessions with novice teachers, modeling principles of effective instruction, and instructional support behaviors are greatly informed.

Observational Learning Theory

Observational learning theory contends that individuals acquire new knowledge and regulate patterns of behavior based on observing responses to and consequences of their own actions and the actions of others. "Cognitive processes play a prominent role in the acquisition and retention of new behavior patterns. Transitory experiences leave lasting effects being coded and retained in symbols for memory representations. Because acquisition of response information is a major aspect of learning much human behavior is developed modeling. . . . The initial approximations of responses learned observationally are further refined through self-corrective adjustments based on informative feedback from performance" (Bandura, 1977, p. 192). Think about a confrontation with an angry parent you may have had as a classroom teacher. As you reflect on the incident, what cues and social-behavioral response patterns helped you bring about positive outcomes, and avoid negative outcomes? You can use observational learning to devise personalized, appropriate strategies to deal with these important interpersonal conflicts.

Cooperative Learning Theory

Proponents of cooperative learning (Slavin, 1983; Johnson & Johnson, 1987) argue that if control in the classroom is decentralized there are a number of positive learning outcomes for students. Two basic categories for dividing up student work tasks are small-group work and peer-assisted activities. These two teaching/learning strategies require fundamental changes in instructional processes, in classroom management, and in basic reward systems. Teachers relinquish authority and transfer that authority, along with responsibility for individual and group learning outcomes, to groups of students. Slavin noted that the single most important component of cooperative learning strategies resulting in improved achievement scores for individual students was that group rewards were contingent upon total learning scores of all group members. Thus, there were incentives for group members to urge fellow learners to perform well so that as a group they received desired rewards. Weigel, Wiser and Cook (1975) reported that in addition to enhanced learning outcomes, getting students to work together cooperatively rather than competing individually may help to reduce interstudent and intergroup prejudice and hostility. Given the increasingly diverse makeup of student populations, cooperative learning experiences among students from varying racial, ethnic, and socioeconomic backgrounds should help to reduce conflicts and provide opportunities for students to develop important group process and teamwork skills in accepting and tolerant social environments.

Schema Theory

Schema theory explains how individuals acquire, organize, and facilitate use of knowledge by using particular cognitive structures. Various schemata then come to represent the knowledge that an individual acquires from experience and the interrelationships of these bits of knowledge to other situations and experiences. "Schemata are prototypes in memory of frequently experienced situations that people use to construct interpretations of related situations (Cervero, 1988, p. 40). Cognitive theorists and researchers (see, for example, Hart, 1993; Hallinger et al., 1993) have developed a variety of types of internal cognitive models describing structures individuals use to deal with new situations and information, and their experiences with them. Phonetics, semiotics, mathematical symbols, academic disciplines, social scripts, and teaching strategies are examples of how individuals store the consequences and interpretations of their experiences in meaningful and accessible forms. Anderson (1984) and Anderson and Pearson (1984) list six functions of schemata. They provide learners with a basis to: (1) assimilate information; (2) make inferential elaborations that fill in gaps in messages; (3) allocate attention to important elements; (4) search memory in a systematic fashion; (5) summarize information; and (6) make inferences that enable them to reconstruct original messages despite missing information. By knowing that schemata vary across individuals and across content area specializations, principals can work with their staffs to rethink the structure, scope, and sequencing of teaching and learning activities in their schools.

Using schema theory and cognitive psychology, Prestine and LeGrand (1991) provide a description of the linkages between *what* one knows and has access to and *how* such knowledge was acquired. They argue that it is important to understand how administrators really learn their craft and how they access their knowledge in daily practice. Understanding the cognitive processes and products has important implications for the preparation of principals and other educational leaders. Thus, schema theory and cognitive psychology provide a general explanation of how principals acquire, access, and put into action their professional knowledge. In addition, these frameworks help principals as they work with their staffs to understand their own learning and the learning of others. How is this framework related to real practice in a real school setting? Schema theory, for example, describes how individuals cumulatively acquire information, how such information is organized in the mind, and how various cognitive structures facilitate access to and use of acquired knowledge in particular situations. Schema theory provides an explanation of the connections among prior knowledge, experiences, and new information. For principals, then, knowledge acquisition and professional expertise evolve; they are the products of multiple sources of knowledge. Principals weave together what they acquire from experience, theory, and empirical knowledge—and through reflection on their knowledge, their actions, and their outcomes, they develop personalized and useful schemata that inform and guide them in their daily work.

Instructional Leadership Knowledge: Experiential

Perhaps the least examined source of professional knowledge is experiential knowledge. This cumulative and seemingly amorphous body of acquired knowledge has traditionally been discounted by academics because it lacks the verifiability and objectivity that scientific-empirical knowledge confidently assures. In addition, experiential knowledge is generally devalued in professional preparation programs because personal experience often suffers the disadvantages of being idiosyncratic and unexamined; thus it is viewed as unrepresentative, often simplistic, and at times, limiting. Nevertheless, as Hart points out, "Experience has many advantages, such as vividness, immediacy and relevance" (Hart, 1990a, p. 159). Given the limitations and advantages described, in what ways can experiential knowledge be a valuable source of professional knowledge for aspiring educational leaders?

The notion that experience, either one's own or that of others, is closely linked to learning is not new in educational literature. John Dewey stated, "Education in order to accomplish its ends both for the individual learner and for society must be based upon experience—which is always the actual life-experience of some individual" (1938, p. 89). Experience as a foundation upon which learning and subsequent acquisition of knowledge is based does not mean that all experiences are equal contributors to one's stock of knowledge. Based on observational learning theory, all experiences have the potential to contribute to further growth and learning. However, Dewey noted that some experiences can be miseducative in that their ultimate effect is to arrest or distort an individual's growth and subsequent opportunities to learn. Dewey proposed that the principles of *continuity* and *interaction* discriminate between those experiences that are worthwhile and those less valuable. "Continuity of experience means that every experience both takes up something from those which have gone before and modifies in some way the quality of those which come after" (p. 35). When new knowledge and experiences are linked in meaningful ways to prior knowledge, there is a greater likelihood that what is learned from the new experience will be integrated, coded, and subsequently retrieved for use in new situations. Interaction occurs among the person, the experience itself, the meaning given to the experience, and the situational context (internal and external environments).

Based on individualistic interpretations of experience, people build up unique, biographically based, personal stocks of knowledge that are useful to their performance and that become bases for responses to environmental factors. Over time these responses become learned behaviors and are further reinforced. So long as the environment is fairly stable and predictable these learned responses are not problematic; however, with dynamic and uncertain environments, automatic and routinized responses may be inappropriate and even organizationally dysfunctional. The task for a principal, or any administrator, is to check continually sets of learned responses for situational validity (Bredeson, 1991a; Osterman, 1989).

Cell (1984) describes three skills that individuals develop and use as they learn from their experiences. These skills are *generalization, selection,* and *interpretation.* Generalization is the cognitive process we use to scan for recurrent patterns in our experiences. Selection is how we determine those things we pay attention to. Interpretation is how we organize, record, and retrieve the messages from our experiences. From these three skills, "we gradually create and recreate a complex set of beliefs, knowledge, and evaluations of ourselves and our world and our interrelations with it" (p. 62).

It is useful to examine another personal experience that became part of one principal's individual stock of experiential knowledge. The incident described contributed in multiple ways to the professional knowledge base that subsequently informed future instructional leadership actions in the principalship. Personal experiences are not isolated from other sources of knowledge. In fact, they are often supported by empirical findings, explained in formal theory and expressed through knowledge-in-action. For each of us, as it will be for you, it is the singular vividness, immediacy, and relevance of our experiences in situations of practice that contribute to unique, biographically based stores of experiential knowledge. Together with empirical and theoretical sources of knowledge, they shape us as professionals and provide the substrate for professional ways of knowing. The following experience illustrates the educative value of personal experience.

Hiring in Haste

One of the primary instructional leadership responsibilities of a high school principal is to hire teachers. Starting July 1st as a first-year high school principal, I was eager to exercise my leadership skills in this area by interviewing, selecting, and recommending six new teachers to the school board for approval. The superintendent who had recently sent my name forward to the school board for approval had left for another job one week after I arrived. In a small, rural, consolidated school district when the superintendency is vacant, the high school principal is the senior administrator to the board. Wanting to begin the school year smoothly with a full complement of staff as well as to assure board members that I was a capable administrator, I listed vacancy notices, screened candidates, and by mid-August had all teaching positions at the high school filled, except the mathematics vacancy. There was no folder full of eager job applicants with secondary math certification. From the half-dozen candidates, only two emerged as viable candidates to be interviewed. The former superintendent informed me, just prior to leaving for his new position, that I should interview the candidate who lived in the district and whose wife was already on the teaching staff. He went on to explain that the board would never hire him because they really would like to get rid of his wife. If they were both employed in the district, the board believed this couple would never leave the district.

This meant there was only one viable, out-of-district candidate left to consider for the math vacancy. After interviewing the only remaining candidate on the day before classes started in August, I remained less than enthusiastic about hiring him. However, my anxiety about starting the school year without one of two high school math teachers weighed more heavily as I considered my personnel options. At 11:00 P.M., the evening before classes were to begin, I recommended to the board that we hire him. I told the board members that I was uncomfortable with my recommendation, but that I was more uncomfortable thinking about starting the year without one key staff member and with very limited possibilities of being able to find anyone for the position before the end of the first semester. Despite my lukewarm recommendation, the board hired the new high school math teacher.

Not long into the fall semester it became readily apparent that the new teacher had significant problems with lesson planning, classroom management, and positive working relationships with students and fellow teachers. Complaints about his performance were coming into my office regularly. My worst suspicions from interviewing this candidate were unfortunately being confirmed. As principal, I now had an even bigger problem. In his first year of teaching, this teacher needed a great deal of supervision and support to improve his performance. If his classroom performance did not improve by second semester, I had to notify him by March 15 that he would be nonrenewed for the coming school year. I was a first-year principal, who had to observe and evaluate twenty other faculty members; spending extended periods of time with one poorly performing teacher meant that I had even less time to become more knowledgeable about the overall instructional program in the school. After multiple observations, follow-up conferences, and very specific recommendations for improvement, I saw little evidence that the new mathematics teacher's classroom performance would improve significantly. I began to "keep book"; that is, I began to collect supplemental data to support my decision to recommend nonrenewal of this teacher to the school board. I had been candid with him in my postobservation conferences, stating that if significant improvements did not occur I would recommend nonrenewal for the coming year. Despite my candor and what I thought to be honest and very direct attempts to help him improve his teaching performance, I did not find a teacher eager to improve, but rather a defensive and bitterly outspoken critic of my own leadership capabilities.

In early March, as I prepared to go to the school board to recommend nonrenewal, I received a letter of resignation from him. His letter indicated that he wanted to leave the area and find a better job. He even asked for a positive letter of recommendation. I told him that I would write a letter, but that it would include all of my observations regarding his strengths and weaknesses. The immediate problem of dealing with a poorly performing teacher had been resolved, but the experience of hiring in haste and the instructional leadership problems it created for me as a first-year principal remain vivid, immediate, and relevant in my personal experience.

What exactly did I learn? Why did this lesson from experience become an important source of professional knowledge? This particular experience taught me that forcing myself into a decision corner and resigning myself to an unsatisfactory solution to one problem—filling a teaching vacancy—had a domino disruptive effect. Complaints about this teacher's classroom performance from students, parents, and school board members, the teacher's failure to respond positively to recommendations to improve his teaching performance, and his inability to work cooperatively with other faculty members created more problems than I could possibly have anticipated. Quite simply I had learned that, despite the importance of having a full staff to begin the school year, forced choices and expediency in personnel decisions rarely resolve immediate problems satisfactorily and frequently generate more serious, long-term problems. Were there other lessons? Honesty, directness, and extra resources were central to my sense of how effective instructional leadership needed to be exercised in dealing with a poor teacher. I realized, however, as the school year progressed that neither the teacher nor his colleagues were going to applaud my supervisory efforts. In fact, I was surprised that even very accomplished teachers, who expected high levels of professional performance from their colleagues and who might otherwise have complained to me privately about this teacher's performance, retreated to the neutral ground of teachers' collective silence. Even the strongest teachers became wary of my supervisory and evaluative behaviors once the possibility of nonrenewal became apparent to the marginal teacher and to the local teachers' union. My unique responsibilities, and the role others had defined for me as the principal were revealed. In the next section, we examine the relationships between definitions of professional expertise and those of professional practice.

DEFINITIONS OF PROFESSIONAL EXPERTISE AND PROFESSIONAL PRACTICE

The way in which professional expertise for principals is defined has direct implications for how one prepares for such a professional role and how acquired professional knowledge (empirical, theoretical, and experiential) is then turned into administrative behavior. In this section we will examine several frameworks to clarify what we mean when we refer to such terms as *professional expertise* and *competence* of school principals. After a brief discussion of various definitions of expertise and competence, we will examine the relationships among these definitions and strategies for professional preparation, the relationships between ways of knowing and the formation of expertise, and finally, the types and scope of transitional experiences that characterize the process of development from aspiring professional, to novice practitioner, to expert. This learning-socialization process will be examined in detail in Chapter 10, "Becoming a Principal."

Professionals are often defined as individuals who use specialized knowledge and skills to deal effectively with problems within particular fields. What distinguishes a novice from an expert is not that experts are always right in their professional judgments, or that experts never make mistakes. Clearly, experts commit their share of mistakes as they work through various problems of practice, but experts have integrated various sources of knowledge into an accessible and utilizable framework that systematically helps them avoid the most common problem-solving errors made by less-skilled practitioners—inappropriate scanning, incorrect synthesis, inadequate synthesis, premature closure, and anchoring.

Lawyers defend or prosecute accused criminals. Medical doctors treat gravely ill patients. Architects design and allocate space for clients. Teachers remediate reading problems for at-risk students. Assistant principals implement strategies to reduce truancy. Principals work with unenthusiastic professional staffs to rethink graded organizational structures. In each situation of practice, the professional uses specialized knowledge, competencies, frameworks, and norms of practice to define problems, to consider strategies and alternatives to deal with these problems, and to take action. Despite the common usage of the terms, expertise and competence, there is a fair amount of variance in how they are defined. We will use these terms interchangeably throughout this book. It is important, however, to recognize that different understandings of professional expertise have implications for how school leadership is defined and legitimized, how principalship expertise is transmitted, and ultimately, how such specialized knowledge is put into practice. We use the work of Short (1985) and Kennedy (1987) to illustrate relationships among definitions of professional expertise, training and preparation for professional expertise, and practice.

Short describes four conceptualizations of competence, a term he considers to be somewhat overused and, at times, abused by well-meaning reformers calling for educational excellence, school improvement, professional development, and accountability measures. At issue is whether competence comes to be understood as a static or as a dynamic entity. As a *static entity*, competence is enumerated in proficiencies in particular behaviors and actions, in deliberations on choices among competing actions, and in standardized levels of capability in specified areas of knowledge and behaviors. The lists and taxonomies in Table 2.1 illustrate principalship competence viewed as a static entity in which all a novice administrator needs to do to gain professional expertise is become proficient in requisite skills and recognize his primary tasks and responsibilities. Effective principals have the requisite skills and recognize their primary tasks, but their expertise comes from their ability to see connections between situations of practice, their professional knowledge, requisite skills and responsibilities, and purposes and goals of their actions. This is a *dynamic entity* view of professional expertise; it is holistic, transactional, and integrative of many ways of knowing and acting.

Mary Kennedy (1987), in her review of literature related to professional expertise, cites the work of Harrisberger (1985), who criticized contemporary curriculum used to prepare engineers because approximately 80 percent of the training is made up of "ics": mathematics, physics, dynamics, and electronics, while the engineering expertise required in situations of practice for engineers consists largely of "ings": consulting, designing, planning, and evaluating. Kennedy provides four operating definitions of expertise: the performance of technical skills, the utilization and application of theory and general principles, the prescription of critical analytical skills (such as case method) for examining and interpreting situations of practice, and deliberate action that stresses reflexivity among skills, analytical processes, actions, and the situation. Each of these definitions of professional expertise has particular meaning in the principalship. As you read through the following examples, think about your current professional work and try to analyze it in terms of Kennedy's four definitions of expertise. If you were asked to prepare a chart that graphically represented your reliance on these four types of competence, which types of competence would tend to dominate your daily work?

Professional Competence Defined as the Acquisition of Technical Skills

Examples reflecting each of Kennedy's four definitions of expertise appear in textbooks, commission reports, training modules, and the curriculum of university preparation programs for school principals. If school leadership expertise is believed to be a static entity or simply the acquisition of specified technical skills, typologies ad infinitum will prevail, and in fact have. There is a constant blitz of new metaphors, frameworks, and images to capture our imagination and attention. Each is an example of the perennial reshuffling of the "deck of technical rationality cards." By reshuffling the cards, the educational players continue to hope they will draw three cards to complete their inside straight—that just the right combination of proficiencies, the ideal model, and the perfect process to prepare candidates for the realities of the principalship in the twenty-first century will fill in their hands.

As Table 2.1 attests, the proliferation of lists of professional competencies for school principals continues unabated. A quick review of the works the National Commission for the Principalship (1990) and the National Policy Board for Educational Administration (1993) provides the clearest example of educational leadership in the principal viewed as technical competence. The performance domains specified in the two works titled *Principals for our Changing Schools* were developed by a task force of educators representing school principals, professors, members of professional associations, and other policymakers. Twenty-one   competencies are organized into four performance domains—functional, programmatic, interpersonal, and contextual.

Functional Domain

Leadership
Information Collection
Problem Analysis
Judgment
Organizational Oversight
Implementation
Delegation

Programmatic Domains

Instructional Program
Curriculum Design
Student Guidance and Development
Staff Development
Measurement and Evaluation
Resource Allocation

Interpersonal Domains

    Motivating Others
    Sensitivity
    Oral Expression
    Written Expression

Contextual Domains

    Philosophical and Cultural Values
    Legal and Regulatory
    Policy and Political Influences
    Public and Media Relationships

When expertise in school leadership is defined as the aggregation of various technical skills, educational administration preparation programs tend to decontextualize important skills from the realities of situations of practice that are often characterized by indeterminacy, instability, uncertainty, and competing values. This reality makes it difficult for new principals to know when it is appropriate to apply the skills they have learned. Finally, preparation programs grounded solely in technical skills traditionally ignore an important source of knowledge that contributes to professional expertise and the processes for integrating sources of knowledge, experiential knowledge and knowing-in-action. An alternative model, then, for preparing aspiring principals would be similar to what Joyce and Showers (1980) suggest: a model consisting of direct instruction about specified skills, simulated practice, and assisted practice of learned behaviors in school settings. When we point out the limitations of defining expertise in the principalship as learned technical skills we do not mean to suggest that particular skills are unimportant to expert practice; practitioners without technical knowledge or skills would be incompetent. Technical skills and proficiencies are necessary, but not sufficient for successful leadership in the principalship; for example, a principal could be technically expert in computerized scheduling of classes, but fail to conceptualize a daily schedule that meets the needs of students and maximizes the talent of teachers. A principal may be technically expert in budgeting and know all of the district, state, and legal parameters for effective fiscal management; however, being able to prepare a budget is not the same as being effective in the allocation of resources to maximize student achievement in the school.

Professional Expertise Defined as the Application of Theory

When educational leadership is defined as the application of theory and general principles of administration as reflected in the notion of "administrative qua administration" guided by empirical inquiry and formal theory (Culbertson, 1988), the curriculum in preparation programs consists primarily of scientifically validated models and frameworks that form the only legitimated professional knowledge base for aspiring administrators. Preparation experiences and instruction then are likely to consist of two teaching-learning strategies:

They can show students how to apply individual principles to particular situations, that is, how to recognize cases as examples of principles [Seager, 1985]; or they can help students integrate knowledge from across the disciplines into a single body of working knowledge [Stark & Lowther, 1986]. (Kennedy, 1987, p. 157)

The application of general principles from theoretical models as the guiding definition of professional expertise is the view most often criticized by practitioners. Armed with the general theory of leadership that leaders initiate structures to define important work tasks in the school, principals go into schools and discover that situations of practice are complex and embedded in unique contexts that diminish the effects of their leadership efforts. Principals recognize that schools are loosely coupled—that teaching and learning processes are not tightly linked to the organizational structure and its rules, procedures, and authority structures (Bidwell, 1965; Weick, 1976). In addition to the neutralizing effects of structural looseness, principals find their leadership constrained by union contracts, by socioeconomic conditions, and by deeply embedded cultural norms. For example, a principal may initiate a process to monitor student achievement systematically, but find that such assessment processes violate norms of teacher control over teaching and learning.

Professional Expertise as Critical Analysis

Educational leadership defined as critical analysis provides systematic methods through readings, case study analysis, and simulation activities to address problems of practice, however, without suggestions for preferred courses of action. Armed with prescriptive, theoretical, and critical analytical schemata, educational administration students and practitioners confront multidimensional situations of practice in which problems are defined and solutions to them are generated and enacted. However, critical lenses do not indicate how decision makers should choose from among alternative actions. Case study analysis is a common instructional strategy for bringing real-life situations of practice into principal preparation programs (Ashbaugh & Kasten, 1991). As a student you may be quite able to identify a central problem and ancillary issues in a scenario involving a conflict between two teachers over the placement of a student with a learning disability. Opportunities for depth-analysis, reflection, and no-risk decision making help you gain understanding, perspective, and rudimentary problem analysis skills. However, in order for you to develop greater expertise as a principal, the analytical skills gained in case study activities must move beyond abstract exercises. Real expertise is gained as you apply these problem-solving skills to new situations of practice that are personal and that have real consequences for the decisions you make.

Theoretical frameworks and analytical methods thus provide lenses, but they seldom provide the specificity to guide particular courses of action or to account for the vagaries of situational indeterminacy. Again, experiential knowledge and knowing-in-action are excluded. There is no place for transactional influences between knowledge and the practitioners and situations of practice.

Finally, expertise in the principalship defined as deliberate action assumes that leadership competence develops with experience but that experience can only contribute to expertise if practitioners are capable of learning from it (Kennedy, 1987). Preparation programs based on this definition of expertise would provide students learning opportunities early on and continuously throughout their training programs, with increasingly complex and multidimensional factors, to try out leadership strategies, test actions and ideas, and connect those experiments to desired outcomes in schools. This is preparation to be a reflective practitioner. Sources of knowledge inform professional expertise and practice. Application of professional expertise in turn expresses that knowledge. There is a reciprocal relationship between knowledge, beliefs, and professional practice.

TRANSFORMING KNOWLEDGE INTO ACTION

Competent practitioners usually know more than they can say.
(Schon, 1983, viii).

In a kindergarten room with twenty-one five- and six-year-olds doing finger painting, a kindergarten teacher engages each child, one by one, in an experiment about what happens when yellow and blue paints are mixed together and swished around on the paper. A guidance counselor listens and skillfully responds to the anguish of a pregnant teenager threatening to run away from home and quit school. An assistant principal ejects an unruly fan from a basketball game, as 1,000 other fans—some jeering, others cheering, look on. To witness any of these vignettes in the daily work lives of educators is to see professional artistry in action. If one were to ask these professionals to describe what they needed to know to do what they did so effectively, they might find it difficult to verbalize their demonstrated expertise with any degree of specificity or accuracy. The inability to adequately represent professional artistry in words suggests that some types of professional knowledge are dynamic, spontaneous, and interactive with the situation of practice and best represented in professional action, rather than in static constructions such as words, theoretical models, or codified rules of practice. Schon (1987) refers to these forms of professional artistry as knowing-in-action. When we are able to describe our actions verbally, we transform our expressive ways of knowing into *knowledge-in-action*.

Schon (1983, 1987) argues for an epistemology of practice that legitimates ordinary practical knowledge. This knowing-in-action has been described by other researchers and scholars as tacit knowledge (Polanyi, 1966); nonlogical processes (Barnard, 1938); intuition/feelings (Guba & Lincoln, 1981), and it is mediated by reflection-in-action, where experts turn thought back on action and make ongoing adjustments in their actions to perform successfully. Schon states, "In much of the spontaneous behavior of skillful practice we reveal a kind of knowing which does not stem from prior intellectual operation" (1983, p. 51). This is not to say that such behavior is random or illogical. Are there examples of knowing-in-action in the daily work of principals? Are there things effective principals do that demonstrate high levels of expertise and keen professional knowledge but nevertheless become problematic in attempts to make seemingly familiar behaviors verbally explicit? If such knowledge is difficult to articulate propositionally, you can see the problem scholars have in delineating exactly what knowledge should be incorporated into a professional knowledge base to guide preparation programs for school principals.

Knowing-in-action is an important contributor to effective administrative performance and to continued professional development. Failure to recognize the importance of knowing-in-action creates problems for practitioners and for the people who prepare them. Newly credentialed principals, who go into schools and begin their professional work, inevitably find that theoretical, empirical, and experiential sources of knowledge, which make up their individual professional knowledge bases, are necessary but not sufficient for administrative success. New principals find what Schon (1983) described as indeterminate zones of practice characterized by uncertainty, uniqueness, and values conflicts. Theoretical models, empirical research findings, and past experiences do not quite match the problems and tend to provide only partial information or explanations to guide administrative choices and actions. Frequently, new principals despair and lose confidence in these sources, especially the theoretical and empirical, because by themselves they do not provide the "right solutions" to their very "specific" problems.

Schon uses the metaphor of conversation to describe how knowing-in-action and reflection-in-action help practitioners appreciate the problematic features of practice while at the same time enable them to recognize the importance of integrating multiple ways of knowing into purposeful designs to deal with complex issues and problems at hand. "When someone reflects-in-action, he becomes a researcher in the practice context. He is not dependent on the categories of established theory and technique, but constructs a new theory of the unique case" (1983, p. 68).

Knowing-in-action is an iterative process in which principals can simultaneously and spontaneously make use of prior schemata and bring those to any new situation of practice. Knowing-in-action doesn't mean flying by the seat of your pants. Principals, like other professionals, use various tools, such as media, language, behavioral repertoires, values, overarching theories, and role frames to help them structure meaningful frameworks for reflective conversations with unique, sometimes uncertain, and often conflict-ridden situations. In these conversations of practice, principals interactively frame problems, define their parameters, entertain alternative solutions, experiment, make adjustments, and shape the situations in order to deal with particular problems effectively. Taken together, these activities are expressions of professional knowing-in-action. "When a practitioner keeps inquiry moving, however, he does not abstain from action in order to sink into endless thought. Continuity of inquiry entails a continual interweaving of thinking and doing" (1983, p. 280), in which professionals keep alive multiple perspectives in the midst of action. "Through countless acts of attention and inattention, naming, sensemaking, boundary settings, and control," principals become worldmakers and sensemakers of situations in which they constantly attempt to match professional expertise and know-how to the problems confronted. "They are in transaction with their practice worlds, framing the problems that arise in practice situations and shaping the situations to fit the frames, framing their roles and constructing practice situations to make their role-frames operational" (Schon, 1987, p. 36).

PUTTING LEADERSHIP KNOWLEDGE INTO ACTION

Knowing is not enough! Principals enact their knowledge and express professional expertise not as exemplars of a static knowledge base, a credential status, or a formal role. Rather, meaningful leadership is anchored in multiple sources of professional knowledge—theoretical, empirical, and experiential. This professional knowledge is integrated and applied through knowing-in-action and generates context-specific understandings which, in turn, inform action. Effective leadership involves holistic, integrative, and systematic processes in which leaders seek to join self, others, and multiple perspectives in a continuing and mutually evocative conversation with problems of practice; thus meaning and understanding are constantly being generated—and linked to action. Next we examine common problem-solving errors made by novices.

USES OF KNOWLEDGE AND COMMON PROBLEM-SOLVING ERRORS

In Chapter 1 and earlier in this chapter, we introduced a view of the school principalship grounded in the research finding and experiential belief that knowledge takes many forms and is acquired in a series of iterative steps by the new professional. One last aspect of knowledge and its uses in analysis and problem solving by principals and other professionals in schools requires attention. Common problem-solving errors to which all people fall victim have been identified by researchers; these errors follow identifiable patterns. Professionals can learn to become wary of these errors and structure safeguards against them as their expertise grows.

We have chosen to close this chapter, therefore, on a cautionary note: All people are subject to cognitive, problem-solving errors, and we must be vigilant to guard against these errors.

We end this chapter with a brief discussion of the most common problem-solving errors revealed by researchers focusing on the professions (Barrows, 1988). They include (1) inappropriate scanning (seeking data or information that will not be helpful), (2) incorrect synthesis (reaching unwarranted conclusions), (3) inadequate synthesis (failure to come to a conclusion that is warranted from the data), (4) premature closure, and (5) anchoring (failure to attend to new, relevant, but unfamiliar information—being anchored in past decisions). These errors occur in all kinds of preservice professional education programs when problem-solving is the focus of learning. Schon (1983) particularly cautioned against the danger to administrators of "selective inattending," because their work is so complex that it is tempting to pay attention only to quickly recognizable problems that concur with experience. This is often the problem in case study analysis discussed earlier. Ramsey and Whitman (1989) identified these problems in medical schools, and Hart, Sorensen and Naylor (1993) found them reoccurring during problem-based learning experiences in preservice training for school principals.

Inappropriate Scanning. This first error presents a tempting diversion for students during problem-based learning. Because they lack experience and have limited knowledge, students (or anyone else for that matter) may go on a "wild goose chase," asking questions and seeking documents that lead them astray or obscure important issues with a deluge of unimportant details. The key is to know enough about the professional knowledge base and the problems of administrative practice to ask the right questions, as did Agatha Christie's famous detective, Hercule Poirot.

One example of this error is found in the search for information that will have no simple, practical use for the educator. For example, educators often survey parents about the instructional techniques used by their child's teacher. These parents probably have never observed the teacher; they report what their children have told them about instruction filtered through each child's experience. Each child's experience, however, may be so profoundly different that the survey (simple yes/no responses or attitude-intensity responses on a scale of, say, one to seven) offers absolutely no avenue for the conveyance of real and accurate information about the child's school experience.

Parent surveys are popular, hence a parent survey—inappropriate scanning. New educational leaders demonstrate a remarkable faith in surveys. Hart, Sorensen, and Naylor (1993) found students eager to survey parents, interview teachers, or talk to the PTA, as much to show that they value input as to gather useful information.[2]

Incorrect Synthesis. Pressure always accrues on "leaders" to be "decisive." Data are gathered; decisions are warranted. As one teacher once said to one of the authors, "Sometimes a leader just has to make a decision and stick by it." An ambivalence develops in school leaders. Should they ponder and weigh the evidence, thus demonstrating analytical talent and thoughtfulness? Should they take the information available and act decisively, thus demonstrating the ability to make hard decisions? Contrasting and admirable values conflict: (1) leaders are thoughtful, analytical thinkers; (2) leaders are decisive; they act. These pressures accrue and lead to the second of the common problem-solving errors identified by researchers—incorrect synthesis.

When incorrect synthesis occurs, people take disparate facts and distill them mistakenly to reach unwarranted conclusions. The facts may be straight

[2]All the examples in this section are drawn from Hart, Sorensen, and Naylor (1993) and from Hart (1992).

and true, but the synthesis of the facts is wrong. The desire to bring "research" or "data" or "feedback" together quickly may exert undue pressure on a professional to "be a leader." One of the authors remembers keenly the efforts of a teacher who used this pressure to try to force a premature decision about instructional techniques and curriculum decisions related to mathematics instruction. Each reader can probably recall a personal experience in her career as a professional educator when data were used as a leverage (sometimes a bludgeon) to force a preconceived decision. Incorrect synthesis thus springs from situations when facts may be straight but the chain of logic linking them to a conclusion falters.

One innovation in the preparation of school leaders may heighten vulnerability to the incorrect synthesis problem-solving error. Many programs are appropriately and innovatively integrating problem-based learning or case study learning into their curricula. But these innovations require problem-solving expertise on the part of instructors and organizers to prevent common problem-solving errors in trial-and-error practice from being reenacted in professional preparation programs. Students and scholars alike must understand, recognize, and rectify errors that emerge when professionals take disparate and unrelated (or ephemerally related) data and combine them into a rationale for action.

Because the focus of case study or problem-based learning often is "getting the facts" or defining the "problem," students feel pressured to come to a diagnosis and then move quickly to an action plan or intervention (premature closure). Incorrect synthesis thus presents a serious challenge. A principal has "facts." These hard facts may come in the form of surveys from parents (with abysmal return rates and ambiguous questions) or as directives from disillusioned school board members, but the principal will assuredly face data in many forms. Like the novice chess players described by Simon (1993), the student of administration may fail to see critical patterns, or may see patterns that do not represent the complexity or true nature of reality. The result: reaching unwarranted conclusions based on misinterpreted or incompletely interpreted information. This is the heart and core of inaccurate synthesis.

Students of administration sometimes label problems "simple" when viewing them from a teacher's perspective only. One student faced with a problem posing a conflict over student placement and instruction said, "I don't see what the problem is. The principal should tell the teacher what to do, and the teacher should do it." Another commented, "Seems like a typical school to me." Another error occurs when students see diagnoses or choices in black-or-white terms—either this or that. Students sometimes adopt "decision tree" methods for defining and attacking problems; they confine themselves to two alternatives at each level, and proceed quickly to the wrong diagnosis.

Inadequate Synthesis. Failure to reach warranted conclusions also mars problem-solving processes for administrators. In this case a logical chain of reliable data, carefully accumulated, may lead to a conclusion that a professional fails to reach.

In the attempt to leave options open or appear open minded, some professional novices phrase their conclusions tentatively, provide verbose and diffuse justifications for every possible recommendation, or ignore important actions that defy convention but are warranted by the data. These situations exemplify inadequate synthesis. A logical chain of evidence points to several logical alternatives, but another decision is reached. Often, this happens because data contradict dearly held beliefs or preconceived explanations for a problem that educators have identified. For example, one of the authors was involved in an intense and emotional conflict between mathematics teachers, special education teachers, and parents over outcome-based education. A score of 80 percent on a carefully designed, computer-administered diagnostic test was required for students to move on to a new concept of mathematics in the program. One student had failed the competency test on the sequencing of real numbers many times in the first few months of school, and his teachers and parents were in open warfare over the "real meaning" of this failure. Parents were signing petitions to abolish competency-based mathematics instruction. The PTA was up in arms. The parents and both special education and mathematics teachers were accusing each other of indifference and malfeasance. The special education teacher solved the dilemma with a simple diagnosis. The student suffered from a sequencing disorder leading him to assign an "a" to the highest number, a "b" to the next number, and so forth for the purposes of the computer-assisted multiple-choice testing system used by the program. Consequently, regardless of the "real" value of numbers, the student logically ordered them thus: a = largest number, b = second-largest number, c = third-largest number, and so forth. He was destined to fail the examination that randomly assigned numerical value to "a" through "d" choices on the alphabet.

Premature Closure. The most common problem-solving error observed by Hart, Sorensen, and Naylor in their studies of administrative students' problem-based learning was premature closure. The minute they saw similarities between a problem or case and some event in their own experience or their own preconceived notions about teachers in particular or education in general, some students labeled the problem and jumped immediately to a preconceived solution. With insufficient evidence, professionals and students alike often want to bring closure to a problem that may be critically different from anything in their prior experience but that bears superficial resemblance to previously "solved" problems.

One student exemplified this error by proposing a solution to one problem with the statement, "Teachers seem to be self-serving; they don't want to teach. . . ." Teacher alienation was labeled as teachers' ennui, boredom, and not caring. School circumstances, professional conflicts, environmental difficulties, or student problems could all have contributed to, or even caused, teacher alienation, but the student chose premature closure: This is a problem springing from teacher indifference.

Another student, confronted with the same problem set, committed a different version of premature closure. She framed the situation in terms of her own district and school. Her solutions duplicated current practice in her district. The problem was simple (we've faced this before), and the solution was readily at hand (previous action or policy). Closure was swift and merciless.

Anchoring. Students who reached premature closure also failed to respond to new, relevant information that they found inconsistent with their previous thinking or experience. This is akin to saying, "Don't confuse me with the facts; I've already made up my mind." Recognizing that he had been making this error for weeks during problem-solving sessions, one student lamented to his principal coach, I've just discovered the "tip of the iceberg." Another applied her preconceived image of a principal to any and all situations, "One reality of being a new principal is if you go in with a strong hand, you won't accomplish anything." Her notion of someone who did not have a "strong hand" led her to formulate tentative and ambiguous action recommendations (and far too many) in the situations she confronted. She, too, tended to appeal to her home districts' policies and procedures as the answer to all dilemmas.

The preceding examples are drawn from studies of preservice educational administration students who aspired to become school principals or to fill other educational leadership positions. Their experiences are not unique, nor were they poor students. In the chapters that follow, we examine additional features of knowledge and of the knowledge-to-action links that make for more sophisticated and professional administrative leadership on the part of new school principals.

Regardless of individual levels of expertise and professional knowledge, all professionals make mistakes. Principals you know and work with make mistakes. As a principal you will make your own share of mistakes. Our position is that preparation for the professional practice of a school principal is not a journey toward perfection but one anchored in the imperfect realities and endemic ambiguities of professional knowing and doing in schools. The difference between experts and perpetual novices is that, even when mistakes are made, experts continue to learn and gain greater expertise by seeing important patterns that will help them make choices and take appropriate actions in the future. In a conversation with a skilled carpenter one of the authors came to understand that professional expertise was not a matter of error-free practice. Even skilled carpenters on occasion will mismeasure, miscut and misalign various structures. However, what experts have, and novices eventually acquire, is an ability to evaluate outcomes, to learn from mistakes, and to make appropriate adjustments when required. Professional expertise involves the use of particular knowledge and skills reflexively so that when something isn't plumb, you recognize the flaw and then fix it.

CONCLUSION

Like professionals in any field, educators need to be very cautious when they separate, for purposes of discourse, professional knowledge and professional action. It is important to stress that successful leadership in today's schools requires the synergy of both knowledge and action, each informing the other. In this chapter we examined the ways in which principals apply their professional expertise to their everyday work. After a brief review of the origins and history of the modern day principalship, we described selected knowledge-base organizers for principals. Next we illustrated the connections among three primary sources of principals' professional knowledge (empirical, experiential, and theoretical) and described how these sources of knowledge inform principals' instructional leadership practices. We then examined in detail four definitions of professional expertise. These included professional expertise defined as: (1) the acquisition of technical skills; (2) the application of theory; (3) critical analysis; and, (4) deliberate action. Next we described how highly expert principals transform their professional knowledge into appropriate leadership behaviors and actions. We highlighted reflection-in-action and reflection-on-action as important cognitive processes guiding principals' use of their professional knowledge in situations of practice. Finally, we described five common problem-solving errors that all professionals, principals included, must guard against in the use of their professional knowledge in their work. In Chapter 3 we turn to an examination of the social context of schools to describe the unique social and organizational dimensions of teaching and learning environments that affect principals' professional socialization, thinking, and work.

SUGGESTED ACTIVITIES

1. Review three or four major educational reform reports. To what degree are principals and their work addressed in these reports? Are there major recommendations in these reports that would significantly change what your principal does?
2. Identify a major problem that needs attention in your school. Using the sources of professional knowledge discussed in this chapter, identify specific ways to address this problem. What sources of knowledge will help you address the problem?
3. In Table 2.1 we provide a sample of knowledge-base organizers for principals. Based on your experience and training, what organizers would you list as critical to successful school leadership?
4. We identified five problem-solving errors for practitioners in the professions, including educational leaders. Identify specific instances or problem situations in your professional practice that are not amenable to routine actions or easy solutions. What strategies have you developed to minimize problem-solving errors in your professional practice when you confront such problems?

The Social Context of Leadership

Principals acquire professional knowledge and connect their knowledge to decisions and actions within a specific and unique context. The knowledge-base search carried out by the profession at large that we discussed in Chapter 2 is reflected on a personal level for each principal. In each school, the mix of individual, cultural, and social factors is unique. In this chapter, we build on previous discussions of forms of professional knowledge and the connection between knowledge and action by adding the features of the group in which the knowledge is applied to the mix. Each school is a system made up of multiple elements. Within this system, principals must exert leadership if they hope to influence the teaching and learning that occur in their schools.

The adults and children who work in schools form a social system of formal and informal relationships. When a new principal joins the school she may be the only new member of the group, or she may be one of several new members. Like all new members of an established group, the new principal will have to learn many formal and informal rules and expectations in order to be fully accepted as a productive, full-fledged member. Productive membership for principals includes the ability to influence the beliefs, values, and actions of others in the school.

At the same time, a principal aspires to leadership. He hopes to have an impact on the work of teachers and students and on the teaching and learning that take place in the school he is assigned to lead. He wants to contribute to the effectiveness of the school as a whole and to the positive experiences people have within it. Those who appointed him expect him to have an impact on the school. Consequently, he will need to learn about the school's social and technical systems, not only so that he will fit in but also so that he can effect positive connections and professional actions, using the best qualities of the school to help other educational professionals in the school achieve their important work goals—helping children and young adults learn and grow.

This chapter introduces some central features of schools as social systems that interact with the technical demands of teaching and learning, and principals' experiences within them. We focus on some techniques that principals use to enhance their roles as leaders within these social systems. In the following sections, we explore the interactions of principals as members of the social systems of schools. The features and patterns of their interactions and the important principles that will help them achieve their leadership goals will be introduced. Later, in subsequent sections of the book, we will explore in greater depth the theoretical and research traditions underlying and supporting these principles.

ELEMENTS OF SCHOOL ORGANIZATIONS

Patterns that shape people's beliefs and actions become embedded in their social groups. Schools, like other social groups, have discrete elements: (1) social structures, (2) a core technology, (3) goals, (4) participants, and (5) environments (Leavitt, 1965; Scott, 1987). Together, these elements are the components of the social and technical system within which principals work.

A school's internal social structure (formal *and* informal), the goals people generally accept, individual participants, and the social aspects of the environment, all can be considered part of the social system. Technologies and the technical environment can be included in a rough representation of the technical system. While this summary is a gross oversimplification of the complexities and multiple levels of school organizations, it will suffice for our discussion here. Social structures include norms or expectations that are considered right and good, and behaviors common to people within the school (though they may or may not correspond exactly to expressed norms). They encompass the orientation and behavior generally accepted and excepted of group members. Technologies encompass all the ways in which work customarily is accomplished in a school (how we teach and pupils learn). Goals include the outcomes sought deliberately and subconsciously—the reasons schools exists—and may be very unclear or hotly contested.[1] Because goals are pursued by individuals and groups, they become part of the accepted and expected elements of the social system. The participants include a wide range of people—from students, teachers, and administrators to parents, community members, and special interests groups. Different perspectives on schools as organizations include different sets of participants. Principals' perspectives on who is or is not a participant shape many of the decisions they make as school leaders about the roles and responsibilities they assign to people. Finally, environments form a critical component of schools' social and technical systems. The beliefs and aspirations of the immediate community, the fiscal environment of a state, changing expectations for teachers' work and professional control, and the expectations of right and proper roles for schools in society strongly influence the system within which principals work (Bredeson, 1989).

---

[1]For example, the Clinton administration at the beginning of the 103d Congress expressed support for a move toward secondary vocational education on the German model—apprenticeships in private organizations. Educators and policy makers argue whether this support stemmed from an educational goal or an economic goal.

These right and proper roles spark sincere and intense debate. For example, if schools are the "great leveler" predicted by nineteenth century public school advocates, principals are expected to make decisions that reduce differences among students and maximize their social mobility (Cremin, 1990). If schools are agents of social change, curriculum focused on social criticism and awareness, social activism, and community service requirements might dominate the school. If schools are agents of global economic competition, principals work to maximize the overall performance of students on tasks deemed necessary for future economic development and to identify and nurture top performers to push them toward ever higher achievement. If schools are centers of community service to children and youth, principals focus their efforts on collaboration with social work, health, and other services for young people and their families. You can undoubtedly think of other elements of expectations for schooling and their relationships with expectations held for principals as well.

Because no two schools have all these features of school social and technical systems in common, no two schools present the same challenge to a principal. This complexity is a hallmark feature of professional work: that each case or endeavor presents a unique set of challenges to which the general knowledge base of the profession must be applied (Schon, 1983). For this reason, a principal needs to have a broad repertoire of knowledge, skills, and actions available to her as a resource so that she can respond to the unpredictable challenges that arise in the schools she is assigned to lead.

Social Structure

The first component of school organizations with which principals interact is the social structure. Relationships among people within the school form the social structure. These relationships include two parts, the normative and the behavioral. The normative structure (what ought to be) describes what people in the school believe their actions rightly should be. This part of the school social structure encompasses the "values, norms, and role expectations" (Scott, 1987, p. 15) that people use to shape their judgments about actions, people, and events (the orientation and behavior referred to earlier). Values are criteria of rightness and goodness; norms of behavior describe rules about the appropriate ways to achieve goals; and role expectations combine values and norms into standards by which to judge people who fill common roles in the school (i.e., principal, teacher, or counselor). In this discussion, we use the common definition of role as an established social position with generally agreed-upon tasks and associated behaviors, and accepted and expected relationships with other roles in the group. For example, the role "elementary school teacher" evokes some very clear skills and behaviors, attitudes, and personal characteristics; in a specific school, those accepted and expected skills and behaviors would be consistent with generally held role expectations, but they would be more elaborate as well as specific to that school and community.

These roles tie closely into values. For example, in schools we value cultural and social diversity among students and often include appreciation of diversity as a curriculum goal. We then establish ways in which cultural diversity can be meaningfully included in our curriculum and set up processes for monitoring progress toward shared goals in this area. Mission statements begin to include diversity; curriculum and instructional guides enumerate diversity goals; teachers conduct inservice sessions; and faculties develop faculty and student handbooks to outline the school's goals and the roles teachers, students, parents, the principal, and others will take in achieving desired goals.

The combination of norms, values, and role expectations forms a structure, because people within the school accept these relationships as right and good, and they act on the basis of their acceptance. Taken together, these relationships form the culture of the school and, consequently, the emotional and psychological climate in which children, youth, and educators labor to achieve their goals.

Principals and other professional educators work within these strong beliefs about what is right and good, rules of behavior that shape the standards by which people are judged. Patricia Wasley (1991) vividly portrays the ways in which these norms shape what people do in schools in her book on teacher leadership. For example, teachers have worked very hard in many schools to establish rules that reinforce their professional role and deemphasize old "babysitting" expectations that used to characterize teaching work. These rules come in many forms: duty-free lunches, freedom from playground supervision, assignments on after-hours activities responsibilities, and freedom from cleaning responsibilities within their classrooms. These rules reinforce strong beliefs about teachers' professional roles, but they also come into conflict with some attempts at major change in instruction and schools. In one example of teacher leaders—Mary and Barbara, who have designed computer-assisted, group-structured mathematics instruction—Wasley illustrates this principle. A group of teachers visited from another school, and Wasley described the conflicts they faced between their desire to emulate an innovative and supportive instructional reform and their commitment to work rules firmly established and accepted in their school:

> They [the visiting teachers] ask a variety of questions about scheduling. Mary makes it clear that in order to conduct this experiment, she and Barbara gave up their duty-free recess time, which causes the visitors to lapse into momentary silence. They do not feel that their group would be willing to do this. They ask about the absence of bells, about evaluation of the kids' work, about whether the kids are learning more this way than in regular classroom instruction. . . .
>
> She notes that because they do not allow any students to be pulled out of the classroom, and because all of the students are working in groups anyway, there is less awareness about learning deficiencies, which is better for those students' self-esteem. (1991, pp. 116–117)

Two beliefs and values manifested in rules are represented in this quotation. First, teachers' duty-free recesses must be protected (or are not sacrosanct). Second, students work in groups free from close oversight and evaluation (or students' progress is not closely evaluated unless they are individually evaluated). These values conflict and the rules that embed them in schools are consequential, not trivial. Values and the rules that emanate from them shape the way children perceive themselves, the way teachers evaluate and perceive children, and the way teachers' work days are structured, among other differences. Reflect for a moment about values that have had similar powerful effects on educational decisions in schools in which you have worked. How strong was agreement among teachers? Were community values influential?

Regardless of the work rules constructed to legitimate and enforce those values and beliefs, individual behavior is difficult to predict. People consistently fail to behave in perfect accordance with their beliefs. One problem with much of the school leadership research results from this conflict between how principals say they behave and how their subordinates (teachers and others) say they behave. This is why scholars who study organizations like schools examine both normative and behavioral structures and do not expect them to be exactly the same. The behavioral structure includes all patterns of behavior that customarily occur within the group. Structure is formed as actions are repeated over and over until they become an understood and tacit part of regular events.

The development of tacit and understood behaviors happens gradually. In the example of cultural diversity in the curriculum, change might at first require very deliberate actions and procedures guided by and nurtured by a core of committed teachers and administrators. Over time, these actions, supported by the achievement of desired outcomes, would become habituated in the work and lives of teachers, students, the principal, and others. Diversity would be a given.

Many examples of the gaps between the behavioral and normative social structures in schools can be found in commonly recounted experiences. Teachers may say that they believe in sharing lesson plans, worksheets, and other materials and ideas freely with other teachers. If they repeat this assertion frequently and to many audiences, sharing among teachers is part of the *normative structure* of the school. The *behavioral reality* may be, in contrast, that teachers share lesson plans and worksheets only with new teachers or others they expect will have a legitimate reason for having limited curriculum resources of their own. And, in particular, teachers may never share with very experienced teachers, especially those who fill mentor or lead teacher positions on the basis of their expertise as teachers and are compensated for their work (Hart, 1990b; Little, 1990a).

Teachers freely explain why the behavioral and normative social structures differ under these conditions. In one such situation, a teacher said, "Why should I give them (teacher leaders) something they will just turn around and use as evidence they're superior teachers? Let them share their materials. They're getting paid for it" (Bredeson, 1994; Hart, 1990a). Teachers may resent being asked to share materials they have spent much time and creative energy developing with teachers whom they see as substandard or teachers who do not share materials with others.

Other examples of incongruencies between what people say they believe and what they actually do can be readily found. Many educators describe differences between assertions (and sincere beliefs) that all children can learn and subtle or overt actions teachers and counselors take that label students and discourage them from pursuing goals and aspirations. The opposite may also be true. The teacher's pet is one example. Literature, popular television shows and movies, and many of our own personal experiences would not be so full of stories about teachers whose favored pupils transgress rules of behavior with impunity were this not the case. You can probably recall any number of favorite stories and legends ranging from *Little House on the Prairie* and *Anne of Green Gables* to "Ferris Bueller's Day Off." These stories are not limited by culture or national boundaries and appear across time and political space. Successful principals learn to recognize the subtleties in the social structure of a school and deliberately deal with (or within) them.

Other scholars describe the behavior that shapes the structure of schools (and therefore educators' experiences) as either professional or bureaucratic. If you believe that schools are bureaucratic organizations fundamentally, you look for direct connections between instructional choices and children's learning. (See Chapter 5 for a discussion of bureaucracy.) Firestone and Bader (1992) point out that behavior in bureaucratic schools would establish connections between the instructional process and the product—students' test scores—to provide the justification for your rules and for the design of work for teachers. Were you the principal in the example given by Wasley, you would worry about the group work and computer-assisted instruction that made it impossible to measure each pupil's performance separate from the learning of others. If you believed that schools are professional organizations fundamentally, Firestone and Bader point out that you would pay more attention to teacher thinking and look for ways in which teachers' reflections on their work affect what happens to individuals and groups in their care:

> The effective teacher (from this point of view) has an approach to planning that is both subtle and spontaneous but also understands how to read cues in the situation and when to deviate from the plan. (Firestone & Bader, 1992, p. 15)

If you as an educator value and trust a behavioral view of instruction that gives explicit guidelines on how teacher behavior *A* is 90 percent likely to produce student behavior *B*, this last view of teaching and schools would leave you uncomfortable about how to behave as a principal. Firestone and Bader summarize the differences these beliefs about the nature of teaching make in school policy:

> Bureaucratic organizations are based on the premise that they require less teacher knowledge because teachers' work will be guided more extensively by central administrators and staff experts. This is apparent in state teacher-certification policies. While forty-four states require teacher candidates to take some kind of test to become certified, these are typically paper-and-pencil tests of basic skills in communications, mathematics, and other areas.
>
> Professionalism requires a higher standard because it is based on the premise that teachers must be capable of exercising more discretion. (Firestone & Bader, 1992, p. 16)

Finally, Firestone and Bader summarize the way a principal's beliefs about teachers and schools fundamentally affect how she seeks to organize a school: "The bureaucratic and professional views of teaching derive from different conceptions of how teachers should teach and imply different designs for schools and districts" (p. 34).

Norms and behavior never are exactly the same for anyone, even in a tightly knit group, and it probably is unfair to imply that they should be completely congruent. Neither are they ever completely contradictory. If they were, the cognitive dissonance would be unbearable, and people would be unable to function. Norms and beliefs set goals to which people aspire and limits beyond which people who work and study in a school dare not stray. They set patterns and shape decisions and actions, but they are not absolutes that control people absolutely. While people consistently strive to meet expectations, they also consistently fall short, or they disagree with some of the injunctions the group seeks to enforce. Consequently, principals and teachers may expect that their colleagues' behavior is somewhat, though not completely, unpredictable. As Scott so aptly put it, the "outcome is not bedlam, not total confusion or chaos, but a reasonable approximation of order" (Scott, 1987, p. 17). Behavioral and normative social structures define what actions are expected and what goals, beliefs, and behaviors are acceptable and good, but they do not *predict* behavior with perfect accuracy in any individual instance. They can be used by principals and others, however, to predict patterns of behavior and to understand and explain long established patterns and beliefs among the people who work in a school. New principals in particular (but all new members of a school) must learn as much as possible about the social structure to smooth their own integration into the group.

An astute and socially analytical new principal will always face some incongruence between what people in a school say they believe and what they do every day. Some argue that this gap between statements about ideals in professional practice and actual behavior is evidence of hypocrisy and cynicism. But the standards we often hold for ourselves and others as ideals remain out of reach in the real world, even as we accept the challenge to continually move toward those ideals. The actual behavior of people in a school, rather than their beliefs about that behavior, make up their daily experience. A pattern, a behavioral structure, emerges from activities and actions repeated over time. Principals can rage and rail against the laziness and hypocrisy of others. On the other hand, they can seek to know more about the dearly held professional beliefs, goals, and aspirations of the educators with whom they work and then seek ways to marshal those ideals and norms to bring actions closer into congruence with actual practice (Hart, 1993). By choosing to use norms of professional achievement as tools, we believe that principals can use the social system of the school as a powerful leadership resource and help others and themselves achieve their cherished professional goals.

One aspect of social structure, its degree of formality or informality, deserves particular mention before we turn to technologies, because it greatly affects principals' interactions with the rest of the school. In very formal organizations, the rules of normative behavior for each person in an assigned formal role (i.e., the job descriptions) are explicitly spelled out in great detail, and the expectations held for each person within the role are clearly articulated. The opposite is true of more informal social structures where roles and relationships are based on long-established or widely accepted beliefs and expectations, or where roles and relationships evolve as people enter and leave the organization (Hart, 1993).

Schools may fall anywhere along a continuum from highly formalized to highly tacit and new principals face the important task of understanding how formalized or tacit roles are. Teachers and principals may be subjected to rigid, highly prescribed contractual obligations, or they may be expected to behave on the basis of widely recognized and accepted professional norms and expectations.

Educational scholars examine differences in social structure from many perspectives. Recently, the enthusiasm for school reform has directed this attention toward teachers' work and careers and toward educators' professionalism. In *Building a Professional Culture in Schools,* Lieberman (1988) brings together a series of essays examining the difference between formal job descriptions and professional cultures. In one essay, "Teacher Leadership: Ideology and Practice," Lieberman, Saxl, and Miles highlight the tensions between cultures and tacit understandings about what is right and good for school professionals and a formal codification of expectations. Criticizing the policy reports on school restructuring, they said:

> The leap from report to reality, however, is a difficult one, for there are few precedents, few models, and no guidelines. We are literally learning by doing. What is needed, then, is a beginning description of this work and some understanding of the people involved—what they know and do, what the dynamics of their interactions look like—as these new forms come into being. What are these new structures? (p. 148)

Both formalized, contractual roles and tacit role expectations control judgments about what is right and good in schools. In subsequent chapters, we will examine research data about principals' interactions with schools and discuss ways in which principals can function to positively affect schools within both these kinds of structures.

Principals fill a unique niche in the social structure of schools. There is only one principal, and she may or may not share administrative and leadership responsibilities with others in a school. The principal's position, by its prominent nature, is highly visible, and members of a school hold strong opinions about appropriate actions by the principal. Those who aspire to the principal's role face a level of visibility and criticism that may be new to them in their professional lives.

Additional pressures arise from new forms of school structures. These new forms were referred to earlier in the works of Lieberman and her colleagues. New professional work structures, new social structures, may hold promise and inspire commitment on the part of many educators. They also bring with them the ordinary stresses that accompany any major change in work designs and social relationships (Hackman & Oldham, 1980).

These stresses are universal. For example, new forms of site-based decision making place demands on principals to provide leadership for teams of professionals. They expect principals to disperse leadership (sometimes called distributed leadership) across the school while tapping others' professional resources of knowledge and skills.

At the risk of overemphasizing a point, these changes challenge the formal and informal expectations about right and good behavior in schools at very basic levels for teachers and administrators. They should not be treated lightly, nor should the impacts of change on committed educators be dismissed as resistance to change or cynical self-interest. Choice initiatives that provide parents and students the option of moving from school to school challenge principals as educational entrepreneurs and may reconfigure the leadership challenge from oversight of processes to the garnering of educational resources (Kerchner, 1990). Career ladder plans, mentor teacher programs, and teacher leader reforms reconfigure the norms and expectations about who will supervise professional development, evaluate personnel, and oversee educators' work (Lieberman, 1988). Some accuse these new school structures of assigning administrative work to teachers (Hart, 1987a). Others credit them with empowering all educators within the school organization (Bredeson, 1989, 1993, 1994).

All these new configurations redefine the social structure in school organizations, and principals must be prepared to rise to the occasion and help others achieve in these schools (Bacharach, 1990; Murphy, 1990). Less dramatically but no less importantly, each school functions with its own unique set of normative and behavioral structures that a principal must tap into if he hopes to be successful in influencing school outcomes. No leader functions without the group he is charged to lead.

Technology

Technology is a broad term. Because of the recent spread of computer technology and its importance and tremendous promise in education, we tend to think of technology in terms of computers or at least in terms of mechanically powered instruments or tools. However, for this discussion of principals' interactions with their schools, technology encompasses all means through which people in an organization do their work. This is the common definition in organizational theory. In schools and in harmony with this definition, technology includes all the established methods used to teach or promote learning.

Technology thus includes all *instructional processes*—direct instruction, lectures, microteaching, Socratic questioning, projects, research papers, essay writing, and work sheets to name just a few. Technology also includes all *ways of organizing teachers' and students' work* to achieve learning goals—small groups, individual assignments, competition between individuals or teams, cooperation between individuals or teams, computer-assisted instruction, computer design, drill and practice; and *ways of assessing outcomes*—standardized tests, multiple-choice tests, essays, short answers, portfolios, criterion referenced tests, performances, exhibits, design contest, and so forth.

As we pointed out earlier, people often oversimplify technology to mean the use of computers in the classroom. This oversimplification is understandable, given the optimism and hope that surround attempts to improve teaching and learning through computers for drill and practice, as simulations for experimentation, or as artificial intelligence. General concepts of organizations, however, provide a more useful, broader view of technology that helps frame teaching and learning in schools while including computers. In the organizational view, technology is the means through which the work is done—"every organization does work and possesses technology for doing that work" (Scott, 1987, p. 18). Thus technology includes the skill and knowledge needed to complete the work as well as the machines (perhaps computers) that may assist in its completion. Principals work with all these technologies to help promote the success of the schools they lead.

The technologies of teaching and learning in schools remain ambiguously understood, poorly routinized, differentially accepted, and questionably efficacious (March, 1976). The single example given from Wasley's works earlier in this chapter illustrates these conflicts. This brief treatment of technology illustrates the complexity of teaching and learning technology and the delicate interaction of the technology with the social system discussed above. James March (1976) persuasively argued that education's technology is unclear and its goals ambiguous. No doubt they are diverse; choices about the appropriate use of various technologies in any given educational setting remain difficult and add to the need for principals skilled in understanding the technical systems of schools. The dominant Western culture accepts the elegant lecture or the stimulating group discussion as good teaching. Measures of good teaching often break down, however, when evidence that a given method results in learning is sought.

Educators usually require no ties to actual learning as evidence that "good teaching" results in learning. This issue is hotly contested in relation to teacher evaluation. Instead, teaching is evaluated by student (recipient) satisfaction, self-reported intellectual stimulation, or by observations of the teaching by experts (teacher evaluators or principals) as evidence that the particular teacher has been successful. Common measures of system (school system) success are decoupled from the elegant lecture and the stimulating group discussion. We require high scores on standardized achievement tests without evidence that elegant lectures and stimulating discussions result in high performance on these tests. This situation supports March's assertion about our unclear technologies and ambiguous goals.

As we pointed out in Chapters 1 and 2, the technology of administration is equally contextual and indeterminate. While we have accumulated a large body of knowledge about issues important to administration in education (Hoy & Miskel, 1991) and long lists of behaviors that characterize "effective" principals, the exact use of that knowledge in any given school is problematic and relies on the professional judgment and leadership repertoire of the principal and other school leaders (Weick, 1978). In Chapter 9, we return to this feature of the principalship in our discussion of principals' effects on student and school outcomes. The reliance on a repertoire of skills and knowledge is not a negative feature of school leadership. The need to tie a body of knowledge to unique situations and forge appropriate actions is a hallmark of professional work.

Participants: Social Roles in Schools

The participants in a school include all the people who work in or attend the school. They also include (depending on beliefs about parent and community participation or control) patrons and members of the community who exert influence over a school's policies, conventions, and resources and over beliefs about appropriate and desirable goals and actions. The experiences of teachers and their beliefs about good education, the talents and orientation of the principal; the educational and cultural background of students and their preparation for school; expectations for student achievement by age, race, and gender; and the characteristics and resources of parents and patrons shape the school's social system.

Participants bring with them a myriad of professional and personal experiences, talents, skills, and personalities. These individual level features, including the principal's, represent an important resource. Whenever you think of participants as part of the social system of schools, you should include these individual level characteristics. Your own skills, talents, shortcomings, and beliefs will always be a part of that mix, not separate from it.

Any social system consists of specific social roles and accepted expectations for those filling these roles. Roles are familiar to everyone who has studied or worked in schools and pose no mystery. One need only say teacher, principal, counselor, student, community, or parent to evoke images about the behaviors, beliefs, and relative power position of each person who is labeled by role.

These images, while they share features in common across a country or culture, also are specifically contextual for a given school. The ways in which roles are constructed and the ways people choose to act within their various roles shape the school. The phrase, "That's not the way we do things around here," holds great power because of established expectations about what is right and good for a particular person, in a particular role, in a particular school.

Principals act within these specific contexts not in spite of them. When a person accepts an appointment as a principal, she moves into a role that predates her and exists independent of her own particular goals and talents. One principal trying hard to establish her leadership in a school lamented, "These teachers just don't understand my vision for this school!" (Hart, 1994). She failed to understand that a school is a complex social system long before a new principal joins it, and very few principals open a new school with a tabula rasa—a blank slate free of professional, district, or societal expectations and beliefs.

Scholars who study roles and their functions in social systems such as schools identify basic characteristics that shape the way individual roles function. These role characteristics reveal important aspects of principals' work: (1) Roles exist within systems, (2) roles require shared expectations, (3) roles do not require perfect agreement from individuals, (4) socialization teaches roles, and (5) role stress occurs.

Roles Exist within Systems

First, roles exist within the social system, not independent of it, and they designate a commonly recognized set of people such as principals, teachers, accountants, and parents. Each person who is successful in a role behaves within a range of acceptable behaviors defined by the group. Even though people in the role may demonstrate a range of behaviors, there will always be a core of absolutely necessary behaviors that the role incumbent must demonstrate. People filling roles are not exactly alike and may fulfill their roles in individual ways, but core absolutes remain as necessary components of role fulfillment. Principals, for example, may spend more or less of their time directly teaching or observing teaching, but they must be the frontline communicators with parents and the community.

We often make unfounded assumptions about what "teachers," "principals," "counselors," or "students" are and do. The word "teacher," for example, evokes images that exist independent of schools. Within schools, teachers perform a systematized work role that requires accepted and widely known patterns of behavior from everyone assigned that role. Disagreements about teachers', principals', or students' acceptable and expected patterns of behavior either are treated as reasons for renegotiating expectations or problems that need attention.

These features of human endeavor strongly affect principals' work. Recent research on some school reforms like career ladders, restructuring, and shared governance reveals how powerful these assumptions about appropriate behavior within a particular context can be. While leadership by teachers is an expressed goal of many reforms, some complain that teachers are doing administrators' work when they take over the supervision of new teachers, and debates about what is "teaching" work rage (Bredeson, 1989; Hart & Murphy, 1990a). Many conflicts also have been reported when reforms place teachers in competition with each other for leadership positions.

> The Master Teacher selection process, entailing a certain amount of cooperation, also created ambiguity. Allowing each person to determine his or her own standards for what constituted a "master Teacher," then merging those choices into a list of those who had met everyone's standards, resulted in a group that met the entire district's shared understanding of what constitutes good teaching. . . . However the [name of the panel] offended the norms of equality that teachers held so fervently [and] crippled the process. . . . (Firestone & Bader, 1992, pp. 106–107)

Teachers who come to work too early and leave too late, for example, may be subjected to social isolation by others as "rate busters." Principals who spend time in classrooms in districts where principals have been seen as managers rather than instructional leaders may be chided or isolated by other principals, accused of "making things difficult for the rest of us."

Other examples abound. Within a given school, for example, no observations of classroom teaching and evaluation of teaching performance may be done by anyone but the principal. In other schools, mentor teachers perform this task and spend much time and energy on the professional development of teachers in their early career years. Teacher evaluation may involve specific procedures and types of interaction, and principals or teachers who deviate from these patterns, even if they do not violate official policy, will feel the discomfort of sanctions by others in the school. In other schools, all probationary teachers may have mentors who observe and evaluate them on a regular basis. In some schools, teachers never enter one another's classrooms. In others, teachers and students move freely around the schools, and groups form around tasks and goals rather than class assignments or age grades. These role identities (expected behaviors) often structure people's interaction patterns and, consequently, their images of themselves in a particular situation in a school and a principal's ability to promote change.

Roles Require Shared Expectations

A second feature of roles in social systems explains how roles are induced, reinforced, and evolve. Roles emerge as people share expectations for role behavior during interaction. New members of a group learn what behaviors are expected of them through these interactions. As teachers talk in the faculty lounge, for example, they share stories about student discipline, principals' absences from the school, the use of the photocopy machine, "a fair day's work for a fair day's pay," or any number of possible behaviors that communicate to new teachers what is expected. Members of the group thus teach and reinforce behaviors in new members by acting and by communicating their expectations. This enforcement process often is unconscious, based on patterns of basic assumptions about the way the school or other social group has come to function. Norms (the orientation and behavior generally accepted and expected of group members) and values (what the group accepts as right) enforce these roles energetically.

Roles Do Not Require Perfect Agreement between Individuals

A third role feature helps differentiate between roles and unique individuals whose importance we emphasized earlier in this chapter. While all members can identify the norms and values of the group and may comply with the restrictions on behavior associated with a role, they do not always personally agree with all the norms and values enforced by the group. Complete consensus is not necessary in order for roles to be enforced by group pressures. The operant condition is that everyone can identify these norms and values as characteristic of a role, even as he voices certain differences with the prevailing assumptions.

Socialization Teaches Roles

Fourth, the socialization process teaches roles to newcomers, including new principals. We discussed the socialization process in detail in Chapter 1. Through socialization, abstract social structures exert influence on a real person. When this person—a new principal, a new teacher, or a new student—reads expectations and actions appropriately, interprets the signals she gets from others in the role, and models others' behavior, she takes on the fundamental characteristics of an established role. Sociologists call this process internalization. Role models, mentors, and supervisors play critical parts in this process of "role-taking."

Sometimes a new principal adopts many conventional behaviors but also applies new knowledge, skills, and behavior to the school and acts in ways not previously expected of the principal. He asserts a new role for the principal while also successfully adapting to the expectations and beliefs of the group and becoming an accepted new member. When this happens, change occurs as a result of the principal's joining the group as the new member. This result is referred to by sociologists as socialization-as-interaction rather than internalization. If interaction and change occur, "role-making" takes place.

Both role-making and role-taking can result when a new principal joins a school (Turner & Colony, 1988; J. Turner, 1988). During the complex socialization process, a person might substantially alter her "situational role identity," her sense of her professional self as a principal or as an educator in general (Louis, 1980). She also might work to alter some core expectations of the existing group in the school by demonstrating contributions that could be made by altering conventional expectations and accepting new knowledge or new ways of doing things. Or she might steadfastly retain her own concept of what principals are and do, regardless of the feedback from the school or its particular context, and remain isolated and poorly integrated. Each of these outcomes could result from a new principal's work in a school. The last outcome could severely limit her ability to influence the school and force her to rely solely on formal authority (see Chapter 1).

When a new principal comes to a school, he is taught the "way things are done around here," the beliefs and behaviors that everyone adheres to in the school, district, or community. The new principal reads, interprets, and models others' behavior, but he also may influence some of the behaviors that other's expect by modeling new possibilities for the principal's role. The "way things are done around here" may be unethical, antiquated, or wonderfully productive. It is up to the principal to gather information and assess the utility and professional desirability of these conventions and to draw new connections among the elements of the instructional system (Dwyer et al., 1983). The delicate relationship between innovation and violation (leading to problems) will form the topic of many of the exercises and discussions in this book. This balance in part shapes the personal development of a principal while also shaping the impact the principal has on the school (Louis, 1980; Nicholson, 1984).

Enforcement pressures on new principals and other new members of a school pushing for conformity often are exerted unconsciously, based on assumptions that have guided people in the school for a long time and that continue to dominate their everyday functions. These basic assumptions may be norms about the orientation and behavior that are generally accepted and expected. While professional actions based on knowledge and on a careful diagnosis of an educational problem or opportunity may be more or less right, it usually is a mistake to attribute bad or good motives to people who defend conventional practice and established solutions to conventional problems. After all, patterns of social behavior help people solve common problems over time. When social situations or educational problems change, the parents, teachers, and students involved should not be expected automatically to see that new solutions will be superior to their established solutions. New principals judge other educators unfairly if they assume that their opponents, those who resist a new solution, do so out of laziness or ignorance. Resistance to change in ways of working out problems is a predictable feature of social life, because it protects valued social norms. In fact, scholars who study work redesign in all aspects of work find that even those who design new ways of doing their own work experience discomfort when they actually try them out.

They often make adjustments to innovations to alleviate this discomfort, even when new processes are proven to produce better results. These small, incremental changes have been labeled the "vanishing effect," because they can eventually result in a return to conventional practice with no conscious attempt to undermine change (Hackman & Oldham, 1980). Change is difficult for all people, especially when it alters the fundamental processes of a venerable profession such as education. Teachers, principals, and students may view change positively, as long as it does not affect their roles and what they do on a daily basis. We return to this discussion in greater detail in Chapter 6 when we explore the nature of principals as formal leaders.

Role Stress Occurs

A fifth role feature asserts that role stress results when actions and behaviors critical to successful role achievement are in conflict with actual behaviors or expectations. Role stress takes the form of conflict, ambiguity, and overload and may result in role strain that negatively affects a principal's performance and attitudes (Bredeson, 1993; Diamond & Allcorn, 1985; Dubinsky & Yammarino, 1984; Latack, 1984; McEnrue, 1984). Regardless of good intentions, new principals often find the transition from teacher to principal and the complexity of leadership and administration difficult to accommodate.

One manifestation of role stress is role conflict. Role conflict occurs when a person fills more than one role at the same time, and simultaneous demands simply cannot be met. In Chapter 6, we examine in detail the work of school principals and the conflicts that are products of competing role expectations. Role conflict also occurs when coexisting expectations conflict. For example, a superintendent may expect a principal to implement a site-based decision-making system at his school and empower teachers to make curriculum decisions. At the same time, the superintendent expects the principal to adopt the state's core curriculum. Either the principal must violate the expectation that curriculum decisions are made at the school level, or he must violate the expectation that the state has the sovereign right to mandate curriculum for the students in its schools. Site-based decision-making reforms often confront principals with this or similar dilemmas.

Ambiguity causes a second form of role stress. Role ambiguity occurs when a person is unsure what is expected of her in a given role, or the role itself is unclear. In the first circumstance, a new principal might feel ambiguous about the expectations of the board of education that hired her, because one board member said that there needed to be a lot of changes, and another board member praised the outgoing principal for her leadership and innovation. In the second case, a principal's role under a newly implemented and nebulously structured, shared decision-making model might be truly unclear to her. Should she simply call meetings and collate agenda items? How should parents be represented? Can parents override the professional judgments of teachers? Is the principal responsible and accountable for decisions and actions taken by the team? Should everyone have a vote equal to that of the principal, or should the group simply provide input and discussion so that the principal can make a better decision?

A third type of role stress, role overload, occurs when too much is expected for any one person to be able to accomplish it or when the person in a role lacks the knowledge or skills needed to accomplish the tasks. There simply may not be enough hours in the day to do the tasks expected, or the principal may not know how to do what is expected of him. A school district may adopt a new teacher career ladder plan, for example, that requires every principal to complete a special evaluation of all teachers in the school in addition to the customary teacher evaluation procedures. If the career ladder evaluation requires a planning meeting with the teacher, classroom visits along with systematic observation, analysis of teaching, and postobservation conferences, and if the principal's other duties are not reduced, overload may result. Under these circumstances, principals understandably have said, "Something's got to give" (Bredeson, 1989).

Many new teachers feel role overload when none of their lesson plans are prepared, none of their responsibilities are routine, and relationships with students, peers, and administrators are not established. This kind of overload comes from lack of experience and still-developing skills. It also results from the common practice in some schools of giving new teachers the leftovers—five different lesson preparations in six periods in three classrooms, for example. This also happens to new principals, who sometimes are assigned to lead the most problematic schools in their districts.

Roles and the beliefs bordering on ideologies that people hold dear about what is right and good for "teachers," "principals," or "parents" sometimes frustrate and irritate principals and others who would like to change (improve) a particular school or affect the quality and achievement of schools in general. The desire to influence a school, to make it a good place for children, youth, and adults to spend their time and a place where learning is valued and fostered, drives the careers of many principals and aspiring principals. This goal is facilitated by a deep understanding of the role conceptions held by the people with whom they work. The expectations of the society at large for right and good behavior by people in fundamental roles in schools are currently being debated, and outcomes of these debates will shape the nature of educational careers in schools for decades to come.

Environment

Environment forms another central feature of organizations; principals contend with internal environments (within the school) and external environments. The external environment can include the community, school district, state, and nation. Environments also include elements of both the social and technical systems.

Each school exists in a particular context. The physical setting; teaching, learning, and administration technologies; immediate culture; and surrounding political environment affect schools in many ways. Schools must adapt on a regular basis to these environments, because they are not self-sufficient. Relationships schools establish with their immediate communities, with the legal entity of the district, and within their states affect their ability to function in the most fundamental ways. For example, states and districts distribute the financial resources that make schools possible. Many states have equalization formulas to help alleviate differences in wealth, but voted leeways in the tax structure are available to most districts as an additional revenue source. The relationships between school and community that shape people's willingness to tax themselves to provide additional resources make a big difference in the financial resources available. The state's political environment further complicates this relationship by placing schools squarely in the middle of other political fights for resources (e.g., equalization, "Robin Hood" bills that take from "rich" districts and give to "poor" districts).

The fight for resources is only one part of the environmental pressure on schools at the local and state level. Beliefs about the right and good roles children should grow up to fill and the appropriate culture they should adopt also affect curriculum and instruction in schools. The recent past is replete with examples of these pressures: attempts to censor health books that portray male and female roles in ways unacceptable to a local culture (boys helping in the kitchen; women at the office); scientific creationism laws; or sex education curriculum and programs resulting in the distribution of condoms in public high schools. The list of politically correct issues imposed on schools is almost endless—especially when political correctness is so completely contextual and so dependent on widely varying cultural values in different segments of the population.

The preceding examples illustrate that the "number and variety of . . . connections" between schools and their environments is indeed impressive (Scott, 1987, p. 19). Environments shape schools through their impacts on each of the other four elements of organizations in Leavitt's model—participants, technologies, goals, and social structure. Participants emerge from many other experiences that build their expectations and beliefs, their skills, and their values and norms. Most teachers graduate from teacher education institutions that expose them to the prevailing theories and practices of teaching. More fundamentally, teachers are socialized about what "good" teachers do—long before they go to college—through years and years of experience in schools. One way this exposure or socialization shapes their practice comes through expectations about what good teachers do. Teachers hold the attention of groups of children, dispensing knowledge in interesting and engaging ways; they assign tasks that test the children's acquisition of the knowledge they dispense; and they design tests that assess the degree to which children have learned. When computer technologies disrupt these expectations, for example, the technical environment affects schools.

Technologies respond to environmental effects. In the most conventional sense, the pressure to integrate computer technologies into classrooms frequently comes from state legislatures that fund educational technology projects or from state education agencies that will provide grant money for computer hardware. The much-touted information highway in which citizens, schools, and universities can participate will exert ever-increasing influence in the future. The instructional processes considered exemplary are defined by states, districts, and experiences of parents and other educators. The well-crafted lecture, the inspirational oration in front of the class, the hamsters in the elementary classroom all emerged from the influences of the environment.

Teacher evaluation procedures offer an apt example of the impacts of environments on schools and ways in which districts further reinforce our beliefs about what teachers do as lecturers and questioners who call on children to recite what they have learned. One of the authors learned this lesson early in her own teaching career. Having spent weeks planning an elaborate group activity unit for an eighth grade social studies class that involved individual and student team projects and independent study, she embarked on the unit just as the regularly scheduled teacher evaluation visits were set by the district. One day, the principal came to her class. He walked about among the student groups, watching them work, observing her guide them, answer questions, and point them toward resources that would help them accomplish their tasks. After ten or fifteen minutes, the principal approached me. "This is very exciting," he said, "and the students seem to be learning a great deal. But I have to complete your evaluation, so I'll come back later when you're teaching."

Schools import their core technologies by hiring consultants to define "principles of effective teaching," or "management by objectives," or "outcome-based education," or "team tournament learning," or "site-based decision making." Consequently, each school becomes dependent on the input of these resources about teaching and administration into the school from the environment. In addition, schools often hire teachers who belong to the local teachers' union, which has its own elaborate agenda about desirable teaching technologies as well as about resources and their distributions.

From the preceding discussion, it should be apparent that no aspect of a school's social and technical system is free from the influence of the environment. This dependency includes goal formation. Goals, too, often emerge from the environment that provides the dollars that pay for schools. This symbiotic relationship sometimes frustrates educators who would like to be free to make decisions and set goals on the basis of their best professional judgment and who sometimes see policy input from government, parents, and community leaders as interference. The reform rhetoric and legislative action of the past decade aptly illustrate the impacts environments have on school goals. The National Governors' Conference, state legislatures, and the national government have actively involved themselves in educational policy making—requiring accountability measures, establishing strategic plans for education in the twenty-first century, appropriating funds for targeted reforms ranging from teacher career ladders to class size reductions and from teacher testing to school site decision making (Bacharach, 1990; Murphy, 1990). Regardless of your personal and professional perspective on these reforms, the environmental impact on principals' work should be apparent. Educators who insist that these decisions are economic rather than educational, or political rather than professional (and who mean this assertion to be a criticism) remain caught in a perspective on schools as self-contained and isolated from the impacts of social forces surrounding them.

TEACHERS' CONCEPTS OF THEIR ROLES

Reformers and scholars often assail one overarching and distinguishing feature of teaching—its deadening predictability from year one to retirement. Dan Lortie's landmark study of teaching provides a look at the core values and norms that he argued are associated with teaching. Lortie (1975) found that teachers as a group accept and enforce norms of equality (We are all equal and our jobs are all equal), civility (We don't argue or contend with one another openly, even when we disagree violently), and privacy (I can close the door and teach as I like). Other scholars see Lortie's norms affecting the outcomes of many attempts to implement reforms and innovation in education (Berman & McLaughlin, 1978; Malen & Hart, 1987).

Teachers' talk provides examples of the ways they view teaching and how it affects schools and principals' work. "If I ask for help, they will think I don't know what I'm doing or that I'm doing a bad job"; "We're all good teachers, so we all deserve the same pay for the same work"; "It caused a lot of pain and anguish when people were not chosen for the career ladder" (equality/civility—taken from unpublished interviews with teachers). "Merit pay causes contention between teachers"; "You don't want to get a reputation in the faculty as a troublemaker" (civility—taken from unpublished interviews with teachers). "These evaluation visits are nothing but a dog and pony show"; "This is my classroom"; "The national reformers can say what they want, but when push comes to shove the professional teacher is going to close that classroom door, and she will determine what goes on in there" (privacy—from a panel discussion at a national organization of teachers and teacher certification officers).

The view that all teachers see their work in the same general terms shows signs of cracking, however. Recent studies of teachers' responses to some of the changes in school structures, teachers' work, and teachers' incentives and rewards show that many differences exist within the teaching corps in their work preferences and valued incentives. Young people just beginning their careers and teachers in their first few years are more likely to see differential rewards for the best teachers in a positive light if they were excellent students in college and received high ratings from their immediate supervisors for their teaching. This may be in part a function of the very low beginning salaries that dominate teaching. Teacher mentors and leaders in a variety of new work designs and reward systems also express support for increased opportunities to earn more money and exert decision-making leadership in schools. Discouragingly, the "best and brightest" teachers in early career also are the most likely to see themselves as "trying out teaching" and to look around for other jobs (National Governors' Association, 1986). They also leave the profession in greater numbers than their less able counterparts. Most disturbing, teachers who express the greatest support for the current reward structures are those with the lowest grades and lowest performance ratings in their early careers (Hart, 1992; Hart & Murphy, 1990b; Murphy, Hart & Walters, 1989; Schlechty & Vance, 1983). Other studies illustrate real diversity among teachers in their beliefs about teachers' proper role in the selection of new teachers, the evaluation of working educators, participation in formal, school-wide decision making, and authority to establish policy (Frieson, Carson & Johnson, 1983; Hart, 1994). Scholars also relate considerable decision deprivation among teachers in a variety of classroom, personal, and organizational level areas (Bacharach et al., 1990; Duke & Imber, 1985; Sorensen, 1991).

These studies demonstrate a diversity among teachers as adult professionals that foreshadows a need for principals who can help develop and implement an increasing variety of performance and reward options for teachers—horizontal and differentiated, as well as hierarchical (Bacharach, Conley & Shedd, 1986). Teachers in a particular school may enforce a traditional perspective on teachers' work, making it difficult for those who move to innovate teachers' roles, or they may as a school move to develop "norms of collegiality and experimentation" that have been identified with effective, high-performing schools (Little, 1982). Some teachers see all activities related to decision making, school-wide activities and policies, and the supervision of other professional educators as "administrative work" while others see these tasks as a natural expansion of their work beyond the closed door of the classroom and beyond the role "telling and dispenser of knowledge" (Hart, 1990a).

PRINCIPALS' CONCEPTS OF THEIR ROLES

Thinking back on their work in schools, most educators remember many different and sometimes competing views of the principal's role. Goldhammer (1980), for example, argued that principals' roles all relate to some kind of leadership: statesperson leadership, educational leadership, supervisory leadership, organizational leadership, administrative leadership, team leadership. Yet these abstract concepts must be manifest in actual behaviors. Behaviors relate to defining the school's broad philosophy and mission; guiding achievement of school educational goals; supervising teachers who are committed to these goals; creating a supportive school structure and climate; maintaining these conditions over an extended period of time; and cooperating with teachers, other administrators, and staff.

Principals' perceptions about their roles often follow patterns that reflect reform movements of general societal patterns. Principals were good managers when management by objectives (MBO) was the watchword of exemplary school leadership. They were social engineers and guardians of the public morals during the Progressive Era. Principals were instructional leaders when literature on effective schools was most prominent (see Chapter 9). Principals were visionaries or shamans in the New Age era of organizational culture. Some say that the "administrator of the future" will combine "instructional and managerial leadership" (Heller, Pautler & Andrews 1987). Others now argue that effective principals will be "Total Quality Managers." The tasks associated with these new role conceptions will be the tasks on which principals judge themselves. Research on principals' work and expectations demonstrates, however, that the things principals say are important often differ dramatically from the things they say they spend most of their time on. While principals say instruction and curriculum are the most important activities in schools and instructional leadership is their most important responsibility, they report only a small proportion of their time spent on these activities. This self-reported emphasis on roles decoupled from the core functions of schools has remained stable for decades (Hoy & Miskel, 1991; Leithwood, Steinbach & Begley, in press).

Other lists of principals' role expectations include such things as resource provider, instructional leader, communicator, and visible presence (management by walking around or MBWA) (Andrews, 1987). They also include the preparation of board or state reports, political leadership in the immediate community, and responding to a multiplicity of demands by internal and external pressure groups (Cuban, 1988). When fundraising and entrepreneurship (Kerchner, 1990) are added, the lists become almost incomprehensible.

Despite these changes in labels, rhetoric, and role expectations, researchers find little change in principals' behaviors over time (Greenfield, 1985a; Duke, 1987). Principals' concepts of their own roles in schools may be tied so deeply to their interaction with other roles—the central roles of teachers and students particularly—that major changes in leadership role concepts may not be possible decoupled from other roles in schools. Reform initiatives empowering teachers, students, and parents, and restructuring and site-based governance profoundly affect the work of students, teachers, and principals and the interaction among their roles in schools. Although core behaviors associated with particular roles remain, traditional roles are giving way to emergent, dynamic sets of expectations for students, teachers and principals (Bredeson, 1994). As an illustration, reflect for a moment on how you would complete the following sentence: "A school principal. . . ."

STUDENTS' CONCEPTS OF THEIR ROLES

One of the most hotly debated issues in education centers around the role of students in schools and the parallel expectations held for teachers. Students function in many school settings as passive recipients of knowledge, doers of tasks assigned by teachers who dispense knowledge that the students then memorize. This view is under rigorous attack from many quarters while being defended with equal vigor by traditionalists.

Students remain in a poor position to alter their roles in schools, however. Those students who adopt expected behaviors and accept established authority relationships among students and adults in schools tend (to no one's surprise) to fit in, to do better in the current structure. The educational literature is filled with debates about the relative appropriateness of this status quo. Not all students learn well from text books and class lectures, yet the primary teaching strategy in American high schools is in the lecture-recitation format.

Current methods of teacher evaluation reinforce this role for students. Calls for accountability, career ladders, and merit pay schemes often have resulted in the adoption of teacher observation instruments and expensive training programs for evaluators and raters who visit and observe teachers, then fill out these instruments, rating teachers on each item. These observations require teachers to perform for students and observers and promote direct instruction models that place students in the role of knowledge receivers.

Experiences like these enforce roles on students by enforcing behaviors and roles on teachers. Throughout modern history, a substantial proportion of students have seen their roles as survival, especially through their teenage years. Movies like "Ferris Bueller's Day Off," comic strips like "Funky Winkerbean," and lines like "When I think back on all the crap I learned in high school, it's a wonder I can think at all" in Paul Simon's song illustrate a broadly held view about students' place in schools. These may not be productive roles, and these characterizations may be extreme, but students' concepts of their roles certainly shape their activities, learning, and performance while they remain in school. Role expectations are powerful and enduring; students carry these sets of role expectations into adulthood as they become parents, school board members, teachers, and principals.

COMMUNITIES' AND PARENTS' CONCEPTS OF THEIR ROLES IN SCHOOLS

Beliefs about the right and proper role of community leaders and parents in schools currently are under the greatest pressure for change and are among the greatest sources of contention in schools. In Utah, for example, the state's strategic plan for education requires schools to include parents in all aspects of decision making in schools and mandates school choice in some form. The Chicago School District experiment—with local school councils having the power to hire and fire principals, make governing decisions about school operations, and allocate discretionary monies averaging approximately $400,000 per school—remains under fire from educators, some parents, labor unions, and politicians (Rossmiller, Bredeson & Fruth, 1993). Wisconsin is experimenting with new roles for high school students through the Wisconsin Apprenticeship Program and "school to work" initiatives building on European models of apprenticeships for secondary school students.

These differences of opinion on roles, governance, and curriculum are not new to schools. William Jennings Bryan, defending the Tennessee law that forbade the teaching of biological evolution in the schools, argued in 1925 that the "people who pay for the schools have the right to determine what is taught in them." Expertise, "truthfulness" and professional knowledge, and academic freedom paled to insignificance in this debate (Hart, 1983). In the early part of this century, school board members discussed the appropriateness of teaching foreign languages in their schools!

Cultural diversity in the United States contributes to the growth of divergent views about parents' right and proper role in schools. The conflict between community and cultural values and the "best interests" of children would have all students pursuing knowledge and lifestyle choices that erode traditional community expectations about what girls and women should do and about what aspirations young men should have. Many Americans have responded to conflicting role concepts by fleeing the public school systems where they feel their preferences receive insufficient attention. From the all-white schools of the 1960s to the Christian schools of the 1980s and 1990s, these parents demonstrate strong opinions about the right of educators to make critical decisions about their children's education and life experiences. When the president and his wife chose to place their daughter Chelsea in a private Quaker school in Washington, DC, they exercised this same choice.

CONCLUSION

Schools, like other organizations, function as complex social systems in which the social and behavioral structures, goals, technologies, participants, and environments interact. Principals appointed to lead these schools face a unique environment in each one, and the ability of a principal to bring professional knowledge to bear in a particular setting will shape the outcomes of this leadership.

People's perceptions exert tremendous influence because educators, parents, and students act on the basis of their beliefs and perceptions rather than on any abstract and objective reality. It becomes important, therefore, for new principals to understand each element in the sociotechnical system of schools and to develop ways to capitalize on the features of each in pursuit of desired outcomes. In the next chapter, we will explore in greater depth the interaction of the formal leader—the principal—with the school system and examine the ways in which new principals can seek to maximize their ability to affect positively the schools in which they are assigned to lead.

SUGGESTED ACTIVITIES

1. In your present assignment, what technologies (methods used to teach and learn) dominate? Are present but unusual? Are new and developing? How might they be affected by the social structure? What might this mean for the principal?

2. The technology of calculators, for example, is the product of history, social structure, role expectations, and professional knowledge. In high-performing organizations, the tools of technology used by practicing professions are appropriate to primary work tasks defined by knowledge level, expertise, and clients' needs. A familiar criticism leveled at education is that its technologies are no longer appropriate nor sophisticated enough to meet the challenges of educating children in the late twentieth century. Think about the technologies of teaching and learning—instructional processes, organization of work, and assessment of outcomes. What technologies no longer serve the primary mission of teaching and learning?

3. If you were sponsoring a garage sale of old, no longer useful educational technologies, what would you put out in the driveway to get rid of?

4. Identify necessary actions or behaviors that people in your school expect of the principal. Identify things your principal does that people acknowledge as educationally sound and good but that are not *expected* for the principal to be successful. Compare these role expectations with those in other schools and school districts.

5. Identify examples in which you have felt role conflict as a teacher—between what you learned is best instructional practice, for example, and what you find yourself doing in your present circumstances. Other examples of role conflict?

6. Identify pressures from your immediate environment that affect your school. Who must interact with these environments? How intrusive or powerful are they?

7. Prepare a list of outside consultants who affect the technology of schools.

8. President William Jefferson Clinton called for the adoption of an apprenticeship system for vocational educational modeled after the German system that would completely restructure vocational education in the United States and reconfigure funding very differently than the Perkins Act in force when he took office in 1993. Describe the "political" versus the "educational" components of this move. What other professional issues related to central school goals are affected in your school by the immediate environment, your state, the nation?

9. List five words that characterize your view of "teacher." Write a short paragraph describing what you or teachers in general do that exemplifies this word as it encompasses the behavioral and normative structures of the teacher's role.

10. What are the prevailing expectations in your community schools about: sex education, textbook selection, student discipline, extracurricular activities, grade changes, curriculum selection, and so on?

11. What "reforms" are popular in your school district and state that will change the role of parents in your school? What conflicts do educators have with parents over their roles? How are decisions labeled as "educational" or "political" in your school?

12. Identify examples of inconsistencies between the norm or expected and expressed standards of behavior and actual behavior by educators in your professional experience.

13. Describe circumstances as an educator when you felt ambiguity about your role. Were you expected to individualize instruction or provide cooperative learning? Were you to maximize the potential of each child or teach equality and patience? Should you mainstream all special education students or provide special services in central locations? Others? Remember, role ambiguity is not just confusion that can be alleviated, it is legitimately unclear expectations?

The Principal and the School

When a new principal is assigned, everyone in the school feels the impact of change. To some degree, the principal's role affects all the people who work and study in a school. Consequently, the interaction between the school sociotechnical system described in Chapter 3 and the new principal has far-reaching effects throughout the school.

Because of this pervasive effect, a beginning principal needs a broad base of knowledge and skills on which he can draw to build a healthy relationship between himself and all elements of the school. Principles of interaction between formal leaders and the groups they are assigned to lead provide one source of knowledge that can enhance a principal's likelihood of success. This chapter continues our discussion of ways in which beginning principals can facilitate their own passage to professional growth with a study of the interactions between formal leaders and the groups they are assigned to lead. The perspective taken here may not appeal to those who ascribe to more traditional, heroic views of leadership. Some writers even argue that we need an "antidote to the 'romance of leadership' " (Firestone, in press) in order to break out of hero models and better understand the actual human power we have come to label leadership. Research on leaders, particularly leaders in professional groups working with highly educated and independent adults, affirms that successful leaders draw on the knowledge and skill of all group members and function interactively. Influence is reciprocal (Manz & Sims, 1987). More specifically, the effort to enhance teacher empowerment in school reform leads some scholars to question the traditional axiom that leadership is directional—from leader to followers. Reitzug (1994, p. 286) summarizes a dilemma raised when a debate about the direction and nature of leader-to-follower influence is mounted:

> Other than the authority vested in socially constructed organizational structures that designate certain individuals as leaders, what warrant do leaders have for assuming that their "dreams or vision . . . should be somehow 'better' than the dreams or vision of any other organization member?" (Angus,

1989, p. 75). On the other hand, if leaders do not attempt to influence follow-ers to pursue courses of action that they perceive to be correct, are they not shirking responsibility for organization direction?

Empowering leadership, Reitzug asserts, comes in the form of a supportive environment for critique, facilitation and stimulation of critique, and behav-iors that make it possible to act on critiques by providing resources encour-agement and support. Reitzug goes on to cite Foster's assertion (1986) that leaders empower people to evaluate and judge the importance of goals and helpful conditions in the organization in order to promote followers' devel-opment, much as Burns (1978) argues that great leaders "transform" their fol-lowers by helping them discover the best in themselves.

However supportive, empowering, or heroic one's view of leadership, the appointment of a new principal creates a period of "apprehension and fear of the unknown with high expectations being held" by principals, teachers, and district superiors alike (Weindling & Earley, 1987, p. 67). Changes in the peo-ple filling formal leadership roles such as that of principal are commonly referred to as leader succession or administrator succession. In addition to the traditional concern over the appointment of principals new to the profession, which is happening at a high rate, researchers find that school leaders are often transferred from one assignment to another. In Great Britain, turnover rates stand at 7 percent per year. Since the Education Reform Act (1988) passed in that country, bringing with it sweeping changes in the role of the head teacher (principal), many say they want to retire (possible at age 55) or leave the pro-fession. Some speculate that the turnover rates may consequently increase sub-stantially (Baltzell & Dentler, 1983; Weindling, 1991; Weindling & Earley, 1987).

Relationships between the principal, other adults, and the children and youth who work in a school form over the early weeks and months of a new leadership assignment. The processes that shape these interactions develop over time into dependable and expected patterns—the roles in social systems discussed earlier. People use these patterns to judge the legitimacy of current events and future actions. Consequently, the interaction of a new principal with people in the school sets the stage for the future influence she might have on their beliefs and actions.

In Chapter 3, we explored the social and technical systems into which a new principal moves. A newly assigned principal can collect information about the school that gives him a view of these elements of the system and information that will help him understand what the established relationships, expectations, beliefs, and "ways we do things around here" are. In this chap-ter, we present a perspective of principals in schools as part of social, interac-tive groups with established patterns of belief and behavior shaping their rela-tionships, decisions, and actions. Using this perspective, and analytical techniques discussed later in the book, we next describe processes principals can employ to gather, analyze, and use data to shape their actions and deci-sions.

The accumulated experiences of an extended professional career eventu-ally may come to seem commonplace to the experienced principal, yet the commonality of common events makes them no less important. In Chapter 2, we introduced five problem-solving errors common to new principals and other professionals. These errors often occur *because* events seem commonplace and simple, so solutions appear similarly simple. H. L. Mencken is purported to have said, "For every problem there is a solution: simple, neat, and wrong." Others warn that experienced professionals also fall victim to too hasty decisions based on assumptions that common events will be essentially identical to past experiences. He calls this tendency "selective inattending," and his research with professionals in many fields has led him to caution that experienced professionals, too, must be vigilant for subtle differences among events. Divorced from context and the mix of variables each school presents, technical skills and domains of knowledge remain almost irrelevant. Embedded in context, skills and knowledge become powerful inputs into professional knowledge-in-action (Schon, 1983, 1987).

The gap between the formal study of school leadership and the vivid and demanding experience of taking charge in a school remains large, however. Immediate demands to schedule classes, hire staff, plan (and pay for) extracurricular activities, complete budget and statistical reports, and buffer the district office from parents' complaints can overwhelm early resolutions to make a difference for kids, to contribute to the quality of teaching and learning in schools, and to build connections in the instructional system. These demands on new principals often push them to abandon the formal skills and knowledge acquired in teaching and in a graduate preservice university-based school leadership education in favor of short-term adjustive behaviors that delay or suppress conflict. The press to conform to existing patterns of practice is intense. Under these pressures, principals taking on their first professional assignments must find ways to connect and integrate their professional knowledge and experience. They must carefully assess their own and the school's salutary core values and beliefs and apply them to the dynamics and unique challenges they face (Porter, Lawler & Hackman, 1975).

These decisions are not easily made. A principal (new to administration or new to a particular school) will find inchoate relationships and interaction patterns between herself, her superiors, and the school social system at the time of her appointment. As these relationships form and become stronger as a result of her interactions with people—superiors, teachers, parents, students—she will be able to influence their shape if she chooses. They begin to form during the uncertainty preceding a change in principals, throughout selection, and into the taking-charge time when the new principal is deeply embroiled in a complex social process and when time to reflect on her experience may be difficult to find. As a principal seeks to become a functioning leader and understand her relationships with others in the group, she ultimately is concerned that her experience be rendered meaningful through insight (McNeil, 1969).

The mix of principal and school is unique each time a principal is appointed; this uniqueness poses dilemmas for a new principal. If we examine changes in leadership only from the perspective of the principal, we miss the history of events and cannot account for people's conduct. But if we focus too intently on outcomes and ignore the dynamic mix of people, processes, and contexts that shape the process, people, and places (schools and districts) in which changes occur, we lose track of the qualities and power of the individual new principal. We lose his uniqueness and creativity. In this chapter, then, we build on the previous discussion of sociotechnical systems and talk about the new principal's interaction with this system.

Any focus on the effects of the lone heroic leader, the individual free agent, isolated from the context in which action occurs is naive at best; however, even those who subscribe to contingency theories of leadership (See Chapter 6), emphasizing the favorableness of the environment for effective leadership, study the leader's actions. The social relationships between formal leaders and their hierarchical subordinates and superordinates play an important part in their influence on the school. Leadership scholars emphasize multidirectional leadership effects:

> The findings of . . . researchers . . . provide firm evidence for the view that influence-processes between superiors and subordinates are two-way rather than one-way. It might still prove to be the case that leaders influence their subordinates more than subordinates influence their leaders. But the studies make clear the manner in which subordinate actions can cause leaders to perceive subordinates in certain ways and consequently to employ certain behaviors towards them rather than others. (Smith & Peterson, 1988, p. 40)

In Chapter 2, we introduced several popular models of the principalship. Cultural and symbolic leadership provided one of these models. Some interpretations of this model portray groups as especially dependent on leaders' almost mystical effects on the groups they lead. Research in schools challenges the universality of this assumption. Describing the "cultural politics of executive succession" by superintendents, Firestone (1990) found that current enthusiasm for dramatic leadership achieved by manipulating organizational culture was not supported by his case studies of superintendent succession. He questioned the assumption that the superintendent is a free actor when choosing the direction of cultural change in school districts. Roberts (1989a, 1989b) affirmed the ambiguities of cultural leadership as it is currently defined and echoed these conclusions in a series of case studies of new high school principals.

INTERDEPENDENCE

In Chapter 1, we argued that all principals must undergo professional socialization and induction to the profession of school administration. In this chapter, we examine the integration and socialization of the new principal into a specific social setting—a unique, functioning, dynamic, frustrating, fulfilling, wonderful school. In Chapter 10, we discuss in detail the process of becoming a principal and focus primarily on the principal and the intrapersonal processes of learning one role and moving into another. In this chapter, we examine principal socialization as an organizational interaction process. During the early taking-charge stages of socialization there are identifiable outcomes. Principals learn social roles just as all people learn how they should behave in a given setting with a given audience. They may be officially powerful, but principals, too, are socialized; they learn the social role that will buy them access to legitimacy in a given setting (Goffman, 1959; Merton, Reader & Kendall, 1957).

The learning process involves adjustments and adaptations to the expectations of the school on the part of principals. These adjustments make cooperative effort possible and represent an orientation toward common needs and goals. Through the adjustment process, people come to internalize the values, norms, and beliefs of others in the same school and to see things as others see them. As a new principal adopts the generally accepted explanations for events, she is "socialized" but not enslaved.

When principals enter districts or schools as new members of the social group, they experience a form of adult socialization—organizational socialization. Organizational socialization differs from professional socialization (Schein, 1986). It teaches people the knowledge, values, and behaviors required of them in a particular role within a particular context. These values and norms may be very different from those a person learned as part of his professional socialization.

To the chagrin of college professors, organizational socialization—immediate, salient, and persuasive—often overpowers the effects of carefully structured professional socialization (Bucher & Stelling, 1977; Duke, 1987). Guy (1985) asserted that the need to fit in to the immediate work environment makes organizational socialization more salient and immediate than the experiences that precede it, no matter how carefully organized. The organization controls a person's evaluation and reward structures and provides social and personal reinforcement for compliance to immediate social norms and expectations. Organizational norms consequently tend to displace those learned during professional socialization. New principals and the others who work in schools consequently are interdependent. The new principal has formal leadership power but depends on those in the school for the power of the group to act. You should be prepared to experience these processes each time you receive a new assignment throughout your educational leadership career.

Vivid descriptions of what happens when a person enters an established organization as a new member resonate with new principals:

> [Experienced members] must . . . find ways to insure that the newcomer does not disrupt the ongoing activity on the scene, embarrass or cast disparaging light on others, or question too many of the established cultural solutions worked out previously. . . . The manner in which this teaching/learning occurs is . . . the *organizational socialization process* [emphasis in the original]. (Van Maanen & Schein, 1979, p. 211)

As the teachers in one principal succession study repeatedly pointed out, principals come and principals go, and teachers often find very effective ways to buffer themselves from the impact of principals' "leadership" no matter how visionary it may be (Cosgrove, 1986). Organizational socialization binds the members of work organizations into communities with far deeper interdependence and ties than those forged through temporary connections with educational institutions or with organizations a principal has now left.

The School: A Source of Principal Influence

By now, you may be discouraged, wondering if a principal can have any real impact on a school and the outcomes of the teaching and learning that take place there. Even though the effects of groups on individuals extend to everyone, including principals, this does not mean that principals lack influence. By examining the socialization of leaders, we acknowledge that leaders are part of a social context that wields a combined source of power over their beliefs and actions greater than the power of either previous professional socialization or their own formal authority:

> If the . . . qualities of the individual are said to be derived from experience in society, there is no logical sense in beginning serious scientific inquiry into the effect (the role-related, social self), while ignoring the cause (society, and ipso facto, socialization) . . . . The nature of the "society" presented in socialization must be described. (Wentworth, 1980, p. 8)

At the same time, the group possesses great power in concert that astute and skillful school leaders can bring to bear on tasks and problems in schools. In a way, this power of the school amplifies any power and influence a principal might hope to exercise on his own.

Organizational socialization then, reveals the multidirectional effects of leaders and organizations, recognizing that a newly assigned principal is a newcomer who must be integrated into the school social group, validated by social processes, and granted legitimacy by teachers, students, parents, patrons, and superiors before she can have a significant impact on actions taken by others. Authority granted by the social group in the school differs from other forms of influence. Blau (1964, p. 200) distinguishes this socially validated authority as *leadership:*

> It may be suggested that the distinctive feature of authority is that social norms accepted and enforced by the collectivity of subordinates constrain its individual members to comply with directives of a superior. Compliance is voluntary for the collectivity, but social constraints make it compelling for the individual. In contrast to other forms of influence and power, the pressure to follow suggestions and orders does not come from the superior who gives them but from the collectivity of subordinates. These normative constraints may be institutionalized and pervade the entire society, or they may emerge in a group in social interaction. The latter emergent norms define leadership.

In contrast to the authority and power granted by the collective, the authority rooted in formal position is limited in scope to the performance of duties that meet a minimum standard. Only actions required by policy and direct demands can be controlled by principals' relying on formal authority, a theme we repeatedly recite through this book. The exercise of this kind of authority unnecessarily sets a principal up for insubordinate responses from teachers and others. For example, imagine that you are the principal of a school in which your ability to influence the beliefs and behaviors of others is limited to positional power, that is, formal authority. How could you influence others to coalesce around shared goals and values? How could you influence commitment to create innovative, self-renewing teaching and learning environments? The works of Etzioni and Blau provide answers to these questions. It would be impossible on the basis of formal authority alone.

School effects on new principals seeking to influence the school in turn deserve increased attention for a number of reasons. First, interaction on the job may be the most important factor in helping newcomers become effective members of work organizations (Louis, Posner & Powell, 1983).

Second, new leaders learn new roles, whether or not the new leader and his superiors influence that process deliberately. If we care about the outcome, we might as well learn as much as possible about this process and affect its results if possible. Providing additional support for an approach to the taking-charge process that acknowledges the power exerted by socialization in creating effective leaders in schools, the role-learning outcomes of socialization serve as primary criteria for later success. Furthermore, principals must learn respected attitudes, values, and beliefs in the school context in order to gain the acceptance of others in similar and superordinate leadership roles and of people in the school. You will recall that this process is called *moral socialization*. The social structure of the school organization is a powerful mediating force affecting work activities and outcomes. Moral socialization, as well as technical socialization, exerts critical force over the eventual professional identity of principals (Greenfield, 1985b).

Third, socialization's influences on leaders are well documented over time and context. Managers' attitudes, self-concept, and professional identity resulting from socialization experiences have long been a focus of study. A new principal who ignores these influences over his professional life risks leaving much of his own professional development and his influence on his school to chance (Berlew & Hall, 1966–67; White, 1978).

A Principal in a School: Tapping the Power of the Context

The traditional leadership literature relies on methods and assumptions that address the outcomes of principals' interaction with schools in general and the traits of leaders and schools that predict these outcomes. (See Chapter 6 for more information about this research.) When the power of context is considered, this approach seems to reflect an exaggerated concern with organizational control, image management, and status quo pattern maintenance (Nicholson, 1984). In contrast, a perspective relying on the interaction of leaders with powerful groups advances understanding and practice in three ways. First, it enhances the likelihood that educational leaders will identify circumstances when the decision to change principals might be advantageous. Second, it allows educators to understand and affect the social dynamics of changes in the principalship across time. Finally, it promotes an understanding of the effects of interaction between school groups and individuals on principals and school outcomes. While we will return to this last advantage in greater detail in Chapter 10, all three of these advances in practice deserve elaboration.

In schools, studies of principals' appointments and leadership provide a look at dynamics that may trigger or suppress major shifts in ideology and practice (Blumberg & Greenfield, 1986; Hart, 1988; Ogawa, 1991; Starbuck, Hedboerg & Greve, 1977). We noted in Chapter 2 that Blumberg and Greenfield provide one view of principals' work relying on moral and visionary craftsmanship in many forms. They present rich case studies of principals who functioned differently, yet effectively, within schools relying on very different major qualities—action oriented, resourceful, goal-oriented, personally secure, tolerant of ambiguity, limits' tester, power sensitive, analytical, and taking charge. Bredeson (1988b) provided a portrait of five effective principals and Dwyer and colleagues (1983) similarly focused on *five principals in action,* illustrating how very differently "effective" principals function in different schools. These case studies go far in advancing understanding of the context-rooted and interactive nature of the principalship.

Affirming the long tradition of this view and its importance in understanding organizational leadership, the earliest studies of administrator succession relied on case studies of complex interactions within organizations. Cases revealing the dynamics of leader succession processes within organizations, including schools, continue to offer intriguing new insights (Fauske & Ogawa, 1987; Gephart, 1978; Gouldner, 1954; Guest, 1962; Ogawa, 1991; Oskarsson & Klein, 1982; Salaman, 1977).

We do not mean by this affirmation of the interactive nature of school leadership that a principal's main task is to fit in, adapt, and secure acceptance in the school. Were this the case, the teachers' protectionist views expressed in Cosgrove's research (1986) would be reinforced. A principal may adapt and prosper personally without contributing to school growth and development—without improving the connectedness of the instructional system in the school and the achievement of desired goals. Schools also need creativity and new ideas in order for the critical connections in the instructional system we discussed earlier to be made. These two apparently conflicting needs make the effects of interaction between a principal and a school a critical factor shaping future events and outcomes. They are most intense and vibrant during the early weeks and months after a principal is appointed, what scholars call the *succession period.*

As we stated earlier, the need to fit in and the need to effect change seem contradictory, yet this challenge is universal to human interactions (Wentworth, 1980). These needs do work at cross purposes if principals fail to find a productive balance between them in each unique situation. One must not assume that all social learning is positive. The acceptance on the part of a new principal of established solutions that have not been productive or are blatantly unproductive is a negative outcome of interaction. Although thorough learning and acceptance of the existing culture through socialization may:

> [a]lways be immediately *adjustive* for an individual in that such learning will reduce the tension associated with entering an unfamiliar situation, such learning, in the long run, may not always be adaptive, since certain cultural forms may persist long after they have ceased to be of individual value. (Van Maanen & Schein, 1979, pp. 212–213)

Taking charge is a powerful experience for which few principals are adequately prepared. We emphasize the process and return to it throughout the book, because the taking-charge or succession time period has been shown to shape principals' future effects. Many scholars contend that the socialization of managers assures a uniformity that suppresses creativity and the diverse options that might be necessary to address the complex dilemmas and needs of schools—that managers of all kinds, including principals, are "oversocialized." Socialization also has been named as an important factor in the seeming intransigence of educational administration when changes are attempted in preservice graduate school education programs. This intransigence is a real, but not insurmountable, challenge. It requires recognition that in a mature group, "leadership comes to be seen as a shared set of activities rather than a single person's trait, and a sense of ownership of group outcomes arises" (Schein, 1985, p. 197). Others assert the social nature of new principals' part in schools more radically—that leadership is an attribute not of individuals but of social systems (Dachler, 1984). The knowledge that social groups possess a singular power related to leadership but distinct from individual influence can expand understanding and, we hope, improve the practice of educational leadership.

Consequently, this chapter should not be interpreted as a clarion call for principals to concentrate all their efforts on fitting in. Rather, we hope that you will gain insight into the probable outcomes of your actions and the general social dynamics for which you can prepare. Organizational leaders always face the tension between the need to become integrated and legitimate members of the groups they lead and the need for their unique creativity and individuality to contribute new energy and productiveness to the group.

The Mix of People, Leaders, and Events: Shaping and Predicting the Outcomes of Interaction

People in transition from one role to another within an organization and people new to an organization experience organizational socialization. Unlike primary socialization, as babies and young children experience it when they have no existing beliefs, values, and behavior patterns, a new principal enters her organizational socialization experience as a complex adult member of several different groups—one who has formed strong beliefs and values. Both deliberately and unconsciously, school organizations apply a number of tactics to integrate new members, and principals experience these tactics more or less aware of their potential effects. The decision to leave the socialization of newcomers to chance, dependent on the mix of people, issues, power, and events that happen to coincide is, of itself, a tactic. Writers describe a number of categories of socialization tactics likely to affect new members. This list of tactics is by no means exhaustive, and districts may change their tactics continually, depending on developing circumstances. Tactics can be grouped as context, content, and sociality factors (Van Maanen, 1978).

Interest in socialization includes the interaction of all these tactics and their effect on the new member and the group. Scholars also examine the substantive changes in new members that occur. What core social beliefs and values might have to be adopted before new members can function as an accepted part of the group? How completely must these core values or behaviors be adopted? How dependent or independent is the new member:

> The novice can be relatively powerless in an ultimate way, yet actively influence the face-to-face process of socialization. The novice then may also inject control and power into the socialization relationship. This is to say, the members' culture is not presented in a vacuum. It is presented *to* someone so that its precise quality is historically and concurrently modified in the interaction between member and novice. The content of socializing activity is thus modified by the very structure of the interaction situation. Socialization is then related to the context of its presentation. (Wentworth, 1980, p. 69)

When the new member also is the functional leader of the group, this influence clearly is enhanced. At the same time, the primary work group in schools is made up of teachers. Their norms and expectations have a tremendous impact.

Context

In large school districts, several (sometimes many) new principals are hired each year and many more are given new assignments. For example, in Chicago over 25 percent of building principals recently were replaced with new principals. When you receive your first assignment, the district may provide introductory experiences structured in a number of ways that provide a context for your socialization. These contexts can be structured as collective (the group of new principals) or individual (by yourself) experiences (Ross-miller, Bredeson, & Fruth, 1993).

Collective socialization tactics require specific choices about what to teach the corps of new people at the outset of their assignments; *individual* socialization can be structured deliberately by the district by training mentors to provide specific guidance and assigning them to newcomers or through the serendipitous outcome of benign neglect. During collective socialization, new principals go through a series of activities together (perhaps training in instructional supervision strategies or district personnel or other policies). Individual processing takes new principals through their experiences alone. While those socialized independently tend to be less homogeneous than members of a cohort (unless old-timers exert the dominant influence), the new principal is more likely to feel lonely, and the quality of the experience can be highly varied. The continuity of experience a collective process promotes is no guarantee of predictable outcomes, however. Even though principals may be "processed" together, they will experience that process differently. Past experiences and personal characteristics exert tremendous influence.

Each context tactic has advantages and disadvantages. Individual socialization leads to relatively high levels of role conflict and ambiguity, but it also enhances innovation. Collective and highly structured activities promote commitment and job satisfaction, but they suppress creativity and change. None of the studies in education reviewed for this chapter applied institutionalized, planned processes to any great extent, but the use of mentors to assist new principals is growing (Jones, 1986; Daresh, 1986). For principals and other managers, individual socialization is most likely.

The context in which principals undergo socialization may also be more or less *formal*. Formal socialization, designed to incubate specific norms and expectations, occurs during traditional administrator retreats, in principals' meetings, and in evaluations that stress conformity and compliance. Other contexts depend on informal arrangements. Mentors play a large part in formal and informal socialization tactics. Sometimes a new principal works almost exclusively with an assigned mentor who has been given training and a specific charge about desired outcomes (Dansereau, Graen & Haga, 1975; Dienesch & Liden, 1986; Hunt & Michael, 1983). These arrangements receive considerable praise (Daresh & Playko, 1989). Other times, mentor relationships develop informally. Reliance on mentors sometimes leaves the quality of the working relationship between mentors and newcomers to chance, and changes in formal mentor-protege assignments are difficult. Outcomes are highly vulnerable to quality control problems, particularly when mentors receive little or no guidance about their role or the goals the district wants them to pursue.

While they add a needed personal touch to socialization, mentors may constrain innovation. Some scholars argue that, by turning the socialization of newcomers over to long-time members of the group, organizations virtually guarantee the reproduction of existing roles (Van Maanen, 1978). Even when mentors and new principals have a good working relationship, the results may be undesirable. Think back on your own initial socialization as a new teacher. How would you assess the competing focus of role reproduction (organizational socialization) and role innovation (personalization) in your first teaching assignment? These same competing pressures will occur when you become a school principal.

Formalization has its advantages and disadvantages that you should be aware of as you take on your first principalship. Highly formalized socialization processes sometimes produce a "custodial" response, making the new principal feel obligated to recreate the existing order. Newcomers try to play the established part exactly as it was designed and filled by others. This outcome may be a greater danger in long-established, highly uniform organizations like schools where organizational inertia is more entrenched.

Informal socialization may stimulate more creativity and innovation, but it also produces "more extreme responses in either the custodial or innovative directions than formal socialization" (Van Maanen & Schein, 1979, p. 240). As a new principal, you should be aware of the relative advantages and disadvantages your particular experience presents for you. Later in this volume, we will explore specific data-gathering, analysis, and planning techniques designed to help you capitalize on the socialization context in which you find yourself.

Content

When a succession occurs, the new principal must master a specific knowledge content in addition to the general content of her professional preparation for the role. Established and ordered steps for learning the content of a new job assignment are labeled *sequential* content socialization. In order to achieve full membership in the new role, principals undergoing this type of content exposure must pass through established steps without deviation. Few districts have more than a few days of established, sequential content to which new-comers are exposed.

Another form of content socialization is labeled *random* socialization. A content of knowledge must be mastered by the new principal, but the steps required to master the content are flexible, ambiguous, or continually chang-ing—or they may depend on the order in which problems come up in the school. Some researchers find that, by sequencing the content, an organization builds high commitment among new members (Nota, 1988). In educational administration, the content of new learning is seldom ordered beyond simple orientation meetings at the beginning of a school year.

The timetable in which a newly assigned principal must master content can also vary by being *fixed* or *variable*. A fixed time such as five years of doc-toral studies or a twelve-week instructional leadership course tightens the con-trol of the organization. It also limits the duration of newcomer status. After formal education is complete, however, educational administrators report almost totally random and variable socialization. This situation leaves their status as fully established members of the corps unclear. A number of research papers coming out of the Danforth new principals' studies report that princi-pals move unevenly through the process as they become (or fail to become) accomplished school leaders. Some of the principals never move from control-oriented positional power to personal power and the final stage of leadership (Parkay, Currie & Rhodes, 1992).

Sociality

Sociality refers to the relatedness, connection, and modeling available through the socialization process. Are there many others like you in the prin-cipal's role on which you can model your behavior? Perhaps your high school football coach whom you admire very much is the principal of another school in your district. Are you the first African American, Native American, woman, Asian American to serve as a school leader in your area? Are you the first blind school principal anyone in your district ever worked with?

When principals follow in someone's footsteps and strong role models exist for them, they experience *serial* socialization. By contrast, *disjunctive* socialization leaves a newcomer without significant role models. New princi-pals can experience disjunctive socialization if they differ significantly in per-sonal characteristics from those who commonly are principals. Women and ethnic minority members, for example, report significant stress in their new leadership roles. They often feel that they must negotiate their way through more ambiguity with less support than their more conventional peers because few people like them have preceded them in the role (Ortiz & Marshall, 1988; Valverde, 1980). Female secondary school principals report that their staffs and community members often doubt their ability to deal with unruly students and serious discipline issues.

While it may sound lonely and difficult, disjunctive socialization also has its advantages. It *may* make it possible for the new principal to build a whole new role. An absence of role models leaves new principals more free to innovate and more ambiguous about what is expected of them in the new role. Consequently, disjunction is a two-edged sword. Researchers find strong evidence that, when innovation is needed, "the socialization process should minimize the possibility of allowing incumbents to form relationships with their likely successors" (Van Maanen & Schein, 1979, p. 250). Just as mentors can suppress innovation, role models can limit thinking and constrain options. While principals without role models need social support, they may be forced to tap their individual creativity more deeply and spark new ideas in others with whom they work.

A second aspect of sociality employed during organizational socialization demands that the new principal either strengthen or abandon his professional self-image as an educator. Acknowledging the power of shedding old images, educators increasingly recommend that teachers be encouraged to demand instructional leadership from principals and that instructionally oriented teachers be recruited into administration. The first recommendation would require "traditional" candidates to divest themselves of beliefs about principals as evaluators, schedulers, organizers, risk managers, and budget directors. The second recommendation would require that educational leaders recruit new principals who possess strong instructional skills and values. A powerful new corps of principals exerting these values might force divestiture of less instructionally oriented images among established principals! When a new work assignment reinforces the professional identity of a person, the existing sense of self at work is invested—affirmed and supported—through *investiture*. When the new work assignment challenges a person's professional identity and causes a substantial adjustment in the self-concept, *divestiture* occurs (Duke, 1987; Van Maanen & Schein, 1979).

By drawing on sociality, districts tap a power that comes from the group. When a principal abandons her status as a teacher, for example, she also abandons central operating assumptions and devalues old skills. Divestiture might force a new principal to acquire new skills or apply existing skills to the new situation; investiture might encourage her to press for innovation grounded in her experiences in the new school. Superiors should be aware of the potential impacts of these effects, and you should consciously check your own experience to test whether your core professional values are in harmony or discord with these experiences.

Investiture and divestiture remain difficult concepts to differentiate during socialization, however, partly because they depend on self-concept as much as on organizational processes. The nebulous features of investiture and divestiture as socialization tactics deserve elaboration. Because every principal enters a new assignment with an established professional identity, some pressure on this self-concept will occur. We know little about the levels of pressure that may be most productive and—if so, under what conditions.

A new principal should not minimize the impact of taking charge in her first assignment as a principal. Citing Fromm (1941), Nicholson and West (1988, p. 1) put it starkly.

[O]ne might even argue . . . that one of the main functions of culture is to cushion and protect us from our fundamental insecurities about change. . . . The most anxiety-inducing questions about the meaning of our existence, the uncertainty of the future, and the nature of identity, are solved for us, partially at least, by the mechanisms of cultural transmission—the socialization of values, beliefs and behaviors and the institutionalization of social relationships.

Socialization Stages

Earlier in this chapter, we referred to the Danforth Foundation's sponsorship of a series of studies on new principals. Some of the most useful findings to emerge from these studies were reported by Parkay and his colleagues and illuminated stages through which principals pass as they mature as school leaders. Regardless of the profession, newcomers appear to move through a series of stages as they experience socialization in a new setting. As you think about the stages of your own first assignment as a principal, keep in mind how the stages relate to each other and how one moves from one stage to another. Draw upon your past experiences in moving from student to teacher. Reflect for a moment: In what ways might this change in role be similar to a move into the principalship? What differences do you see?

Linear models (like the one proposed by Parkay et al., 1992) see new school leaders moving through stages along a continuum until they reach equilibrium, integration, and influence in the new school. *Iterative* and *cyclical* views of stages see the process continuing perpetually, as principals anticipate their next school assignment (Miskel & Cosgrove, 1985). Parkay and his colleagues identified five stages in the taking-charge experiences of principals that they classified as survival, control, stability, educational leadership, and professional actualization, but three stages are more common. These stages differentiate periods of learning and uncertainty, gradual adjustment and influence, and stabilization and maturity. In the discussion that follows, we include the five stages of Parkay and his colleagues within three general categories. Next we discuss socialization stages from an organizational interaction perspective. Chapter 7 presents the stages and processes of leader success and its impact on schools. In Chapter 10, "Becoming a Principal," we focus more specifically on the intrapersonal dimensions of socialization stages.

Encounter

Quoting Van Maanen, Parkay et al. (1992) call this first stage in a new principal's taking-charge experience a " 'breaking-in' phenomenon" that "represents a prototypical crisis period. . . ." New principals often describe this time in their experience as "traumatic chaos." Parkay and his colleagues labeled it "survival." During this time, new principals sometimes have difficulty using communication to influence the interpretations of others. Roberts, studying the same principals as Parkay and others, found during these early times:

> Stories circulating among faculty members were not principal-initiated, positive, culture-building tales but rather complaints in which the new principal was often the target. Making changes without sufficient communication, being

critical of all instead of a guilty few, being negative about faculty in an article, constantly point out errors, and even being inappropriately silent. . . . Most who faced these difficulties reacted defensively. . . . In only a couple of cases were new principals able to handle such complaints from faculty in a sensitive, constructive manner which resulted in a positive outcome. (1989a, pp. 16–17)

Further, new principals in this stage experience some of their most serious challenges from strong, resistant, and experienced teachers whose place and power in the school culture is firmly established. As one new principal put it,

> Little in my background or training adequately prepared me for the dilemmas that I faced in my first year as principal. . . . Decisions were usually easy—all I needed to do was fall back on school district policy, contract law, sound accounting practices, state financial regulations, and the liberal application of rational and logical thought processes. . . . I felt totally confident that I had been well-prepared by training and temperament to confront any problem I might encounter and astound everyone with the Solomon-like wisdom I was to exhibit. (Aldrich, 1984, p. 75)

This first stage for new principals inspires mixed emotions as excitement and anticipation are combined with confrontation with a new work setting. We do not mean by the use of the term *confrontation* that new principals should plan to be confrontational, nor that teachers, parents, and students will necessarily be so. We do mean that strong new members with formal power over established members of a group pose a threat, however benign, to existing relationships within a school, and savvy new principals should plan for a cautious (if not a deliberately manipulative) response from teachers, students, and others. During this first stage, the beginning principals study researchers found that the least successful new principals focused their efforts on establishing tight control over the various components in their schools and provided little leadership linked to values and integration into the culture (Roberts, in Parkay & Hall, 1992).

While we have differentiated professional socialization (pre-entry) from this discussion of organizational socialization stages, we should acknowledge that some scholars find the process more seamless. This perspective includes anticipatory socialization in the complete process of "getting in" to a new school social group, from preparation through selection and early entry. Success during this stage depends on the extent to which the expectations of the new principal, and of the district and school, are realistic and the degree to which the newcomer is well matched with his new role (Watts, Short & Well, 1987). During this stage the new principal is initiated to the new job and into a group of colleagues and interpersonal relationships. Through interaction processes, the group and the new principal come to see how he fits into the school, uses time, and works toward common goals (Feldman, 1976). As one new principal put it, you will face a situation of "new principal/old community" (Artis, 1984, p. 107).

During this first stage, the new principal must confront and accept the reality of the new social setting. Expectations are confirmed or disconfirmed, conflicts between personal values and needs and the climate of the school are confronted, and the aspects of self that the new setting will reinforce or suppress are discovered.

The anticipation and confrontation stage requires much learning of a new principal. This learning should be cognitive and affective. Cognitive learning during entry into the new school, sometimes is called sensemaking, and surprise functions as the most powerful feature. The demands of "surprise and sensemaking" on a new principal during encounter seem dependent on three main factors: (1) the amount of change—differences in status, role requirements, and work environment between the new and old positions; (2) contrast—the carryover of people from old to new settings; and (3) surprise—unmet positive and negative expectations. Reality usually differs markedly from expectations. Stress coping during encounter also focuses on feelings. Some have compared this transition to the grieving process, but most, acknowledging that job change is stressful, assert that it is far less traumatic. If the beginning principals' study is any example, however, you would be well advised to be sensitive to your own stress levels during this important stage of a new principalship (Hopson & Adams, 1976; Louis, 1980; Parkay et al., 1992; (Richards, 1984)).

During encounter, anxiety over whether their contributions will be valued and people will like their work confronts new principals (Nicholson & West, 1988). Women feel significantly higher levels of presuccession or pretransition anxiety about performance and the value of their contributions than do men. This first stage of the first principalship can be one of "excitement, optimism, and discovery" (Nicholson & West, 1988, p. 98), but you should be prepared for negative surprises to outweigh positive—particularly those related to people and the environment.

Accommodation and Integration

During the conclusion of the first stage, as principals move on toward more integrated leadership, they focus on control, on "setting priorities and seeking ways to manage the overwhelming flow of new demands" (Parkay et al., 1992, p. 16). Principals seem afraid of losing control and being labeled ineffective. As a defense, many principals rely on their formal sources of power when this occurs.

The accommodation stage involves a gradual completion of the process of fitting in. The new principal must reach accommodation with his new work role, the people with whom he interacts and the culture of the new school. This phase technically is organizational socialization at the work site (Nicholson & West, 1988).

Principals and other managers find that successful accommodation gradually leads to a stability where management tasks become effective and efficient routines. As unfamiliar events that previously were sources of frustration become more routine and familiar, they cause less stress. Parkay and others found principals in this stage less intent on proving their leadership by promoting change for its own sake and more interested in the importance of doing a good job for their new schools.

During adjustment, principals become more familiar with and less concerned about their relationships with their mentors and supervisors (Weiss,

1978), group dynamics (Moreland & Levine, 1983), the characteristics of their jobs (Dawis & Lofquist, 1984), evaluation, and their personal influence (Feldman, 1976). Some scholars even see changes in individual identity and personality (Mortimer & Lorence, 1979; Brousseau, 1983; Kohn & Schooler, 1983) as a result of these adjustments. The tasks of the new job are assessed. Interpersonal relationships with teachers, peers, and superiors emerge. The new principal learns to cope with resistance to change on the part of established members of the group. The differences between the group's evaluation of her performance and her own evaluation are confronted—and the new principal learns to cope with ambiguity.

Stabilization—Educational Leadership and Professional Actualization

This last stage in a successful transition from new principal to school leader is described by Parkay and his colleagues in two steps as educational leadership and professional actualization. Total harmony between principal and school is not necessarily the result of educational leadership, but principals take concrete steps toward career and professional growth and advancement for teachers and for themselves and press hard for effective outcomes for the school. When they successfully achieve professional actualization, principals no longer feel compelled to impose their own vision of a school on an unwilling faculty. At this stage, principals are working in harmony with their staffs. Personal visions have evolved into publicly shared and valued visions. "My school" becomes "our school" (Bredeson, 1993). Faculty and principal are able to transform their established routines toward a more effective instructional system. "Faculty members believe that they have been truly empowered and work collegially and harmoniously to improve the school" (p. 58). The principal, validated through the power of the whole, works to bring out the best in the "incipient vision the faculty has for the school" (p. 18).

As a cautionary note, only a few principals move completely through the five stages to actualization in three years. Principals do move from coercive behaviors and positional power to personal power and behaviors facilitating learning and growth for themselves and others. The first year of a new principal's professional career reveals the "handwriting on the wall" (Parkay et al., 1992, pp. 61–62), predictive of a principal's eventual development and success. Integrated and stabilized new school leaders assess and evaluate their decisions and actions by what is best for the school, not by a preestablished vision with which they enter their new leadership role. They respond more to an internal locus of control than to worries about how they are perceived.

Other writers are less heroic in their terms but no less specific in the social and output outcomes they describe. They evaluate the outcomes of the final stage in the new principal's self-image—formation of new relationships, adoption of new values, and acquisition of new behaviors—all related to personal, not organizational, outcomes.

During this third stage of socialization, the newcomer locates herself in the context by learning which behaviors are congruent with expected behaviors. Increased commitment to the organization, an altered or reaffirmed self-image and values, and new interpersonal relationships develop. Feelings of mutual acceptance should result (Wanous, 1980).

As the school and principal adjust and move toward stabilization, changes in the environment, the school, or individual educators within the school usually mix up the balance, so many writers treat stabilization and preparation for the next change together, since "it may not be uncommon to find that stabilization never occurs" (Nicholson & West, 1988, p. 14). They caution that we too often treat principals and the schools in which they work in terms of work outcomes, assessment, management control, job satisfaction, and job design focused on stabilized work structures and relationships, treating people as if they have "no past and no future."

For new school leaders, this stage (a preparation for change) requires that they negotiate two new sets of relationships simultaneously—one with superiors and one with faculty, staff, and students (Duke et al., 1984). It may involve a continuing informal negotiation among all these people akin to the "social contracting" relationship of leadership (Fulk & Cummings, 1984). The cyclical nature of the stages also requires that people continually project into the future, combining their appraisal and assessment of current work performance with preparation for future transitions.

Context

Principals interact with new schools in a context that sets the stage for their taking-charge experience. No discussion of the principal in the school would be complete without a view of the existing social world that a new principal joins. Very rarely will a new principal be assigned to open a new school, and even then established patterns within districts and common assumptions about schools often constrain the "newness" of the school culture (Ogawa & Bossert, 1990).

Consequently, new principals enter an existing social world. But this pre-existing set of expectations and beliefs does not completely eliminate the opportunity to exert influence. Even if the norms and expectations in a school prescribe behavior so tightly that creativity is seen as a "breach of the rules" (Wentworth, 1980, p. 58), the prescription "does not exert an irresistible hold" over the newcomer. Each new principal brings a personal perspective, outside influences, and creative skepticism to the experience. Neither the principal's prior qualities, nor the school's prior qualities explain the outcomes when a new principal takes charge (Smith & Peterson, 1988).

The *personal* context of interactions between a school and a new principal is simple: the new principal. New group members—their talents, preferences, characteristics, thinking, and experiences—form the personal context in which a new principal takes charge. In addition to learning as much as he can about the school, a new principal facing a first assignment should consequently spend time getting to know himself and understanding professional and personal identity. Some new principals focus on their careers and the evolving development of their work as educators. Others find insight in theories of adult learning and development. Still others prefer some combination of these views to help them better understand and use their strengths, weaknesses, and present career circumstances to help facilitate a strong start to their careers as principals (Manning, 1977). In Chapter 6, we turn to more traditional concepts of leadership that attend to traits and characteristics. These traditions provide some insight, but our intention in this discussion is to emphasize that new principals should attend to their personal traits, characteristics, and beliefs *embedded within, and in interaction with, a context.*

The social structure or organizational culture at the time a new principal takes charge makes up the primary context, the human system into which he seeks integration. Culture is an elusive concept when applied to organizations. While it may feel "right" to many people who work in schools, researchers report that principals have trouble applying culture to their decisions and using it to help them do their work better. This may be because culture is so fundamental to organizations that organizations *are* cultures. To tap the power of the existing culture and use it to his advantage, a new principal must come to understand and be able to use the fundamental values, beliefs, and assumptions about goodness and worth that drive and energize the group, made up primarily of teachers. We will return to this theme in our discussion of data-gathering and analysis techniques you can apply to this process (Parkay & Hall, 1993; Pondy et al, 1983; Smircich, 1983).

Human systems theory provides another useful framework for a new principal seeking to understand a school context. The principal is in a formal leadership position, at the top of the school level organizational hierarchy. The expectations and responsibilities of that position influence people's responses to her, and she should attend to the inherent features of that structure that affect her interactions with people. Interactions with individuals and groups also will shape the effects of her taking-charge experiences and socialization. While many formal and informal interactions can be planned, serendipity plays a part, and the new principal needs to be especially attuned to "firsts" that will provide important information.

We pointed out that teachers, parents, and students will react to a new principal or new member of the group in part as a result of the expectations they hold for the role he fills. This "level" response will trigger judgments and reactions. Three central features of human systems strongly affect these responses. They are: similarity of group members; frequency of interaction or contact among them; and the tendency of people to interact with people like themselves and limit the frequency and intensity of their contact with people who are different (Gecas, 1981).

In the early stages of contact between the new principal and the school, the first and second of these features—similarity of members and the impact of contact on positive feelings—exert the greatest influence. The similarities among teachers, the community, and the principal and the frequency of contact among them positively affect feelings, increasing liking among the members and creating positive responses. But the nature of these contacts and expectations and beliefs about contact strongly influence these outcomes (another reason the new principal should invest time and energy getting to know the context). Communication by itself may not be a balm when problems arise. Monane points out that unconditional belief in the salutary effects of communication is unfounded, that positive effects depend on the *legitimacy* of the interaction. Neither increased similarity nor increased contact are "independently or jointly productive of positive affect in systems where hostility is the legitimate expected" outcome of contact (Monane, 1967, p. 28–29). For example, among the Apache and Navajo, contact between sons-in-law and mothers-in-law is frowned on and produces negative feelings when it occurs. While expectations within schools may be less dramatic, they have the same effects. Firestone and Bader (1992) describe difficulties among superintendents, school boards, and teachers, arising from expectations about principal classroom visits and interactions with teachers about instruction, for example, that exert influence independent of the objective quality of the visits themselves.

These characteristics of social systems raise questions for new principals about challenges they will face around diversity. A new principal belonging to any underrepresented group faces additional and different challenges from those faced by his more "conventional" peers. Opportunity and diversity among school leaders are important values, but when perceptions that a new principal is "too different" limit contact, block communication, and reduce perceptions that the appointment is legitimate (Hart, 1988; Pounder, 1988, 1989; Valverde, 1980), the new principal faces a serious uphill battle. Surface characteristics, especially those reflecting differences in gender, race, and ethnicity, present initial barriers that can be overcome but increase the challenge. Differences in training and experience also can create initial barriers. The experience of one author provided an example during an interview for a principal's position. I had received two graduate degrees from a large, (often-labeled "radical") university; the superintendent who interviewed me and later hired me wondered aloud during my second interview if I would be too liberal and too different for this rural, consolidated school district.

Finally, people tend to increase their interactions with people who are like them and limit their interactions with those who are not. This tendency poses problems for new principals, their superiors, and their new colleagues. School and community members' perceptions that a new principal doesn't "fit" may lead to isolation and the perceived need to protect standard practice and traditions from his influence. The new principal might intentionally or unintentionally intensify perceptions of his differences by drawing attention to them with his behavior, because he does not realize how he is perceived. On the other hand, a new principal might highlight similar experiences as an educator, parent, or member of the community, and de-emphasize differences to help others get to know him and the contributions he can make to the school.

In loosely coupled systems like schools, two very different features should dominate early interactions. First, it may take more effort for the principal to establish the legitimacy of her authority and the authenticity of her role (Blau, 1964; Dornbush & Scott, 1975) with teachers, parents, and supervisors and, eventually, with the school as a whole than it would if linkages were tighter. Second, and conversely, early, positive (or negative) responses by superiors or influential teachers and parents to the new principal and her ideas could trigger similar responses from others over time, especially those with whom she has close and frequent contact. Ogawa (1991) found, for example, that the unhappy and negative interactions between a newly assigned (yet very experienced principal) and a beloved school secretary badly damaged his relationship with teachers and the community. Loyalty to former principals and comparisons of leadership styles and personalities present challenges to acceptance of the new principal. A few people in the school may even equate acceptance

99

*The Principal
and the School*

and support for the new principal as disloyalty to the former principal. This is especially the case when the predecessor, well liked by teachers, is forced out of his position (by the school board or superiors).

Outcomes or Effects

When all the factors in the interactions between the new principal and the school come into play, some outcome patterns emerge. While we caution always that general patterns do not absolutely predict outcomes for each individual experience, these patterned outcomes provide a framework for you as a new principal to watch for the effects of early socialization stages in the school. A *custodial* response from you as the new principal of the school would be the most stable outcome for that school. This means that no real change would take place and the inherited past would dominate. We also caution that a custodial response is intrinsically neither positive nor negative. It means simply that the new principal functions as the custodian or guardian of existing values and practices. All aspects of the principal's role remain virtually unchanged, and the new principal is much like her predecessor. She essentially replicates her predecessor, learns the requirements of the job, and uses customary strategies and actions to meet these requirements. When role models have close contact with the newcomer, the steps and content of socialization are systematically laid out, and the newcomer shapes a new professional identity (divestiture), a custodial response is promoted.

Another category of outcomes predicted when a new principal takes over is *content innovation.* When a new principal accepts traditional norms and goals while changing tactical alternatives, tasks, and the knowledge base on which she draws to get her work done, the outcome often is content innovation. In other words, the role remains essentially unchanged, but significant change in the content of the actions taken occurs. When new ideas and innovation are stressed during collective socialization experiences and role models are absent, this outcome is more likely.

The most innovative outcome of a new principal's taking-charge socialization experiences is *role innovation.* When role innovation occurs, missions and goals may be refined or redefined and the role of principal itself may be reshaped. This outcome is more likely when socialization is individual, informal, random, and disjunctive, and it affirms a strong professional identity. In other words, when a new principal experiences his assignment alone, without formal planning from others, in random order, without dominant role models, and with a strong professional identity intact, he may reject most of the norms governing conduct and performance and make a genuine attempt to redefine the ends as well as the means (Schein, 1971).

CONCLUSION

This discussion introduces only briefly the features of early experiences and possible outcomes a newly assigned principal may expect to encounter. For example, we have touched only briefly on the strong personal development effects of custodial responses. Two dimensions of managerial work—novelty and discretion—also exert influence over outcomes. The greater the novelty of the role experiences a new principal confronts, the greater the likelihood that she will develop new skills and perspectives. The greater the discretion, the more likelihood that she will attempt role innovation. Older, higher-status, generalist managers are more likely to say they are role innovators (Nicholson & West, 1988). Since both principal growth and school improvement are desired outcomes when new principals take charge, Nicholson and West report a research finding of great interest:

> [H]igh role innovators are more likely than low innovators to report having experienced personal change as a result of their last job change. This indicates, in the terminology of the theory of work role transitions, that "exploration" is more common as an adjustment mode than pure "determination." (p. 110)

The creative and innovative work that can result when principals receive new assignments deserves as much attention as does the effect of macro level education reform (West, Farr & King, 1986).

We cannot close this chapter without emphasizing that, in any given situation, each of the possible categories of outcomes we have discussed could be very productive and appropriate. The need for educators (new principals and their superiors alike) to invest careful thought and deliberate action to facilitate desired outcomes drives this discussion. Successful new principals find their experiences facilitated by traditions of trust (Bredeson, 1993) and through friendship and strong affective bonds with their peers, teachers, and superiors (Sherman, Smith, Howard & Mansfield, 1986). Schools and students pay a high price for disaffected and unhappy new principals. Wanous (1980) estimated that negative early socialization outcomes are among the five most important factors creating feelings of alienation and resignations among people in organizational settings. "The meanings of job change are highly personal. We would need to take an individualized biographical perspective to fully appreciate how they fit into the lives and careers of managers" (Nicholson & West, 1988, p. 211). This approach has been termed a "worthwhile endeavor" for future research.

> If job change has the power to effect changes in identity as well as in organizational performance then how the transition process is managed has a vital bearing on the well-being and effectiveness of organizations. It would appear that few organizations recognize this. (Nicholson & West, 1988, p. 212)

One final factor affecting the quality of succession and transitions is the quality of feedback and recognition given to new leaders—an area in which Nicholson and West found most organizations to be deficient. Principal socialization research paints a similar picture; some new principals report going months on end with no contact with their superiors and absolutely no feedback about how they are perceived (Duke et. al, 1984; Greenfield, 1985a, 1985b). In Chapter 10, "Becoming a Principal," we examine in further detail the intrapersonal dynamics of moving into the principalship.

1. Looking back on your first few years as a teacher, what were some of the "dos and don'ts" teachers taught you in the faculty room and lunch room conversations that you didn't think about as a student teacher or new teacher? In what way did these rules of behavior influence your ideas or ideals? If you have taught in different schools or communities, what rules of behavior (norms) distinguished one school from another, and how did these differences affect what people did?

2. How do your socialization experiences as a teacher suggest some strategies for you entering a school as a new principal?

3. Describe a situation in which a new principal "taught" something unexpected to a group of teachers, a community, or a school and the positive outcomes of that surprising new information. Describe a principal who "knew all the answers" before coming to a school and refused to learn from the context. What were the results of these principals' experiences?

4. Take material collected in the assignment for Chapter 1 and analyze potential outcomes for yourself and what you would add based on this information—depending on whether you decide custodial, content, or role innovation outcomes are most desired in this assignment.

5. School leaders always face the tension between "fitting in" and expressing new ideas and individuality. Think about principals you have worked with as a teacher. What factors or circumstances increased this source of tension for these principals? How did each deal with it? Have you observed individuals who have not been successful in dealing with this tension? What were the primary reasons for the lack of success at fitting in while maintaining a sense of unique professional and personal identity?

6. As you envision yourself in a principalship, what strategies are you likely to use to become successfully integrated as a formal leader in a new school?

CHAPTER 5

Principals and Their Work

School principals play vitally important roles in the creation and nurture of successful teaching and learning environments. The lists of job responsibilities, functional tasks, competencies, personal attributes, and professional behaviors required to be an effective principal in Table 2.1 suggest, however, near super-human qualifications for practicing principals. We all know principals who currently hold these positions in schools and—as good as most of them are—none is superhuman, so how do principals come to understand their roles? How do they continue to construct positive and effective professional work lives in schools?

We noted in the introduction to this text that our approach to under-standing the principalship would be quite different from more traditional pre-sentations in textbooks and workshops. Our presentation is centered on social learning and role-making processes as opposed to delineation, description, and prescription of functional tasks, competencies, and proficiency domains. These representations and descriptions are important, but insufficient. In addition, understanding of just what it is that effective principals do and how and why they spend their time in particular ways to bring about desired educational outcomes is crucial to each new principal's thinking about and preparation for the principalship. Our review of the work of the school principal recognizes the importance of previous studies and documentation of job analyses from multiple perspectives and notes that these descriptions are more thoroughly covered in other sources (see, for example, the works of Lipham, 1981; Lipham et al., 1985; Peterson, 1978; Kmetz & Willower, 1982; Martin & Willower, 1981). We will briefly summarize major findings from this literature to provide a suc-cinct overview of principals and their work. In this chapter we provide you with an opportunity to combine the three sources of knowledge—empirical, theoretical, and experiential described in the first two chapters.

First, we present a brief historical account of the evolution of the princi-palship. Next we examine various sources of influence that have affected the social organization of schools and the work of principals. Specifically, we examine the impact of the organizing principles of the industrial revolution, the work of organizational-management theorists, and the theory movement in educational administration. Finally, we summarize the contributions of empirical research on the school principalship. Together these sources provide a comprehensive description of how principals carry out their primary responsibilities; they also indicate that despite various personal, professional, and situational factors a number of common themes characterize the work of school principals.

FROM PRINCIPAL TEACHER TO PRINCIPAL

Historic Roots of the Modern Principalship

The growth of the principalship and job responsibilities for school administrators paralleled the development of schools and formalized methods for teaching in Europe and in the United States. Some of the earliest descriptions of the work of school administrators can be found in the writing of Johann Sturm (1507–1589). In 1537 the magistrates of Strasburg, Germany needed a rector to organize a local gymnasium, a secondary school for boys. They hired Johann Sturm, a classically trained renaissance scholar, to organize a curriculum, develop teaching methods, and hire and supervise teachers for approximately 600 male secondary school students. With this specific charge in mind, in 1538 Sturm published *The Best Mode of Opening Institutions of Learning*.[1] In this particular work and in numerous other books, essays and treatises published over the next 45 years,

> [w]e find such modern problems discussed as principles of education, school organization, educational values, teachers' salaries, relation of parent and school, entrance requirements, discipline and conduct of pupils, how to bring education within the reach of poor boys, class instruction against individual instruction, responsibility of the teacher, and the like. (Ensign, 1923, p. 182)

Johann Sturm was an exception for his time and many of his ideas for organizing schools and the curriculum were not adopted to any significant degree across Europe until several centuries later.

In the English public schools—residential-private boarding schools—we also find antecedents of the modern day principalship. By the eighteenth century the term *headmaster* was in common use and the roles and responsibilities for these headmasters were focused primarily on discipline and supervision of student life of boys attending school away home (Ensign, 1923). This provides at least a partial explanation for the importance of discipline in the evolving role of principals codified in the legal principle of "in loco parentis."

Early colonial education in the United States was influenced by English experiences in schooling. At Phillips Andover Academy in 1786 the contract

---

[1]Johann Sturm Latin text.

between Eliphaet Pearson and the trustees referred to "Principal Pearson" (Ensign, 1923). Prior to the 1850s in the United States, most schools, both public and private, tended to be small with only one or two teachers. Thus, there was little need for full-time principals to deal with administrative matters beyond the classroom. Responsibilities for curriculum development and organization were generally assigned to the "principal teacher."

In education, the transformation of the word *principal* from an adjective to a noun came with the rapid growth of cities and the ever-expanding school-age population. Douglass (1932) attributes the development of the formal position of school principal to (1) the increased size and complexity of schools, which presented greater problems with organization and management; (2) the expansion of secondary education; (3) the change in the nature and quality of secondary school students; (4) the increase in the body of professional knowledge related to principles and techniques of school administration; and (5) the changed attitude generally toward the idea of specialization in education. Because these changes required more extraclassroom work than any one "principal teacher" could adequately handle, school boards began to relieve head teachers of classroom duties so that they could assume the increasing demands for administration and coordination.

> Thus, scholarship, the traditional characteristic of the head master, organizing ability, and certain qualities of leadership came to be demanded of him who was to head the teaching staff of the new American secondary school. (p. 188)

By 1870 the growth of cities resulted in larger and more diverse school-age populations enrolled in larger and more complex schools, both elementary and secondary. As urbanization occurred across the United States a greater demand developed for secondary schools. In large secondary schools in cities with diverse student populations, "principal teachers" increasingly spent more time carrying out administrative responsibilities. Despite the desire to retain a role combining both teaching and administrative responsibilities, the sheer numbers of students and teachers and the time required for principals to carry out major organizational and administrative reporting tasks in large city schools resulted in school boards' relieving principal teachers of classroom teaching responsibilities. In 1890 there were approximately 2,500 high schools serving over 200,000 students. By 1910 there were over 10,000 high schools with over 900,000 students (*Digest of Education Statistics*, 1991). Today there are over 128,000 elementary and secondary principals and assistant principals in the United States.

Similarly, elementary school principals found themselves largely carrying out expanded responsibilities in addition to their classroom duties. Many tasks were largely clerical. In 1845 principals reported their primary duties—58.8 percent record keeping and reporting, 23.5 percent organization and classification of students, 11.8 percent maintenance of equipment and the building, and 5.9 percent discipline and care of students (Pierce, 1934, pp. 210–211).

Traditional clerical and administrative responsibilities as well as organizational structures of schools influenced the evolution of the role of the school principal today; however, the principal's job is more than just an outgrowth of history. The principalship traces its heritage to various antecedents, but it is not limited to them. Besides the broad historical factors influencing the role of principal, the school in which you become a principal also has a history of principals; this history brings with it sets of expectations and beliefs about your leadership role. Many individuals inside and outside your school will actively attempt to shape your administrative role. As a principal you will need to combine requirements of the job itself (functional task and duties) with your personal skills, competencies, and characteristics within the particular social settings.

As a new principal you will assume a historically important education role. The imprint of professional and organizational history is a powerful source of influence on your future leadership. Management theory is an important source of job information that you will find useful in shaping your role; it is useful in terms of understanding the managerial dimensions of principals' work and it suggests a number of common themes in administrative work.

Management Theory: Influences on the Work of Principals

Schools are unique social organizations with rich individual histories and missions related to teaching and learning. Although this special organizational focus shaped particular constraints and opportunities in the organization, operation, and administration of schools, schools and the people who work in them share a number of common characteristics with other social organizations. Similarities across types of organizations suggest that leaders in those organizations can learn from one another by borrowing ideas, models, theories, and practices.

Woodrow Wilson (1887) laid out a compelling argument on why leaders should look for successful ideas across organizational and national boundaries.

> If I see a murderous fellow sharpening a knife cleverly, I can borrow his way of sharpening the knife without borrowing his probable intention to commit murder with it, and so, if I see a monarchist dyed in the wool managing a public bureau well, I can learn his business methods without changing one of my republican spots. (p. 220)

Wilson's injunction is that adaptation of salient ideas and methods is not inherently contaminated by its source so long as leaders keep their sights on legitimate ends. Neither should models and methods be borrowed and followed mindlessly. Wilson said, "We can borrow the science of administration with safety and profit if only we read all fundamental differences of condition into its essential tenets" (p. 219).

What are some of these borrowed ideas related to the work of school principals? To whom have school administrators looked for ideas and frameworks for understanding their work? When employing the ideas and methods from other organizations, have educators in general and principals in particular remained wary of mindless mimicking? Do principals read all fundamental differences of conditions in education into the essential tenets of leadership in schools? In the next section we address issues rasied by these questions.

Organizing Principles of the Industrial Revolution

The latter half of the nineteenth century was a period of dramatic social change, with rapid growth in the numbers of students and schools resulting in greater demands on principals. The industrial revolution was in full flower, affecting every aspect of society—schools and the principalship included. In *Future Shock,* Alvin Toffler (1970) describes six organizing principles that undergirded the industrial revolution. Looking to business and industry, which were themselves undergoing similar structural and organizational changes, the principles of *standardization, specialization, synchronization, concentration of resources, maximization of production units,* and *centralization* of control structures were viewed by educators as helpful organizers in their efforts to deal effectively with an increasingly demanding and seemingly unwieldy public educational system. Educators applied these principles to such pressing problems as the development of an appropriate curriculum for diverse student populations, changes in sizes of schools (from small, rural settings to large, urban schools with hundreds of students), and mandates to provide educational programs from kindergarten through high school. These problems and many others increased the need for planning, organizing, and coordinating at building and school district levels by principals.

The six organizing principles of the industrial revolution ultimately came to define both the context and content of principals' work. Take a moment to think about how these organizing principles of the industrial revolution have influenced, and continue to shape, the organization, operation, and administration of schools as you know them today. A few suggestions may stimulate your thinking. Graded structures, standardized curricula, state licensure, subject matter specialization, school consolidations, carefully sequenced and synchronized teaching-learning activities, the concentration and maximization of resources to enhance uniformity and efficiency, the uniform salary schedule, and the need to centralize control structures to monitor and coordinate the organization have greatly affected school structures and the role of principals within them. Even with the outward changes brought about by perennial calls for educational reform, the shell of the generative industrial metaphor remains in schools.

Management and Organizational Theory

In Table 2.1 we displayed selected examples of knowledge base organizers to illustrate various ways in which professional knowledge for principals has been articulated in typologies, training models, and formal theory. Many of these ideas and categories can be traced to the early works of organizational and management theorists. We will briefly discuss the contributions of five noneducator theorists whose ideas are evident in the frameworks presented in Table 2.1: Henri Fayol, Max Weber, Frederick Taylor, Mary Parker Follett, and Chester Barnard. As you review the ideas of these early theorists, think about how these ideas have become integrated into the social framework of schools and the work of school principals. (Excellent summaries of the works of these theorists have been done by Hoy and Miskel, 1991, and by Campbell et al., 1987. We also refer you to the original writing of classical organizational theorists.)

Henri Fayol (1841–1925) is credited with being the first to develop a general theory of administration for organizations. His work with coal mining and foundry industries in France became the context for applying his basic principles of management (division of labor, centralization, scalar chain of authority, unity of command, and order). His theory of management, based on hierarchies of authority and responsibilities, described six key activities in organizations—technical, commercial, financial, security (protection of property and persons), accounting, and managerial (that is, planning, organization, command, coordination, and control).

Max Weber (1864–1920), an affluent German intellectual and sociologist, is often referred to as the father of organizational theory. Weber's notion of bureaucracy as an ideal type of organization was initially conceived as an antidote to patronage, institutional chaos, and ambiguity. Bureaucracy was designed as a model for creating greater efficiency and goal attainment. The major principles of bureaucracy are (1) division of labor; (2) hierarchical organization; (3) selection of employees based on technical qualifications determined by examination; (4) officials who are subject to strict rules, discipline, and control; (5) impersonal orientation; and, (6) organizational incentives to encourage employees to make administration a career. These principles of organization were intended to enhance expertise, make decision making more rational, increase compliance and coordination among organizational units and members, assure continuity and uniformity, and encourage organization and career loyalty. Today, however, the word *bureaucracy* carries with it negative connotative baggage. Many of the dysfunctional aspects of bureaucracy are the result of exaggerated applications of the primary elements of bureaucracy. For example, the *division of labor* can lead to boredom in one's job; an *impersonal orientation* by members of the organization contributes to interpersonal distance and low morale among employees; *hierarchy of authority* may block communications and task accomplishment; and, *rules* often become goals themselves—thus leading to hyperlegalism, with more time being spent on the development of rules and enforcement strategies than on the major tasks and purposes of the organization (Thompson 1967). To varying degrees each of these dysfunctional aspects of bureaucracy can be found in many of our school systems today. For example, children with special needs may be seen as the responsibility of special education teachers. Union contracts and local district policies may stifle curriculum reform and faculty work. Central office administrators may remain aloof from the real work of teaching and learning.

Frederick Taylor (1856–1915), the father of the scientific management movement, published *The Principles of Scientific Management* in 1911. Trained as an engineer, Taylor was convinced that the application of scientific principles could eliminate much of the waste and inefficiency in organizations. His ideas on efficiency, grounded in time studies, piece-rate systems, and carefully defined worker tasks and time allocations, were the foundations of scientific management principles applied to work settings. Many of Taylor's ideas came to education through the work of Franklin Bobbit in an article titled, "Some General Principles of Management Applied to the Problems of City-school Systems" and published in the 1913 yearbook of the National Society for the Study of Education. As Callahan (1962) notes in *Education and the Cult of Efficiency*, school administrators could do little to resist the ideological tide of efficiency so convincingly and enthusiastically supported by captains of business and industry, local school boards, the press, and the general public. The principle of efficiency became mainstream as younger administrators entered the field of school administration. They "accepted the prevailing conceptions (as most students do, after all) and they in turn carried the business orientation to all corners of the nation and to their students, who did the same" (p. 246). Callahan goes on to describe the outcome of this blind application of scientific efficiency as a tragedy for American education.

> Educational questions were subordinated to business considerations; the administrators were produced who were not, in any true sense, educators; that a scientific label was put on some very unscientific and dubious methods and practices; and that an anti-intellectual climate, already prevalent, was strengthened. (p. 246)

Thirty years later, Callahan's words are equally powerful as educators in the 1990s deal with the rhetoric of management gurus hawking their latest organizational palliatives and consultative wares across bookshelves and board rooms.

One voice, that of a political philosopher, Mary Parker Follett (1868–1933), pierced the veneer of scientific management. Follett recognized the importance of the human side of organizational life. Reflecting on her experiences in industry, government, and education, she espoused a human relations viewpoint based on the belief that organizational problems and challenges are best met by building a system of harmonious and supportive relationships among all people who share an interest in organizational outcomes (*Creative Experience*, 1924). Her ideas are often compartmentalized under the rubric of "human relations" in many traditional texts on administration, although Follett's writings contributed significantly to political and organizational theory. She viewed the work unit as a functional whole in which all participants have vested interests. According to Follett, authority derives from function, not position. Finally, she believed that leaders and followers reciprocally influence each others' actions, an idea that permeates this book. Her contributions to management theory were way ahead of their time. They resonate in the literature on employee empowerment, quality circles, and Theory Z so popular in management theory today.

Another influential writer who shaped early management theory, Chester Barnard, a vice-president of Bell Telephone of New Jersey, developed a classic theoretical formulation of the interdependent relationship between the formal and informal side of an organization. In *Functions of the Executive* (1938), Barnard argues that effective leaders understand that structural and process dimensions in organizations are interactive. As leaders they act on this belief and help others understand the interdependence of these two dimensions to task accomplishment.

We provide only selected examples from the work of classical organizational and management theorists. The work of these theorists and the conceptual frameworks they espoused influence the ways in which we think about schools as organizations and how we envision the role and work of school principals. Besides providing you with a brief overview of the theoretical concepts, our purpose in providing an abbreviated review of major organizational theorists is to stress that the work of school principals has been shaped by many sources of influence, even those of noneducators. Many of these ideas continue to shape the work of principals to the degree that they apply to current role expectations, norms of professional behavior, and deeply embedded beliefs about leadership and followership in schools.

Educational Administration Theory

Based on the works and theories of earlier scholars, especially Herbert Simon's *Administrative Behavior* (1957), the theory movement in the field of educational administration evolved. Under the auspices of the W.K. Kellogg Foundation, the Cooperative Program in Educational Administration was founded to improve preparatory programs for educational administrators. Jack A. Culbertson (1988) credits the work of individual scholars in the consortium with playing a leading role in translating and transmitting simplified versions of logical positivism to the field of school administration. Through their scholarship, they activated the theory movement in educational administration and directly influenced both the conceptualization of administrative work of principals and preparation of candidates for the principalship. Culbertson links the work of this early group of educational administration theorists to the philosophical traditions of logical positivism.

> Diffused in simplified form into educational administration in the 1950s by such leading scholars as Simon, Getzels, Griffiths, and Halpin, the ideas heightened hopes for a science of administration. Research became more theory-based; leading scholars moved away from "ought" generalizations; changed relationships between scholars in educational administration and the social sciences brought new inquiry; more conceptual content buttressed training programs; and new journals for disseminating the products of the theory movement were launched. (p. 17)

Getzels' social-process theory is a good example of the impact of the theory movement on descriptions of the principal's job. The theory, which was strongly influenced by the work of Talcott Parsons, brought the social system concepts of formal "role," "institution," "individual," and "personality" to the study of and preparation for the principalship. This set of interrelated concepts, which evolved into a general model linking the social system structural features to social behavior of individuals within those systems, informed inquiry, theory, and practice. The formal role of the principal became defined in terms of role expectations (normative rights and duties).

> When the role incumbent puts these rights and duties into effect, he is said to be performing in his role. The expectations define what the actor, whoever he may be, should or should not do under various circumstances while occupying the particular role in the social system. (Getzels, Lipham & Campbell, 1968, p. 61)[2]

Lipham, Rankin, and Hoeh, in *The Principalship: Concepts, Competencies, and Cases,* (1985) then used the social systems framework to describe requisite skills

[2]For a detailed account of the roots and development of organizational theory, see Hoy & Miskel, 1991.

and competencies for successful leadership. Social systems theory framed the principal's job itself. The authors state:

> For many years, a pervasive antitheoretical bias permeated professional programs for preparing administrators. Recently, however, most programs for preparing principals assume that concepts and constructs concerning educational issues and goals, administrative organization, instructional leadership, decision making, educational change and other theories are essential for effective performance of principals. This realization resulted in the competency-based approach to administration (Lipham, 1975) wherein great effort was expended toward not only defining and describing the theoretical concepts needed by principals but also toward devising the means whereby the understandings could be translated into specific skills and behaviors that could be taught, learned and assessed. (p. 295)

This blend of technical and theoretical competence helped both to define and to inform principalship practices.

Social systems theory represented one philosophic tradition that guided theory, research, and practice in school administration. Quite a different theoretical position is represented in the writings of Tom Greenfield (1975). Greenfield rejected the dominant administrative theory paradigm, which held that administrative practice and our understanding and explanation of it were codifiable in objective, universal principles, and law-like generalities. He argued that the very character of knowledge in educational administration is one that is socially constructed and grounded in temporal values, preferences, and human intentions, not in "objective reality."

As a reader of historic and contemporary management literature, you doubtless have already noticed that the language of management theory and administration is gender biased. "Fathers" abound in the literature of educational administration and the principalship along with *The Man in the Principal's Office* (Wolcott, 1973). The views and experiences of women in organizational theory are greatly underrepresented. The perspectives of racial and ethnic minorities are absent from traditional management theory and literature.

In addition to the influence of historical antecedents, classic organizational theory, and theoretical developments in the field of educational administration, empirical research on the work of school principals has also greatly informed our understanding of this unique leadership role. Various methods of inquiry have contributed substantially to the knowledge base upon which preservice preparation programs and professional practice are based. In the next section we will examine empirical research on the work of school principals.

EMPIRICAL RESEARCH ON PRINCIPALS AND THEIR WORK

Job analysis is one strategy for gaining a better understanding of how individuals enact their roles in organizations. Job analysis helps us clarify various roles, responsibilities, and relationships among individuals in complex social organizations. Miner and Miner (1977) state, "The methods used to gather information about a job vary greatly in comprehensiveness and systematic rigor" (p. 162). These methods typically include: (1) observations of job occupants; (2) surveys of job occupants using interviews and questionnaires; (3) examination of work materials; (4) assessment of the work environment—physical, mental and social; and (5) personal experience in the job. Since each method has advantages as well as limitations, combining the findings from these methods provides a more complete description of the work of school principals.

The job analysis strategies described by Miner and Miner parallel methods used by researchers and practitioners to study the work of school principals. A brief summary of findings from selected studies provides an empirical backdrop for a discussion of principals' work. Our discussion of studies is grouped into four general methodological categories: observational studies; survey research (written questionnaires); qualitative studies (interview studies, case studies, ethnographies, and naturalistic accounts); and first-person accounts. Our summary is not meant to be encyclopedic; it is selective and illustrative. More detailed and comprehensive descriptions can be found in the works of authors cited in our reference list.

Observational Studies

Observational studies, both structured and unstructured, of the work of school principals provide a rich, descriptive portrait of daily administrative routines that are enormously complex and demanding. The work of Peterson (1978), Martin and Willower (1981), Kmetz and Willower (1982), Bredeson (1985, 1987), Kelley (1987), and Pierson (1989) represent systematic inquiries through direct observation of the daily routines and activities of principals. Taken together the findings support the view that the principal's job is characterized by the brevity and variety of daily activities, fragmentation, uncertainty, discontinuity of work routines, long hours, a preference for verbal communication, high levels of interpersonal interaction, a high volume of activities (which are rapidly paced and frequently interrupted), role overload, and extensive responsibilities with limited control and authority. These detailed descriptions of school principals' work provide useful information for candidates preparing for the principalship and for individuals already occupying the role, although they provide little guidance about what principals should do to optimize the impact of their leadership on desired student and school outcomes. Working conditions are dominated by competing demands, multiple role expectations, and the highly interpersonal nature of daily routines. As a result, principals are busy persons, who are more often attentive to immediate and pressing demands than they are to important technical core (teaching and learning) issues. The press of immediate events pushes principals to be more reactive than proactive in matters of instruction and learning. Finally, much of the real work done by principals remains nearly invisible because it is verbal, interpersonal, and predominantly focused on service to others (Bredeson, 1987; Gronn, 1982).

Such a job description might discourage even the most zealous applicant for a principalship. Nevertheless, educators continue to seek this important leadership position in education. Perhaps it's a bit like an incident in Dik Browne's comic strip "Hagar the Horrible." Looking for volunteers for a Viking mission, Hagar circulates a similarly challenging description of the demands and dangers of such a position. Hagar tells a young Viking applicant, "Forget it, Kid! It's a *Suicide Mission*" However, to the astonishment of Hagar and Lucky the applicant persists by asking, "What's the pay like?"

Structured observation efforts, based on Mintzberg's model of managerial behavior and other descriptive studies provide important details about the general job tasks of principals. From these studies we have learned much about general job tasks, professional responsibilities, role enactment, and various ways in which principals currently define their leadership roles, yet the job portrait remains an incomplete one. Survey research has also made important contributions to a more complete analysis and description of principals' work.

Survey Research

Written questionnaires have been employed extensively to investigate various questions related to principal work life. For example, the National Education Association's Department of Elementary School Principals and later the National Association of Elementary School Principals sponsored and conducted surveys in 1928, 1948, 1958, 1968, 1979, 1986, and 1989. The National Association of Secondary School Principals (NASSP) published the results of extensive national surveys on the work of principals at the middle school (Valentine et. al, 1981) and at the senior high school (Byrne et al., 1978). In Foskett's (1967) study of elementary principals, a mailed questionnaire was used to chronicle specific dimensions of the principal's job. Essentially the purpose of these inquiries was to prepare an inventory of static job dimensions and characteristics (for example, time spent on job tasks and role priorities) as

TABLE 5.1. Percentages of Total Time Spent on Fourteen Tasks

Tasks	Percentages
Preparing reports—e.g., attendance, budget, etc.	6.85
Written communications	8.43
Telephone	5.95
Teacher concerns—problem solving, social, program, etc.	9.65
Student supervision/counseling	10.55
Discipline—referrals, parent conferences	8.13
Extracurricular activities	10.85
Meetings—staff/central office	6.20
Supervision of noncertified employees	4.55
Contract management	3.75
Curriculum development/supervision	7.95
Teacher evaluation	9.55
Special education conferences, staff	3.63
Professional growth—conferences, reading	4.05

opposed to a search for understanding of particular behaviors, purposes, or meanings attached to those categories of job activities. As researchers discovered through observational studies, surveys of principals portrayed their work as highly ambiguous, subject to definition by multiple role senders, and norm driven (individually and situationally constrained with a large number of "conditional rules": is's, oughts, musts, and don'ts). A 1984 NASSP study conducted by Drake and Wagner illustrates the types of findings and job descriptions based on these survey data (Drake and Roe, 1986, pp. 162–163).

Gottfredson and Hybl's study (1987) provides a more recent example of a structured job analysis of principals' work based on data collected from a national sample of principals (1,153 respondent principals) in both public and private schools at elementary, middle, and high school levels. They conclude:

> Despite individual differences in job descriptions within each kind of school, the magnitude of the differences in the importance of job factors often leaves little doubt about the most important aspects of the jobs of principals; in schools of various types—or even of schools in general. Staff Direction and Visibility, and Observation and Feedback, and Planning and Action are highly important facets of the jobs of principals *in general.* It seems safe to regard these as key parts of the job and to be concerned that *all* principals perform these functions adroitly. (p. 61)

FIGURE 5.1. Actual and desirable time use.

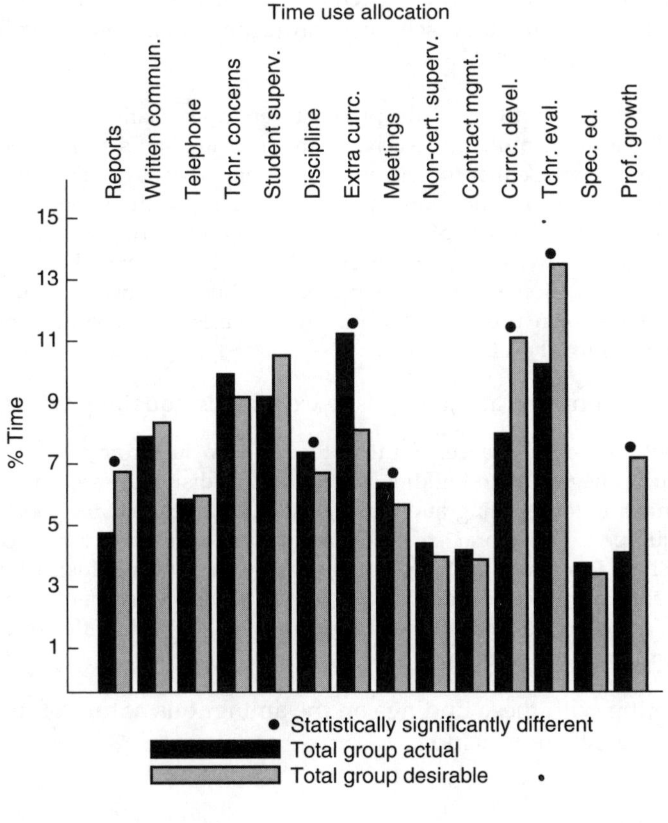

Qualitative Studies

In addition to the contributions of descriptive observational studies, other sources of qualitative data contribute to our understanding of the work of principals. Survey interview studies, naturalistic and ethnographic studies, and autobiographical studies provide a deeper look into the everyday work of principals.

Survey interviews, structured and open-ended, are important sources of descriptive information on principals' work. Literally hundreds of studies have employed interview methodologies to gain insight into the job of being a principal. A good example of the texture of comments provided in interview data can be found in *Elementary Principals and Their Schools: Beacons of Brilliance and Potholes of Pestilence* (Goldhammer et al., 1971). Though over twenty years old, the descriptions contained in this report are very contemporary in their depictions of the work of principals.

> No one can intelligently administer a school in today's world without recognizing the difficult problems associated with the task. Some principals obviously are near the point of helplessness; other principals, however, have found successful ways to meet their responsibilities and thus they provide excellent leadership for their schools. (p. 1)

As revealed in the title, the interviewers reported on a wide range of conditions in elementary schools across the nation. The most vivid descriptions of the context and quality of the principal's job come in their portrayal of the extremes of the elementary school continuum: "beacons of brilliance" and "potholes of pestilence."

> In the "beacons of brilliance," the principals are charismatic leaders; they seem to instill enthusiasm in their teachers. The teaching staffs seems to be working as teams because their morale was high, their services extend beyond normal expectations. Teachers and principals, along with parents, constantly appraise the effectiveness of schools in an attempt to devise new programs and strategies to overcome deficiencies. Programs are adaptable and emphasis in the instructional program is placed on children's needs. Principals are confident they can provide relevant, purposive learning without having to lean on traditional crutches. (p. 2)

The work environment at the opposite extreme is equally graphic.

> The "potholes of pestilence," on the other hand result from weak leadership and official neglect. The buildings, dirty and in disrepair, are unwholesome environments for learning and child growth. The schools are poorly staffed and equipped. The morale of teachers and pupils is low; where control is maintained, fear is one of the essential strategies employed. Instructional programs are traditional, ritualistic, and poorly related to students' needs. The schools are characterized by unenthusiasm, squalor, and ineffectiveness. The principals are just serving out their time. (p. 2)

Resonating with these findings on the ambiguous nature of the principal's role these researchers conclude.

Perhaps the most critical problem faced by the elementary school principal today is the general ambiguity of his position in the educational community. There is no viable, systematic rationale for the elementary school principalship to determine expectations for performance; no criteria exist through which performance can be measured. (p. 4)

Such descriptions of excellent and poor schools would be less chilling if they did not parallel a more recent description by Jonathan Kozol in *Savage Inequalities* (1991). He provides similar, contrasting portraits of the inequities among schools in the United States.

Before I leave, I do as Christopher asked and enter a boy's bathroom. Four of the six toilets do not work. The toilet stalls, which are eaten away by red and brown corrosion, have no doors. The toilets have no seats. One has a rotted stump. There are no paper towels and no soap. Near the door there is a loop of wire with an empty toilet-paper roll. "This," says Sister Julia, "is the best school that we have in East St. Louis." (p. 36)

A student describes another school to Kozol during his visit. "We have a school in East St. Louis named for Dr. King," she says. "The school is full of sewer water and the doors are locked with chains. Every student in that school is black. It's like a terrible joke on history" (p. 35). Even though the federal courts have ruled that a child's education is ultimately the responsibility of the state, poor school districts, such as East St. Louis, remain poor because there are few incentives for states and communities to redress the inequalities of opportunity for students that result from great disparities in local wealth.

In seeking to find a metaphor for the unequal contest that takes place in public schools, advocates for equal education sometimes use the image of a tainted sports event. We have seen, for instance, the familiar image of the playing field that isn't level. Unlike a tainted sports event, however, a childhood cannot be played again. We are children only once; and, after those few years are gone, there is no second chance to make amends. In this respect, the consequences of unequal education have a terrible finality. Those who are denied cannot be "made whole" by a later act of government. Those who get the unfair edge cannot be later stripped of what they've won. Skills, once attained—no matter how unfairly—take on a compelling aura. Effectiveness seems irrefutable, no matter how acquired. The winners in this feel meritorious. Since they also are, in large part, those who govern the discussion of this issue, they are not disposed to cast a cloud upon the means of their ascent. (p. 180)

In addition to vividly emotional descriptions, qualitative researchers provide insights into the work of principals. For example, role overload for principals is a frequent theme described in qualitative studies. The literature suggests that new demands and responsibilities are continually being added to the principal's role, such as director of parent or community councils, director of breakfast and lunch programs, facilities manager for school sports teams, teacher career ladder supervisor, and many more. Few, if any, of the former role demands are ever taken away. "We continually add to a principal's job, never subtract" (Bredeson, 1989, p. 15).

The work of Blumberg and Greenfield (1980) presents case studies of eight principals based on interview data, individual and group, collected over time. Eight distinctive and idiosyncratic images of individual role making and role taking in the principalship are presented. These included principals characterized as Politician, Humanist, Broker, Catalyst, Juggler, Organizer, Rationalist, and Helper. Blumberg and Greenfield note that

> we were not so surprised to find that there was a great deal of similarity among the problems they faced on a day-to-day basis. . . . Schools are in many ways not much different today from what they were like even fifty years ago. It was not surprising, therefore, to find that the character of the problems and issues concerning these men and women did not differ much from one school to another. . . . Stripped of particularistic social, economic, and racial distinctions, the eight schools being served by these principals are extremely similar relative to organizational configuration, instructional objectives, group norms, and role relationship among participants. (1980, pp. 253–254)

Naturalistic and Ethnographic Studies

Though significantly fewer in number than questionnaire and interview studies, naturalistic and ethnographic investigations, which combine methods of inquiry and rely on multiple data sources, help to provide what sociologist Clifford Geertz called "thick descriptions" of the work of school principals. One of the best known ethnographic studies of the principalship is Wolcott's *The Man in the Principal's Office* (1973). This ethnographic account describes the daily work routines of an elementary principal, Ed Bell, and details how he allocates his time among various administrative tasks. The descriptions in this narrative account of Ed Bell's work provide more than a listing of job responsibilities; they provide the context for administrative work, the meanings the principal attaches to his leadership in the school, and the values and purposes that guide him in his work. The following passage is illustrative.

> The consequence of Ed's problem-centered orientation brought his actual behavior somewhat into harmony with the expectations of those about him. It also provided him with a practical goal against which he could personally measure his administrative success. He also attempted to give at least token recognition to virtually every event, comment, or complaint that came to his attention. Unable to draw on any special body of knowledge or set of unique skills to a position in which he had to perform adequately but wished to perform exceedingly well, Ed brought instead a conscious, almost tangible quality of super-dedication to try to do anything for everybody. He remained ever on-call and available for action, as evidenced by long hours spent at school each day, numerous responsibilities and assignments accepted, new programs tacitly encouraged, and an endless procession of new staff, pupils, parents, and outsiders inducted patiently into the operation of the school. Remote as these functions may be from a ritual quest for a more professional role, they nonetheless present a job description of infinite duration that renders service to the institution and provides a man some personal sense of having done a day's work. For whether Ed was engaged in a twelve-second encounter with a hurt thumb, a twelve-minute search for a record player for a substitute teacher, or a twelve-day administrators' workshop with his colleagues attempting to define an ideal elementary school, his behavior seemed to be guided by an unwritten rule that is at once the *raison d'etre* for the role of the

elementary principal and the perfect obstacle to ever achieving a radical change in that role: *every problem is important.* (p. 316)

Another detailed description of the marriage between person and position is John McPhee's *The Headmaster,* a biographical account of Frank Boyden, headmaster of Deerfield Academy, a private secondary school. The portrait of this principal and his work is vivid.

> Boyden's strategy has sometimes seemed petty, but more often it has seemed inspired. It is best exemplified by his showmanship and his pantoscopic attention to detail. It has been said that a thousand details add up to one impression, and at Deerfield it is the headmaster who adds them up. He thinks in pictures. Once a picture seems right, he wants to keep it that way. Anything that mars it or changes the focus irritates him. (p. 226)

The image Frank Boyden carried in his head was a personal and professional guide to leadership in Deerfield Academy.

Autobiographical Descriptions of the Principalship

The literature abounds with first-person accounts of the work life of principals. This genre of descriptive literature by definition provides more personal, journalistic accounts, than it does systematic examinations of the work of school principals. Nevertheless, these pieces do provide a substantial body of descriptive information. "Life in the Fishbowl: Revelations and Reflections of the First Year," by Davis (1988), is a good example of this genre. Using the analogy of life in a fishbowl, Davis describes how everyone is constantly watching, measuring, and judging the new principal. If the new principal is an outsider, those watching and evaluating have no context and little knowledge about her administrative behaviors and actions. Thus, those watching and evaluating tend to measure the new principal's performance against that of former principals and against various organizational standards (some manifest, many others latent). As observers and stakeholders, people both in and out of school hold many expectations of principals. These sets of expectations, which often come in the form of criticism, influence the new principal's initial socialization to the role. It is important that principals not personalize the criticisms or the seemingly endless conflicts and contradictions in various sets of role expectations. Rigorous scrutiny of who you are and how you will behave as principal is a natural part of leader succession in organizations. In Chapter 7 we deal extensively with the social and organizational processes of leader succession. At times the anxiety of teachers and students may be expressed in surprising or even in personally hurtful ways.

Recognizing that this anxiety is rooted in psychological reactions to organizational change, especially a change in leaders, will help you as a newly appointed principal respond in ways that allay concerns and fears while at the same time making your mark as an educational leader in the school. As you think about moving from classroom teacher to principal, the idea that your life will be placed in a fishbowl will evoke anxiety. In Chapter 10 we will deal more explicitly with personal strategies for coping with the stress of professional role transition. As a teacher you might have used pithy humor, sarcasm, or perhaps even sharp retorts when criticisms were leveled at you and your work. In the transition from teacher to principal, your reactions to criticism and to conflicting expectations are likely to be somewhat more restrained. As Davis advises, new principals need to "catch bullets of criticism" rather than return the volley.

Finally, Davis goes on to describe how much of organizational learning for new principals occurs quite unsystematically. "I found that a major part of the growth process in being a new principal is in making mistakes, bad decisions, or in just muddling through" (p. 22). These realities of entry into the principalship can result in feelings of uncertainty, personal and professional inadequacy, isolation, and general role confusion as well as exhilaration and a sense of professional empowerment. Davis likens the entering principal to a ship's captain who steps on to a vessel already rigged, supplied, and staffed and with its compass and sails set. Once you take the wheel, you experience both the challenges and the exhilarations of navigating the ship.

Using principal succession as a frame for examining early experiences and social learning by principals, Ann Weaver Hart's chronicling of her first year as a junior high school principal provides a rich, systematic, first-person account of principals' work. Participant observation was the primary data source in this investigation. Documents and interviews, both formal and informal provided additional descriptive data.

> When I arrived, I found an unpromising context. Incongruities were sharply etched in the minds of important people in the setting; my own (and the selection agents') conviction that I possessed the "orientation, skills, and values" necessary to function as principal was not shared by many. Early responses from the setting were negative; they evolved into cautious optimism; they ended in cordial integration, acceptance of differences, permission to lead, willingness to act. My experience is best described as a process of recognizing incongruence, countering incongruence, and experiencing leadership validation and attribution. (Hart, 1988, p. 336)

Narrative accounts such as this one connect us in meaningful ways to the range of experiences and emotions of the novice principal. In addition, they provide valuable empirical markers that highlight key features of the work terrain of school principals.

CONCLUSION

In this chapter we described principals and their work. We began our discussion with an overview of the history of the modern principalship. We then examined intellectual, social, historical, and organizational factors that influence how principals conceptualize, organize, and subsequently carry out their work as educational leaders in their schools. We highlighted the imprint of management and organizational theory, the impact of the social/economic organizing principles of the industrial revolution, and the conceptualization of organizational and leadership theories in educational administration as major sources of influence affecting the work of principals. Next, using a job analysis framework, we reviewed the findings from empirical research on principals' work. These included descriptive accounts of principals' work from observational studies, survey research, qualitative inquiries, and first-person narratives. From these studies we developed general descriptive themes that characterize the work of school principals.

In Chapter 6 we move to a discussion of principals as formal educational leaders and the challenges they face as they strive to exert positive influence on teaching and learning in schools.

SUGGESTED ACTIVITIES

1. Researchers and scholars have employed various methods to observe and gain a better understanding of principals' work. We believe that your own understanding of the principalship would be greatly enhanced through these methods. For example, shadow your principal for a full working day—keep a running log of activities, interactions, and decisions. Do your observations of your principal's work day support the description and generalizations of other researchers? As you reflect on your principal's day, what surprised you the most? Other strategies that you might use to examine principals' work include personal interviews, questionnaires, and/or examination of the principal's physical work environment.

2. We describe six organizing principles of the industrial revolution. To what degree are these principles still influential in your school? Identify specific examples.

3. Educators often look to other organizations for ideas that would help them address pressing problems and challenges in schools. What are some of the ideas currently being transported from other social sectors to education? Evaluate the strengths and weaknesses of each.

4. Using one of the theories of organization and management described in this chapter, write a brief (1–2 pages) organizational sketch of your school. Are there important factors and characteristics about your school that are not explained by the theoretical framework you have chosen? What are they?

5. There are often discrepancies between what principals say are their most important leadership responsibilities and how they actually spend their time. Discuss this with your principal. How does the principal deal with this source of tension? What suggestions does he or she have for you as an aspiring administrator?

6. Read a first-person, descriptive account of a principal's daily routine. What are the joys of professional work as a principal? What are the major frustrations? What aspects of the principal's work does this personalized account highlight? Does this have any influence on your current view of the principalship?

7. If you are currently involved in a clinical or field-based experience as an aspiring principal or assistant principal, keep a daily log of your observations, impressions, and feelings about your successes and your challenges. If you were invited to a graduate class on the school principalship, what aspects of your work day would you highlight? Why?

Principals as Formal Leaders in Schools

Educators, policy makers, and parents generally agree that leadership in schools makes a difference in the quality of teaching-learning experiences and outcomes for students and for staff. Even though there is widespread agreement that the principal's leadership is crucial to school success, educators exhibit a

> reluctance to admit the importance of leadership. Ascribing to any one person such extraordinary powers for good or ill smacks of undemocratic elitism. To some who worship at the altar of total egalitarianism it may seem safer to design an elaborate job description, in the hope that any qualified administrator will grow into the job, than to rely on more subjective yardsticks of leadership. (Hechinger, in Lipham, 1981, p. v)

Despite this pervasive reluctance to acknowledge the potential for influence that principals possess, the assertion that principals are crucial leaders in successful schools is not anathema to democratic, empowered teaching and learning communities. Rather this assertion recognizes that educators (teachers, principals, and support staff) contribute in different ways to the overall school mission and its successes.

In this chapter we describe ways in which successful principals simultaneously meet the multiple, and sometimes contradictory, demands of various formal leadership roles, while they maintain a focus on school improvement and student outcomes in their daily work. Our discussion of leadership builds on earlier chapters dealing with the social context of leadership, the principal's role in schools, and sources of influence that have shaped the school principalship. We begin with a brief discussion of the formal leadership roles of principals from two major perspectives—social role theory and power. Next, we discuss selected analogies used to describe formal leader roles and the relationship of these suggestive comparisons to perspectives of organization. We then turn to a brief review of research on leadership and the major themes and frameworks that guide scholarship and practice to better understanding of principals' formal leadership. In the final section we examine the effects of educational reform, school restructuring, and teacher empowerment on the principal's formal leadership roles in schools. In Chapter 9 we discuss the instructional leadership roles of principals and examine the impact of principal leadership on school improvement and individual student outcomes.

THEORETICAL PERSPECTIVES: SOCIAL ROLE THEORY AND POWER

School principals are important social actors in education today. We described in Chapter 5 how the increasing size and complexity of schools in the United States, especially in the late nineteenth century and throughout the twentieth century, required that someone in the school spend time on managerial issues that significantly affected teaching and learning in the school. The size of the average school changed from a small institution with only one or two teachers to large and complex organizations with dozens of teachers and hundreds of students. These students came from diverse backgrounds and had unique educational and social needs. School boards, superintendents, and teachers looked first to "principal teachers" and then to full-time principals to assume primary administrative responsibilities within these dynamic organizations. As teachers, principals, students, school boards, parents, and community members established over time who would do what in schools, the formal leadership role of the principal emerged. Social and cultural norms, institutionalized practices, and school board policies all contributed to the legitimation of the principal as the school's formal leader.

Social Role Theory

Social role theory provides an apt explanatory framework for an examination of principals as formal leaders in schools. As we discussed in earlier chapters, the organizing principle of social role theory is that "social behavior is not random and meaningless; rather, behavior tends to be 'patterned,' i.e., predictable, meaningful, and consequential for the participants" (Allen & van de Vliert, 1984, p. 4). A social role is the product of three factors: (1) social position (a specific location in a social system with sets of role behavior expectations), (2) normative role expectations (prescriptions about what a position incumbent should and should not do under given circumstances), and (3) the individual and her or his behavior within the role.

Principals occupy a unique organizational role. That role is defined by the location of the position itself and the social and organizational status that comes with it; by others' expectations of the principal; and by how people in the principal's role choose to strike a balance between role taking (as prescribed by organizational demands—job descriptions and workplace realities) and role making (personalization of a role based on individual needs, dispositions, and preferences). The interaction of social position or status, normative role expectations, and individual role enactment greatly influence principal leadership. The combined effects of role expectations and individual role enactment shape major differences among principals in their formal leadership.

This impact on principals' leadership can be depicted as a Venn diagram in which three major sources of information and belief combine to shape the outcome—principal leadership (see Figure 6.1). The three circles (circles A, B, and C) that encompass the principal's leadership role are: (A) the principal's perception of his leadership role, (B) other people's perceptions of the principal's role, and (C) the principal's awareness of the perceptions and expectations of others for him in the job. The greater the shaded area of overlapping circles representing role perception, the more congruence there is among people in the school concerning the principal's formal leadership role. Little—or in some cases, no—overlap of circles would suggest very different expectations and beliefs about the principal's leadership among individuals. These differences in role perception often result in role conflicts.

To illustrate, think about the role of principal as disciplinarian in a school. If the principal believes that discipline is a shared professional and personal responsibility in the school, she will expect teachers and staff to participate actively in the design and implementation of all discipline procedures. General agreement among the principal, teachers, students, and parents that discipline is a shared responsibility would likely result in consistent actions by teachers, students and the principal. Together they would work collaboratively to promote a healthy, disciplined school environment. In this case, in Figure 6.2 there would be a large shaded area of overlap among the circles representing the three contributors to role perceptions. This would depict high agreement on the principal's role in discipline and low likelihood for conflict with others based on differing expectations.

On the other hand, if the principal believes everyone in the school should actively participate in discipline, but teachers, parents, and students believe

FIGURE 6.1. Principal's role as defined by role perceptions.

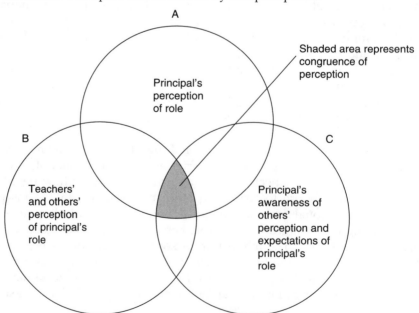

the principal is responsible for all discipline, there would be less congruence among staff regarding the principal's role in discipline (Figure 6.3). Teachers could send students to the principal's office whenever they felt the student's behavior should be monitored and corrected, parents would blame the principal for breaches in expected student conduct, and teachers would feel free to ignore misbehavior they witnessed outside their own classrooms because "it's the principal's job." Students would know that they could deviate from acceptable behavior expectations as long as the principal could not catch them.

The Venn diagrams illustrating the principal's role offer one way to view the principal's role in schools. Schein (1971) provides another view of social role theory in his general model of organization. He uses three empirically discernible perspectives to describe roles in organizations. These perspectives define interactions among people in the school on the basis of tasks, authority, and human relationships—functional, hierarchical, and interpersonal. The functional perspective focuses on the primary tasks. Traditionally, the leadership role of principals has been described with lists of functional tasks performed. *Principals for our Changing Schools: The Knowledge and Skill Base* (National Policy Board for Educational Administration, 1993) is an example of the leadership role of principal based on a functional perspective.

The hierarchical perspective is "essentially a matter of who, on paper, is responsible for the actions of whom" (Van Maanen & Schein, 1979, p. 219). Organizational charts are hierarchical representations of formal lines of authority and accountability legitimated by past practice, policy, and legal statute. Principals have authority to sign documents, approve requisitions, conduct staff evaluations, and implement school board policy. This authority is vested in the principal's hierarchical position in the school and district.

The third role perspective is interpersonal. This perspective represents people's inclusion in the organization and their relationships with others. Fig-

FIGURE 6.2. Principal's role in discipline congruent perceptions.

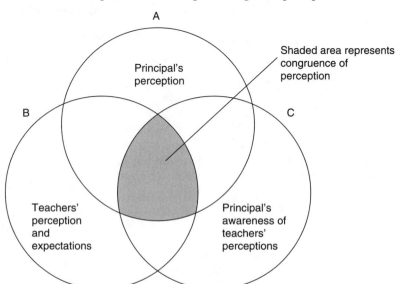

ure 6.4 illustrates the interpersonal role of a school principal. The circle represents the principal's relationships with colleagues in the school. The radial dimension displays the depth and intensity of the principal's inclusion in the school. Inclusionary relationships involve "social rules, norms, and values through which a person's worthiness to a group is judged by members of that group" (Van Maanen & Schein, 1979, p. 222). (In Chapter 10 we describe the socialization process of becoming a principal.) Newly appointed principals (outsiders) are on the periphery of the group. As shared experiences evolve and trust is earned, the newly hired principal becomes more integrated, more included. In Figure 6.4, this inclusion would be represented as movement toward the center of the circle along the radial dimension.

> Movement along the inclusionary dimension is analogous to the entrance of a stranger to any group. If things go well, the stranger is granted more to say in the group's activities and is given more opportunity to display his or her particular skills, thus becoming in the process more central and perhaps valuable to the group as a whole. (Van Maanen & Schein, 1979, p. 222)

Principals, in their formal leadership roles in schools, act simultaneously from the functional, hierarchical, and interpersonal perspectives. Successful principal leadership requires knowledge of primary tasks, an understanding of organizational structures and distinctions in authority and influence, and an appreciation of norms and shared values that characterize unique school cultures. Principals also monitor their own inclusion in the school.

FIGURE 6.3. Principal's role in discipline incongruent perceptions.

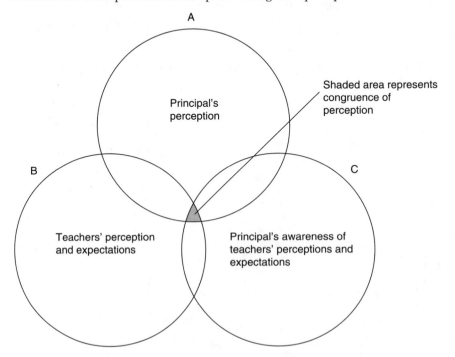

Power and Leadership

The social model of the school that Schein's functional, hierarchical, and inclusionary perspectives represent may underestimate the role that power plays in principals' interactions with others. Power and leadership models consequently provide additional insight for a new or aspiring principal seeking to enhance her leadership potential.

Yukl (1989) describes leadership in terms of power, that is, a person's "potential influence over the attitudes and behavior of one or more designated target persons" (p. 14). According to Yukl, position power gives principals formal authority, control of resources and rewards, control over punishments, control over information, and control over the physical environment, technology, and organization of work in schools. Personal and political power are also important sources of leader influence for school principals. Personal power, often called charismatic power, springs from the personal characteristics and personality of the principal and his knowledge and skills that contribute to the school. Political power relies on bargains, negotiations, and coalition formation to establish a network of power bases, debts, and agreements. Principals who use this power draw on the cumulative power of others in concert.

Bennis and Nanus (1985) also describe a symbiotic relationship between leadership and power.

> Power is the basic energy needed to initiate and sustain action. . . . Effective leadership can move organizations from current to future states, create visions of potential opportunities for organizations, instill within employees commit-

FIGURE 6.4. Interpersonal Perspective of Principal's Role Dynamic of Principal's Inclusion in School Social Group Membership
(Adapted from Schein, 1971—Inclusionary Domains of Organization.)

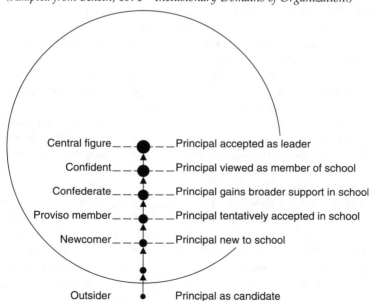

ment to change and instill new cultures and strategies in organization that mobilize and focus energy and resources. . . . Vision is the commodity of leaders, and power is their currency. (pp. 17–18)

As the sources-of-power typology suggests, principals have substantial influence over the attitudes and behaviors of teachers, students, and others in schools because they occupy a formal social position. This position gives them legitimate authority in the school. It defines what Corbett (1990) called, the "rules, roles and responsibilities and relationships" among the principal and other role holders. The fact that principals have access to and control many of the material, financial, informational, and political resources imbues them with significant power and thus potential for leadership.

TRADITIONAL LEADERSHIP STUDIES

We believe that each principal needs at least a passing familiarity with traditional leadership studies in order to talk the talk of leadership across settings and understand how his own views of leadership fit into the larger traditions. In the following sections, we divide concepts of leadership into four common categories: (1) traits, (2) situation, (3) behavior, (4) and contingency, context, and culture.

Leaders' Traits

Early studies on leadership sought to identify traits of leaders that distinguished them from those who were not leaders. The reasoning was that we then could look for people with those traits when selecting leaders. These studies identified intelligence, alertness, verbal facility, originality, judgment, scholarship, knowledge, athletic accomplishments, dependability, initiative, persistence, aggressiveness, self-confidence, desire to excel, activity, sociability, cooperation, adaptability, humor, socioeconomic position, and popularity (among others) as traits of leaders (Bass, 1981). Stogdill (1948) divided the many desirable leadership traits appearing in the proliferation of lists into five categories: capacity, achievement, responsibility, participation, and status. He concluded that traits failed to identify leaders.

Results of trait studies also were contradictory. Some traits identified as advantageous in one study showed up as dysfunctional in others. Leaders were sometimes assertive and aggressive, sometimes mild mannered and restrained. Some were quick and decisive; others were reflective and diplomatic (Hoy & Miskel, 1991).

A genre of the trait theory of leadership is "the great man." In this tradition, scholars attempted to identify "great leaders," who were nearly exclusively white males. These great men were then studied to discover what particular traits, training, experiences, and behaviors contributed to their greatness. Failure to appreciate the context of leadership and other contingencies rendered the great man theory of leadership impotent. Nonetheless, the great man view of leader is deeply embedded in our culture and in our perceptions of leadership. To illustrate our point, we reflect on a familiar scenario in our teaching in educational administration. As a stimulus to discussion of research and scholarship on organizational leadership, we often begin by asking students in our classes to identify people, contemporary or historical figures, who are great leaders. Though a few women are listed, Mother Teresa, Margaret Thatcher, Joan of Arc, and Indira Gandhi, our experiences have been that these student-generated lists are nearly always dominated by the names of great men!

Although the trait approach yielded inconsistent findings, it later reemerged in various guises. For instance, the National Association of Secondary School Principals recently developed the Assessment Center to assess the extent to which candidates for administrative positions possess requisite skills. The Assessment Center is being widely adopted by school systems. Such approaches to administrator screening are based on the assumption that the skills needed to lead are known, carrying on the traditional search for leaders with necessary traits (McCleary & Ogawa, 1989). The National Policy Board for Educational Administration recently commissioned a series of papers that portray the principalship as a series of competencies. Those who possess these competencies should, by this logic, be good principals (*Principals for Our Changing Schools: The Knowledge and Skill Base,* 1993). Critics are quick to point out, however, that traits not only predict performance poorly but the methods we use to assess traits and competencies are suspect (Phillips, 1984).

The Situation

Abandoning the frustrating search for leaders' traits and "great men," some scholars turned to circumstances, or situations, to explain the behavior and success of leaders (Campbell, Dunnette, Lawler & Weick, 1970; Campbell, 1977). They postulated that contextual variables such as organizational size, structure, climate, roles, and subordinate characteristics influenced leadership (Hoy & Miskel, 1991).

Researchers began to examine situation as a salient variable associated with effective leadership. First, they looked at such structural properties as size, hierarchy, and formalization; then they asked about the influence of organizational climate (openness, participation, and group atmosphere). Next, researchers turned to the characteristics of roles, which included such factors as position power, type and difficulty of assigned tasks, strategy, and procedural rules (Smith & White, 1987), and the characteristics of subordinates (followers). These studies questioned the influence of knowledge and experience, tolerance for ambiguity, responsibility, and power of subordinates on leaders. Some people assert that situations can be designed to create relationships and behaviors that substitute for leaders, permitting and enhancing healthy information exchange, promoting productive decision-making processes, and providing for the exercise of authority without a designated leader (Fiedler & Garcia, 1987). However, most reject the assertion that the situation makes the leader, calling it "unduly restrictive and counterproductive" (Hoy & Miskel, 1991, p. 256).

Leaders' Behavior

When the situation approach came up dry as an explanation for outcomes, people turned to leaders' behavior. Definitions of leadership reflecting this focus have a distinctly action-based flavor. For example, Hemphill (1964) wrote: "To lead is to engage in an act that initiates the process of solving a mutual problem." Others defined leadership as behaviors that facilitate the attainment of organizational goals. Like the trait-centered definitions that preceded them, behavioral definitions of leadership resulted in contradictory assertions. Fiedler (1957) described leadership as a function assigned to certain organizational members—directing and coordinating group activities; Katz and Kahn (1978) defined leadership as the influence exerted on the behavior of organizational members that exceeds compliance with "routine directives." The former assumes that leadership is bound to certain roles, while the latter suggests that leadership can exist independent of formal roles.

Beginning with the work of Ohio State University researchers to whom we referred under the duality of leadership (Fleishman, 1953, 1957; Halpin & Winer, 1957; Hemphill & Coons, 1950), leader behaviors were observed and catalogued into two main categories: consideration for people and initiating structure that fosters task accomplishment. A number of other studies (Bales, 1954; Blake & Mouton, 1964; Bowers & Seashore, 1966; Cartwright & Zander, 1968; Getzels & Guba, 1957) identified similar couplets of leader behaviors (Hoy & Miskel, 1991). You will remember that more effective leaders were found to be high on both dimensions: attending to organizations' tasks while taking care of members' feelings.

Contingency, Context, and Culture

Disappointed with attempts to predict leadership outcomes with situations, writers turned to a contingency approach. They sought ways in which the effectiveness of task- or relations-oriented behaviors were contingent on contexts such as task structure, the leader's position power, leader-member relations, and subordinates' characteristics (Fiedler, 1957; Vroom, 1976).

Yukl (1989), upon reviewing this array of definitions and conflicting research findings, suggested that researchers should design studies that would illuminate the ramifications of this range of definitions. Hoy and Miskel (1991) and Immegart (1988), writing in the educational administration literature, drew similar conclusions. Hoy and Miskel closed their chapter on leadership by proposing a "schema of variables for the study of leadership." They included leadership traits, situational characteristics, leader behavior, and leader effectiveness. Immegart offered a model of leadership that included nine factors, arguing that "the number of aspects, dynamics, and variables that are examined in leadership research must be increased" (p. 274).

The complex interplay among organizational and personal factors has increased interest in symbolic views of contingencies shaping leaders' influence. Firestone (1989) found evidence that the "chief executive may be a . . . link between national and organizational cultures" in schools. This link may, he argued, be the reason so much evidence exists that superintendents are hired by school boards with specific agendas (Carlson, 1962; Bredeson & Faber, 1994). Pfeffer (1981) characterized organizations as essentially two-dimensional—symbolic and substantive. Using this model, principals exert little influence on the substantive dimension of schools. Instead they manipulate symbols to maintain the school members' compliance and the legitimacy of the school in the external environment.

Others see the distinction between substantive and symbolic to be artificial and inaccurate. First, this distinction looks at the impact of leaders on culture, tending to ignore the effects of school culture on new principals. This focus is criticized and examined further in subsequent chapters of this book. Second, culture is cast as either something that organizations have—a variable—or as something that organizations are—a root metaphor (Smircich, 1983). The latter position leads to the conclusion that "organizations are understood and analyzed not mainly in economic or material terms, but in terms of their expressive, ideational, and symbolic aspects" (Smircich, 1983, pp. 347–348). If culture is the organization, then culture is necessarily inseparable from any part of the organization. The allocation of resources and production processes—the substantive dimension—reflects organizations' cultures. Administrators' contributions are real, and the success of the school may hinge on their effectiveness in the symbolic, cultural domain (Miskel & Cosgrove, 1985).

Smircich (1983) would concur with this view. She described one treatment of organizational cultures as systems of shared thought or systems of knowledge and belief. The patterned behaviors in cultures develop as people act and know within a school's system of knowledge and belief. Principals might exert influence by affecting how others make sense of school reality. Principals' influence in the cultural dimension thus exceeds attribution; they should be able to affect performance by affecting school culture. They shape defined reality, meanings, beliefs, and expectations on which people act. Cultural effects appear to be multidirectional, not always flowing from leader to group. Moreover, accumulating evidence indicates that interpretations influence substance.

Some experimental research supports this view of multidirectional cultural effects. For example, Green and Novak (1982) manipulated feedback from supervisors to workers and found that information about work from superiors affected subordinates' performance and attitudes about their work. These results are confirmed in other studies (Griffin, 1983; O'Connor & Barrett, 1980).

This attention to organizational culture is reflected in a body of work on the induction and professional socialization of new principals undertaken by the scholars associated with the "Beginning Principals Study" referred to briefly in preceding discussions (Curcio & Greene, 1989; Daresh, 1986; Hall & Hord, 1987; Parkay, Rhodes, Currie & Rao, 1989; Playko & Daresh, 1989; Roberts, 1989a, 1989b; Roberts & Wright, 1989). This research fails to support the predictions of Schein, Smircich, and others who see cultural leadership as a powerful tool for principals. The researchers hoped to find social, personal, and cultural linkages recognized, exhibited, and manipulated by beginning principals as part of their ascension to leadership in high schools (Roberts, 1989a). Focusing on the new principal's impact on school culture, not on the culture's impact on the new principal, these researchers were disappointed in their findings. While school culture should exert important influence on successor principals' leadership as well as other school factors (Blanch, 1989), new high school principals' concerns, they found, centered on "being the boss, being in control, and being responsible" (Roberts, 1989a, p. 19). Culture is a complex phenomenon, deeply embedded in a social whole (Smircich, 1983). It may have been much too soon to observe any effect of principals on culture in one year, yet Roberts and her colleagues found principals not only lacking influence on, but paying little heed to, school culture.

FRAMEWORKS FOR LEADERSHIP

We draw on the findings from traditional research on formal leadership in organizations to lay the foundation for a discussion of complementary models educators write about and apply to the work of school principals. In the following sections we introduce five frameworks used to describe principals' leadership. These include: (1) the skills, processes, and responsibilities of effective leaders; (2) technical, human, and conceptual leader skills; (3) processes of leadership; (4) leader responsibilities; and (5) principals as managers.

Skills, Processes, and Responsibilities of Effective Leaders

Perhaps the most common description of the formal leadership roles of school principals draws on the functional perspective. Several of the selected knowledge-base organizers listed in Table 2.1 are examples of formal leadership organized around the various functional work tasks associated with the principal's established and conventional role. See, for example, the work of Kimbrough and Burkett, 1990; Lipham, Rankin, and Hoeh, 1985; and Hughes and

FIGURE 6.5. Principal leadership: A three-dimensional perspective.

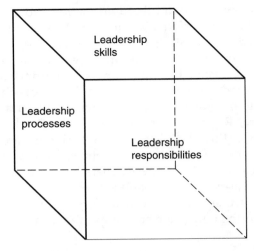

Ubben, 1989. Essentially, these lists of tasks help principals locate and understand their places, their work, and their relationships with others in the organization. They function almost like an annotated bibliography for administrators. Many principals use these compendiums much as one would use a home medical encyclopedia.

Figure 6.5 shows an attempt to organize various perspectives of leadership into a three-dimensional hybrid of leadership skills, processes, and responsibilities. Imbedded in the figure are the ideas of such classical management theorists as Henri DeMan, Henri Fayol, George E. Mayo, and Mary Parker Follett, as well as the works of other theorists—Talcott Parsons, Karl Weick, and Thomas A. Sergiovanni.

Leadership Skills

Other writers prefer to view effective principal leadership as the application of three basic skills—technical, human, and conceptual. Technical skills for principals include basic knowledge and its application in such areas as human development, teaching and learning, law, budgeting and school finance, and technological matters in the school. However, we all recognize that monodimensional, technical experts are not necessarily good organizational leaders and they may even unintentionally alienate people in the organization. A three-dimensional perspective recognizes that human and interpersonal skills are also needed. The ability to understand, work with, and motivate others in schools is critical to successful leadership in schools.

Empirical research on leadership since the 1950s has often been organized around variations on a two-part theme, a concern for task accomplishment and a concern for people. We return in detail to this theme later in the chapter in our discussions of the traditional duality of formal leadership and contingency approaches to leadership studies. Technical skills are the foundation of task-related work. Human skills are the currency principals employ to work with people.

A third variation emerged with renewed interest in cognitive psychology and focused on conceptual skills. Conceptual skills are essentially the leader's capacity to see the connections between various parts of the whole. For example, a series of parent complaints about a fourth-grade reading text may require principals to use all three leadership skills to respond appropriately to expressed concerns. This is more than a public relations issue. An effective principal will understand the technical aspects of the complaint. She will be able to evaluate the quality and appropriateness of reading techniques and their application in the text. She also will understand that concerned parents need to be able to discuss their misgivings with teachers and principals. She knows that a decision to change a reading text in one grade has implications well beyond the fourth-grade teacher and these parents. It is costly, thus using resources that could have gone elsewhere. It may disrupt a coherent K–5 reading program, thus affecting all other teachers and students. Other parents may like the text and object to a principal's too quick reaction to complaining parents. These very real problems occur every day in schools over issues such as literature selections for student reading, evolutionary biology and creationism, sex education, AIDS education, and many other issues. Conceptual skills help principals project and predict multiple effects of a single incident and draw connections within the school's curriculum, teacher autonomy, district policy, and overall parental involvement and support of the school. Effective leaders blend appropriate technical, human, and conceptual skills.

Leadership Processes

Another functional description of the principal's formal role as school leader is provided by Hughes and Ubben, 1989. These authors describe principals as organizers, delegators, coordinators, and evaluators within five major task areas: (1) curriculum development, (2) instructional improvement, (3) pupil services, (4) finance and facilities, and (5) community relations. These are the basic leadership processes depicted in Figure 6.5. These task areas are rooted in the work of Henri Fayol (1841–1925). Fayol studied administration in the coal mining and iron industries. He listed planning, organizing, command, coordination, and control as primary elements in his theory of administration. Essentially these generic management processes are viewed as mechanisms for enacting technical, human, and conceptual skills and for attending to the primary responsibilities of formal leaders in schools.

Leadership Responsibilities

Principals, like formal leaders in any complex social organization, have four major responsibilities. First, principals are responsible to promote goal attainment (student cognitive, emotional, and physical development). Second, principals participate in the maintenance of cultural patterns. Schools are social institutions created to model and teach others commonly shared values, beliefs, history, and social norms. Third, principals work to maintain the practices and resources that support coordination of organizational structures and processes in order to accomplish desired goals. Establishing a curriculum sequence, basic safety, and order in the school are examples of how principals take responsibility in this area. Finally, principals must balance their role as organizational buffers who protect their school from intrusive external forces while helping teachers and others be responsive to the needs of children. This requires that they adapt school goals and processes to changing demographics and social dilemmas that affect teaching and learning in the school. Substance abuse, child abuse, and the effects of poverty and crime are examples of external factors that require adaptation within schools.

As formal leaders, principals are responsible for coordinating and addressing perennial organizational problems. Jacques (1989) described these problems as organizational imperatives. As you review this list of imperatives, think of the implications of these role demands for principals as school leaders. In what ways does each shape the formal leadership roles of principals?

1. Articulating mission, goals, strategies, and main functions
2. Arranging functional alignments
3. Identifying mechanisms of coordination and control
4. Constituting accountability and role relationships
5. Institutionalizing planning and communication
6. Relating rewards and performance
7. Achieving effective leadership

Even though these imperatives (problems) are not the sole responsibility of principals, they do provide helpful organizers for viewing principals' formal leadership in schools.

Figure 6.5 represents a summary of leadership perspectives organized around technical skills, general management and leadership processes, and primary responsibilities. As a beginning principal, you may find these organizers helpful as you think about your future role as a formal leader. The perspectives might also suggest important questions for you to consider as a novice administrator. For example, from the technical skills perspective, what specific technical skills do you need to be an effective principal in the areas of curriculum development, instructional improvement, pupil services, finance and facilities, and community relations? From the leadership-as-expertise-in-administrative-processes approach, in what ways will basic administrative processes (planning, organizing, coordinating, evaluating, and controlling) help you define and enact your leadership role in school? Finally, from a synthesis of various perspectives, how will you balance and blend functional tasks, processes, and organizational imperatives into an effective personal leadership style that focuses on student outcomes and school improvement? We turn next to formal leadership viewed as managerial behavior.

PRINCIPALS AS MANAGERS

The work of Henry Mintzberg (1973) provides another lens for viewing the formal leadership roles of principals. Observing the work of executives, Mintzberg developed a taxonomy of ten managerial roles under three broad categories of activities—interpersonal (leader, liaison, figurehead), informational (monitor, disseminator, spokesperson), and decisional (entrepreneur, disturbance handler, resource allocator, negotiator). See Chapter 5 for a review of research by Willower and others using this taxonomy to describe the work of elementary and secondary school principals.

Mintzberg's taxonomy of managerial roles provides interesting metaphors you can use to understand the ways in which many principals operate in their managerial roles. We provide a brief description of this taxonomy. Should you be interested in exploring this approach further, you should refer to Mintzberg, 1973.

Figurehead. Based on formal authority vested in their role, managers perform symbolic and ceremonial duties of both a legal and social nature. For example, they sign documents, preside at meetings, greet visitors, and participate in such school rituals and ceremonies as graduations and retirement celebrations.

Leader. Mintzberg describes this role as one that integrates organizational activities to accomplish its basic goals. Leaders help to guide and facilitate the work of others.

Liaison. In this role managers help establish and link people and groups both in and outside the organization.

Monitor. Monitors seek information from multiple sources and pass this information along to subordinates. Generally this information is analyzed to discover problems and opportunities in the work of the group.

Disseminator. As conduits for organizational information, managers pass along needed information to others.

Spokesperson. Based on a comprehensive knowledge of the organization and its environment, managers transmit information, ideas and values to people outside the organization.

Entrepreneur. In this role managers initiate and design efforts to improve processes or outcomes in the organization. New ideas, new equipment, and reorganized structures are some of the tools of the entrepreneur.

Disturbance Handler. In this role managers deal with crises and unforeseen events in the organization. Conflict, tragedies, and the unexpected events call for someone to be the disturbance handler.

Resource Allocator. A major source of power for managers rests in their control over and distribution of resources—money, personnel, material, equipment, physical space, and services.

Negotiator. In the resolution of conflicts, managers may act as gobetweens. A manager's authority and access to resources are used to resolve internal conflicts and disputes.

Although Mintzberg studied executives, not school principals, these roles are applicable to formal leadership by principals (see Kmetz & Willower, 1982 and Martin & Willower, 1981). Yukl stated:

> All of the managerial roles apply to any manager or administrator, but their relative importance may vary from one kind of manager to another. A manager's roles are largely predetermined by the nature of the managerial position, but managers have some flexibility in the way each role is interpreted and enacted. (1989, pp. 62–63)

Defining leadership as managerial role taking suggests social role determinism. From our perspective, Mintzberg's taxomony of managerial roles is descriptive and heuristic, not deterministic and prescriptive. The managerial profile of principals is a function of the interaction of role taking (situational demands and role expectations) and role making (individual preferences and behavior in role enactment).

FORMAL LEADERSHIP: THE TRADITIONAL DUALITY

Decades of scholarship have yielded important findings on leadership. Over the years the descriptive labels have changed across studies; however, two major dimensions of leadership behavior persist—*concern for organizational tasks* and *concern for people.* This duality is rooted in the scientific management theory movement and the human relations movement; it became the organizer for empirical, theoretical, and practical work in the area of school leadership. Hoy and Miskel (1991) provide an excellent summary table of major contributions to leadership studies using these two dimensions of leadership. The Ohio State Leadership Studies, for example, identified "system oriented" and "person oriented" behaviors of leaders (Stogdill, 1963). Along a similar vein and using the Leadership Behavior Description Questionnaire, Halpin (1966) distinguished two general types of leader behaviors—"consideration" (leader concern and behaviors directed at welfare of subordinates) and "initiating structure" (the degree to which the leader structures his or her role and the work of others to accomplish group goals and tasks). The findings of other researchers and theorists supported this dual factor description of leadership behavior. See, for example, the works of Barnard (1938) on effectiveness and efficiency; Getzels and Guba (1957) on nomothetic and idiographic behavior; Cartwright and Zander (1953) on goal achievement and group maintenance; and Bales (1954) on the task leader and social leader.

Using these two basic dimensions, concern for task (low to high) and concern for people (low to high) Hersey and Blanchard (1977) and Blake and Mouton (1985) developed instruments and frameworks to assess and describe basic leadership styles. In addition the two-dimensional matrices examine leader effectiveness by analyzing the relationships among leader style and situational variables such as the nature of the task, the maturity of the group, and leader-follower relations.

The *high-task-and-low-people* leader keeps eyes on the task even at the expense of feelings and concerns of others. We often equate this style with authoritarian leadership. The *high-task-and-high-people* leader integrates concern for task with concern for relations in a synergistic way to accomplish organizational goals and to engender enthusiasm and commitment from individuals in the school to those goals over time. The *low-task-and-high-people* leader's primary concern is for building harmonious work relationships and meeting the needs of people in the school. Task accomplishment is clearly subordinated to smooth working relationships and satisfied subordinates. The *low-task-and-low-people* style is really a leaderless style. In this laissez-faire approach to management the leader simply assigns people to various tasks and then leaves them alone.

LEADERSHIP BY ANALOGY

While the leadership duality perspectives provide a way of viewing principals' actions based on their concerns for tasks and people, they present a rather colorless view of a richly detailed school dynamic. Consequently, many students and practitioners of the principalship turn to analogies and metaphors to help them think more vividly about the principals' work. This metaphorical thinking extends to principal preparation programs.

It is unlikely that there would be any major disagreement among practitioners and theorists that one of the primary purposes of administrator training programs is to prepare leaders. However, with some 300 to 400 definitions of leadership currently in the literature (Bennis & Nanus, 1985), the consensus on leadership breaks down once attempts are made to define and then put various conceptualizations of leadership into practice. Thus, we are left to view formal leadership as a glass that is either half-empty or half-full. The half-empty perspective suggests that the conceptual confusion evinced by so many competing definitions of leadership thwarts our efforts to build a strong conceptual and empirical knowledge base for the preparation of school leaders. In contrast, the half-full perspective permits us to look at leadership through multiple lenses focusing less on conceptual problems and more on the heuristic possibilities various lenses offer. Our perspective on the leadership is that the glass is half-full. In this section, we will examine heuristic possibilities embedded in selected analogies to describe the formal leadership roles of principals.

"Metaphors and other suggestive analogies are rich and powerfully evocative languages which are at the very heart of organizational leadership" (Bredeson, 1988a, p. 1). Analogies are cognitive-linguistic devices that allow "the transfer of coherent chunks of characteristics—perceptual, cognitive, emotional and experiential—from a vehicle which is known to a topic which is less so" (Ortony, 1975). We have selected analogies for leadership from the works of Senge (1990), Deal and Peterson (1994), and Sergiovanni (1987) to illustrate the use of metaphor to describe principals' leader roles. Each suggestive comparison illustrates the principle of transferability of characteristics and qualities from phenomena and concepts we know well to those we know less well. The connections we make between the two help us understand formal leadership roles of school principals.

Developer of Learning Organizations: Designer, Teacher and Steward

Peter M. Senge (1990) maps out new territory for leaders of learning organizations. Learning organizations infuse adaptive and creative learning strategies at all levels to cope with changing realities affecting them; to sustain themselves in turbulent, hostile environments; and to succeed in uncertain and highly competitive business environments. To create and sustain "learning organizations," Senge argues that a new type of leader is required. Leaders of learning organizations differ markedly from traditional leaders, often viewed as hard-charging, heroic organization figures, "who set the direction, make the key decisions, and energize the troops" (p. 8). In learning organizations, leaders are less like commanders leading the charge and more like designers, teachers, and stewards. Schools are not the business organizations Senge refers to in his writings, but they do face similar organizational challenges requiring creative leadership. Let's examine ways in which principals as formal leaders may take on the roles of designer, teacher, and steward to create and sustain schools as continually improving and self-renewing learning organizations.

Principal as Designer

Senge asks you to imagine that your organization (school) is an ocean liner and that you are its "formal leader." He then asks, as formal leader, "What would your role be?" He goes on to suggest that most of us are likely to imagine ourselves as captain, navigator, engineer, or director of the ship. The leader roles we imagine ourselves in are rooted in more traditional views of leadership. Historically, we have viewed leaders as heroic individuals who grasp the controls, take charge, set the coordinates, and sail on forcefully to their destinations. A review of the literature on the school principalship bears out similar images of heroic, take-charge leaders.

Senge acknowledges the importance of captains, navigators, engineers, and directors, but he also recognizes that each of these roles is too limited compared with the role of an effective leader in a learning organization. He uses a different metaphor to describe the person who exerts significant influence on the behaviors and actions of others. "No one has a more sweeping influence than the designer" (p. 10). Think for a moment how principals as formal leaders act as organizational designers in their schools and communities. As designers, principals help to formulate, articulate, and nurture the governing ideas, images, purposes, and values that have enduring influence on the school. As designers principals also are involved in developing policies, practices, and structures that translate their school's vision and values into successes for teachers and students. Finally, the designer in a learning organization works to ensure that self-renewing learning processes are institutionalized so that adaptive and generative learning is a professional work norm, not just a process used in strategic planning exercises or under the direct supervision of the principal. Bureaucratic and cultural linkages are design elements that effective instructional leaders use to positively influence teaching and learning in schools. We discuss this role extensively in Chapter 9.

Principal as Teacher of Teachers

Earlier in this text we described the historical evolution of the "principal teacher" to the school principal. According to Senge, organizational leaders are teachers.

> Leader as teacher does not mean leader as authoritarian expert whose job it is to teach people the "correct" view of reality. Rather, it is about helping everyone in the organization, oneself included, to gain more insightful views of current reality. This is in line with a popular emerging view of leaders as coaches, guides, or facilitators. (p. 11)

Principals as teachers need not be omniscient paragons of pedagogy. Rather, they are coaches and facilitators who help students, teachers, and other staff understand the mental models and basic assumptions about teaching and learning in particular schools and communities. "Leaders as teachers help people *restructure their views of reality* to see beyond the superficial conditions and events into the underlying causes of problems—and therefore to see new possibilities for shaping the future" (p. 12). In the "teacher" leader role, principals bring attention to the realities of school life at three distinct levels—individual events, patterns of individual behavior, and systemic structures—and help others understand the relationships among the three. Senge states,

> Event explanations—who did what to whom—doom their holders to a reactive stance toward change. Pattern-of-behavior explanations focus on identifying long-term trends and assessing their implications. Structural explana-

tions are the most powerful. Only they address the underlying causes of behavior at a level such that patterns of behavior can be changed. (p. 12)

By design and through their actions, principals as teacher-leaders model for others the behavior of simultaneously attending to interrelationships among events, patterns of behavior, and school structures.

Principal as Steward

The role of steward emphasizes the ethic of service. Leader as servant is antithetic to many traditional conceptualizations of leadership. Images of a submissive servant being governed by the wishes and needs of others is hardly the stuff of dynamic, take-charge, heroic leaders. In learning organizations, stewardship operates at two levels. For example, principals as "servant leaders" are stewards for the people they lead and for the larger purposes and mission of the school. Individuals who dedicate their lives to teaching in schools invest heavily in their school. Recognizing this personal and professional commitment, the steward-principal appreciates the effects his behaviors and leadership initiatives have on his colleagues. Steward-principals are also servants to the larger purposes and mission of the school. "Doing what's best for children" is a common, guiding principle for professionals in schools. However, schools are complex social organizations that operate in less than perfect environments where groups representing diverse goals, values, and interests compete for scarce resources. When, for example, teachers participate in a work slowdown by refusing to take extra duty assignments or to hold parent-teacher conferences in order to force the school board to negotiate the teacher contract, these actions affect the school. The principal's role as steward requires her to attend to what's best for children and for the teachers. Since the needs of teachers and students are not always perfectly congruent, principals may experience role conflict as they attempt to serve children's and teachers' needs simultaneously. Stewardship requires creative leaders to use Stephen Covey's (1989) habit of thinking "win-win." Though it is not always possible, stewards serve their colleagues and their schools by raising conflicts and contradictions in their work to mutually satisfying outcomes.

Senge's metaphoric description of leaders as designers, teachers, and stewards offers examples of analogies that expand our ideas about the formal leadership roles of principals. Metaphors provide us with fresh insights and perspectives that help us reframe our understandings of leadership by transferring what we know about familiar roles to ones we want to understand better. Next we discuss metaphors for leadership contained in the work of Deal and Peterson, 1990; 1994.

Symbolic Leadership Roles: The Principal as Symbol, Potter, Poet, Actor, and Healer

"One of the most significant roles of leaders (and of leadership) is the creation, encouragement, and refinement of the symbols and symbolic activity that give meaning to the organization" (Deal & Peterson, 1990, p. 13). This shared sense of meaning is often described as organizational culture, the "feel" a school has when you walk through the front doors. Think for a moment about schools you have attended, visited, or work in currently. Besides obvious differences in size, architecture, and location, what aspects of character and culture make each a unique environment? Your perceptions of these factors will likely include those "deep patterns of values, beliefs, and traditions" (p. 7) that give shared meaning to the daily routines and everyday life of students, teachers, and administrators in the school.

The linkage and reflexivity between leadership and culture in schools is crucial to organizational effectiveness. Through technical and symbolic leadership roles, principals shape their school's culture. Technical leadership includes eight functional roles: planner, resource allocator, coordinator, supervisor, disseminator of information, jurist, gatekeeper, and analyst (Deal & Peterson, 1990; 1994). These role descriptions are consistent with traditional lists characterizing principals' leadership roles. See, for example, Drake and Roe, 1986; Lipham and Hoeh, 1974; and Small, 1974. While carrying out these roles, principals are also influenced by the existing culture.

> Most principals must work with a cultural tapestry that is already woven. They must somehow reinforce thin spots or tears, shape it to cover different or changed surfaces, or even try to reverse the fabric without unraveling the shared meaning. (Deal & Peterson, 1990, p. 14)

Note the use of metaphor in this description of cultural leadership. Next, we discuss suggestive comparisons (symbols, potters, poets, actors, and healers) describing five symbolic leadership roles of principals (Deal & Peterson, 1994).

Principals are symbolic leaders in part because they hold an important title and formal role in schools. Who principals are, how they are selected, what they do, how they dress, what they believe, and what they value are powerful symbolic messages. Think about principals you know. What symbolic messages are conveyed in terms of the factors listed above? What symbolic leadership roles do they assume in their schools? Based on our experiences as classroom teachers, we have learned that students in our classes scrutinize us closely. In addition to observing our overt behaviors and personal styles, they notice seemingly insignificant details about the moods we are in, the mannerisms we have, even the color and style of our clothes. Together these details create an image that carries important symbolic messages about who we are and what we value. In a study of the communication patterns of principals, Bredeson (1988a) presented five portraits of leadership: *Blessed with Communications Skills, I'm a Teacher, Too, A Corporate Executive, Discipline is # 1,* and *The Counselor.* Each vignette projects an image of leadership, characterizes each principal's interpretation and enactment of his or her role, and reveals important symbolic messages to people inside and outside the school. In another study, Kelley and Bredeson (1991) concluded,

> As each principal communicated messages through his words, actions, and rewards, whether intentional or not, he also transmitted symbolic cues to everyone in the organization. What the principals paid attention to, what they talked about, what they did, and who and what they rewarded were the symbolic threads of the patterned design of symbolic leadership. (pp. 20–21)

Effective symbolic leadership connects people in schools to common experiences and shared purposes. "The management of symbols is not only a critical leadership function for principals in schools, it is also a measure of shared meanings, values, ideologies, and a sense of vision for the future" (p. 21).

Edgar Schein (1985) provides an excellent analysis of the connections between organizational culture and symbolic leadership. He describes primary mechanisms leaders use to influence organizational culture. These include (1) what leaders pay attention to, measure, and control; (2) leader reactions to critical incidents and organizational crises; (3) modeling and coaching of desired behaviors; (4) allocations of rewards and status; and (5) criteria used in recruiting, selecting, promoting, retiring, or dismissing of personnel (pp. 224–225). The central message conveyed through these symbolic leadership mechanisms is, *"Watch what I do."*

The potter image of leadership suggests that school cultures are malleable in the hands of the principal. The analogy suggests many comparisons between the craft of potting and effective leadership. Imagine for a moment, an artist at a potter's wheel. Based on what you know and have observed about this art form, in what ways is throwing pots similar to what principals do to shape school cultures? Here's a list of some of the structural characteristics and qualities of pottery making that might be transferred to leadership in schools: clay (type, color, and quality); mineral composition; a potter's wheel; the use of water; processes—centering the mass of clay; shaping the clay mass; building and refining the object; glazing; and firing. What does each suggest to you in terms of the composition, processes, and skills leaders use to shape school culture? As skilled potters, principals work with cultural ingredients (shared values, symbols, rituals, ceremonies, myths, and routines) to shape, refine, and reinforce school culture.

As poets principals use language in evocative ways to create shared meanings, reinforce values, and sustain guiding images for their school. For example, principals use *words* (community, family, and village); *mottos* ("A Place for Everyone," "Celebrate Diversity," "We Care," "Each One Teach One," and "All Children Can Learn"); and *stories* (poignant, humorous, or telling events in the life of the school) to communicate core values, beliefs, practices, and norms. Principals are not the only poets and storytellers in schools. In a study of school restructuring and teacher empowerment, Bredeson (1993) reported that words, mottos, and stories were used by teachers and principals to reinforce shared cultures. One principal stated,

> My school had to become our school. For example, if I weren't here and a parent came in to see the school, my guidance counselor or teachers could tell them about the school. It's theirs. Teachers can all tell the story. They've all bought into it.

Principals are also actors who assume major roles in various social and organizational dramas acted out in and out of school. Some of these roles are predictably scripted. These include graduation ceremonies, student awards banquets, retirement celebrations, and open houses. More improvisational skills are required when crises and unforeseen events arise. It is the principal's performance in these scenes that reveals to observers key values, beliefs, and meanings in the school. The dialogue is important, but everyone watches what the principal as actor does.

Finally, Deal and Peterson describe principals as healers. As dynamic social organizations, schools are responsive to critical changes in their internal and external environments. Educational reform initiatives have resulted in changes in the roles, rules, responsibilities, and relationships that govern the behavior of teachers and principals. These changes have created stress and anxiety for them in schools.

> The principal as healer recognizes the pain of transition and arranges events that make the transition a collective experience. Drawing people together to mourn loss and to renew hope is a significant part of the principal's culture-shaping role. (1990, p. 30)

The death of a colleague, a school closing, the aftermath of a teacher strike, and work role transitions in restructured schools are examples of events which require the healing skills of an effective principal.

Mystics, Neats, and Scruffies

Our third example of analogies for leadership is from the work of Thomas Sergiovanni. In his text, *The Principalship: A Reflective Practice Perspective,* (1987), he categorizes principals under three basic mindscape types—mystics, neats, and scruffies. The categorizations represent different conceptualizations of schooling, of professional practice, and of their relationship to theory and formal knowledge. *Mystics* see educational administration primarily as a non-science informed primarily by professional practices, not by theory or research. To mystics, formal knowledge is of little use, the world is hopelessly phenomenological, everything is relative, and idiosyncratic personal knowledge, which is primarily intuitive and tacit, counts most. "The principal functions as a clairvoyant" (p. 5). *Neats* see administrative practice as an applied science in which theory and research are tightly linked to professional practice. "Neats seek to establish the one best solution to a problem and the one best way to practice. The principal is presumed to function as a highly trained technician" (p. 5). Role ambiguity, situational uncertainty, and complexity make the world of practice a messy place for neats and mystics. Neats prefer facile solutions and "right actions," while mystics consider situations of practice phenomenologically idiosyncratic. Building on the work of Donald Schon (1983), Sergiovanni describes what he sees as a fundamental mismatch between formal knowledge, professional practice, and the realities of today's schools. He concludes, "In the actual world of schooling the task of the principal is to make sense of messy situations by increasing understanding and discovering and communicating meanings" (p. 7). This is the work of *scruffies*. To scruffies, the practice of administration is "characterized by interacting reflection and action episodes" (p. 4).

> The scruffies' view of the principalship is that of a science of the practical—a science that stems from theories of practice and which provides principals with practical as well as theoretical mindscapes from which to work. The concept *reflective practice* is critical to this new science. (p. 6)

Our purpose in this section has been to illustrate the heuristic possibilities of selected analogies. Each metaphor describes a slice of leadership reality for school principals. These suggestive comparisons provide insight into principals' formal and informal leadership in schools. As a student of educational administration, you must recognize that the analogies used to describe leadership roles for principals have important implications for research, theory, and practice. Metaphors are more than just nice (Ortony, 1975). Metaphors are value laden and have evocative power to shape our attitudes about who can be leaders, how leadership is exercised, and to what ends leader influence will be used. In addition to the more obvious suggestive comparisons from the examples described above, it is important to recognize that many metaphors are so deeply embedded in the ways we think about schools and leadership in them that we no longer even think of them as metaphoric. That's just the way things are.

The literature in organizational theory and leadership is grounded and expressed in traditional male experiences and perceptions. Traditional organizational theory texts refer to the "father" of a movement and tradition. The language of male experience, especially corporate industrial, sports metaphors, and military experience provide our metaphors of management and leadership. Given our cultural history, we should not be surprised that one set of perceptions became dominant not only in practice and opportunity, but also in conceptual and intellectual terms. Based on your experience in schools, do a quick review of the language we currently use to express major educational activities, processes, and concepts. Here are a few examples to prompt your thinking: bottom line, targets, strategic planning, quarterbacking the team, attacking problems, and cutting our losses. You might be thinking that language and images are innocuous and not really that influential in shaping the way we think about leadership and organizational purpose. If so, in what ways would changing the dominant images affect our thinking about leadership? For example, images about mothers and the experiences of women. In addition to being male-oriented, the predominant themes in organizations are white, middle-class experiences. How might our thinking change if those images were grounded in the experiences of other cultures?

The use of analogies to describe formal leadership roles of principals is important. We believe that metaphors are at the heart of how principals put their leadership into practice. "Through metaphors, leaders mediate meaning, create understanding, and connect individuals to collective interests and ideals. If there is any one language of leadership, it is expressed through the management of metaphor" (Bredeson, 1988a, p. 4). As conceptualizations of schooling change, other images will emerge to capture meaning and provide insight into the leadership roles of principals in schools. Metaphors are central to "the process of 'imaginization' through which people enact or 'write' the character of organizational life" (Morgan, 1986, p. 344).

REFORM, RESTRUCTURING, AND THE PRINCIPAL'S FORMAL LEADERSHIP ROLE

Since 1983 and the release of *A Nation at Risk* (National Commission on Excellence in Education), education has been on the proverbial front burner of policy wonks, legislators, and educational professionals. Though some critics would argue that schools have not changed enough, a significant body of evidence exists that today's schools are different professional work environments from those of a decade ago. These differences are especially apparent in day-to-day working relationships among teachers and principals (Fullan, 1991). As leadership responsibilities and traditional mechanisms of control are shared among teachers and principals, the traditional role of principals is continually redefined. Bredeson (1994) describes principals who are rejecting traditional leader roles in favor of group-centered leader behaviors. These principals pay careful attention to individual and group needs; they emphasize consultation and facilitation rather direction and control; they model leader behaviors and coach others; they nurture accepting and supportive climates; they encourage others to be self-monitoring; and they relinquish control not by abdicating responsibility but by empowering others.

Since it is unlikely that reform efforts and change processes in schools will subside in the near future, the formal leadership role of principals will continue to be reshaped and redefined. Barth (1988) suggests that the move toward a more collegial model of leadership in schools requires principals to take the following behavioral steps: (1) articulating a vision to the staff; (2) relinquishing control when appropriate; (3) entrusting others with control and not withdrawing that trust; (4) involving others in decision making; (5) assigning responsibilities wisely while accounting for individual differences in ability and commitment; (6) attributing successes to teachers; (7) sharing failures; and (8) admitting ignorance.

> The 21st century is expected to see continuing expansion of collegial involvement and a more 'flattened' organizational structure for decision making in the schools. In their role as leader of leaders, principals will need new skills in order to more effectively facilitate and empower teachers and other members of the school community. They will need to be able to help shape and nurture the leadership capabilities of everyone involved in the school's work. (*National Association of Elementary School Principals, Principals for 21st Century Schools*, 1990, p. 11)

CONCLUSION

In this chapter we examined the formal leadership roles of school principals. We began with a presentation of social role theory. We described social role as a product of three factors—social position, normative role expectations, and individual characteristics and behaviors within the role. Next we introduced Schein's model of organizational role grounded in three empirically discernible perspectives: functional, hierarchical, and interpersonal. We then examined the principal's formal leadership role through a three-dimensional framework of skills, processes, and organizational imperatives. Mintzberg's taxonomy of managers provided further insight into ways researchers and practitioners have defined the formal leader roles of principals. We also used selected analogies to illustrate the heuristic possibilities in viewing schools and leadership in them through the lenses of various suggestive comparisons. We then briefly reviewed traditional constructs applied to leadership studies.

Finally, we briefly discussed the impact of current school reform on the role of principal as leader.

In Chapter 7 we turn to school dynamics that bring this formal leadership role into direct contact with change processes in a school environment when a new principal is appointed.

SUGGESTED ACTIVITIES

1. What functional tasks do principals assume that distinguish their professional work from the work of others in schools and which define them as formal leaders?

2. Use each of the categories in Mintzberg's taxonomy and name and describe a principal or other school leader who seems to you to operate from this orientation. Compare your descriptions with others in your seminar or course.

3. Identify four major responsibilities that your principal has as a formal leader. Draw diagrams illustrating how the principal and others understand each responsibility. To what degree are there overlaps in perceptions of each responsibility? Identify any area in which role conflicts are likely. Compare your diagrams with others in the class.

4. In Figure 6.4 we illustrate the concept of principals' inclusion in a school through interpersonal relationships with colleagues. Again, draw a figure that illustrates the principal's inclusion in your school. Compare this with other illustrations. What specifically might the principal do to change her or his relationships as depicted in your drawing? When your principal assumed the role of formal leader, was he or she new to the school? To the district? How does being an outsider versus an insider to the school, to the district, influence the principal's inclusion?

5. Jacques (1989) identified seven organizational imperatives that require leader attention. In what way does each shape what your principal does? Which of these organizational imperatives are most attended to by your principal? Compare this with other students' principals.
   a. articulating mission, goals, strategies, and main functions,
   b. arranging functional alignments,
   c. identifying mechanisms of co-ordination and control,
   d. constituting accountability and role relationships,
   e. institutionalizing planning and communication,
   f. relating rewards and performance,
   g. achieving effective leadership.

6. Various analogies have been used to describe the roles and responsibilities of principals as formal leaders. What suggestive comparisons would you use to describe principals as formal leaders? Compare your leadership analogies to those of your colleagues. Identify the strengths and limitations of each analogy for describing principals as formal leaders.

Leadership and Leader Succession

When you take charge in a school for the first time, you must strive for success under tremendous personal and professional pressure. To make this a positive experience, you need to know about the context and personal factors that influence succession effects, ways in which you can adapt for these factors, and the potential positive or negative impacts combinations of factors might have. You also can benefit personally by knowing in advance the features of various stages through which you are likely to progress during your succession experience. This chapter is designed to fill these needs. We are concerned in this book with improving your leader succession experiences. Information about the processes you can expect, the factors that influence those processes, and the potential outcomes of your succession will help you take action to improve the likelihood of your success.

Leader succession for principals is both a personal and a professional experience. Personally, you will be in transition from teacher or assistant principal to school leader, from a member of the team to team leader. The people, school, and immediate community usually will be new to you, and people may or may not know much about you. Often what they know will be based on second- or third-hand information interpreted and filtered before it reaches the school. If you are familiar with the people in the neighborhood and school, they may already hold strong opinions about what kind of principal you will be. Personal relationships change dramatically under these conditions. Many first-time principals report feeling isolated from sources of personal support and disconnected from their new peers (Weindling & Earley, 1987). We return to this theme in more detail in Chapter 10 when we examine the personal issues raised on becoming a principal.

Professionally, you will face expectations that place the well-being of many young people (or at least accountability for their well-being) largely in your hands. You must adjust to these new expectations. Teachers, parents, students, and superiors watch and wait to see what your impact on the school will be. Early in your tenure people wonder if your leadership will improve or degrade their working and school experiences, promote or frustrate the accomplishment of their professional goals. Many teachers simply hope you will see to administrivia in the school with minimal fuss, buffer them from parents, and leave them alone.

These leader change or succession experiences occur commonly in schools and other kinds of organizations. You can expect to take on between five and six new leadership assignments in your career (Gabarro, 1987). The attention and emotion generated when a new principal is appointed and the time and energy invested in selection processes illustrate the importance succession has for the people involved (Miklos, 1988).

While we acknowledge that critics question the efficacy of leadership in general, we find substantial evidence of principals' direct and indirect influence on schools (see Chapter 9) and of the impact of succession on that influence. For this discussion, it suffices to point out that schools identified as successful in reaching their goals often report that the principal is a key figure in that process. As we come to know more about principals' influence on school effectiveness, we can improve the preparation, induction, and professional development of school principals (Leithwood, Steinbach & Begley, 1991). We seek new ways to enhance the success of talented aspiring school leaders and improve their preparation, induction, and support during the critical taking-charge period. When you take on your first professional assignment, you will be more successful if you integrate and apply your professional knowledge and experience in a unique context while undergoing both professional and organizational socialization. For new principals, critical relationships and interaction patterns among peers, with their superiors, and within the school are just emerging at the time of their appointment. When you move on to new assignments, a careful assessment of the attitudes and behaviors to take with you and what dynamics and unique challenges face you at the new school substantially improve your chances of success. This chapter is devoted to providing a structure for understanding and capitalizing on the succession period in four areas: (1) effects, (2) context, (3) personal factors, and (4) stages.

The mix of principal and school is unique for each succession. This poses a dilemma for you as you work to improve your own succession outcomes. If you focus too intently on your own point of view, you may miss important cues from the school that can guide your actions. If you discount your unique talents and focus on fitting in with the group, you risk diluting your qualities, power, and potential contribution to the school.

As we emphasized in earlier chapters, each newly appointed principal enters the principalship hoping to be a leader and to make a difference in the school. Scholars of leader succession designed their studies based on the belief and assumption that new leaders can affect performance. In addition, some people assert that changing principals per se will have a positive impact on school performance. Many school districts have automatic transfer policies for principals. School district administrators transfer principals to a new school after five or seven years as a matter of course, but the research on succession provides very mixed support for these policies. You should keep several questions in mind as you read the rest of this chapter. Are automatic transfer policies functional or dysfunctional? What situations might shape the outcomes of succession, so that administrators can work to improve the likelihood of positive effects? How do various factors such as economic well-being, race, gender, and school size influence principal succession outcomes? What is the experience like?

Many people believe that a change in leaders will make a positive difference, so the first of these approaches to studying succession makes sense in light of these beliefs. One of the first things superintendents or school boards do when student performance is poor or declines in a school is to change principals. Sports teams are famous (or infamous) for this intervention. The case of George Steinbrenner who oft replaced managers of the New York Yankees, stands as an apt illustration of this belief in salvation sought through leadership change. Much of the early research seeking answers to the question whether succession per se affects performance involved win-loss records of sports teams.

Studies in schools revealed that social and economic factors and personal characteristics and behaviors of principals affect the relationships between succession and school outcomes. Studies in other kinds of organizations examined social and personal factors affecting the impact of succession on performance, as well. These third and fourth approaches to leader succession eschew the rationale that leader change alone yields positive outcomes and accept the assumption that multiple, interactive social and personal factors combine in very different and powerful ways in each principal's succession.

Stage frameworks provided a final approach to understanding leader succession. The context of succession events, the content (knowledge or facts) learned during succession, and the passage of time shape this approach. Because succession events appear to be time bound, scholars in this tradition reasoned that more complete understanding of the stages of effective successions could be used to influence the quality of other successions (Manz, Adsit, Campbell & Mathison-Hance, 1988).

SUCCESSION EFFECTS

The question whether succession per se is a salutary or disruptive event in schools and other organizations remains unanswered. Based on a review of literature on succession, the answer seems to be, it depends. Brown (1982) found studies supporting every possible outcome. Carroll (1984) argued that researchers should find conditions that result in different effects, such as changes in supervision patterns (Koch, 1978). As Pfeffer and Davis-Blake pointed out, "the consequences of successions are likely to vary dramatically depending on the conditions surrounding them" (1986, p. 81).

Positive Effects

Case studies formed the basis of early accounts of positive results from leader succession. Two very different cases illustrate. One of the first well-known cases with a positive outcome was written by Guest (1962). He observed a new manufacturing plant manager who was successful in taking charge. He used informal contacts to improve interactions and communication. By establishing and nurturing personal relationships, he was able to accomplish substantive and structural changes.

A second succession case with a positive outcome was prepared by Salaman (1977), who studied a succession in a small manufacturing plant. In this case, the retired manager threatened the successor's success by exercising influence. The power of the predecessor to influence the process and outcomes of leader succession is vividly portrayed in this case. Workers praised and idealized the predecessor, illustrating Gouldner's (1954) description of the power of the "Rebecca Myth." When this myth functions, group members for various reasons—anxiety, fear of the unknown, or simply change in role behavior by the new leader—idealize the predecessor, regardless of her objective qualities or past popularity. (This phenomenon is named after Daphne de Maurier's *Rebecca*.) Despite this mythical pressure the charismatic new leader in Salaman's case overcame its negative effects and succeeded.

More recently, studies in schools and other educational organizations provide rich case descriptions of succession successes. Thorum (1994) studied the succession of a program director in a community education program. Using a combination of interview data and the participant observation journal of the educational leader, she delved into the interaction relationships in which the values, hopes, and goals of a group of educators and the authentic goals of a new leader interacted to yield a positive outcome. She concluded that the language of leaders and followers presents a major barrier to understanding leadership effects as interactive, iterative processes in the professional group she studied because these words carry with them assumptions about unidirectional effects by leaders on followers.

Principal succession, too, has been described positively. Cosgrove's (1986) cases included several principals whose successions were judged positively by teachers. Parkay and his colleagues (1992) also provided descriptions of principals whose successions led to a mature, autonomous, and healthy relationship between the new principal and the school.

Negative Effects

Conclusions that succession disrupts a school and is dysfunctional also have been reached. Some case studies and many correlation analyses yielded bleak predictions about the impacts of your succession on a school. Gouldner (1954) was among early writers reaching this negative conclusion. He watched the new manager in a gypsum mine violate highly entrenched beliefs, norms, and expectations. People reacted negatively; the new leader increased tension and stress by relying heavily on hierarchical authority.

More recent studies support Gouldner's conclusion. Fauske and Ogawa (1987) and Ogawa (1991) followed the retirement of an elementary school principal and the first year of his successor. They wondered how a faculty makes sense of the impending changes, comes to know the successor principal, and interprets the meaning and outcome of the succession. The successor principal was an experienced administrator whose entire career was spent in the same district. His appointment resulted from a routine transfer policy that required all principals to move regularly to new schools. While the new principal's charm, facility with names, and apparent influence at the district office earned him kudos early on in his tenure, his failure to respect important norms, value the neighborhood and culture in the school, and accept the influence and status of established members of the group led within a year to an unsettled and unhappy situation. He entered a power struggle with the beloved school secretary who had served in the school for many years, he pressured faculty to work while ill in order to make him look good (low teacher absenteeism rates), he spent a great deal of time away from the school running personal errands and tending to his real estate business, and he bragged about his important tennis partners, expensive cars, and exclusive neighborhood far from the school. At the end of his first year, the teachers remarked, "The prince has turned into a frog."

In another service organization, a psychiatric unit in a hospital, Oskarsson and Klein (1982) reported similar experiences. They highlighted a variety of dangers attendant to leader change. Succession brought apprehension. Strong differences of philosophy between the group and the new leader caused conflict, withdrawal, and unproductive behavior. They concluded that once a group begins to view itself as beleaguered, the successor's task is particularly difficult. Like the principal in Ogawa's studies, the new leader came to be viewed as an intruder. Unlike the frog prince in the preceding study, the hospital group in this study stopped their work to address relationship problems and try to reestablish productive working patterns.

Succession studies that ignore context and simply analyze performance records also yielded negative conclusions about succession effects per se. The win-loss records of athletic teams provided some of the earliest succession studies. The logic of these studies is seductive. Turnover in team managers compared with win-loss records should reveal any relationship between leader change and performance. When a team loses consistently, the manager often is fired, so the record matches the logic. Scholars asked whether this convention serves any purpose other than catharsis for owner and fans. The performance records of athletic team analyses provided no support for the belief that changing leaders improves performance (Grusky, 1963). Baseball teams with the poorest performance records, for example, had the highest succession rates. Grusky argued that succession is a vicious circle—poor performance leads to succession, disruption, and poor performance. Gamson and Scotch (1964) called this process "ritual scapegoating." School superintendents—more vulnerable to political attacks and shifting power bases in school organizations—also suffer ritual scapegoating, especially in large urban school districts where the average tenure of superintendents is less than three years.

No Effect

Perhaps more discouraging to new principals than claims that succession improves or degrades performance is the contention that it makes no difference. Cosgrove (1986) found many teachers who hold this opinion: "Principals come and principals go, but we'll still be here." In her study of ten principals (five successors and five ongoing for a control group) over a year's time, she found the stage framework developed by Miskel and Cosgrove (1985) useful, emphasizing prearrival factors and postsuccession effects. She found, however, that most of the differences she observed between succession and non-succession schools were related to individual principal differences or teacher preferences rather than to succession. While she saw succession effects extending beyond the first year, she also reported very negative effects when a principal delayed too long in making changes he felt were warranted. She also concluded that teachers influence the effects of principal succession. Hart (1993) interpreted these findings as support for an interactive perspective on succession effects.

The win-loss records of athletic teams also led some to conclude that the "ritual scapegoating" explanation may fit reality better than attributions to the leader. Pfeffer (1981) and other writers who study leadership accept this explanation, asserting that principals and other managers like them are so alike and the connections between behavior and organizational performance are so diffuse, that leadership fills only a symbolic, attributional role. We make sense of the difficulties of collective life by attributing performance to a leader, so that we can get on with things. The group offers up the leader as a "ritual scapegoat" to best atone for a poor performance (Eitzen & Yetman, 1972). Because major league baseball teams are so evenly matched overall in talent and resources, their performance can be explained as an artifact of probability, not team leadership—the regression effect. Strong teams' performance tends to regress downward toward the mean, and weak teams' performance regresses upward toward the mean, and, as with students in school, past performance is the best predictor of future performance (Allen, Panian & Lotz, 1979).

Data on student performance have contributed to skeptical assessments of principal succession's effects on schools. Miskel and Owens (1983) examined principal change effects on a variety of school outcomes—structural linkages, perceived organizational effectiveness, job satisfaction of teachers, and student attitudes. They found no evidence of principal succession effects on these school outcomes. Rowan and Denk (1984), however, sought to isolate the principal succession effect and the circumstances under which leader succession may be advantageous. As is discussed in Chapter 8, their data showed negative, disruptive effects of succession in high socioeconomic status (SES) schools and positive effects in low SES schools. Ogawa and Hart (1985) asked if principal succession makes a difference, not whether the differences was positive or negative, and found evidence that a change in principal may account for a small but discernible difference in student performance on mathematics and reading tests.

The plethora of diverse results from research leaves those of us in school leadership unsettled. Many explanations have been offered for these apparently contradictory findings. First, each succession is unique; outcomes depend very much on complex, interacting factors. Attempts to explain these outcomes for a group would result in arithmetic means that suggest no differences—the effects would wash out in the math. The enormous constraints that situations place on principals and other formal leaders also offer an explanation (Lieberson & O'Connor, 1972). Schools and other long-lived organizations become tra-

dition bound, and inertia makes them slow to change, even under the influence of a powerful and prominent new leader (Hambrick & Mason, 1984; Hannan & Freeman, 1984a; Samuelson, Galbraith, & McGruire, 1985). We began
this book by arguing that the dynamics and quality of your interactions with
the school you are assigned to lead will shape the outcomes of your succession experience. Others put it more directly:

> The inherent social disruption caused by successions may be one reason why
> a new manager's ability to develop effective working relationships discrimi-
> nates so strongly between the failed and successful successions. (Gabarro,
> 1987, p. 166)

These findings provide further support for the importance of your efforts to
understanding ways these effective relationships can be developed. Your first
step will be to come to know the context of your succession, the new school,
and the factors in that context that will affect your succession.

CONTEXT

As Miklos (1988) pointed out, participants see principal succession as an
important school event. The interpretations teachers, parents, and students
place on the change and the features of the school, its needs, and people's
goals, hopes, and aspirations (as well as the challenges) make each experience
unique. We cannot emphasize too often that preparing for leader succession
requires that you nurture creativity, flexibility, analytical skills, and the ability to adjust to changing circumstances. No algorithm for success exists.

A university provided the setting for one influential study examining the
impact of context factors on leader change. Gephart (1978) studied the forced
succession of a study body president and concluded that a process he called
"status degradation" functions when members of the group decide that a
leader must go. The insight Gephart offered was that, regardless of relevant
objective performance factors, social-psychological processes structure the way
in which people come to share a common explanation for events. In his case,
this was a forced change in leadership. Along with the concepts of ritual scapegoating and attribution discussed earlier, status degradation helps us understand how groups make sense of their experiences related to the important
events surrounding leader succession.

These conclusions emphasize the importance of people's perceptions in
shaping their actions. In the section on succession effects we discussed sensemaking as a source of evidence that succession has no substantive effect on
organizations. Yet, you should not discount people's explanations. Explanations and attributions contribute understanding to difficult circumstances and
people's choices and behavior. Attribution functions in many ways: "The conditions and consequences of the perception of self-as-cause have become a
major focus of contemporary attribution theory. Especially relevant . . . are the
self-attributions individuals make with regard to personal control over events
that affect them" (Turner, 1988, p. 19). People thus attribute cause to themselves and to principals, teachers, parents, and groups. These attributions are

both positive and negative. How many parents, when their children get in trouble in school or the community, blame the children's choice of friends? The power of the construct in part lies in the kernel of truth at the core; friends can get young people in trouble. Yet, almost all the parents probably blame the others' children rather than examining multiple causes and influences; they oversimplify the situation and limit their intervention choices. Positive effects also emerge from attribution. When teachers and students attribute positive influences to a new principal's leadership and ideas, they then may act on these attributions, creating effects through their actions (Hart, 1988).

Other case studies and large survey research studies reach similar conclusions (Crow, 1990b; Lamoreaux, 1990). They reinforce that interpersonal factors are those most often identified by new principals and aspiring principals as the critical factors shaping their work. Crow's survey respondents focused on the importance of interpersonal and school climate issues. Lamoreaux's educational criticism portrayed a strong personal vision, interacting positively with a receptive group, as the influential factor in principal succession. He said that her "vision . . . is a vision of caring, of sharing, and of relationships. It is a vision that she models when working with students and staff" (Lamoreaux, 1990, p. 18).

Similarly, Hart studied the interpretations of the new principal (1987a, 1988). She asked how a newly appointed principal makes sense of the dynamic interplay of self and the established social system of the school. Providing one person's "native view," she too found that the social structure of the existing organization, its needs as perceived by current members, and its sacred and tacit practices exert tremendous influence over perceived outcomes (Crow, 1993). These perceived outcomes are critical to new principals' being accepted by teachers, students, parents, and other administrators as legitimate leaders who can act on the behalf of their school group to achieve shared educational goals (Corbett, Firestone & Rossman, 1987).

In an attempt at open-eyed realism, some principals and scholars ask, "What do you expect, given the similarities among principals and constraints from the family and community?" Pfeffer (1978, 1981) offered contextual constraints to explain the failure of principals to affect school performance: (1) administrators' similarity, (2) the nature of administrative work, (3) the organizational and external environments in which administrators operate, (4) power, (5) succession systems, (6) size, (7) school performance, (8) sources of social support for new principals, (9) predecessor status and assessment, and (10) symbolic dimensions of school organizations.

Administrators' Similarity

The first contextual constraint on the influence of principals is the similarity of people in the candidate pool. By the time you are selected, socialized, and trained you are remarkably like other principals, especially because they already have been sorted and socialized as teachers. Selection processes contribute to the homogeneity of administrators, because superiors tend to select candidates who are like them, with whom they are comfortable.

Homosocial reproduction operates in all types of organizations, including public schools. Baltzell and Dentler (1983) noted that educational administrators, particularly superintendents, favor candidates who possess similar social and personal characteristics when they select principals. In short, school administrators tend to look alike.

While this tendency provides an explanation for the relative exclusion of women and members of minority groups from educational administration, it is not an acceptable excuse. As a new principal or a candidate for a principalship, you should be aware of the subconscious influence this process exerts, and we will return to this theme when we discuss specific actions you can take to highlight your talents and potential as a leader. Top leaders in education are obligated to acknowledge this powerful social tendency (divorced from objective measures of "quality" or "potential") as they address equity issues in school leadership. Educational leadership in the United States has been dominated by white, Protestant, males (Valverde, 1980; National Commission on Excellence in Educational Administration, 1987; Tyack & Hansot, 1982). School leaders may or may not have colluded in the continuation of this pattern; we tend to believe that most have not, but the responsibility to combat it consciously now rests with all school leaders. Expanding the participation of teachers, staff, parents, students, and community members in the selection of principals offers greater diversity of perspective and the likelihood of serious consideration of candidates traditionally overlooked in principal search processes.

Formal education and training provide another explanation for the similarity of administrators. Here, Pfeffer also provided insight into the homogeneity of the administrator candidate pool. He observed that most administrators undergo similar formal training and informal socialization experiences. In preparation for public school careers, the vast majority of administrators in the United States complete university-based, graduate training programs. Educational administration programs generally vary little, although many educators and faculty are working together to rectify this shortcoming (Ogawa & Pounder, 1991). Educational administration programs usually provide exposure to such topics as school law, school budgeting and finance, educational politics, managerial and organizational theory, curriculum, instruction and instructional supervision, the principalship, and personnel administration. You will note that we, too, rely on these standard curriculum organizers in much of our discussion about the history of educational administration and the work of the principal in Chapter 5. Similar language and common understandings give stability and economy to dialogue about principals' work, but they carry a seductive complacency, as well. As professionals, we must be alert to the two-edged sword of common experience and language. Social critics, revisionist scholars, and other writers play a critical part in pointing out these dangers (Bredeson, 1988a; Giroux, 1991). Uniformity of experience, training, inquiry, and images of schooling result in administrators who act on the basis of similar knowledge and assumptions, limiting the questions they ask, the way they define problems, and the solutions they consider.

Antecedent professional socialization amplifies the homogenizing effect of university education. For example, almost all school administrators were classroom teachers. Principals name teaching as part of their professional socialization experience (Bredeson, 1991a; Duke et al., 1984). After leaving the classroom, principals typically follow a common career path. This path leads from assistant principal to principal (with elementary and secondary stopovers in some districts) and, in some cases, to the superintendency. Studies of administrator socialization show how administrators develop common orientations during these shared experiences (Pitner & Ogawa, 1981; Greenfield, 1985a, 1985b). The result: School leaders tend to act from a common set of assumptions and beliefs (Tyack & Hansot, 1982). Bredeson (1991a) identified significant differences between male and female teachers in the extended teacher roles they assumed in their schools. Traditionally, male teachers take on two to three times as many extracurricular assignments, especially coaching duties. These extra duties put them in front of larger numbers of parents and make them more visible to key decision makers in school districts. Highly visible public performance translates into positive indicators of leadership potential for many who select principals. We are not suggesting that coaching is the only route to the principalship; we are saying that extended teacher roles beyond classrooms support the career advancement of men and women.

The Social Nature of Administrative Work

The social nature of administrative work also constrains the impact of principal succession. We introduced the influential work of Mintzberg, Willower, Peterson, and others revealing the verbal, highly interactive, and activity-focused daily work of administrators in Chapter 5. Pfeffer (1978) suggested that organizational elements such as formal job descriptions and informal role expectations limit administrators' discretionary behavior. In addition, principals typically avoid making important unilateral decisions such as resource allocation or personnel selection even when they are empowered to make them.

Examples of these constraints abound in schools. Teachers often expect principals to buffer them from parents and to leave them alone as much as possible. Most principals have very limited control over resource allocations and personnel decisions. Union contracts, superintendents' edicts, and board policies often prevent principals from making unilateral decisions about instructional programs and materials. Site-based school councils, teacher career reforms, and other changes in schools further separate principals from direct control over core instructional decisions and require them to learn group influence and facilitation skills to affect decision and postdecision outcomes. We approach these features of school organization from a neutral stance in this discussion; they simply *are,* and they may, in fact, be very positive features overall. Influential principals learn to use them and develop a repertoire of talents and skills that turn contextual constraints into mechanisms for action. Group-centered leadership, which we discussed in Chapter 6, is an example of how principals in restructured teacher-empowered schools turn apparent contextual constraints to the school's advantage (Bredeson, 1994).

A third source of constraint on principals' influence is the settings in which they work. Circumstances over which administrators have little or no control exist in schools and in their environments. These circumstances influence operations and performance. Instructional technology, management technology (e.g., school records, scheduling, grading, communication networks), social norms (the way we do things around here), and standard operating procedures typically are deeply embedded in schools. Together they define school culture, which is not easily changed by principals, especially if it is a strong culture. Weaker school cultures are more amenable to the influence of leader succession (Parkay & Hall, 1992; Wright, 1992).

Examples of setting factors abound. A principal new to a school inherits a faculty that is likely to have well-developed norms that guide the day-to-day operation of the school. She also will find that instructional programs have been implemented and textbooks have been adopted, purchased, and used. The physical layout of the building can limit instructional programs.

School traditions and rituals also are influential factors in school settings. For one of the authors, the impact of social norms became apparent when he unwittingly violated a long-standing student tradition. The food services director of the school had requested that changes be made in the holiday dinner celebration. The entire student body assembled in the gymnasium for a holiday meal. To speed up serving the elaborate meal (whole, carved turkeys; homemade desserts; breads; stuffing; potatoes and gravy; and assorted vegetables) the cooks made a simple request—to have *all* students go through buffet serving lines. As a new principal and a seasoned church supper aficionado, I agreed to the new plan. Two days later, I retracted this decision. The senior class officers came to my office and explained the importance of one aspect of this school tradition. Seniors were seated and had their dinners served to them by the junior class. The seniors had waited for years for this special consideration. Understanding the importance of this tradition, I agreed and arranged with the cafeteria staff to carry on the tradition, even with its minor inefficiencies.

Factors outside the immediate school environment such as contracts with suppliers, school choice or vouchers, and government regulations also influence the structure and operation of schools. Because these constraints persist over time, they greatly reduce the discretion and, therefore, the influence of principals. These constraints include the norms of local communities, the policies of state and federal agencies, court rulings, and innovations in instructional technology. Not only must principals respond to forces in the environment, they also find decision-making alternatives constrained by the interests of powerful constituencies. Parent advocates for students with disabilities compete with school sports boosters for the resources and attention of educators. For example, when an administrator hires teachers, only those candidates who hold a teaching credential and, often, only those who have passed muster with the personnel director can be considered.

Power

Power is another situational variable. We introduced the relationship between power and leadership in Chapter 6. While it sometimes is de rigueur to admit that power functions in school organizations because of pervasive norms of at least surface protestations of equality, the power dimension plays a critical role in principal succession. In addition to its relational power inherent in kinship, reward power, coercive power, legitimate power, expert power, and referent power moderate overall effects of succession (Smith & Peterson, 1988). Many scholars have studied the relationship between corporate ownership, controlling interests, connections, organizational performance, and succession. These studies reveal that the greater the external control of an organization's management the greater the frequency of executive succession (Allen, 1981; Allen & Panian, 1982; McEachern, 1975; James & Soref, 1981). School districts in the United States are strongly controlled by elected or appointed boards of education, and thus exhibit strong external control characteristics.

Research on power during succession receives little attention in educational administration. Power is not an acceptable quality; educators respond to more noble motives. Contrary to this conventional wisdom, however, political power does affect elections and, consequently, superintendents' and other educators' careers (Beischel, 1994; Firestone, 1989; Kayon, 1993).

Succession Systems

School districts may have formal or informal systems for identifying and developing future principals. Traditionally, these systems amounted to a conversation between the incumbent principal and a young male teacher about his interest in administration, but more formal systems that allowed more diverse criteria to exert influence also existed (Carroll, 1984; Friedman, 1986; Hall, 1986). Hall (1987) found that a major interest in the development of succession systems springs from perceived needs to identify and develop future leaders within organizations and help them develop into viable candidates for available positions. According to Hall (1987, p. 236), a number of organizations fail to develop succession systems, relying instead on the "one-position staffing" system: "How can we find the best qualified individual for this particular job?" When organizations rely on this method, they must find people already prepared to meet the demands of the new position. A more appropriate system would be replacement planning (emphasis is placed on future positions and needs rather than on specific jobs) and succession planning (emphasizing a future orientation and focusing on principals' learning needs). Reviews of personnel selection processes in education, however, reveal a disappointing paucity of carefully organized systems for the development and selection of principals. While other kinds of organizations invest tremendous resources in finding, preparing, and selecting leaders, education falls short in this area (Gips & Bredeson, 1986; Bredeson, 1991a).

Testing this belief in the power of succession systems and the hypothesis that quality succession systems will lead to superior reputations and performance, Friedman (1986) examined the characteristics of succession systems and performance in organizations: (1) level of formalization; (2) presence of checks and balances; (3) sufficient resources allocated to the system; (4) availability of information on people and positions; (5) use of technical competence criteria; (6) use of political criteria; and (7) formal staff role. He found that the level of formalization per se played no role in either reputation or organizational performance. When top management was involved in nominations, other managers were rewarded for developing subordinates, and other checks and balances came into play in succession processes, positive relationships were found. Sufficient resources, information systems, access to information, and influence on selection by a professional staff were positively associated with performance. The perceived rigor of a selection process also affects the reputation of the successor principal (Hart, 1988); the more rigorous the perception, the more positive the impact on reputation. Political criteria and insider appointments also were positively associated with outcomes.

Another common flaw in planning for succession is: "The monitoring and remunerating of executives on the basis of their performance as developers of people, a powerful means by which to ensure adequate attention to succession and development issues, is a relatively uncommon practice" (Friedman, 1986, p. 201). Cultural criteria (taking part in the ongoing social system, fitting in) are more important than political criteria (loyalty, network ties) during the decision making. Fitting in is a commonly used criterion for identifying and grooming future school administrators. Principals report that they chose an administrative career only after someone encouraged them. They also report that the pressure to be a team player and look, talk, and act like the other administrators is very strong (Campbell, Fleming, Bennion & Newell, 1987). When your superior invites you to consider an administrative career, the allure is enticing. "My principal thinks I am leadership material." Many educators who might make important contributions are never approached, however.

Size

School size is a situational factor of succession examined at some length with ambiguous results. Studies have attempted to determine whether the size of the school is linked to the frequency, form, or outcome of succession. Because size and succession rates are confounded by other situational variables— school history, technological differences, neighborhood differences and SES, retirement policies, and principals' benefits—the direct relationship that might be suggested by simple correlations has been challenged (Sonnenfeld, 1986). Studies of the succession rates and experiences of school superintendents indicate that turnover is increasingly prevalent among superintendents, especially in large urban centers where the environment is particularly turbulent (Beischel, 1994; Kayon, 1993).

Other attempts to isolate the effects of size on succession link size with situational variables such as inside-outside succession or performance. Large schools, like smaller schools, are susceptible to the succession effect. In education, size functions as a variable in succession at the district level. Operating to restrict opportunity in small districts, size may also contribute to the perception that insider successions are more fair (Hart, 1987a; Oskarsson & Klein, 1982). So that you can better interpret some of the feedback you might receive, you should be aware that the size of the district or school in which your first succession to leadership occurs could well affect the nature of people's judgment about the fairness of your selection, regardless of the screening and selection processes pursued and your qualities and qualifications.

Stable School Performance

While size receives much attention as a situational variable in the context of succession, the stability of the school's performance environment may be far more critical. In school districts, for example, infrequent superintendent succession is more common in rural, close knit, stable communities where districts also tend to be small. Their urban counterparts—larger, more diverse, and more subject to conflict—have higher succession rates. In these complex environments, ritual scapegoating is blamed by some urban superintendents for high turnover (Scott, 1982). Kayon (1993) and Beischel (1994), for example, focus on rates of turnover in their research.

Poor performance often is blamed as the precipitating factor in involuntary succession (Fredrickson, Hambrick, & Baumrin, 1988; Friedman, 1986), yet studies of the dismissal of chief executive officers find that organizational performance explains less than one-half the variance in CEO dismissal and turnover rates (James & Soref, 1981; McEachern, 1975; Salancik & Pfeffer, 1980). Superintendents often leave office because of a political battle with school board or community leaders (Beischel, 1994; Kayon, 1993). Multiple-factor models acknowledge that the personal characteristics and perceived self-interests of governing boards (concern for friendships, image, wealth, reputation, etc.) and the sociopolitical features of the district moderate outcomes. In public institutions such as schools, these public governance and political factors exert tremendous influence. Sociopolitical features include such things as the board's expectations and attributions, board members' allegiances and values, the availability of alternative administrators and the incumbent administrator's power (i.e., control over community interest groups and key contacts). Predecessors exert important influence. They therefore are included in comprehensive models of succession (Fredrickson, Hambrick & Baumrin, 1988; Meyer, 1979; Pfeffer, 1981; Salancik & Pfeffer, 1980).

Sources of Social Support for New Principals

Peer support creates a favorable situation for succession. If new CEOs can bring along with them a number of important subordinates, for example, their own success appears to be enhanced (Grusky, 1969). Weindling and Earley (1987) found that many faculty members expect new heads to bring in their own people. Given the personnel staffing systems in most schools, new principals rarely have the opportunity to bring on a team of supportive staff. Over time, with key appointments, they can build a cohesive team. Those who accompany a new leader may have a decided advantage.

Peer support plays a critical part in the success of newly appointed principals. Weindling and Earley's (1987) interview subjects identified supportive assistants as a primary source of support for new heads. Duke and others (1984), too, contended that an assistant principal and helpful colleagues in similar positions in the district provide important peer support during the transition following succession. In private industry, in public administration, and in school administration the presence or absence of peer support is an important situational factor facilitating and hindering leader succession.

In yet another sense, peers provide support that enables new managers to bridge the organizational transition between themselves and their predecessors (Brady & Helmich, 1985). Allies within the existing social group can be invaluable to a manager as they assist in this difficult process. Often these allies are not peers but individuals who, because of their experience and history in the school, can help the new principal understand the existing school culture and the political climate of the local community. These people may be support staff as well as professional colleagues (Hart, 1988; McGivern, 1978). Whether you benefit from the perspectives of professional colleagues or support staff, insiders and peers who are willing to share their views about the school prior to your arrival can provide you with invaluable insight. You should treat their input with respect as you seek many points of view on the new school following your succession.

The growing interest in principal mentor systems as a means of supporting the professional growth and development of new principals acknowledges the importance of peer support for early success. Some states have built mentor principals into their requirements for administrator preparation programs. In Ohio, for example, new principals have a formal mentor arrangement with educational administration faculty through colleges and universities. Others have increased their requirements for mentors providing guidance to principal interns and for principals in their first assignments. These compulsory mentor-protege relationships pose many problems, however, because they violate some of the fundamental qualities of naturally occurring relationships. Programs relying on mentor-protege relationships abound. Others rely on paired peers for some of this support (Daresh & Playko, 1989).

The efficacy of these programs for improving principals' performance early in their careers remains largely unestablished. They do reduce tension and provide easy access to new information early in an administrative assignment, however.

Predecessor Status and Assessment

The predecessor can exert powerful influence over the succession experience. One of the authors experienced this dynamic first-hand when he was appointed principal of a school in which the deposed principal was working as a teacher. The school was divided into camps of teachers who supported the predecessor and those who did not, and these camps exerted powerful influence over seemingly trivial decisions and events (such as the missing graduation tassels). Other direct examples abound. Gordon and Rosen (1981) found that a popular predecessor is not an easy act to follow; members of the group compare the newly appointed leader unfavorably with their valued predecessor. The idealization of the predecessor becomes a difficult obstacle for successors. This is especially true if the predecessor was forced to leave. Understanding the circumstances under which the previous principal left is helpful to new principals as they seek to become accepted by teachers, students, and staff in the school. If a very popular principal was forced from her position, those loyal to her may actively and passively resist a new principal's initiatives. Time, trust, and administrative expertise will contribute to acceptance and effective leadership, and knowledge that these responses are not "personal" in the ultimate sense will help the new principal avoid feelings of resentment while working to secure people's affirmation. Weindling and Earley (1987) found that school leaders experience their successions in part as a function of their predecessors' style and behavior. Heads most frequently rated serious difficulties associated with consultation and communication with faculty members, for example, as a result of the practices and style of previous heads. Their subjects argued that the most important factor in adjustments to predecessor-successor differences was a function of their ability to learn as much as possible about the style of their predecessors and then deliberately set up transition changes that capitalized on qualities and failings alike.

A poor-performing predecessor or one who is unpopular with his constituency also can create a favorable environment for a succession. Some practitioners even go so far as to declare that the first rule of leader succession is, "Follow an unpopular leader."

The Symbolic Dimension in Succession

The power of this maxim leads to another dimension of leader succession grounded in the culture of schools, which we discussed in Chapter 6. While succession literature has not traditionally addressed the symbolic context of organizations, case studies of leader succession provide tantalizing stories of the impact of symbols and organizational culture on perceptions and outcomes. Writers use the words and concepts of symbol, meaning, and understanding but seldom emphasize this aspect of the succession process. Your impact will affect the hopes, aspirations, and fears of people in the school to which you have been assigned, and these feelings and beliefs deserve the greatest possible respect, regardless of your assessment of their "objective" reality.

The effect of a crisis mentality on people's attitudes and behavior during succession, for example, is tightly coupled with belief. A group, believing it faces an imminent crisis, will tend to move to replace a leader who appears to lack a specific solution to the problem. The quality of the solution is less important than its specificity Hamblin (1958). Once the decision to purge a leader is reached, people use a variety of methods that feature meaning and belief as tools to bring about succession. Status degradation is among these symbolic processes, as is ritual scapegoating, and these processes may have no concrete benefit (Gamson & Scotch, 1964; Gephart, 1978).

How the new leader is selected also carries with it symbolic meaning. Those who participate in and make the final selection contribute a meaning to the succession through their own characteristics and reputations. New principals often receive reputational credit (as competent and desirable leaders) when those who participated in their selection are seen as credible decision makers. Not only do group members assess a new principal more favorably if the selectors are seen as competent, groups often project the characteristics of the sponsor onto the successor. Additionally, other selection factors influence group beliefs, including the perception that the selection process was rigorous, wide ranging, and competitive. In schools, superintendents' talents or agendas thus can transfer to principals whose appointment they control or substantially affect (Hart, 1987a; Hollander, Fallon & Edward, 1977; Hollander & Julian, 1978; Knight & Weiss, 1980). You have no control over perceptions of your selectors' expertise. At the same time, you have many skills, experiences, and knowledge resources needed by the educators in the school to which you are assigned and similar to those of the educators who appointed you. Succession gives you an opportunity to "show your stuff," to give those with whom you will work a chance to see that you possess the knowledge and skills they need. Reputation is not everything, but a good reputation presents an opportunity you should seize if it is available to you.

The rationale and motives driving a succession are another function of meaning and symbol. When people see the reasons for change as legitimate (death, voluntary retirement, the promotion of the predecessor), they are less likely to criticize the successor. This effect of legitimacy improves a group's attitudes toward changes that might follow. Many teachers assume that change will come with a new principal. A voluntary retirement is considered highly legitimate, but principal behaviors still affect outcomes (Ogawa & Smith 1985). The legitimacy of precipitating causes for succession also is complicated by the availability of promotional opportunities. Frequency of opportunity is a critical variable shaping reactions, symbolizing their own promotion opportunities and, subsequently, their responses to a new principal. If opportunities are infrequent, new principals face more resistance and resentment than when other opportunities may come along at any time. Teachers who aspire to the principalship sometimes feel that an outsider appointment limits their opportunities. "Your appointment made me feel like there was no place for me in the district" (Hart, 1987a).

Schools enfold the actions, beliefs, and interpretations of educators and pupils. Greenfield argued that these are the "stuff from which organizations are made" (1975, p. 71). As a new principal, your understandings of this "stuff" will influence the reality created by the women and men, boys and girls, whose labor you are assigned to lead. Miskel and Cosgrove (1985) asserted that your most critical function may be to influence the perceptions of teachers and pupils, the beliefs and dreams on which they choose to act.

PERSONAL CHARACTERISTICS AND BEHAVIOR

In addition to context, your personal characteristics and behavior affect the taking-charge and leadership process. These traits and behaviors interact with context, and it is wise to learn ways to emphasize traits and behaviors viewed positively by your school and district. We have no control over many personal characteristics that affect principal succession; nevertheless, if you are aware of the impacts of personal leader characteristics in succession, you can be better prepared to deal with them as you move into your first administrative role. Next we discuss four characteristics that strongly effect the taking-charge process and two behavior patterns shown to make a difference: (1) gender, (2) race and ethnicity, (3) insider-outsider status, and (4) kinship or personal ties; and (1) task-centered behavior, and (2) change-oriented behavior.

Gender

The gender of a principal affects the responses of school community members to her or him and the outcomes people attribute to the new principal (Shakeshaft, 1989). As we stated in Chapter 6, regardless of any conscious bias, people are more likely to attribute a group's performance to a leader's behavior when the leader is male. This factor is an "unconscious ideology" (Rice, Bender & Vitters, 1980). The gender of newly assigned leaders influences the interaction of group members and group performance, and these effects are culturally dependent (Garland & Price, 1977; Hollander, 1978; Smith & Peterson, 1988; Terborg, 1977).

Another feature of gender arises in relation to expectations about what it takes to be prepared to be a school leader. Superiors seem more likely to insist that women (as opposed to men) fill assistant or apprenticeship roles. Again, this may be partially explained by decision-makers' prior knowledge and familiarity with the individual. School board members are more likely to know teachers who perform extracurricular duties because of public contact and feedback than they are to know individual classroom teachers (Bredeson, 1991a). In Great Britain, for example, Weindling and Earley (1987) found that twenty-five percent (25%) of men worked as acting head teachers before being appointed to their first headship while forty percent (40%) of women were assigned acting roles first. Women spent significantly more time teaching and as deputy heads and were older at their first appointment. Even people completely outside education enforce these expectations. One woman principal shared an experience talking with a complete stranger on an airplane immediately after her appointment as a junior high school principal. Even though she was thirty-five at the time (the average age for first principal appointment for men), a man seated next to her exclaimed on hearing that she was a principal, "Aren't you awfully young to be a principal?"

Additionally, gender emerges as a factor in employment discrimination for school leaders. "[W]omen with children were three times as likely as men to have been demoted en route to a headship. Men rarely experienced demotion after absence from teaching, even when they had worked outside the education system" (Trown & Needham, 1981, in Weindling & Early, 1987, p. 25).

We also find that women candidates for educational leadership positions are rated somewhat differently than men. In an experimental study that examined the interaction of gender, position, vacancy, and candidate information, Bredeson (1992) found statistically significant interactions among three factors. He concluded that gender and position stereotypes explained significant differences between female and male candidates for the elementary assistant principal and elementary teaching positions. The primary purpose of this study was to examine the relative costs of providing information requested by school district employers that was clearly illegal according to E.E.O.C. guidelines. He found that background information on spouse and family results in lower ratings for women. Since there is clearly a penalty associated with this information, Bredeson recommended that, when requests for illegal information are made by school employers, candidates simply refuse.

Gender receives increasing attention as a leadership factor as more women aspire to leadership roles in schools. Dunlap and Schmuck (1994) recently presented a complex view of women in educational administration and of the interactions of gender and race in shaping women's leadership experiences. Many of the case studies and research reports collected in their volume describe pressures women in leadership face in schools. They feel they cannot join women's school leadership associations, for example, because their male colleagues and superiors label them as radical and unreasonable feminists or complain of reverse discrimination. We recommend that each aspiring principal, whether man or woman, be well versed in the dynamics affecting men's and women's interactions in leadership roles in order to have better personal experiences.

Race and Ethnicity

Within the traditional succession literature, race and ethnicity have received remarkably little attention, given the underrepresentation of people from minority groups in leadership positions. The *Digest of Education Statistics* (1991) reports the breakdown by ethnic and racial categories shown in Table 7.1.

TABLE 7.1. Profile of Public and Private School Principals by Gender, Race and Ethnicity[1]

Principals—Public Schools		
Total		78,889
Gender	Men	55,256
	Women	23,634
Race/ethnicity	White	67,794
	Black	6,770
	Hispanic	3,097
	Asian	529
	Native American	700
Principals—Private Schools		
Total		23,881
Gender	Men	11,640
	Women	12,241
Race/ethnicity	White	22,366
	Black	643
	Hispanic	607

[1]Data from *Digest of Education Statistics 1993*, National Center for Education Statistics, Washington, DC.

Researchers tend to include this factor in investigations of insider-outsider status, but outsider dynamics fail to capture the complexity of leader succession when the new leader lacks the highly visible personal traits people in the school associate with a leader-principal. Hart (1993) drew on social psychology theory and the literature of social criticism to call highly visible gender, race, or ethnicity characteristics "social incongruence." Teachers, parents, and students in the school have a mental picture of a principal or leader that includes the complement of personal characteristics of the kind of people customarily holding leadership positions. As Stogdill (1974) pointed out, these traits tended to be things like tall, white, athletic, male with high verbal acuity. When African Americans, Native Americans, or Hispanic Americans take charge as principals, they automatically encounter challenges to their integration not faced by new principals who possess socially congruent leader traits. The dominant ethnicity of the school matters, as well, as the new principal's characteristics are interpreted in context. Perceptions of social congruence are grounded in the characteristics of current leaders in schools. The numbers in Table 7.1 take on a special importance as we think about the changing demographics in society, especially in urban schools.

We do not want to make too much of differences among leaders, but the challenges faced by principals during succession are shaped within each setting. To ignore these differences is to ignore the reality of leader succession in today's schools. Anyone who doubts the intensity of these differences for the individual leader need only read Pedro Reyes' presidential address to the University Council for Educational Administration annual meeting (1993). In Chapter 12, when we turn to a personal framework for leadership, we address specifically actions that new principals can take to help them use their traits, including race and ethnicity, to make the most of their succession experiences.

Insider-Outsider

Your status as an insider or outsider also will affect the taking-charge process. Definitions of insider or outsider are constructed in the context of each school and district and depend on role stereotypes and customary expectations. Studies examine the likelihood that an outsider or insider will be appointed contingent on many factors. These include the status of the predecessor (e.g., a long tenure as principal, the forced or voluntary nature of her or his turnover); school performance; successor's leadership style (applying contingency theories—see Chapter 6); and growth in the school's area, size, and mission.

One of the most influential bodies of research on insiders and outsiders examined school superintendents (Carlson, 1962, 1972). Although this research was completed some time ago, it remains the most cited material on the insider-outsider and the local-cosmopolitan orientation of educational leaders. A group of dissertation studies completed at the University of Wisconsin-Madison contemporizes this finding. These studies revealed that insiders and outsiders have an equal likelihood of appointment when a board of education is satisfied with the district's performance (Beischel, 1994; Fitzpatrick, 1992; Kayon, 1993).

Insiders and outsiders face different constraints and advantages. Insiders tend to be adapters rather than innovators and may lack a clear mandate from their superiors. Their leeway often is hampered by the previous administration. Outsider appointments are more likely when a board is dissatisfied with the direction of the district. Outsiders are innovators, feel the board expects change, and benefit from strong board commitment.

While these findings are supported by other studies, the factors affecting the success of insiders and outsiders are complex. They may spring from social interactions that facilitate certain behaviors; they may arise from differences in the norms of the school where either insider or outsider appointments prevail; or they may be a function of the cosmopolitan or local orientation of the majority within the school, people who tend to move or remain loyal to a given organization during their careers (Carlson's place-bound and career-bound administrators). In a series of studies including pre- and postsuccession factors and using several data sets, the outsider-insider context in management succession was found to have distinct features that hold across organizations (Helmich, 1974, 1977; Helmich & Brown, 1972). Insiders tend to stay longer in office. Even after controlling for factors other than leader change that affect organizational change, it appears that outsider succession does indeed result in more change than does insider succession (Helmich & Brown, 1972). Other research confirms these outcomes. Fewer subordinates are replaced when insiders are appointed, and fewer changes are made in other roles (Gabarro, 1987). In times of poor performance, or when the environment is uncertain and problematic, scholars find that outside successors are more likely to make strategic internal changes and to be more effective in implementing successful turnarounds in performance than are successors appointed from inside the organization (Helmich, 1974; Helmich & Brown, 1972; Reinganum, 1985; Samuelson, Galbraith & McGuire, 1985).

Insiders have problems and advantages. Insider succession can cause problems when one or more of existing assistant or aspiring principals was an unsuccessful applicant for the position (Daum, 1975; Weindling & Earley, 1987). High internal rivalry raises particular obstacles to the success of an insider. And, as we note elsewhere, old friendships and relationships have an additional effect.

Outsiders also have some advantages, as long as they can avoid being labeled "deviant" by the group. Outsiders can counteract the power of interest groups and cliques, giving greater flexibility and latitude in ameliorating internal conflict to everyone involved. By doing so, they make it possible to redirect the course of the school (Becker, 1963; Gabarro, 1987).

Although little current research on the insider-outsider characteristics has been done in schools, scholars previously have explored the relationship between the principal as change agent and his or her work history. These studies affirm that outsiders are more inclined to view change in their schools as necessary for job advancement, are more career committed, and describe themselves as facile at persuading their superiors of the need for change. Their faculties more frequently describe them as change agents in the school (Ganz & Hoy, 1977). Cosgrove (1986) found that none of her subjects, all insider (in the district) successors to the principalship, felt they had a mandate for change from district executives or the school board. You may wish to systematically seek to learn whether or not some mandate was assumed during your succession.

The insider-outsider characteristic and the selection or prearrival stage (see stage frameworks discussion) also interact. Weindling and Earley (1987) found that some heads felt that a short list of internal candidates was created by superiors to give the appearance that insiders are being seriously considered. This "perceived 'poor' treatment of internal candidates had a deleterious effect not only on the individuals concerned, but also on the staff as a whole." As one head put it long after her own appointment, "It might make them feel better if they were all shortlisted" (p. 71). She saw the short list of insiders as a management strategy designed to control the behavior of those who are passed over.

While the relative advantage of insider or outsider principal succession is strongly contextual, several generalizations are warranted. Outsiders tend to make more changes in rules, structures, personnel, and procedures. They see change as important, both substantively and symbolically, for their success, and they feel that they have a mandate for change. Outsiders are less constrained by previous contacts, internal rivalries, and social patterns, and they owe no personal debts. They also lack important informal information about the school and an understanding of its history. During high intraschool conflict, this lack of knowledge may critically hamper their ability to form coalitions or to act decisively or quickly.

You should be alert to factors that influence responses to insider or outsider appointments. If you move into your first leadership role as an outsider, the presence of a favorite son or daughter passed over for your appointment may restrict your actions and shape early negative attitudes toward you. Your traits, beliefs, and skills may blend or clash with norms in the new school. If you are an insider, past experiences may shape people's early expectations and perceptions, limiting or facilitating your early success—especially if opportunities to demonstrate critical skills valued by the school are scarce. Studies suggest that, unlike the unknown outsider, an insider never really gets a honeymoon period, because the "new" leader is seen as a continuation (more or less) of the status quo (Weindling & Earley, 1987).

When principal selection processes are seen as administrative manipulation, the newly appointed principal, especially the outsider, needs to be aware of the effects of preappointment factors. For example, a suburban school district recently had the opportunity to replace all three of its elementary principals. During the first year, two principals were hired, one as a permanent replacement and one as a one-year appointment for the principal who was on sabbatical leave. During the year, a third principal announced her retirement, opening a third position. The school district, under the leadership of a newly appointed superintendent, was also making significant efforts to move toward school-based decision making. Teachers were asked to participate in all levels of critical decision making to help energize and move their educational missions forward. The disingenuousness of district and superintendent support for school-based decision making became apparent in the appointment of a new principal to replace the retiring principal. In this school, the teachers had become excited about the possibilities of bringing in a new principal. They looked forward to making substantive contributions to the screening and selection process for a new principal. Behind the scenes, however, the decision had already been made. The superintendent extended the temporary principal's administrative assignment. She had done an extremely good job as a new principal, and the staff really liked her. In fact, they persuaded the superintendent to move their original principal (who was on sabbatical leave) over to fill the retirement vacancy. The superintendent agreed that this would be a good way to keep two good principals; however, this decision to accept one faculty's preferences deprived the other faculty of any input into the selection process. With two principals already under contract, the staff at the retiring principal's school realized that their opportunity to influence the future of their school had been taken from them. Given this selection scenario, the outsider principal, within a context of manipulation and teachers' feelings of betrayal, faced a new staff soured by their experiences.

Many questions about insider-outsider succession remain unresolved. The definition of insiders is nebulous, depending on perceptions. For example, you may be considered an insider or an outsider if you originate from another school in the district; this distinction arises out of tradition, personal beliefs, group norms, or the mix of events. The case described above illustrates this ambivalence. In Great Britain, the majority of new heads are appointed from Outside their local education authority *and* their school. Of 188 new secondary heads they surveyed, only ten percent (10%) were appointed from within the school and only forty percent (40%) from within the local education authority (LEA) or district. While "the advantages to be gained from appointing an internal candidate [seem] to be quite small and [are] probably outweighed by the disadvantages," superiors must still contend with the strongly held belief that appointment to leadership roles is an important reward for long and loyal service (Weindling & Earley, 1987, p. 179). The reverse norm functions in most American school districts where outsider appointments are growing in the superintendency but are still fairly uncommon for principals in many school districts (Beischel, 1994; Kayon, 1993).

The research reviewed in the preceding section poses problems for the new or aspiring school principal. You ask yourself: "Am I a trusted insider or a suspect outsider?" "Should I seek information from informants or rely on my own sources and experience?" "Do I owe debts to teachers, peers, superiors, or constituents in the school or district?" "Do I have a mandate for action from my superiors?" "How do I know?"

The research speaks clearly: examine your particular succession experience. Rely on the interpretations and beliefs of the educators, parents, and community leaders with whom you work for your guide to your insider/outsider status. You may feel strongly that you are a team player, an insider. If those with whom you work perceive you as an outsider, your firmly held beliefs have no impact on their sense making or actions. In this setting, it matters not at all what you believe; people act on what they believe.

Relationships: Kinship and Personal Ties

Relationships among people affect succession. These relationships can be personally established or based on kinship ties. Nepotism has plagued many school districts, particularly in small communities where mobility is not the norm. In these communities, for example, it is not uncommon for the high school principal to be the nephew of the superintendent; the elementary school secretary to be the wife of the superintendent or the high school principal; and the business manager to be the sister-in-law of the school board president. Kinship affects generations of appointments to school leadership positions in a community or state, even when overt nepotism is not apparent (Buchanan, F., in press).

Personal relationships among people, included kinship, seem to affect leader appointments more when opportunities are limited than they do when opportunities are abundant (Boldt, 1978). The scarcity of school leadership positions is obvious in communities where there may be only one elementary school and a 7–12 high school whose principal may also be the district superintendent (a common situation in states where sparsity of population results in hundreds of small school districts). Again, we refer you to the *Digest of Educational Statistics* (1991). Currently there are approximately 15,000 school districts in the United States; however, more than half of the total number of students are found in the 100 largest school districts. Thousands of small local school districts continue to operate as the urbanization of society continues.

Personal linkages reveal relationship traits akin to family. Because formal leaders "do differentiate between subordinates" and "group averages of subordinate perceptions do not show the same relations with measures of leader style as do individual subordinate perceptions" (Smith & Peterson, 1988, pp. 36–37), the exchanges between a newly appointed principal and each person in the school will be important to the outcome of succession. While you should not be overly concerned about one person's negative response to you as a newly appointed school leader, the research suggests that you will do well to pay attention to individual perceptions of you and to their impacts on group perceptions. Positive reactions, too, can play an important role in framing perceptions of your leadership.

We previously identified the leader's behavior as an important factor in leader effects. Drawing on the task- and person-centered dimensions of leadership that often dominate discussions of leader behavior, principals and scholars who study them concentrate on behavior designed to accomplish tasks, support personal needs, and initiate change.

Task-centered and Person-centered Behaviors

In Chapter 6, we introduced the technical and human dimensions common to many concepts of leadership. The task-person duality of leader behaviors—so important to the progress of the general leadership literature—resurfaced in succession studies. These behaviors aimed at task accomplishment and human relations shape perceptions of the new principal.

The interpersonal dimension represents a principal's ability to move in an inclusionary role in the school (see Figure 6.4). Quality working relationships are associated with positive performance and personnel evaluations (Liden & Graen, 1980). Positive working relationships are associated with three salient outcomes. First, the new principal and others develop mutual expectations. Second, they come to trust each other in the general effort they all expend in behalf of the work. Third, they develop a bond of mutual influence "beyond that which is accorded the new manager and the subordinate by virtue of their roles" (Gabarro, 1987, p. 101). If a new principal is perceived as unfeeling, critical, or different in vital ways from the teachers and other staff, anxiety and productive collapse may result (Oskarsson & Klein, 1982).

The ability to accomplish tasks also affects judgments about new principals. When seen as competent in crucial tasks, their acceptance by the group is facilitated. Teachers will tend to be more receptive to new principals with clear task expertise, those who have proven themselves on required tasks. Beliefs about task competence are not solely dependent on observed behavior, however. Superiors, mentors, subordinates, and peers influence a new principal's reputation as a person who can get things done (or not). The principal Ogawa and his colleagues studied began his tenure with a very favorable reputation based on stories from other teachers and the district office. This favorable reputation bought him a lot of time on which he capitalized (Fauske & Ogawa, 1987; Hollander & Julian, 1978; Ogawa, 1991).

Interactions between the new principal and people in the school can also create a situation in which the principal comes to be seen as someone who can get things accomplished. If the principal emerges naturally from group interactions as someone who is active in defining tasks and task-related problems, proposing solutions and procedures, and soliciting solutions from others, he will be seen as a natural leader by the group. Some studies reveal that task behaviors are more influential in gaining acceptance for new principals than human relations behaviors, evidence underscoring the enhanced receptivity of groups to competent and knowledgeable successors revealed by experimental research (Hollander & Julian, 1978; Kunz & Hoy, 1976).

In addition to supportive or task-directed behaviors, principal succession often brings with it some expectation for change. Change often requires reframing or redefining core tasks, and leaders often function as the translators and definers of the direction of that change in an organization. Many successions occur as a result of belief in a need for change, and studies affirm that people expect a new manager to make changes. This functional perspective holds inherent appeal, because it addresses the fundamental issues schools care about regarding their leaders (Miklos, 1988; Schein, 1985).

Change-related behaviors by principals and other administrators are also related to succession stages. Observing that change takes place in a sequence of stages alternating between learning and action, three periods of change have been found to be common during succession: (1) early on during the taking-hold stage; (2) reshaping, following immersion in the organization's social and structural nature and intense learning; and (3) consolidation of position by the new manager. In one study of seventeen cases, the greatest period of change followed deep immersion in the organization (Gabarro, 1987; Parkay et al., 1992).

Change is also associated with successor background and situation. Earlier we discussed some of the most prominent personal characteristic factors. Principals also come to a school with a set of skills, beliefs, and expectations learned in other settings. The extent and nature of this experience seem to have a major effect on the way in which change is approached. Prior experience "profoundly influences the manager's actions and what he tends to focus on, as well as the kinds of problems he is likely to face" (Gabarro, 1987, p. 7). Another important situational factor successors use to shape change, experience within the enterprise at hand, influences the pace and scope of change. An elementary principal assigned for the first time as principal in a high school, for example, might be less quick to move on change because of less experience.

In the sense that almost all educational administrators are industry insiders, the relative rate of change might be predicted to be fairly rapid. Only nine percent (9%) of more heads (principals) in one study said no major changes had been introduced in their schools during their first year. The majority of these changes originated with the new head, and they often related to the image of the school, especially when the community had a low opinion of its school. New heads said that the pacing and timing of change played a critical part in their success. Planning for change began immediately upon succession, and many new heads who thought they would delay change found they could not delay. New school heads recognized "the importance of being seen by staff as someone who could get things done." Faculties, too, expected change. Virtually everyone expected that some change would accompany succession. The only exception they found was in a school where an insider was appointed (Weindling & Earley, 1987, p. 103).

Change may be seen as good or bad. In the British study, reactions to change were favorable in six schools, negative in four schools, and mixed in six schools. Five years later, however, the criticism often accompanied the "go slowly" decision:

> Before they take up their post, new heads are often given one of two pieces of conflicting advice: "Go in and make an impact," or "Do nothing for a year." The current research suggests that both are misguided. New heads need to make some early changes which are not controversial and are, in fact, welcomed by the majority of staff. At the same time they should carefully assess the situation and plant the seeds for future innovation. (Earley, Baker & Weindling, 1990, p. 25)

One new head offered this advice to new school leaders:

> Timing is important. You have got to be an opportunist, rather than simply assuming you can introduce any change just when you want to. Seize the opportunity when you see an interest. You have got to have the support of people who are going to make the change. (p. 24)

Some major dilemmas related to change remain for new principals. Although studies reveal the salutary effects of timely and appropriate change following succession, judgments of timeliness and appropriateness require some thought. Tension remains between the need to move quickly and in a timely fashion in order to avoid the loss of opportunity and the need to respond to and thoroughly understand organizational problems and needs. Decisive change may be the more important behavior, as the new principal "may lose credibility because he appears indecisive" Gabarro, (1987, p. 91).

In your unique setting and circumstances, how do you balance the need and expectation for change against the need for information gathering, analysis, and planning? Research suggests a number of principles. Make some changes that improve the quality of work life in the school early. Do not disrupt cultural taboos. Set the stage for changes in the future. Break down the business-as-usual norms that build up when nothing new happens following a succession. At the same time, pursue the information-gathering activities, analysis, and planning laid out in other chapters in this book.

LEADER SUCCESSION STAGES

In Chapter 4, we introduced the notion of organizational socialization and the stages through which newcomers pass in their relationships with a new social group. We also discussed the special situation a formally appointed new leader faces under these circumstances. We presented three general stages: anticipation and confrontation, accommodation and integration, and stabilization as educational leadership and professional actualization. Leader succession research approaches the stages issue a bit differently, providing additional insight to the experience you can expect as a newly appointed school principal.

These stage approaches offer some guidance about actions you can plan that will help improve your experience. In the taking-hold stage, you will feel pressed by the exigencies of grasping the new situation and may have time for little sensemaking and the attendant "double-loop learning" that reflection makes possible. This is a time of concrete experience and active experimentation. The immersion stage provides more opportunity for reflection. Reflection leads to more abstract understanding of the nature of the school (construction of your own theoretical maps of the sociotechnical system), because this period provides the opportunity to learn from the actions of the previous stage and examine underlying social assumptions governing behavior. The reshaping stage is heavily action-oriented—a period of active experimentation and concrete observation exploiting the more reflective learning which took place during the immersion stage.

Acknowledging the interaction dynamics in succession events, recent models provide a fourth approach to understanding succession. These models attempt to synthesize the impacts of leadership, change, and culture on the organization across time. They examine the processes and stages of interaction among people and context variables. These studies point to factors like the breadth and rigor of the search for a successor, the presence of insider favorites with power in the organization, crises brought on by poor performance, the power and expertise of selection agents or sponsors, and successor contacts.

Two process models appear to unify approaches to succession. One model emphasizes stages: presuccession, and postsuccession. The second model combines situational variables. Modifications of these approaches particularly useful to educational leaders resulted in a focus on process, context, and outputs resulting during prearrival, arrival, and succession effects. The important pre-arrival factors in this approach are reasons for the succession, selection processes, reputations of leaders, and orientations of leaders. During arrival, demography, organizational structure, school culture, educational programs, successor actions, community, and school effectiveness are important. Succession effects included changes in reputations, orientations, and arrival factors (which set the stage for the next succession) (Gordon & Rosen, 1981; Miskel & Cosgrove, 1985).

Extensions of these stage frameworks support the point of view that inter-action effects of leader and context are underemphasized in many approaches to succession. The traditional research underrepresents the complexity of the social environment in which succession takes place. In Chapter 10, we discuss this process in greater detail as part of the process of becoming a principal.

Stages of a new leader's entry intrigue writers interested in a wide range of questions related to leadership succession. The actual replacement of the incumbent sometimes divides the prearrival stage into four parts: (1) establishing the need for a succession event; (2) determining selection criteria; (3) selecting candidates; and (4) choosing among the candidates. Practitioners of educational administration (and the authors) recognize these steps as artifi-cially rational and hierarchically ordered. Yet they provide insight into who is involved, the reasons they give for their decisions, procedures followed, the time span over which events take place, and the amount of organizational effort expended—time, energy, and financial resources (Friedman 1986; Jentz, 1982). Stages sometimes appear as anticipation; appointment; inauguration; honeymoon; assertion of personality, style, and programs, working through differences; and equilibrium. The new principal should be prepared for sur-prises and the need to make sense out of these surprises, as well. Unfortu-nately, negative surprises usually outnumber positive ones (Smircich, 1983).

You will want to take care to meet the earliest stages of your appointment and arrival with thoughtful skepticism. The air of expectancy, excitement, and optimistism—teachers looking to the you for a fresh start—should be kept in perspective. Some new principals see this sincere welcome as undue pressure to work miracles, pressure to achieve as the new champion or savior. One new head said, "I think the staff here had unrealistic expectations of me and wanted someone who could 'walk on water.' " (Ordinary mortals need not apply.)

CONCLUSION: COMBINING AND EXPANDING VIEWS OF SUCCESSION

This introduction to the leader succession scholarship illustrates the impor-tance of attending to specific factors that will affect the quality of your own taking-charge experience. While books about the principalship rightly address the functions principals are expected to perform, and the people who appoint principals justifiably expect principals to get the routine tasks done that keep a school running, the symbolic and interactive dimensions of succession set the stage for all subsequent actions involving the principal and the school. In Chapter 6 and in this chapter, we presented evidence that personal characteristics, beliefs, actions, organizational and social characteristics, cultures, inter-action, environment, and context shape the ultimate impact of a principal succession.

Ultimately, each principal's goal is to affect student learning positively. In the next chapter, we examine the factors enhancing the likelihood that this goal will be attained using social-symbolic interaction among teachers, principal, and community. In Chapter 9, we then move to a discussion of the factors shown to enhance principal influence over school and student performance. The relationship between principals' actions, students' learning, and school-wide outcomes is subtle, complex, and indirect. Careful planning will help you succeed in shaping this relationship.

SUGGESTED ACTIVITIES

1. In your present work context, name three contextual factors you see as most powerful in constraining principals' decision-making alternatives. What specific actions to expand these alternatives would you recommend to principals? Why?
2. The district in which you work has a system for selecting and orienting new principals. Describe the *formal* and *informal* succession systems in your school district and the impacts the features of the system might have on new principals.
3. What personal characteristics do you possess that could be predicted to have an impact on your succession to a principalship? What context factors might interact with these personal characteristics that you should attend to and why?
4. Describe your ability to use task-centered and person-centered behaviors with other adults, particularly those you have been assigned to supervise. How might these abilities affect your succession experiences when you become a principal?
5. Interview a principal who has taken over a school for the first time within the past year. Using the stage frameworks and issues relevant to leadership succession presented in the chapter to design questions about the principal's experience. What "stage" would you say this principal is in and why?

Leadership Through Social-Symbolic Interaction

One of the authors received an early lesson in the importance of communication and interaction with school faculty and staff. As a newly assigned junior high school principal, I was surprised to learn that the district and school in which I worked held parent-teacher conferences each semester only during the afternoon. Because so many fathers were unable to attend at that time and so many mothers worked (a great many as teachers in the district), I felt that we should hold conferences during some evening hours. In other school districts I had worked for, conferences were held on two consecutive afternoons and evenings, and school was closed the following Friday to make up the time for the teachers. I suggested during a regular faculty meeting that we try such a model in our school and asked for input and ideas. No discussion ensued and no comments were forthcoming in the following week, so I proceeded to schedule parent-teacher conferences and sent a letter to the parents describing the new hours and our hope that more parents would be able to attend.

A few days before the scheduled conferences, I received a telephone call from the district union officer, followed by a visit from the school representative, informing me that a formal complaint had been filed against me for violating the teacher contract. My position was that these conferences were covered by the provision requiring the teachers to attend to "other activities and duties as assigned" and that the free Friday more than compensated for the evening hours. Their position was that I had made an arbitrary decision. My initial response was frustration and anger. I had asked for input, invited criticism and comment, and received neither. Complicating the situation further, I had already announced the evening hours to parents. An extended conversation with the school union representative revealed that the complaint was filed by a young woman on the faculty who received a call from an out-of-town boyfriend inviting her out on one of the nights scheduled for conferences. He would be in town only during the scheduled evenings, and she would not be able to spend time with him unless the schedule was changed.

Unable to change the conferences, we struck a bargain. All the teachers would keep a record of the parents attending conferences and the times of their visits. We would examine these data after the fall conferences and decide how to schedule spring conferences on the basis of their attendance and needs. Second, I excused the teacher from attendance at the conference during the second night if she would communicate with the parents of her students so that they would know when she could be reached. Because she was a resource special education teacher, she had fewer parents to see. The attendance logs teachers kept revealed that parents preferred the evening hours but attendance was heaviest between 5:00 P.M. and 7:00 P.M. We used these data to shorten the hours scheduled in the spring—one day from 3:00 P.M. to 8:00 P.M. and one day from 1:00 P.M. to 6:00 P.M.

I learned several things from this experience. First, the decision was better informed because it accommodated the needs of both parents and staff. Second, I was able to design a more appropriate schedule for conferences because of the data we gathered. Finally, the experience invited more open communication from the staff about their needs, and many told me they were more willing to communicate directly with me about their needs and opinions than they had been before the conflict over conferences.

In preceding chapters we explored personal experiences of new principals. New principals described how the people in their schools affected their leadership experiences. Interaction with teachers played a particularly powerful part in these accounts. Later we reviewed empirical research yielding strong affirming evidence that the outcomes of a new principal's succession emerge largely out of her interactions with others in the school rather than as a one-way effect of her leadership *on* a school. In this chapter, we provide a look at some theories and concepts underlying empirical research and framing our understanding of personal experiences. They offer conceptual maps for understanding how new principals who wish to exercise leadership in schools can better analyze, understand, and plan their work. We have found them to be useful models for this purpose.

The forces motivating people to interact, the social processes of interaction, and the social structure, environments, and outcomes of interaction all contribute to the organizational effects we group under the general label *leadership*. While we acknowledge and affirm the effects you and other principals will have on the schools in which you serve, this chapter is devoted to expanding your knowledge of the reciprocal nature of leadership and its effects on principals, teachers, and staff. By improving your ability to use this knowledge, you will enhance your impact on the schools you are selected to lead.

This chapter focuses on two issues critical to understanding the implications of leadership as interaction: (1) interaction as the unit of analysis for examining leadership issues during the taking-charge process in schools and (2) processes of interaction shaping leadership and its outcomes. In the first section we draw on the writings of Turner (1988) and Schein (1985) for models that illustrate why interaction is an appropriate focus of inquiry and intervention. In the second section, we discuss several process theories of interaction.

We have repeatedly emphasized that principals function in professional work groups. The interaction between the principal and people in the school consequently takes on an importance of its own; the process itself warrants careful attention.

While each person's experience is essentially unique, the new principal also is a group member. If a principal is new to the district also, she must learn to function within the school and district at many levels. She must interact with established individuals, subgroups, and coalitions.

Interaction can be broadly defined as the overt actions (including language), covert deliberations and plans, and physical presence and gestures of one person that influence others in a continuing cycle of exchange and communication. Note that this definition emphasizes interaction on many levels—conscious and unconscious, verbal and nonverbal. Interaction occurs in schools between individuals, between individuals and subgroups, and between subgroups.

Interaction differs from action because it is meaningfully oriented toward the actions of others. Interactions can be motivated by deliberate and calculated thought, emotion, or tradition and custom. For example, most school districts establish rules and formal processes for selecting principals. The interactions that spring from these processes involve clearly observable and dependable steps. An emotionally driven selection process might occur when a crisis, personal loyalty, dislike, affection, or other emotion affected the choice—"gut feelings." A superintendent may select a new principal because she likes him, regardless of written procedures or custom. You may recall in Chapter 7, we described one such experience in which a superintendent ignored formal plans and his own assertions about site-based decision making and imposed a principal on an elementary school.

Finally, some principal selection processes are established by tradition. They are tacit and customary. Many principals report that they experienced this form of selection. Their principals or other school administrators approached them, told them that they would make fine principals, and suggested that they get administrative certificates. When administrative positions became available, they were appointed (to no one's surprise).

As you take on your first and subsequent school leadership positions (or perhaps reflect on assignments you have had), you will note that people need some motivation to interact and that interactions take on repeated patterns over time, establishing rough structures that people come to expect. One useful way to look at principals' interactions in schools highlights the motivation to interact, the interaction process, and emerging structures.

Motivation, Interaction, and Structure

The complexity of schools and their multiple components pose daunting challenges for principals when they strive to make some systematic sense of their work. This complexity often frustrates new principals so that they throw up their hands in surrender and return to routine and safe patterns learned during their careers as educators. The motivation, interaction, structure model can help you avoid this surrender. Motivation energizes and mobilizes people to interact; interaction highlights how people use symbols and gestures (including language), plans, and physical presence to communicate with others in their group; and structure emerges from the patterns that thereby become established in a school. These patterns allow people to repeat and organize their interactions. Social structures that a new principal can describe, use, and affect thus become more apparent and more easily understood, as well as a source of leadership influence.

Because interactions in each unique school are indeterminate and spontaneous, you can use this model to focus your attention on the dynamics and elements of the interactions that occur during your taking-charge experience.

Motivation

The first element in the interaction model captures factors and processes that stimulate the motivation to interact. Interaction takes time and effort, and people are more or less willing to expend that effort depending on the payoff they expect from their experience, and the level of effort required. Earlier we discussed the propensity of those who select principals (and other managers, as well) to appoint people who are like themselves—thus perpetuating inequities of race, ethnicity, or gender. The tendency toward "homosocial reproduction" influences selection processes in the absence of any overt prejudice, because superiors recognize and trust familiar qualities in other people. Visible differences like gender, race, and ethnicity, then, can suppress the motivation to interact, because interaction requires more effort to get to know the person and requires that one monitor one's own behavior. Teachers often exhibit these tendencies in their motivation to interact with a new principal who differs significantly from culturally established preconceptions of "principal," thus limiting her potential influence.

Motivation can come from many sources. A simple exchange of benefits provides one motive: I'll participate in the school-site council if you'll teach my class once a month. A teacher might be motivated to obtain a desirable room assignment or gain influence over a new principal's beliefs and actions. People may be motivated to interact in schools to affirm their professional identities as valuable teachers; to participate in a ritual, ceremony, or tradition such as graduation; to gain group acceptance (as "leaders"); or to shape the outcome of events (a definition of what really is happening). In the last instance, for example, a superintendent might be motivated to take an active part in principal appointments to shape others' view of her as an instructional leader with high standards, thus leading to the perception that she is improving instruction in a school district.

Interaction Processes

While the motivation to interact begins the process, interaction events and processes reveal what people do when they influence each other. During the interaction process in schools, teachers, students, and principals signal a course of behavior, interpret their own signals, and interpret the signals of others.

They then act in response to their interpretations, and the cycle repeats itself. Student discipline is one of the most common interaction processes in schools in which principals, teachers, students, and parents all interact. In middle and junior high schools in particular, much effort is often directed toward the formulation of school discipline systems that affect schoolwide and within-classroom interactions. The principal's part in these systems can range from that of ultimate enforcer, to whom all transgressors are referred, to that of laissez-faire minimizer, who judges teachers by their ability to avoid sending transgressors her way. Important principles like consistency, strictness, respect, responsibility, and many others get tied up in these student discipline interactions, so much so that many school districts have adopted policies that block high school graduation for students with poor citizenship marks.

The majority of principals' interactions are verbal. Words play a critical part in understanding and influencing others, because we usually assume words mean the same or essentially the same thing to different people. People have the capacity to think, imagine, rehearse alternatives, foresee outcomes, avoid inappropriate responses, and select a course of action, and they can understand and assume the perspective and attitudes of groups or communities. For example, in some districts the dominant attitudes might be "in this district we always have prayer at graduation."

This all sounds very rational, but the process can have very different effects and interpretations. In any interaction, our selective perception frames beliefs about ourselves, how others frame their beliefs about self, how they think and act, and how we interpret interactive situations. We save information about these interactions as stocks of knowledge to be used during subsequent experiences. For example, a principal's visits to classrooms may be seen as interference or as caring attention. These divergent judgments may emanate from unhappy past experiences or reflect conventional practice in a school. Delegation of authority may be judged as empowering or as a sign of weakness. Decentralized decision-making and management styles, using alternative conflict management or dispute resolution processes, may confuse and frustrate colleagues used to traditional hierarchies of authority and control.

Structuring Processes

The third element of Turner's theory of interaction is structure. Over time, interactions are repeated and the group expects strict adherence to established patterns. These structured interactions may be repeated at preestablished times and places as well as in preestablished ways. The norms governing social interactions between teachers and the principal are dimensions of school culture (social structure). Recently, one of the most hotly discussed and debated elements of culture-structure in high schools involved the appropriateness of prayer at high school graduation and baccalaureate ceremonies. While prayers offered by local religious leaders or students were customarily a part of graduation ceremonies some decades ago, new interaction pressures and judicial rulings are restructuring expectations, social processes, school traditions, and the school culture.

For a school culture or social structure to develop and persist, repetition must occur. Some scholars use repetition and the persistence of a practice through succeeding generations of teachers and students to judge the impact of a principal on a school's culture. Culture, repeated patterns of social interaction and expectations, is a powerful mechanism through which principals influence their schools. Consequently, the structuring processes of interactions when a new principal is appointed form the foundation for long-term positive or negative effects on the school that go beyond actual interaction events (Deal & Peterson, 1990; Pettigrew, 1979; Schein, 1985; Smith & Peterson, 1988).

School Culture Structuring Interaction

The preceding emphasis on structured interactions as manifestations of school cultures leads to a second approach you can use to better understand interactions in a school. Organizational culture provides a framework for organizing an analysis of interactions during a change in principals. Scholars sometimes even define organizational culture as an outcome of interaction among group members and between the group and the environment. Using this definition, you might examine several levels of culture in a school: (1) cultural elements common to education and schools in general, (2) cultural elements characteristic of the district and community, (3) cultural elements common to the kind of school to which you are assigned (i.e., K–12, K–6, 9–12, parochial), and (4) cultural elements unique to the mix of people in that particular school.

To understand cultural elements on all these levels, you must look for ways to reveal and analyze basic and unconscious assumptions and beliefs held at the level of shared understanding by the teachers, students, and other members of the school. These assumptions and beliefs may be completely taken for granted, and they guide and shape people's view of their school and its relationship to the district and community. To examine these deeply embedded assumptions and beliefs, you may need to enlist the assistance of an outsider, perhaps a peer principal or a trusted mentor, to discuss events and characteristics of the school that you are discovering, because insiders often take these beliefs so for granted that they are hardly aware of them. Because these beliefs and assumptions have repeatedly helped people solve problems in the past, they come to be seen as reality, whether they accurately represent the challenges of the present or not.

Other less general and abstract meanings for organizational culture on which you can draw exist as well. Schein provides some examples. These include observed, regular behaviors; norms; dominant espoused values; philosophy; rules; and feeling or climate.

First, culture includes *observed and regular behaviors.* When teachers, students, and principals interact, they use patterns of language, and certain rituals surround deference and demeanor among them. These could include such things as customs for greeting or addressing people. Teachers may call each other by their first names yet address the principal as "Ms." or "Dr." They may insist that students address them by their surnames or adopt a casual, first-name greeting. Culture may include the way teachers walk into the principal's open door and receive immediate attention and a hearing for a grievance or professional concern, or the requirement that they make an appointment. It may include expectations about student behavior, and how to act when the principal brings visitors to a classroom.

A second concrete aspect of culture that a new principal can observe involves the *norms* developed within the school. (Remember the accepted and expected behaviors discussed in Chapter 6.) For example, work actions by teachers often include discussions of "a fair day's work for a fair day's pay." We pointed out earlier that, if a teacher arrives too early or leaves too late (according to the school norms for the majority of teachers), he violates this norm, even though he may be a superb teacher, and he may experience isolation, criticism, or other kinds of sanctions from the rest of the faculty. A norm may also include the expectation that grade-level teams in an elementary school plan all field trips and activities together, sharing the tasks of planning and the resources of different teachers. A teacher who planned a field trip limited to his class would violate this norm. Norms function independently of judgments about their relative functional or dysfunctional effects.

Third, culture includes the dominant *values* espoused by those in the school. Examples often touted include things like "high academic standards," "individualized instruction," "fostering diversity," or "every child is a winner." Many schools have begun to hold cultural diversity celebrations. Students and parents are encouraged to perform dances, theater, and music from their culture of origin; food fairs are held to raise money and give students the chance to taste one another's cuisine; and students are encouraged to wear clothing from their parents', grandparents', or ancestors' cultures. Other schools promote high academic achievement by designing academic olympics, holding academic award ceremonies, and providing rewards to high performers each term. Schools also celebrate athletic prowess, the spirit of competition, and individual versus group success through their rituals and rewards.

A fourth commonly experienced manifestation of school culture can be found in the *philosophy* that guides a school or district's policy toward administrators, teachers, and students. While similar to dominant values, philosophy functions at a broader level and frames values. Philosophies with direct effects on the way schools are operated include open-classroom schools, parent co-op schools, magnet specialty programs, outcome-based schools, and integrated-curriculum schools. Sizer's Coalition of Essential Schools and the Charter School Movement provide cohesive, nationally prominent examples of school cultures guided by highly visible and powerful philosophies.

Fifth, culture includes the *unwritten rules* of the game for getting along in the school, "the ropes" that a newcomer must learn in order to become an accepted member. We have referred to this aspect of culture as "the way we do things around here" in previous discussions. Everything from the way students line up to enter the building before school to the distribution of supplies can be included in these rules, and they may or may not seem important or even functional to an outsider. Attempts to change them, however, often result in resistance and emotion far out of proportion to their educational importance.

Culture is conveyed to an outsider by a sixth feature—the *feel or climate* people experience through the school's physical layout and the way in which members of the school interact with students, parents, or other outsiders. The physical decay and sense of personal threat described by many who enter urban schools convey an attitude of disregard, even of hostility, on the part of the school toward all who enter there and toward the children and youth who study there (Kozol, 1991).

We emphasize that careful observations, analysis, and understanding of various aspects of culture do not mean that new principals blindly or passively accept existing cultural norms. As we argued in earlier sections of this book, some aspects of school culture may be very dysfunctional for growth and learning by adults and students. Detailed, careful analysis and shared commitment, however, are needed before principals can initiate change in important aspects of school culture.

The abstract features of embedded assumptions and beliefs and the more general and observable features just described can be accessible to an attentive and systematic analysis by a new principal through the interaction patterns among teachers, staff, students, and parents. All kinds of customs and behaviors can help a principal come to know a new school better. Examples of these behavior patterns abound: Football players never take exams during fall term. Teachers take professional leave days for the duck, deer, or elk hunt (depending on where the school is located), while administrators look the other way. The PTA president always quietly picks the teachers his or her children will have. The interactions among teachers, administrators, parents, students, and staff that are routine and accepted as the "way we do things around here" are the focus of a new principal's analysis from this point of view. In this way, she comes to know more about the patterns that guide the group and can assess the effects of changes she believes should be introduced (Louis, 1980).

The complexity of interactions among people in the school also makes definitive judgments about the essence of and relative usefulness or goodness of particular values within a culture impossible. Leaders often are judged on the basis of criteria drawn from the context, so cultures are good or bad in relation to each value within each context. For example, a school culture valuing ethnic diversity can exhibit healthy outcomes by focusing on respect for different languages, food, clothing, physical types, and family structures. This value for diversity can exhibit dysfunctional outcomes if educational values that disadvantage students in later life dominate elements of the diverse community culture, and the school yields to these pressures by guiding all children from this group away from higher education aspirations (Kerchner, 1990). Evidence is mounting, in fact, that prescriptive models that specify what a "good culture" is (such as that offered by Peters and Waterman, 1982) are either incomplete or wrong (Hitt & Ireland, 1987). Describing the experience principals often have when attempting to influence school culture, Deal and Peterson pointed out that

> a school's culture has been created well before most principals arrive; it will
> exist long after most leave. Only a few principals may have the opportunity to

start afresh in a brand-new school, but even then the new teachers and students will carry cultural imprints from their previous place—as will the principal.

Most principals must work with a cultural tapestry that is already woven. They must somehow reinforce thin spots or tears, shape it to cover different or changed surfaces, or even try to reverse the fabric without unraveling the shared meaning. There is a delicate balance between a principal's doing nothing and doing harm. The Chinese call this balance *wei-wu*, the place between inaction and undue force. This balance is at the center of effective symbolic leadership and cultural change. (1990, p. 14)

This introduction to evidence that interaction between the principal and the school yields useful information to a new principal leads naturally to questions about the nature of interaction. Several different perspectives on the interaction process can provide useful conceptual maps for principals seeking to better understand their leadership interactions.

PROCESS THEORIES OF INTERACTION

Process theories of interaction often serve as research frameworks for leadership studies—to explain followers' and leaders' behaviors or to describe the nature of their relationships. Many process theories explaining motivation to interact depend on a very rational view of choice and behavior. They assume that people weigh the relative costs and benefits of choices and the utility or appeal of outcomes or payoffs they expect. They also assume that values are clear, and that people will remember their losses and gains in past choices and use that memory when making future choices. Rational theories also assume that people have access to the relevant information necessary to weigh various advantages or disadvantages of interaction and the conscious ability to assess the relative utility or value of projected outcomes.

Were this true, educators involved in the selection of a new principal would interact on the basis of unambiguous notions about the purpose of schools, the qualities of each candidate, and the impact on school outcomes each candidate would have. They would know what they want (at least in the near future), remember what principals had succeeded or failed to give them in the past, and know what each candidate was likely to be able to give. They then would choose among the candidates after weighing all these data. Reflect on principal selections you have participated in or heard about. Do any of these features match the processes you are familiar with? How have they been different?

Less rational processes also affect interactions in schools. For example, some perspectives on interaction rely on the understanding of "folk practices" by those who participate in them, concepts of belonging, and the definition of facts. Others explore concepts of self and others, trust, signals, gestures, and information processing that create an attributed meaning. Still another interaction perspective views our concepts of ourselves as constructed myths—stories that represent what we believe we are. Each of these views provides insight into the processes experienced by teachers and principals when a new principal is chosen. In the following sections we describe basic principles, including diverse views of interaction processes, and contributions that individuals can make to improve the taking-charge process for principals.

Exchange

Earlier in the chapter we introduced the concept of exchange and profit as a motivator for interaction. Exchange also results in specific processes between teachers or between teachers and the principal, trading services and benefits. If a teacher volunteers to stay late for a week and supervise the student drama club's rehearsals during the drama teacher's illness, the drama teacher should expect to give some favor or benefit in return. From an exchange perspective, the relationships between a principal and a teacher (or teacher leader and teacher) are personal and depend on the relative benefit each can derive from the relationship. Exchange benefits can take many forms—power, influence, money, advantageous work, or classroom assignments. One dysfunctional outcome of these relationships in secondary schools can be seen in teaching assignments when experienced teachers who have worked with the principal for a long time receive the best schedules (one or two preparations, honors or advanced-placement classes) and new, inexperienced teachers are assigned six different preparations out of a seven-period day, sometimes traveling from room to room. These bargains result in the least experienced teachers' filling the most difficult assignments.

For exchanges to work, people need not win in some imaginary contest. They need only make some profit, and that profit may reflect progress toward goals accepted by others in the school, such as a favorable schedule or room assignment or new textbooks. Exchanges also do not depend on the assumption that people are rational. They do, however, depend on calculations and negotiations over the valued resources a new principal is willing to give up (control over a decision) in order to receive valued resources from teachers (support for a new reading program).

Resources have broad meanings. They include social and personal as well as economic benefits. Obligations developed through exchange become a web of obligations that may be called in at any time and in support of many issues (a problem for insider successors). Teachers who have benefited from a union's assistance during salary negotiations may feel obligated to oppose a school reform plan that the union opposes, for example. The most "crucial distinction is that social exchange entails *unspecified* obligations. . . . [It engenders] feelings of personal obligation, gratitude, and trust" (Blau, 1967, p. 93).

If a new principal is to use the principles of exchange to establish relationships with others in a school, she needs an understanding of its ambiguous and nonrational aspects. Expectations, for example, play a critical part in the value people assign to the resources being exchanged. If teachers value time for professional preparation, then time is a valued currency of exchange. The power of a benefit a principal offers to teachers depends as much on the expectations and values of the teachers as it does on the actual benefit they may receive. People tend to develop their values from their past choices and experiences.

Expectations teachers and principals hold can take a number of forms:

1. general expectations of the total benefits that can be accrued from work and relationships in a school;
2. expectations about a particular person—ways in which he or she can give rewards for actions and ways in which the rewards conform to accepted standards; and
3. expectations that, when the costs of working together are deducted (time, loss of autonomy, etc.), the comparative rewards of the interaction warrant the effort.

In the first case, a teacher may be unwilling to invest in site-based decision making at the urging of a new principal because she doubts that she or her students will benefit or her working life be improved by her investment of time and effort. In the second case, the teacher may disbelieve a principal's assertion that she can provide a promised reward (money for summer time, for example). In the last case, a teacher may look at the balance sheet between costs and rewards and conclude that the costs outweigh the promised benefits. In all three cases, expectations would suppress teacher participation.

At the most personal level, exchange is sometimes seen as a series of favors that make people grateful, lead to expressions of that gratitude, and make doing favors enjoyable: "One good deed deserves another." Many principals and teachers never move past this level in their exchange relationships. Consequently, other teachers sometimes accuse those involved in such relationships of toadying, or they say that a principal is "buying" favors. On a more positive note, exchange can provide a means through which a new principal gradually establishes relationships with teachers and others and becomes an integrated member of the school. He can begin the process of establishing necessary ties binding him to people in the school and linking all to shared values and purposes.

Exchange processes are not limited to the individual level. Group obligations, too, can develop. Exchange theories view this group effect as an outcome of personal (dyadic) exchanges. As a new principal gradually provides valued outcomes for the school as a whole, for example, shared values are marshaled to become currency in a social contract of sorts. Exchange theory postulates that this process creates legitimate power for a new leader and transforms obligations into authority. Loyalty and compliance with the new principal's leadership thus become social obligations enforced by the majority of teachers in the school (Festinger, 1957). If this occurs, a principal will no longer need to rely solely on the personal obligations established through exchanges with a few loyal teachers, nor on the formal authority of position. For example, one of the authors negotiated with the school board for teachers to make up a snow day on a Saturday so that teachers could end their school year on schedule. Going to bat for the teachers is a common exchange for the group in which principals engender teacher loyalty. Buffering teachers from intrusive external pressures, supporting them in conflicts with parents, and promoting teachers' professional image and contributions to the community at public occasions are other examples of leadership through exchange in action.

A number of criticisms have been lodged against the exchange perspective on interaction. First, it isolates incidents, deemphasizing chains of responses and individual preferences. The assessment of value or benefit and the cost of the exchange are unique to each person; it may be hard to tell what a teacher wants as opposed to what "teachers" want. Second, it depends on the assumption that people have unambiguous and well-ordered values—that teachers, parents, and others know what they want and in what order. Third, it relies on people's ability to calculate their choices on the basis of clear values, complete and accurate information, experience with profits and losses, and maximized benefit. In a profession characterized by unclear goals and ambiguous outcomes, such as education this may be unreasonable.

Talk: Verbal Interactions at Work

Another approach to an interaction analysis of leadership relies on detailed analyses of interaction processes among people, especially the analysis of talk. This seems a uniquely suitable method for understanding principals' leadership, because the vast majority of their interactions are verbal. By understanding how patterns of talk among new principals, teachers, and others develop, new principals can seek to influence the effects of the new assignment to a school. By better understanding the patterns of social interaction in their schools, new principals can hope to affect them (Bredeson, 1987, 1988; Gronn, 1983; Heritage, 1984; Kmetz & Willower, 1982; Martin & Willower, 1981; Peterson, 1985).

This form of conversational analysis sometimes is called *ethnomethods*. Ethnomethods can be defined as implicit practices in a group that create a presumption that all in the group share a common world. By concentrating on patterns of conversation, new principals can learn about processes of interaction and implicit assumptions and beliefs held in common by teachers, staff, and students in their schools (Cicourel et al., 1974; Garfinkel, 1967; Heritage, 1984).

The discussion of what is real and what is illusion serves a concrete purpose in understanding talk between new principals and the people who work in schools. If people act on their "realities," illusionary or not, the question of their substantive reality is moot. If a new principal, for example, is viewed as a "hatchet man" by teachers, hired by the school board to "clean house," teacher interactions with the principal, the language used to explain their interactions, and the outcomes that result will reflect that reality. From this perspective, talk among teachers serves as the primary means through which their shared view of reality is established. People must talk together about a new principal and the events leading up to her appointment, interpret the meanings others are beginning to develop, and share their interpretations with each other to establish a group version of what is happening.

Another contribution of talk analysis emerges from the content of the talk and ways in which it can be manipulated by teachers when interacting with the new principal. Newcomers respond in unique ways to a group in part because they receive different kinds of information than do established members. By giving or withholding information or providing information in particular ways, established teachers shape the interpretations and responses of a new principal. Some established teachers may be very assertive, moving to present their view of the school to a new principal in an attempt to affect the thinking of this influential new member. Deliberate stories or myths frequently told to newcomers to teach them a cultural content may provide only part of the story and may or may not match with actual assumptions that operate, so you will benefit by withholding early judgments about the nature of the actual shared reality shaping teachers' work, parents' attitudes, and your interactions with superiors (Jones, 1986; Smith & Simmons, 1983).

Symbolic Interactionism

The exchange of language and gesture—symbolic interactionism—provides another perspective and explanation for the part communication plays in sustaining a shared view of experiences in schools. In addition to exploring the enduring means through which people communicate and interact, symbolic interactionism examines ways in which people develop self-concepts and assess themselves based on their beliefs about how others see and evaluate them. It provides a foundation for exploring how you might come to view yourself and how others in the school can shape that view. Symbolic interactionism relies on symbols in many forms such as talk, physical gestures, smells, dress or adornment, intonation of voice, and facial expression (Edwards & Klackars, 1981).

The roots of symbolic interactionism lie in the collected lectures and writings of George Herbert Mead (1934). Its basic assumption is that individuals, not groups or organizations, create and sustain group beliefs through interactions with others. Each person must be aware of, learn from, and signal other people for communication-interaction to occur.

When a new principal is appointed, then, each person involved will interpret the experience based on current and past events. As events unfold and are interpreted, this abstract model of a principal's succession may be confirmed or modified, and the interpretations of teachers, parents, or superiors help shape the modification.

No single person, not even the principal, can be the focus of inquiry into symbolic interaction, because it requires a number of specific conditions. First, symbols must be exchanged—words, gestures, facial expressions. This exchange requires that someone send a message for which they intend meaning and that someone receive the message. Second, a receiver must interpret the message. Third, those involved must share some common meaning of the gesture or symbol. Fourth, a return message is sent. Someone receives the return message, examines and interprets her internal response, and then, in some state of self-knowledge more or less well developed, sends a message in return. Fifth, people learn symbols through ongoing interactions with others. Finally, concepts of self and group, need for inclusion in the group, and the need to understand what is real shape ongoing group interpretations of information.

This cycle of iterative interaction and interpretation can be easily illustrated by commonplace events in schools. For example, a new principal may be asked by a teacher to discipline a child for disrespectful behavior in class.

The teacher has particular expectations of how this student should be handled. When the principal sends the student back to class without meting out expected punishment, the teacher may protest or feel quietly and resentfully unsupported. A principal may have very different interpretations of what transpired. The teacher may interpret the principal's actions as unsupportive and predict that this will lead to a decay in schoolwide student behavior. The principal, responding quickly to the needs of the teacher and the child, may believe he has dealt fairly and successfully with the problem. The actions and reactions in this scenario are important in themselves and in the symbolic messages they communicate.

A new principal also risks assault on his core self-concept during transition periods such as succession. Self-concept within the formal role of principal may conflict with your individual needs. Teachers may withhold information from you. You may have difficulty assessing yourself because you have difficulty obtaining the necessary information. You also must balance the desire to understand what you should be doing and how well you have done with the costs to the ego you could suffer if you receive negative feedback, and the negative implications of seeking information about yourself in the group when it may be perceived as a sign of weakness or insecurity. This may be a particularly difficult task for a newly appointed principal who is supposed to be strong and to lead (Ashford, 1989).

We perhaps overemphasize the risks understanding brings, when the benefits so strongly outweigh the costs. A shared understanding of reality that captures substantial agreement about what is and what happened has many advantages for a principal seeking to affect a school. A major contribution of a shared factual world that develops between a new principal and his staff—responsiveness—is a natural outgrowth of the frequency and perceived success of their interactions. This power comes from integration, inclusion, and accurate interpretations of communication in all its forms. It allows educators in a school to respond in an understandable way. You need only spend an evening with a closely knit family, a faculty meeting in a cohesive school, or a revival meeting of a small congregation to see the subtleties of communication and interaction.

Another valuable contribution of this shared understanding developed through interaction is a sense of belonging and inclusion. We have reported in several places throughout this text that new principals often report a general sense of isolation and loneliness. This isolation may cause a diffuse anxiety—difficult to identify. Principals have major responsibilities, but they also know implicitly whether they are excluded from the group. Inclusion can reduce anxiety and make it possible for a new principal to function effectively.

Still another advantage that comes from inclusion is the improved ability to predict others' responses to common events. For instance, if a student disrupts an assembly, teachers can count on the nearest faculty members to take action to end the disruption. If a fight breaks out on the playground, the closest adult will stop the fight. Within a profession, trust provides an implicit sense of predictable behavior from others. Common knowledge leads to common actions, springing from trust that others in the group are reliable and that their responses are predictable. Thus, when a new principal establishes that she has had common experiences, possesses critical and valued skills, and shares values and beliefs that drive the actions of others in the school, she contributes to the trust necessary for healthy interaction. Think for a moment about a time when you heard a teacher remark about a principal, "I just don't know where she stands." What emotions and attitudes accompanied this feeling?

While it's important for our interactions to communicate clearly and establish a shared understanding, sometimes it also is important to make a good impression. We all want to put our best foot forward, but no one wants to be accused of acting. Another view of interaction acknowledges the legitimacy of the parts we all play while minimizing the accusation that we are fake or insincere.

Dramaturgy or Self-presentation

Dramaturgy reveals the dramatic, performance dimensions of interaction—the ways people present themselves in a given setting. Resonating Shakespeare's view of the world as a stage, the impact of this perspective springs from the lure of "the presentation of self." This point of view accepts that we all interact with others to some degree as actors on a stage, presenting ourselves in ways we view as most advantageous in a given situation. Furthermore, these presentations change from stage to stage, depending on a person's reading of each context, and some people are better at the presentation of self than are others (Goffman, 1959).

The presentation of self illuminates two important factors that contribute to an understanding of principals' challenges when taking charge in schools. First, principals skillful at the presentation of self will be apt and astute self-monitors; they will observe and attend to the beliefs, shared realities, and driving values in the new school. They will watch themselves and others and monitor their own behavior to assure that it is appropriate and receives positive responses. New principals who are skilled self-monitors "prove themselves" to the group. (You will not be surprised that actors and politicians tend to be good self-monitors.) Second, self-monitors always will be aware of a "front stage" and a "back stage." Front-stage behavior requires careful adjustment for an audience and strict adherence to accepted and expected behavior. Back-stage behavior is reserved for insiders and may allow (or encourage) letting down, dropping some of the monitoring and careful control otherwise expected. It may even serve a bonding function—after-hours talks with faculty, quiet chats in the parking lot after parent-teacher conferences. Astute principals understand both self-monitoring and front- and back-stage settings. They assess the stage, frame their behavior, and act out rituals.

Not surprisingly, self-presentation receives some criticism, in part from the fear that it may be artificial rather than simply adaptive. It may embody the fear that our personalities are self-constructed myths rather than manifestations of different aspects of personality (Collins, 1985).

Self-presentation can be a curse or a blessing to you in a new principal's role. Overused, it can bury potential contributions as you continually play to various school audiences. You might be accepted, yet fail to have any substantial impact. Ignored, the need for self-monitoring can lead to fatal social errors that prevent you from being given the chance to have an impact. New principals must acknowledge that they are not alone on stage performing a monologue. Teachers, support staff, students, and the principal all act out important roles in the school educational drama. Perhaps the metaphor of drama best captures our discussion of leadership as social interaction; leadership is not a solo performance. Implicit in leadership is followership; successful leadership in schools is a professional group production.

CONCLUSION

In this chapter, we introduced some concepts on which we base our assertion that the social-symbolic interactions taking place between a new principal and people in the school and its environment can serve as a useful level of analysis for understanding the establishment of leadership. When interaction is the focus of attention, you will seek different kinds of information useful to you in establishing productive and influential relationships. These perspectives draw on the study of interaction between groups and individuals and among individuals, to understand what happens to the new principal and the school when a new principal is assigned. The motivation to interact, interaction processes, and the structural outcomes of interaction form the major aspects of these frameworks. Multiple process theories of interaction help explain how utility, behavior, exchange, ritual, and information interpretation shape the outcomes of interaction. In Chapter 11, we expand this discussion to include the building blocks of effective school leadership.

SUGGESTED ACTIVITIES

1. On a formal and sometimes superficial level, the teachers and students in a school must interact with a new principal whenever circumstances or assignments require. To be successful, however, you will want to help spark a motivation to interact with you on the part of others in the school. Brainstorm quickly a list of ten circumstances that are likely to motivate others to interact with you, the new principal, on more than a superficial basis. Next to this list, give at least one positive (not based in the demands of formal authority) value or stimulus that you believe would increase others' motivation to interact with you. Finally, how might you contribute to strengthening this motivation?

2. School leaders often find the daily press of activities keeping them secluded in their offices or out of school. How might you deliberately structure your interactions with parents, students, and teachers so that the press of the "busyness syndrome" does not prevent you from regularly interacting with others in the school about the work of the school? Compare your ideas to those of someone else in your seminar or class who works in a different level of schooling. How do your ideas address: (1) the cultural elements common to education and schools in general, (2) cultural

elements characteristic of your district and community, (3) cultural elements common to the kind of school in which you work, and (4) cultural elements unique to the mix of people in your particular school?

3. The motivation, processes, and outcomes of interactions involve many people's observed and regular behaviors, norms developed with the school, dominant values (such as high-academic standards, fostering diversity, or outcome-based education), the general philosophy of education that frames school values, and the general climate or "feel" of the school. Referring to a school in which you have worked, lay out an outline for increasing the level of positive and productive interaction in this school between the principal and others who work and learn there. If you are thinking of yourself as the principal, include in your plan ways to use your own talents and minimize the impact of your shortcomings or areas in which you need improvement.

4. What exchanges, communication techniques (perceptions and beliefs), and human symbols might you use to enhance interaction as a school leader? Ground your thoughts in a particular school for reference.

Principals' Influence on Student and School Outcomes

"In schools where achievement was high . . . invariably the principal made the difference."

—(Boyer, 1985)

In Chapter 6 we described principals as formal leaders who enact their roles in schools as designers, teachers, and stewards. According to Senge (1990), these images can be used to describe the role of a successful leader in any learning organization. As we think about the implications of these metaphors for leadership in schools, we turn our attention to the impact of principals' instructional leadership on school and student outcomes. What do principals do as designers, teachers, and stewards to bring about desired results for students and for school improvement? Do principals in highly successful schools carry out their leadership roles differently than do principals in less successful schools?

Our focus in this chapter is on what principals do to make a difference in student achievement in their schools; however, we eschew the idea that specified leadership behaviors cause predictable learning outcomes. Our understanding of the relationship between principal leadership and desired student and school outcomes acknowledges the complexity of social and symbolic interactions within dynamic educational settings. Further, principals often exercise instructional leadership in unstable environments characterized by contextual uniqueness, uncertainty, and ambiguity. Despite the complexities of instructional leadership and student learning, we also reject arguments from some critics who say that such conditions render principals powerless to influence teaching and learning outcomes in their schools. In this chapter we describe what effective principals do to influence student and school outcomes positively. We begin with a discussion of guiding assumptions related to principal leadership, organizational structures and processes, and various school and student outcomes. We then turn to a brief review of the literature on the effects of principal leadership. Next we present a two-dimensional, instructional leadership framework to elaborate theoretical and empirical findings on the relationships among sources of principal influence and types of influence. In the final section, we examine the influence of principal leadership on school and student outcomes within the context of current educational reform initiatives.

PRINCIPAL INFLUENCE ON STUDENT LEARNING: SOME GUIDING ASSUMPTIONS

Our discussion of principals' influence on school and student outcomes is based on a set of guiding assumptions. These assumptions are the products of professional experience, theoretical propositions, empirical findings, and reflection.

1. In their roles as leaders and through their daily work activities, effective principals positively affect student, classroom, and school outcomes.
2. Principal instructional leadership, student outcomes, and school effects are complex, multidimensional, interactive phenomena that are not easily separable into discrete variables for conceptualization, observation, measurement, analysis, interpretation, and leadership preparation.
3. The influence of principals on student and school outcomes is significant; however, these outcomes are the products of multiple sources of influence and the efforts of many individuals over time, not solely those of principals.
4. The concept of principal effects on student and school outcomes as reported in much of the literature implies causality, although it is examined from distinct philosophical and methodological traditions.
5. Practitioners and scholars generally agree that principals' leadership influences such mediating factors as school governance, school climate, and instructional organization. There is also general agreement that these factors in turn affect student and school outcomes, despite inconclusive empirical findings and some methodological weakness.
6. Any representational rendering of principals' influence on student and school outcomes through narrative description, theoretical modeling, or causal mathematical equations is partial and therefore may underestimate principals' influence on student learning.
7. Any single managerial activity or principal leadership behavior has the potential to ripple across the school, amplifying its effect on teaching and learning processes, and affecting student and organizational outcomes.
8. The instructional leadership behavior of principals affects student outcomes in school and beyond school.

Implicit in this list of assumptions is the belief that principals' instructional leadership behaviors interact with school and student outcomes in highly complex ways. To deal with the complexity of relationships among principals' leadership behaviors and their impact on teaching and learning outcomes, we have developed a two-dimensional framework (Figure 9.1). The framework serves as an organizer for our discussion of the ways in which effective principals positively influence student outcomes in their schools. The two dimensions are: (1) sources of influence, and (2) type of impact. Although we discuss each dimension separately, we recognize the interaction and interdependence of factors within each. Our hope is that the framework helps you think about your own role as an instructional leader.

A TWO-DIMENSIONAL PERSPECTIVE OF PRINCIPALS' INSTRUCTIONAL LEADERSHIP BEHAVIORS AND SCHOOL-STUDENT OUTCOMES

The linkage between effective administrative leadership and successful school-student outcomes has long been the *raison d'etre* of educational administration preparation programs. School principals occupy a unique leadership role in which they can exercise enormous influence on teaching and learning structures, processes, and outcomes. The literature in educational administration and in organizational theory is rich with accounts of leadership effectiveness (Lipham, 1981; Bossert, 1988; Pitner, 1988). You may also want to review the literature on effective schools (Brookover, Beady, Flood, Schweitzer & Wisenbaker, 1979); Edmonds, 1979; Purkey & Smith, 1983). More recently, some of the most convincing findings have come from outside the field of educational administration. "Much of the best research, for example, did not set out to look at principals at all, but at some particular program or innovation. Researchers discovered along the way that it was the principal who made the difference" (Lipham, 1981, p. vii). These findings, coupled with research findings in school administration and organizational theory, have helped to renew the focus on the importance of the principal's instructional leadership role in schools.

Research on effective schools, in particular, spawned various theories and descriptive typologies about within-school factors correlated with student achievement. As various theories of school effectiveness were formulated, the leadership of the school principal consistently appeared as a critical within-school factor. Educational reform reports, *A Nation at Risk* (1983), *Time for Results* (1986), *Investing in Our Children* (1985), *Teachers for the 21st Century* (1986), *Principals for 21st Century Schools* (1990) added fuel to the fires of inquiry focused on an examination of the relationships among student achievement,

FIGURE 9.1. A two-dimensional perspective of principals' instructional leadership effects on school and student outcomes.

| | | Types of Impact | |
		Direct	Indirect
Sources of Influence	Behaviors		
	Beliefs		
	Symbols		

school effectiveness, and the leadership behaviors of building principals. Recognizing that many factors contribute to effective schools and successful student outcomes, a general consensus regarding the importance of the school principal's leadership has emerged.

> If a school is a vibrant, innovative, child-centered place; if it has a reputation for excellence in teaching; if students are performing to the best of their ability, one can almost always point to the principal's leadership as the key to success. (U.S. Senate, 1979)

The descriptive model of principals' instructional leadership influence on teaching and learning outcomes in schools displayed in Figure 9.1 has two primary dimensions. The first is sources of instructional leadership influence. We describe three important sources of leadership influence—principals' behaviors, principals' beliefs, and principals' use of symbols. The second dimension is type of impact. We describe direct and indirect sources of principals' influence on student learning.

Sources of Instructional Leadership Influence: Behaviors, Beliefs, and Symbols

When you assume your first position as a school principal, your role as an instructional leader will already have been partially shaped by various organizational and environmental constraints and opportunities and by the expectations that teachers, central office administrators, parents, students, and others hold for you as an instructional leader. From our earlier descriptions of the work of the principal and principal succession, you know already that these groups hold more expectations for performance of tasks than any one person can reasonably be expected to accomplish. Role ambiguity, role conflict, and role overload are chronic conditions of the school principalship. As a principal you will be presented with literally hundreds of choices about how you will spend your time, what you will do, and what you would like to accomplish. Local conditions, unique situations of practice, and deliberate professional choices combine to shape your role as an instructional leader.

Keep in mind that you are both a role taker and a role maker. When you are hired as principal, the local school board, superintendent, teachers, students, and parents already have expectations for you as their principal. These expectations, enforced by organizational history, deeply embedded values, and norms of behavior, shape and define the leadership role you have assumed. When you accept the position you also accept these sets of role expectations. Later in the text we will discuss information gathering strategies that you can use through the interview selection process to help you better understand existing role expectations and school cultures.

We do not mean to suggest that you have no influence in shaping your role as an instructional leader. Within the boundaries of organizational, environmental, and collegial tolerance, you can shape your instructional leadership role in the principalship. During your initial entry into a school, you can use the stage frameworks for socialization to shape your activities and to determine the information you need to ask important questions. Understanding existing bureaucratic and cultural norms is an important part of your social-ization. As a role maker you may ask yourself, "What's important in this school? What do the people who work here think needs to be done? How should I spend my time? What should I do as an instructional leader? With limits on my time and energy, where is it likely that my efforts as an instruc-tional leader will have their greatest impact?"

The first dimension of principals' instructional leadership influence pro-vides you with an array of leadership possibilities. We describe these sources of influence as possibilities rather than prescriptions because individual pref-erences and capabilities, environmental constraints, and situational uniqueness require principals to use their professional expertise reflexively in situation-ally appropriate ways not in preordained, mechanistic formulas. Next we examine three sources of instructional leadership influence on student achieve-ment and school outcomes—behaviors, beliefs, and symbols.

Behaviors: What Instructional Leaders Do

As empirical evidence accumulated on the importance of principals' con-tributions to school improvement and student learning, researchers began to examine the characteristics of principals and their schools with special inter-est in the differences in within-school factors in high-student-achievement schools and low-student-achievement schools.

A study done at the University of Oregon in the early 1970s is represen-tative of this type of research. In this investigation the research team inter-viewed a national sample of 291 elementary school principals (Goldhammer, Becker, Withycombe, Miller, Morgan, DeLoretto & Aldridge, 1971). Based on observable characteristics within these schools, the researchers were able to discriminate between two general types of principals. High-achieving schools were called "beacons of brilliance" while extremely poorly achieving schools were labeled "potholes of pestilence." Findings from two decades ago, res-onate with Kozol's descriptions of "savage inequalities" (1991).

Effective schools research (Brookover et al., 1979; Edmonds, 1979; Murphy & Hallinger, 1988; Purkey & Smith, 1983) provided a substantial body of empirical evidence on school characteristics associated with higher-than-pre-dicted student achievement based on demographic variables, though they were perhaps less narratively vivid. From these data, researchers developed conceptualizations of one salient school-level factor—instructional leadership. The resultant literature attempts to define (DeBevoise, 1984), describe (Patter-son, 1977; Duke, 1987; Blumberg & Greenfield, 1980), measure (Hallinger & Murphy, 1987); explain (Bossert, Dwyer, Rowan & Lee, 1982); and predict (Heck, Larsen, & Marcoulides, 1990) specific instructional leadership behav-iors of principals associated with high levels of student achievement. (This body of empirical findings does have its critics, however; they point out that standardized achievement scores, typically in mathematics and reading, are very narrow measures of the desired educational outcomes in schools.) By identifying what instructional leaders actually do, the literature provides important professional knowledge for practitioners, policy makers, and pro-fessors of educational administration. To differentiate instructional leadership behavior from other managerial task behaviors, we use DeBevoise's definition.

Instructional leadership includes, "those actions that a principal takes, or delegates to others, to promote growth in student learning" (1984, p. 15). To describe in greater detail what principals do as instructional leaders, we use the selected works of Bossert, et al., 1982; Murphy & Hallinger, 1988; Duke, 1987; and Heck et al., 1990.

A Framework for Instructional Management (Bossert et al., 1982). A group of researchers from the Far West Laboratory for Educational Research sought to better understand the role of the principal as an instructional manager. These researchers conducted a review of the literature and research on the linkages between school-level factors and student learning. They concluded, "The literature on effective leadership has specified a broad range of behaviors that contribute to effective instructional management" (p. 36). Their review indicated that manipulable variables such as time-on task, class size and composition, instructional grouping, curriculum, and evaluation affect student learning. They acknowledged, however, that given the sheer volume of administrative responsibilities, principals are limited in the amount and quality of time they can spend directly assisting and guiding teaching and learning processes with individual teachers.

Bossert and others suggested an alternative approach. They argued that principals could significantly influence two school-level factors—school climate and instructional organization—through routine administrative behaviors. These routine tasks included goal setting and planning, monitoring of student progress, evaluating of instruction and its outcomes, communicating, scheduling, allocating resources for instruction, organizing and coordinating programs and resources, staffing, modeling, governing, and filling in when necessary. The two school-level factors in turn would shape individual classroom instruction and affect student learning.

This approach indicates that principals can directly influence student learning by engaging in systematic instructional leadership behaviors. However, their primary influence on student learning is indirect, that is, mediated through school climate and instructional organization. For example, to build a positive teaching and learning climate, a principal might work with teachers and other staff to create high expectations for students, establish effective discipline policies and procedures, and build supportive work relationships among teachers. In the area of instructional organization, principals need to understand the connections among desired learning objectives, the curriculum, class groupings, scheduling, the use of time, the allocation of resources, and teacher work. For instance, if the learning objective focuses on cultural diversity, a principal might help teachers set goals, facilitate curriculum development, plan and provide inservice training, and evaluate student outcomes as measures of the school's progress toward the appreciation of ethnic and cultural differences.

The framework also suggests that routine managerial behaviors of principals are the products of the influence of antecedent factors (community characteristics, principals' beliefs and experiences, and institutional contexts) and are interactive with school climate, instructional organization, and student outcomes. Principals' management behaviors shape classroom and school instructional organization and climate. These same behaviors are in turn affected by climate, school and classroom instructional organization, and various student outcomes. In our discussion of the dimension of type of impact, direct and indirect, we elaborate on the transformation of seemingly mundane managerial activities into effective instructional leadership strategies.

Instructional Management Behaviors. Based on a review of school effectiveness research, Murphy and Hallinger (1988) set out to develop a research-based definition of the principal's role in instructional management. They constructed the *Principal Instructional Management Rating Scale* and used it to gather data from teachers, principals, and district central office personnel on the instructional management behaviors of 10 elementary school principals in a district serving 8,000 students. From the data collected, they identified eleven specific behaviors clustered in three dimensions of instructional management behaviors—Defines the Mission, Manages Instructional Program, and Promotes School Climate.

Defining the Mission includes two major instructional leadership activities. "The principal's role in defining the mission involves framing school-wide goals and communicating these goals in a persistent fashion to the entire school community" (p. 221). Bringing clarity and purpose to teaching and learning activities in the school is an important leadership task. Through vision, planning, and passion, principals help others in the school community coalesce around a core set of beliefs, values, and hopes for children.

The second dimension, *Manages Instructional Program*, involves the principal's working with teachers in areas specifically related to curriculum and instruction. In this role, principals supervise and evaluate to see how school goals are translated into successful classroom practices. This includes formal and informal supervision and evaluation, classroom visits, curriculum planning, coordination of programs, and working with teachers and other staff to monitor student learning. Principals can integrate the complexities of curriculum planning, monitoring of student learning outcomes, program and staff evaluation, and communications of school and individual outcomes into their routine work. One way principals integrate these administrative processes and tasks is the Management Information System for Effective Schools (MISES), developed by the National Center for Effective Schools. This data shell provides interactive channels that facilitate all of these tasks. It is a fully integrated system, runs on a microcomputer, and costs less than a thousand dollars. Given such affordable and accessible technology, principals do not have to wait for legislative audits, commission reports, or techno-guru evaluation consultants to know if their school is achieving its goals and specific objectives. Microcomputer programs such as this one provide principals with another valuable tool for authentic, school-based instructional leadership.

Promoting a Positive School Learning Climate is the third category of instructional management behaviors discussed by Murphy and Hallinger. Principals protect instructional time by being buffers against intrusions from internal and external forces that threaten teachers' instructional time with students. Principals also promote positive learning climates by their physical presence and visibility throughout the school—in classrooms, at student activities, and at curriculum meetings. Promoting professional growth and learning among the staff, providing incentives for teachers and students to develop and grow continually, and enforcing academic standards are instructional management behaviors that promote student learning.

A Vision of Instructional Leadership (Duke, 1987). In his book, *School Leadership and Instructional Improvement.* Daniel L. Duke (1987) asks the reader to compare the effects of principal leadership on student outcomes to the effects of physicians' practice on their patients' health.

> Physicians generally are not evaluated in terms of patient performance, except in cases involving gross malpractice. They are held accountable for "good medical practice." Is there an equivalent to "good medical practice," to which school leaders may be held accountable? (p. 26)

He then goes on to describe "good instructional leadership practices." Duke believes these are the professional behaviors for which instructional leaders need to be held accountable. Unfortunately, even the best professionals operate in real situations of practice, which at times are anything but routine or ideal. Thus, principals' authority and discretion in instructional leadership practices need to be viewed within the context of environmental constraints. These include school structures and staffs that are already in place, collective bargaining agreements, state mandates, local district policies and legal guidelines, and general systems of rewards and sanctions.

Two examples in the areas of teacher selection and union contracts based on our experiences as principals illustrate Duke's assertions about the direct connection between desired instructional outcomes and principal leadership behaviors embedded in specific contexts. The quality of instruction and its impact on student learning outcomes is directly related to the quality of the teaching staff. For example, your training and experience may have convinced you that creative, child-centered teachers with diverse personal and professional backgrounds are the best instructors. You also understand that one of your most important instructional leadership tasks is personnel screening and selection. As a new principal, you will inherit a teaching staff that reflects a mosaic of past selection criteria and marketplace factors. Depending on staff turnover rates, it may take years for you as a principal to substantially change the composition of your staff by hiring new teachers. Thus, your direct influence on student instructional outcomes through the selection of excellent teachers is dependent on opportunities to fill key teaching positions. Within this context, you may then look to influence the existing teaching staff through staff development activities and training.

In states where collective bargaining exists for teachers, union contracts also affect principals' instructional leadership behaviors. For example, you and your teachers may want to work together to develop a new curriculum that integrates the areas of language arts, social studies, and fine arts. Since there is little time during the school day, your staff decides to spend blocks of time together after school and on a faculty retreat to work on this innovative curriculum. The local parent-teacher organization has paid for a meeting place and will provide meals for the retreat. As an instructional leader you recognize this as an opportunity to build closer professional working relationships among teachers and to develop an exciting new approach to teaching and learning in your school. In some school districts, such initiatives requiring extra staff time would not be permitted under existing union contracts. There may even be specific provisions in the contract that stipulate how much teachers must be paid for any extra time outside the contractually defined school day. Our point is not to criticize collective bargaining in schools. Union contracts are an important part of the context in many school districts and are important sources of influence on principals' instructional leadership behaviors.

We concur with Duke that no one set of behaviors characterizes what all successful instructional leaders do. Situational uniqueness and indeterminacy within the context of professional practice render any prescriptive list of effective instructional leadership behaviors problematic. Multiple contingencies and constraints to effective instructional leadership make such a prescriptive list of behaviors problematic. However, "Research suggests that instructional leaders must see to it that certain predictable functions or situations are handled appropriately" (p. 81). Duke identifies five areas of work activity for instructional leaders that affect student learning and school outcomes: (1) teacher supervision and development; (2) teacher evaluation; (3) instructional management and support; (4) resource management; and (5) quality control. Coordination and troubleshooting are two leadership processes that cut across the five areas. Duke's integrated vision of instructional leadership provides a framework for thinking about and enacting what principals do in the area of instruction. However, what a principal would do specifically within each of the five areas is difficult to specify.

> The situations constitute complex configurations of intentions, activities, people, and interrelationships. They call for a variety of technical skills and professional judgments, adapted to the particular needs of the moment. Since these needs are ever-changing, no single prescription for dealing with a given situation will suffice. (pp. 81–82)

To underscore the belief that specific lists of tasks do not necessarily produce authentic instructional leadership that influences student achievement and improved school outcomes, Duke provides a diagnostic checklist rather than a facile prescription for ailing instructional leaders. The instructional improvement checklist includes a series of questions in each of the five areas of instructional leadership and in two process areas, coordination and troubleshooting. The purpose of these questions is to generate discussion and reflective thinking, not to yield a composite score on a leadership continuum. (See Duke's diagnostic checklist pp. 297–299.)

A Model of Validated Instructional Leadership Behaviors. In an effort to build upon past research findings and to move to the next level of theory building related to instructional leadership, Heck, Larsen and Marcoulides (1990) developed a predictive model of principal instructional leadership variables that influence student achievement. Figure 9.2 contains the structural components of this model.

Synthesizing previous findings on the effects of instructional leadership by school principals on student achievement and school outcomes, the authors built a conceptual, predictive model. Governance, school climate, and instructional organization are described as latent variables (not directly observable) that influence student achievement. School climate and instructional organization directly affect student outcomes while the effects of governance are mediated through school climate and instructional organization. *Governance* is defined as teachers' perceptions of the extent to which a principal (1) involves staff in crucial instructional decisions; (2) involves parents and other groups in school programs; (3) protects faculty from detractors to instruction; and (4) leaves teachers alone to do their work. *School climate,* aimed at improving the educational environment in the school, measures the extent to which a principal (1) communicates instructional goals; (2) communicates high expectations; (3) encourages discussion of instructional issues; (4) recognizes student and school academic successes; (5) informs the community about student academic achievement; (6) works to keep faculty morale high; and (7) establishes a safe, orderly, disciplined learning environment. *Instructional organization,* directed primarily at the work of teachers and students, is defined as teachers' perceptions of their principal's efforts to (1) develop school goals; (2) coordinate and articulate the instructional program across the school; (3) engage in formal and informal discussions of instruction; (4) observe teachers; (5) ensure a systematic process for staff monitoring of student progress toward instructional goals; (6) emphasize test results for program improvement; (7) secure resources to support instructional programs; (8) visit classrooms regularly; (9) provide feedback to teachers; (10) identify professional development needs of the staff; and (11) evaluate curricular programs. *Student achievement*⋅ is defined as consistent student-school performance over a three-year period above or below a school's expected performance band score in reading and mathematics in grades 3, 6, and 12 on the California Achievement Program Test (CAT). Based on these operational definitions, the model posits that "the

FIGURE 9.2. Predictive model of principal instructional leadership variables influencing student achievement. *(Heck, Larsen, and Marcoulides, (1990)—Instructional leadership and school achievement: Validation of a causal model.)*

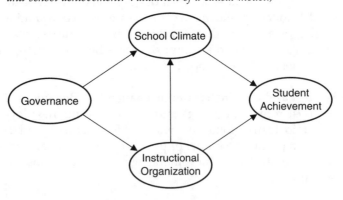

principal may influence school-student achievement through managing the political relationship of the school to its environment, supervising the school's instructional organization and building a positive climate for learning" (p. 101).

In general these researchers provide powerful empirical evidence that principals influence school governance, school climate, and the school's instructional organization to affect student achievement. After controlling for student socioeconomic status (SES) and the language background, the model provided estimates of the effects of specific leadership behaviors in high- and low-achievement schools.

The results of the analysis of Heck and others support assertions that principals exert instructional leadership that affects student performance. Their data indicated that principals in high- and low-achieving schools focused on the same leadership behaviors. However, principals differed in the extent to which they engaged in key instructional leadership behaviors, in what they believed about the efficacy of their own leadership behaviors, and in the sources of influence they used to bring about desired student-school outcomes. Principals in high-achieving schools were more engaged in specific instructional leadership behaviors that positively affected school governance, school instructional climate, and instructional organization than were principals in low-achieving schools. The researchers also looked at individual student test scores. Their analysis indicated that when individual student achievement was the unit of analysis, the leadership behavior, "leaves teachers alone to work" (governance), revealed no statistically significant difference between high- and low-achieving schools. This finding suggests that principals must be engaged in teaching and learning in their schools. Simply leaving teachers alone as a display of confidence in their professionalism does not serve the needs of teachers or learners. For different reasons, teachers in high- and low-achieving schools need the support and affirmation that comes from principal involvement and engagement in the school's learning environment. When the unit of analysis was the school, the researchers failed to reject the null hypotheses related to differences between principals in high- and low-achieving schools in the following behaviors: leaves teachers alone to work, involves parents in school program (governance); communicates instructional goals (school climate); and develops school goals, coordinates instructional program, and emphasizes test results for program improvement (instructional organization). Heck and colleagues conclude,

> The instructional leadership role of the principal is one key element in a conceptual framework that recognizes the importance of the school's social context in determining student achievement. Clearly, instructional leadership is a multi-dimensional construct. How the principal and teachers are able to organize and coordinate the work life of the school shapes not only the learning experiences and achievement of students but also the environment in which this work is carried out. The identification of a set of principal instructional leadership behaviors that are directly associated with school achievement outcomes serves as the basis for developing criteria to evaluate the effectiveness of principal performance and leads to more effective preparation programs for school administrators (p. 122).

The four instructional leadership frameworks we just discussed use distinct perspectives (descriptive, theoretical, empirical, and causal) to convey a similar message. Student and school outcomes are significantly affected by what principals do in their daily work and the priorities they give to particular instructional leadership activities.

What do highly effective instructional leaders do to affect student and school outcomes positively? Each of the preceding frameworks provides organizers for thinking about and for carrying out purposeful instructional leadership activities focused on student learning. To move from general categories of instructional leadership to specific examples of how principals in real work settings exercise influence, we have selected two instructional leadership behaviors common to the four frameworks: (1) establishing and communicating high expectations, and (2) protecting teaching and learning activities and time (buffering). We draw on principals' stories to illustrate how principals focus attention on teaching and learning and establish priorities in their daily work to build a constellation of instructional leadership behaviors that together transform routine managerial tasks into powerful sources of influence affecting student learning.

Establishing and Communicating High Expectations. As a new principal, I had the opportunity to work for two months over the summer and learn hundreds of things about how things were done in a rural, consolidated school district before most students and faculty returned to school. In a review of standardized test results sent to me from a university testing center, I discovered that our students were not performing well on the verbal section of the standardized achievement test. After the teachers and students returned in the fall, I began to work with the other administrators and my teaching staff to address student achievement in the areas of reading and writing. In high schools, it is not uncommon for the faculty to think this is a problem the English department should handle. Thus, as we began our discussions as a staff, I was concerned that attention to the problem not be translated into a professional finger-pointing exercise in which one academic unit was found delinquent.

After several meetings, we decided to focus on improving the reading skills of our students. All teachers in the high school were asked to meet in their respective departments to develop strategies for improving the reading skills of students. Not unexpectedly, some teachers, especially those in industrial arts, physical education, math, driver education, music, and art were puzzled by such a request. These teachers saw no problem in setting high expectations for students in reading and targeting this area of improvement; however, they had difficulty translating those expectations into their work with students. As principal, I was responsible for communicating these expectations for students to others. This included communicating with teachers and support staff who saw themselves as only marginally connected to and responsible for accomplishing the goal of raising our students' reading skills.

Over the next few months, my instructional leadership activities included working with faculty to explore ways in which everyone assumed responsibility for improving the reading skills of students, finding time in an already crowded week for silent sustained reading, planning and conducting after-school workshops on reading in content areas, reallocating money for teachers to visit other schools and to attend professional conferences, and (while other areas competed for our attention and energies) working to keep our collective eyes on our objective—the improvement of student reading skills. Finally, our collective expectations to improve student reading skills were not part of a hidden curriculum, nor were they well-kept professional secrets. Communicating the importance of reading skills to overall student academic success required attention in newsletters to parents, presentations to the school board, and discussions with our students. Creating and communicating high expectations for students in reading became the focus across many routine leadership activities, not an isolated curriculum task that could be worked on after completing all of the other managerial tasks in my day.

Protecting Teaching and Learning Time. The core technology of schools is teaching and learning. This core is influenced by internal and external forces. For example, over the past three decades the curriculum of schools has grown exponentially. New knowledge, new technologies, and new social realities compete for curricular space in schools. Since public schools already have a captive audience of students, private and public agencies come to schools demanding, or in some cases offering, many worthwhile programs that deal with such subjects as marriage and the family, drug and alcohol abuse, sexually transmitted diseases, suicide prevention, and gang violence. Pressures to expand the curriculum, whether from external or internal forces, are very real in schools. Principals must protect their schools from distractions that threaten teaching and learning time. In this instructional role, principals often act as buffers to protect learning time for teachers and students and to uphold program integrity. Examples of external distractions might include social service agencies' sponsoring school lyceums; college and military recruiters' wanting to interview students; and parent, student, and community groups' offering schoolwide events during the school day. Within the school, threats to instructional time may be embedded in various school rules, school district policies, operating procedures, and teacher-sponsored field trips and activities that either take away or waste learning time. Whether from internal or external forces, buffering and protecting learning time and curriculum quality are important instructional leadership behaviors. Buffering does not mean building an impenetrable wall around the school and its curriculum; it means working to build shared values about instructional time and quality and working to balance the need to be responsive to important community and personal interests while protecting the school's program integrity. Our second example illustrates how one of the authors raised teacher awareness of the use of instructional time in the school.

I once asked teachers to examine the teaching-learning time that fell under their direct control in their classrooms. In a 55-minute class, for example, on average how much time was spent taking attendance, starting learning activities, making transitions between activities, and waiting for the class dismissal bell to ring? Their accounting, combined with my own observations, indicated that for some teachers, 5 to 10 minutes of each class were spent on these activities. Multiplied by five classes a day, then by 180 days of school, we discovered that from 10 to 25 6-hour school days were being wasted. Our calculations did not include passing time between classes, early dismissals, schoolwide assemblies, classroom interruptions, and student absences. We then asked ourselves some basic questions about the use of instructional time in the school. How effectively did we use class time before holidays and vacations, the first day back after a break, beginning and ending units of study?

As principal, I raised the issue not as an expression of "Neo-Taylorism," but rather to raise our level of awareness so that we could discuss a critical factor under our direct control. The potential loss of valuable time for teaching and learning can be enormous. Careful supervision and monitoring of time may be necessary for the most incompetent time managers on your teaching staff; however, by simply raising all teachers' awareness of time as a critical resource, principals can positively influence the learning environment in schools. Think about the use of time in your school and its impact on instructional quality. What internal and external distractions threaten teaching and learning quality and time in your school? How would you protect teachers and students from these threats? What strategies would you use to examine critical factors affecting instructional organization?

We want to make one final point in our discussion of principals' behaviors as a source of influence on student and school outcomes. Principals' instructional leadership behaviors do make a difference in teaching and learning environments and ultimately on student outcomes; however, principals' behaviors alone will not produce high-achieving students. Student successes are the products of the commitment, energy, and efforts of teachers, parents, support staff, and the students themselves. Principals' instructional leadership forges the efforts of others into successes for students. Next we describe a second source of instructional leadership influence, principals' beliefs.

What Instructional Leaders Believe

Another powerful source of influence that principals use to affect student and school outcomes positively is what they believe about teaching and learning, about the connections between their instructional leader behaviors and teachers' work with students, and about the effect of their leadership behavior on student learning outcomes. Beliefs are expressions of values. They form the basis of educational visions, plans, and professional behavior. The instructional leadership behaviors of principals we discussed in the previous section are expressions of these basic beliefs.

It should not be surprising that principals' beliefs are connected to their instructional behaviors. After all, principals bring their personal values, unique experiences, and beliefs to their leadership roles in schools. Principals' values and beliefs help them shape their role as leaders and their interaction with aspects of the school's culture affects those same values and beliefs. Salancik and Pfeffer (1978) and cognitive psychologists argue that individuals align their beliefs with their actions to minimize any cognitive dissonance between them.

The effective schools literature includes explicit and implicit statements of belief related to leadership and school improvement. Statements of belief include the following:

- All students can learn.
- The work of teachers and principals makes a difference in the lives of children.
- Learning is the most important reason for being in school.
- A clear and commonly accepted mission is important to student and school success.
- High expectations in academic quality must be upheld by everyone in the school.
- Learning time should be maximized; thus student-teacher time needs to be protected from disruption.
- Instructional programs improve over time, based on systematic monitoring and assessment of program and student outcomes.
- Student outcomes are the products of the efforts of many individuals over time—parents, teachers, staff, community members, and others.
- Safe and orderly school environments are necessary for successful teaching and learning. (Synthesis Update 1990, Effective Schooling Research Bibliography)

Principals who hold these beliefs are likely to behave in particular ways. For example, decisions and actions in curriculum and instructional organization; allocation of resources; priorities in daily work routines; attention to school culture; and relationships among teachers, students, parents, and other community members are grounded in these principles of professional practice.

Earlier in this chapter we introduced the work of Heck and colleagues on instructional leadership. Building on effective schools literature, Heck, Larsen, and Marcoulides (1990) tested causal relationships among latent variables (school governance, school climate, and instructional organization) and student achievement. Their findings provide strong empirical evidence of the influence of principals' beliefs on student and school outcomes.

> Our study indicates that the variables principals attempt to influence do not distinguish between principals of effective and ineffective schools; that is, both groups focus on the same set. On all of our hypothesized latent variables, however, principals can be distinguished by what it is about each variable that they believe to be important to influence. (p. 118)

The beliefs that separated the principals of ineffective schools from those of effective schools included their beliefs about their ability to influence teachers' work in classrooms through governance, school climate, and instructional organization. For example, principals in highly successful schools involved their staffs more in critical instructional decisions, they involved parents more in school programs, and they protected teachers and learners from undue pressures and distractions. These findings provide an empirical linkage to effective schools findings that describe the connections between the work of principals carried out in governance, instructional organization, and school climate, and principals' beliefs and school-student outcomes. Perhaps the most powerful belief that principals can hold is that their routine managerial activities can be transformative in the area of instructional improvement and student outcomes. These beliefs and behaviors do not require heroic acts of leadership, nor do they demand access to unlimited resources. Rather, as Dwyer and others (1983) concluded,

> [P]rincipals' are forceful leaders because they successfully carry out common acts of the principalship, not because they accomplish heroic feats. They require no new program, no innovation, no extensive change. The success of these activities for instructional management hinges, instead, on the principal's capacity to connect them to the instructional system. (p. 54)

Principals are symbolic and cultural leaders in schools; their beliefs are also expressed in personal statements of vision, in their communications with key internal and external constituent groups, in public ceremonies and rituals, and in their daily work to create and nurture positive teaching and learning environments. What beliefs do you find embedded in the following comments by school principals? Persell and Cookson, (1982) describe the link between principals' beliefs and effective instructional leadership.

> If effective leadership can be defined as helping others to help themselves, then an effective principal is one who helps the entire school community realize its potential. Effective principals appear to have a vision of what their school should be like. Without this mental picture, the leadership role can too easily fall into the trap of reacting to negative situations and not creating positive situations. Above all, principals can do their job better if they are secure in themselves and have faith that their decisions will, in the final analysis, prove to be the best alternatives given the set of specific circumstances they find themselves confronting. (p. 28)

Tapping the potential of others, personal vision, security in self, and faith in professional decisions are grounded in beliefs, sustained and improved by practice.

This commitment to the power of belief echoes the school culture and symbolic leadership work we discussed in Chapter 6. Peterson (1989); Firestone and Wilson (1985); and Deal and Peterson (1990) link belief systems to aspects of culture that support quality teaching and successful student outcomes. School culture is defined as

> the unconscious set of commonly shared norms, values, and beliefs that exist in a school to shape behavioral interactions. Indeed, much attention is now focused on the ways principals and others shape the norms, values and beliefs of teachers and students to enhance student learning and other valued outcomes. (Peterson, 1989, p. 15)

What principals believe influences the beliefs and behaviors of others, and thus influences the culture. Firestone and Wilson (1985) reported that principals influence the quality of instruction and student outcomes by working through bureaucratic and cultural linkages that govern teacher behavior and work routines. They concluded that principals, through hundreds of interactions and activities, influence cultures that focus on the primacy of teaching and learning. Principals exert instructional influence in schools by managing the flow of stories and information, by creating and manipulating symbols and rituals, by serving as cultural communicators, and by expending high levels of energy and putting in long hours.

> The principal's task and challenge is to develop a clear vision of the purposes of the school that gives primacy to instruction and to carry it through consistently during those countless interactions. By doing so, the principal uses bureaucratic linkages to create opportunities for teachers to follow that vision and minimizes chances to operate in different ways. At the same time, the principal uses cultural linkages to communicate that vision so that, to a greater or lesser extent, it becomes the teachers' own culture. The initiative for carrying out instructional work then rests with teachers, but they are much more likely to incorporate the principal's perspective. (Firestone & Wilson, 1985, p. 22)

Effective principals do not keep these beliefs to themselves but work to make their vision for learning a shared vision among teachers and students. Effective principals build school cultures that affirm the primacy of high-quality instruction and student learning and that are supported by norms of collegiality (Little, 1982), high expectations and performance standards, and a belief in professional growth, self-renewal, and continuous improvement.

Finally, the work of Tom Guskey (1986) on staff development and teacher change informs the link between behaviors and beliefs. Guskey's model of the process of teacher change indicates that changes in beliefs and attitudes follow changes in teachers' classroom practices and subsequent changes in student learning outcomes. When teachers change their instructional practices and then begin to see gains in student achievement, their beliefs about teaching and learning are changed or reinforced. By extension, we argue that principals' instructional leadership behaviors shape their beliefs about teaching and learning in their schools. The effects of these behaviors on teachers and students in turn moderate principals' beliefs, which then influence what principals do. Principals' beliefs and behaviors are powerful signals to teachers and students. Next we discuss principal influence on instruction through symbols.

Sources of Influence: Symbols

Symbols provide a third source of instructional leadership influence. Who principals are, what they do and say, and how they choose to communicate and shape school culture are powerful symbolic tools for influencing teaching and learning in schools.

The power of symbols reflects the power of convictions. Robert Owens (1987) describes a symbolic leader as one who "[s]tands for something that is important and that gives meaning and purpose to the seemingly mundane and routine work of others in the school" (p. 155). By employing a repertoire of such symbols as high visibility throughout the school, school mottos, public recognition and rewards, and ceremonies and rituals, principals can affect the attitudes and behaviors of co-workers by helping them understand what is valued and rewarded in the organization. These symbolic acts give meaning to the work of individuals and provide cohesiveness to efforts to accomplish shared goals. "Effective leaders may focus on technical change, but their activities are often highly symbolic, as they build the school's culture around their vision for the school" (Peterson, 1989, p. 5).

Even when principals do not consciously use symbols, teachers, students, parents and others, looking for clues as to what's important, scrutinize who leaders are, what they do and say, and what they value and believe. They develop their beliefs about what the principal will do as an instructional leader from this scrutiny. Understanding who the principal is and what she stands for is much like viewing the creation of a mosaic. As little pieces of personality, interests, expertise, purpose, and leadership behavior are added together from hundreds of separate interactions and events in the school, patterns and themes begin to emerge. Values, beliefs, words, actions, and rewarding behaviors add to these themes. From these patterns and themes, a picture of the principal as an instructional leader becomes clearer. Our earlier discussion is suggestive of some of the behaviors and beliefs that contribute to these portraits of effective instructional leaders.

Who principals are and what they stand for provides a model for others in the school. Principals can demonstrate for others the difference, for example, between immediate concerns such as meeting with an angry parent or getting a copy machine repaired, and important long-range issues (instructional focus and goals). They can show how teaching and learning have primacy in school planning, decision making, resource allocation, and daily work. As Edgar Schein (1985) reminds us in his text on leadership and culture, if you want to know what's valued and what's most important in your school, watch what the principal does.

> In order to work at the level of the group's deepest assumptions about the nature of reality and its own identity in relationship to its environment, a leader must have a great depth of vision and extraordinary insight into thoughts and feelings that are normally taken for granted and therefore not articulated. Leadership in this sense means the ability to step outside one's culture even as one continues to live within it. It is not enough just to set goals and sell symbols. The goals and symbols and the assumptions on which they are based must be "correct" in the sense that they will indeed solve key problems for the group and will fit with other deep cultural assumptions. The effective leader needs to use his deeper vision before trying to sell anything. (Schein, 1985, p. 325)

Firestone and Wilson (1985) also describe the importance of principals' symbolic role in schools.

> The principal is in the right place to become a reference point and to establish norms because he or she is close, has relevant experience, and is in a position of authority. As a result, teachers invest a good deal of affect in their view of the principal; the office is a symbolic one that can be used to manipulate the stories and rituals that interpret teachers' work. (p. 21)

Kelley and Bredeson (1991) examined principals' symbolic leadership and its influence on the attitudes and behaviors of teachers. They described how two high school principals, one in a public school and one in a parochial school, used symbols to convey core values, images, and ideologies in their schools. These symbols transmitted via words, actions, and rewards reinforced the philosophy of the schools, moderated the efforts of the schools' subcultures, influenced the attitudes and behaviors of teachers, legitimated authority structures in the schools, and maintained the status quo. They concluded:

> Symbolic leadership is the integration and communication of a principal's thoughts, words, and actions. These integrated messages were communicated through the patterned use of words, actions, and rewards that had an impact on the beliefs, values, attitudes, and behaviors of others with whom the principals interacted. No single word, act or reward in and of itself epitomized symbolic leadership. Yet when seen as an integrated whole of administrative behavior, these individual segments strongly suggest an important dimension of principals' leadership. (p. 19)

This recognition of the power of symbols to evoke strong emotional responses and actions from people is not unique to educators. Thomas Carlyle, a Scottish essayist and historian, wrote, "It is in and through symbols that man, consciously and unconsciously, lives, works, and has his meaning." Principals live the work of teaching and learning through symbols that focus everyone's attention on these important activities even as a plethora of distractions and crises diverts them. In a deliberate way, principals consciously communicate and manipulate symbols to influence the beliefs, attitudes, and behaviors of others. "Symbols are powerful transmitters of important messages which leaders can use for reinforcing, maintaining, and/or creating new organizational cultures" (Kelley & Bredeson, 1991, p. 20).

Symbols often provide cultural shorthand that expresses important values, beliefs, and norms in the school. Three symbol systems in this shorthand—stories, icons, and rituals—can be used by principals to influence positive teaching and learning outcomes in schools. Stories convey the essential features of a school, person, or group through example. Icons represent ideals in physical form (e.g., trophies, the manuscripts of a revered scholar, a small child's bag of marbles treasured long after childhood has passed). Rituals present the group's values and commitments in open ceremonies that reinforce values and bind individuals to the group (e.g., flag ceremonies, a memorial service, the "Hello Day" assembly in which all the coaches dress as cancan girls and perform a la "A Chorus Line"). Symbols have three primary functions. Symbols are descriptive and expressive. They are used to capture the essence of values, ideas, and purposes of a school. Second, symbols are energy controlling in that they can stimulate loyalty, commitment, and give members a focus for their group energies. A third function of symbols is to help maintain the existing culture by providing stability, coherence, and a sense of history—or when necessary, to help the organization adjust to new realities by providing acceptable patterns for change (Riley, 1983; Solomon, 1980; Kelley, 1987).

School sagas or stories often blend real events, myth, and purposeful exaggeration. Whether or not the facts, people, and events described are perfectly accurate in the stories is much less important than the core values or cultural themes the stories express. Once stories are told and then repeated by others as an illustration of an important message, these stories become part of an organizational saga. Depending on the nature of the story, it can even follow individuals into other organizations. One such organizational saga accompanied a colleague of ours throughout his professional career in education. We have chosen this story, embroidered over time by organizational raconteurs, to illustrate the power and enduring symbolic influence of stories.

This particular story, referred to as "One Punch," followed a friend of ours from the school playground to the dean's office at a major university. As an adolescent, our friend found himself in a schoolyard face-to-face with the school bully. Compared with this bully, he was not particularly strong and did not relish getting into a fight, especially since his mother was the school principal. Confronted as he was, he also remembered the advice of his father. If you get into a situation where you can't avoid a fight and you're afraid of what the outcome might be, at least be sure to take the first punch. Pressed against the wall by the school bully, our friend clenched his fist, closed his eyes, and swung as wildly as he could at his tormentor. After one swing, nothing happened. His punch was so accurate that it knocked his opponent out cold. Even though he hated the possibility of a fight and would have done nearly anything to avoid this one, the outcome quickly earned him the nickname, "One Punch." Over the years, the nickname stuck and came to represent decisiveness and clout. In the years to follow, when he was confronted with tough situations, choices, and unavoidable conflicts as a superintendent, military officer, department chair, and dean his reputation as "One Punch" preceded him. When pressed, he would get the job done swiftly and unequivocally. With "One Punch," the outcome was always decisive. Our point here is not to applaud violence, but to illustrate the sustaining power of stories as symbols and the messages they transmit to others.

One of the authors (you may guess which one) served as a principal in a district about an hour's drive from home. People in the community did not know the principal at first, but a powerful story about a devoted, energetic, stern, and beloved principal who had served for decades in the community smoothed the way. "Are you related to Anna B. Hart?" became a common entree to conversations about commitment from, and the influence of, a powerful educator. Almost everyone also mentioned that the new principal did not wear her hair in a bun!

Think about stories in your school. What is it about the stories in your school that keep them alive as interpretations of important ideas, values, beliefs, norms, or traits? How might such stories be used by the principal to reinforce an important cultural norm related to instruction in your school?

A second symbol system is the use of icons—concrete, physical objects that express key elements of a school culture. Buttons, pins, school mottos, logos, banners, trophies, and certificates are icons. They express important values and keep those values in front of students, teachers, and parents. Principals use banners and logos to capture the essence of the school mission; trophies and certificates to celebrate the successes of students; awards and photo displays to reinforce positive behavior; and public recognition and honor ceremonies to challenge teachers and students to achieve. Icons have symbolic value to the degree that they represent something valued in the school. Icons capture the essence of values, beliefs, and goals. Look around your school; what are the valued icons? What cultural messages do these icons express? What symbols represent student achievement? If you were principal of your school, what icons might you use to symbolize teaching and learning goals in the school? Are there negative icons around your school?

Rituals provide a third system of symbols for school leaders. Principals wear various ceremonial hats in their leadership roles. Back-to-school nights for parents, graduation exercises, awards banquets, academic honor ceremonies, and retirement celebrations are highly symbolic public rituals in schools. These rituals hold different meanings for different people, often depending on their roles. For example, both of the authors have experienced graduation ceremonies as students, parents, teachers, and principals. The symbolic rituals were interpreted differently depending on the role we found ourselves in at the time. Rituals provide symbolic occasions for principals as instructional leaders to share and reaffirm important values, beliefs, and norms related to education in their communities. The ritual of high school graduation exercises suggests one such value—intergenerational connection. Parents and grandparents celebrate this important rite of passage for young adults and in doing so remember their own graduations. Teachers recognize how much their students have matured and changed over the years. Students celebrate their success and the release this ritual signifies from the crushing supervision of their lives. In a recent graduation ceremony, school board members, administrators, and teachers wore graduation robes and were part of the graduation processional. The principal who choreographed the ceremony recognized the importance of intergenerational connection in terms of the successes of these graduates and those who had contributed to the accomplishments of these students. Most important, the principal symbolically held out the promise to those who would follow.

Principals influence instruction and its outcomes by what they do, what they believe, and how they use symbols. Next, we turn our attention to whether principals' use of these sources of influence directly or indirectly affect student achievement and other instructional outcomes.

TYPE OF IMPACT: DIRECT AND INDIRECT

Principals make a difference in student achievement and school outcomes. This assertion is supported by theory, empiricism, and experience. Less clear to researchers and practitioners of educational administration is exactly how or precisely in what ways principals affect student learning. Our review of the literature affirmed that the behaviors, beliefs, and symbolic leadership of principals have both direct and indirect impact on student learning. The extent to which the effects of principals' behaviors, beliefs, and symbolic leadership are viewed as direct or indirect is a function of sources of influence, organizational structure and role, our perspective on leadership, and epistemological issues.

It is difficult (and may be a futile exercise) to track the linkages between principals' leadership behaviors and student outcomes. Such mapping is reductionistic in that it assumes that particular behaviors and events are direct causal agents of learning. Suffice it to say, student learning is complex and a search for simplistic causal connections suggests cookie cutter leadership behaviors and the aping of technical skills, with little appreciation for the complexities of leadership or human cognition. It presupposes linear relationships and ignores feedback loops, interaction effects, and the impact of small changes in the system on large future effects (the "butterfly effect").

For example, if we were to say to you as a new principal that if you have a clear vision for student learning, your students will achieve, we would be less than honest intellectually and practically. A clear vision is important to effective instructional leadership, but only if it is appropriate to the school and shared by teachers, parents, and students. In addition, vision is only one of many factors in the overall picture of teaching and learning. Walberg (1990) for instance, developed a theory of educational productivity that highlighted nine factors required to increase the affective, behavioral, and cognitive learning of students. He organized these factors into three groups: student aptitude (ability or prior achievement, development or individual maturation, and motivation); instruction (amount of instructional time and quality of instructional experiences); and psychological environments (curriculum of the home, morale-social learning climate, peer group influence, and television viewing time). The key question for principals and for teachers is, in what ways are these educational productivity factors alterable within the context of schools and under the direction of professional educators? Clearly, some factors are more amenable to direct influence by principals and teachers than others. They do not function in isolation and any single factor, such as a principal's vision of student learning, must be seen within the context and complexity of many other factors that contribute to student learning.

The organizational structure of schools also affects the sources of principal influence and makes this influence indirect rather than direct. The technical core in education, teaching and learning, is only loosely linked to structure and governance in schools. Karl Weick (1976) described schools as loosely coupled when the principles and values underlying the technical core (teaching and learning activities) are incongruent with major governance and structural aspects of the organization. The best example of this in education is the self-contained classroom within a school and a district. Critical decisions in curriculum and instruction may be made by the school board, by central office administrators, and by principals, but these decisions affecting teaching and learning are implemented by classroom teachers. Principals have a unique organizational role in governance and in the operational hierarchy of school, but they are not working directly with children in classrooms on a daily basis. Therefore, principals' efforts and influence on student learning are primarily indirect, mediated through teachers and their work.

> The principal is formally accountable to his superiors in the district hierarchy for all that happens in a school. Yet the teachers who have direct contact with the children, who have the most to do with what happens, do most of their work out of his sight and hearing and with at least a minimal formal claim to autonomy. (Metz, 1978, p. 188)

Leadership perspective is the third factor affecting the direct and indirect impact of principals on schools. Desires to attribute student outcomes directly to principal instructional leadership are in part steeped in a traditional view of principal as heroic leader. Principals influence student achievement by marshaling and coordinating the energies, efforts, and commitment of others toward the accomplishment of shared goals for student affective, behavioral, and cognitive outcomes. Instructional leadership is not something principals accomplish by themselves. If student achievement relied only on the heroic instructional leader behaviors of principals, we would be wasting vast amounts of resources on the professional development and training of teachers, not to mention 60 percent to 70 percent of our educational budgets dedicated to personnel costs. Principals are teachers also, but their primary responsibilities as instructional leaders require them to act more as enablers of high-quality teaching and learning than as primary service deliverers.

What do we mean when we use the terms, *direct impact* and *indirect impact?* Kleine-Kracht's (1993) definition of direct and indirect instructional leadership is among the most concise and useful. She defines direct instructional leadership as hands-on, face-to-face activities such as the "immediate interactions of principals with teachers and others about the classroom, teaching, student performance, and curricula" (p. 188). In contrast, indirect instructional leadership is invisible to others because either they are unaware of what constitutes instructional leadership or they fail to see the connections between various activities and teaching and learning.

> Indirect instructional leadership activities are behaviors that deal with the school's internal and external environment, the physical and cultural context surrounding the classroom, teaching, and curricula, and the meanings that principals' actions have for teachers. (p. 189)

Principals' Direct Impact on Student Outcomes: Empirical Evidence

In *Classrooms and Corridors,* Mary Metz (1978) provides a vivid description of professional work in two desegregated, urban junior high schools. Recognizing the importance of the principal's leadership role to the overall character of the school, she concludes, "The Principal has direct responsibility without direct control over events for which he must answer" (p. 188). Responsibility without control creates role ambiguity and role anxiety for principals. Despite the contradictions implicit in this description of their leadership role, effective principals make choices as instructional leaders to engage in activities that directly affect teachers, classrooms, curricula, and students. You also will find a high tolerance for ambiguity useful.

Principals directly influence student achievement through teaching, coaching, and modeling. The principal's most direct influence on individual students comes from her personal contact with them through occasional teaching and coaching and through modeling of particular behaviors in her daily work. On occasion principals substitute for teachers in classrooms; in these situations, though limited, principals are teachers. Principals also coach students in student government and in preparation for public presentations, through discipline, in ceremonies, through schoolwide lyceums, and as chaperons for student activities. Principals influence students directly by their behaviors that students observe. As we noted earlier in the chapter, everyone in the school is constantly scrutinizing the principal's behavior for clues about important values and learning. Students learn from their principal when they interact with her. Does she listen to students? Does she respect individuals with whom she interacts? If the principal says that she respects diversity of opinions, what do students learn from her reactions to a student boycott of the school cafeteria? Each of these examples, along with hundreds of other daily interactions between principals and students, influences learning outcomes.

Principals, however, are administrators, not full-time teachers and coaches. Their ability to interact with over 1,000 students on any given day is limited. Even though, "[d]irect activity is potentially more effective than indirect activity because it takes into account individual differences among teachers and students" (Murphy & Hallinger, 1988, p. 221), direct influence such as that described above is likely to be a less efficient use of principals' efforts than more indirect methods because of the narrowness of scope and actual number of individual students that a principal can work with on any given day. Thus, principals engage in instructional leadership and supervisory activities that are more likely to have broad and lasting effects in the teaching-learning environment in the school. These include such activities as being visible in classrooms and at school events, providing feedback to students and teachers, working on curriculum with teachers, planning schoolwide events, coordinating teaching-learning activities, troubleshooting and facilitating instructional delivery, participating on multidisciplinary teams to develop individual educational plans for students, working with teachers to use student test data to improve their curriculum and instruction, and helping to select instructional materials. Next we discuss principals' indirect influence on student learning.

Principals' Indirect Impact on Student Outcomes

Many educators and scholars argue that all principal effects are indirect (see, for example, Pitner, 1988; Bossert, 1988; Duckworth, 1983; Ellett & Walberg, 1979; and Murphy & Hallinger, 1988). Essentially the argument is that a principal's influence on student outcomes is mediated through factors within and outside of the school environment. We cite a few examples to illustrate conceptualizations of the indirect impact of principals' behaviors on student achievement.

The framework by Bossert and others (1982) indicates that principals' behavior has a direct effect on two critical school-level factors—school climate and instructional organization. By positively affecting these factors, principals can indirectly influence student achievement. Duke (1987) also concluded that principals "[d]o not exercise direct control over the teaching-learning process" (p. 25). Therefore they employ their administrative skills by coordinating and troubleshooting in four key areas (staff development, resource allocation, institutional support, and quality control) to affect student achievement positively. Murphy and Hallinger (1988) identified principals' work in policy development, monitoring of student progress, and enforcement of policies and practices as indirect instructional management activities.

Through this indirect activity, the principal can influence the work structure within which the staff perform. Indirect principal activity is advantageous in that it does not require constant supervision and therefore consumes less of the principal's time. The major disadvantage in indirect activity is that effectiveness of policy implementation in the absence of direct supervision requires teacher commitment to the policies. Such a consensus is often difficult to achieve. (p. 220)

Heck, Larsen, and Marcoulides, (1990) link instructional leadership to student achievement by positing, "The principal may influence school-student achievement through managing the political relationship of the school to its environment, supervising the school's instructional organization and building a positive climate for learning" (p. 101). Firestone and Wilson (1985) describe how principals work through bureaucratic and cultural linkages that govern teacher behavior to influence student outcomes. Peterson (1989) describes principals as instructional leaders who employ technical and cultural dimensions of schools to positively influence teacher work and student learning. Finally, Kleine-Kracht (1993) provides a description of one high school principal who uses a variety of indirect instructional leadership strategies and existing school structures to influence teaching and learning.

> Thus, in choosing to exert primarily an indirect influence on instruction, the principal of North High School was faced with several significant decisions. He had to select qualified and credible individuals to provide direct instructional leadership. He had to allow these individuals to exercise their responsibilities with genuine authority. He had to possess a clear understanding of the school's purpose and make that purpose concrete in his decisions. Finally, he had to encourage experimentation and innovation. (p. 210)

Recognizing that many school boards, parents, and superintendents want to see principals exert much more direct instructional leadership, she argues for a reconceptualization of instructional leadership. She states that there is

> a popular conception that administrators are instructional leaders only when they are constantly in the classroom, observing teachers, and discussing curriculum. Underlying this popular conception is an assumption that the principal as an instructional leader must know more than his or her followers. If, however, we take a new understanding of the principalship seriously, we might envision the principal as an instructional leader who primarily facilitates leadership in others and empowers them to be leaders. This reconceptualization would require that administrative training programs must also emphasize the development of the competencies and attitudes basic to indirect instructional leadership. (p. 211)

Dwyer and others (1983) support the efficacy of this recommendation in their *Five Principals in Action.* They uncovered many different styles of effective instructional leadership. Direct modeling and physical presence in the classroom, for example, were more appropriate with a young, inexperienced faculty.

Indirect instructional leadership may also have more impact on student learning over time than direct instructional leadership, because teachers do not necessarily accept principals as their instructional leaders (Pellicer et al., 1988). In some cases, teachers construe direct instructional leadership as an administrative political ploy to exert greater control over them and their work. For example, principals can use sanctions and rewards to influence teachers and their work (Blase, 1989).

> According to teachers, the principals' use of sanctions was quite frequently associated with the manipulation of resources (e.g., equipment, materials, space, funds); work factors in classrooms (e.g., class loads, class size, homeroom responsibilities); work factors outside classrooms (e.g., strict rule enforcement, unwillingness to bend rules); opportunities for input in decision (e.g., curricular, extracurricular). . . . The data emphasized that the use of control-manipulative behaviors by some school principals had serious negative effects on teacher involvement and performance; these behaviors were seen to undermine school-based academic and social standards. Anger was the most predominant feeling that teachers expressed in regard to the use of control and manipulation by principals. (Blase, 1989, pp. 735, 745, 746)

Any time teachers perceive that the instructional leadership activities of the principal are intrusive, manipulative, and political, a potential exists for negative effects to school climate and to the organization of instruction, which in turn have the potential of negatively affecting student learning outcomes.

The indirect influence of principals on student achievement also is cited in the work of Rowan and Denk (1984), who examined the effect of a change in principals (leader succession) on student achievement. They reported, "Leadership changes in schools did not affect school basic skills performance until the second year of a new leader's tenure, and more important, the effect differed depending on the socioeconomic composition of the school" (p. 532). In schools with high enrollments of AFDC children, the effect of a change in principals on students' basic skills in reading and math tended to positively affect basic skills performance. In schools with low AFDC student enrollments, the impact of a change in leadership was slightly negative. Thus, the "socioeconomic context for leadership" moderated the impact of a change in principals. The researchers hypothesize that the differences in impact may be attributable to receptivity to change and school improvement initiatives in low SES schools because there is more room for growth and improvement. However, in schools where there are relatively low AFDC student enrollments and where students are already achieving, teachers and staff are less likely to see changes in leaders and in the way they do things as desirable; thus, a change is more disruptive than remediative. Finally, in further analysis of their data they noted that the "effects of principal turnover were merely short-lived displacements in that they were unrepeated in following years" (p. 532). Using a data base that included all California school districts, Ogawa and Hart (1985) also reported modest effects of a change in principals on student achievement.

In conclusion, principals have direct and indirect influence on student learning outcomes in their schools. The issue is one of balance and congruence. The realities of a principal's daily managerial responsibilities limit opportunities for direct influence. Thus, indirect sources of influence promise to complement direct instructional leadership activities. When direct and indirect instructional leadership behaviors are congruent with shared beliefs about student learning and with norms of high expectations for individual learning emphasizing continuous improvement, they combine to create a powerful instructional leadership strategy.

From the outset of this chapter, we have focused on the principal's capacity to influence student achievement within the context of the school. It is reasonable to assume that a text on the school principalship would have such a bias. Sources of principals' instructional leadership influence and principals' beliefs are felt at many levels, within and outside of the school. Next, we briefly describe how principals' instructional leadership, direct and indirect, is felt at multiple levels (student, classroom, school, and beyond the school) and how principal leadership influences student affective, behavioral, and cognitive learning.

When discussing the effects of principals' instructional leadership on student achievement, it became clear that understanding the relationship between leadership and learning was a function of the unit of analysis. The differences we see when individual student performance scores are averaged with group scores provide one example. An individual student's test score may reflect the student's past performance and ability and the impact of a teacher's direct instruction. The relationship between a teacher's performance and a single student's test score is then apparent. However, when individual test scores are averaged for a group, the average group score may render any effect on individual students invisible. Similarly, as student achievement scores are aggregated by classroom, by school, and by district, simple linear relationships often fail to explain the subtle, layered, and complex relationships between teacher instruction and student performance. The findings of Walberg's theory of educational productivity are useful as we examine the interdependence among sources, types, and levels of principals' influence on student learning.

Walberg's theory of educational productivity (1990) posits that there are nine key factors that contribute to individual student learning outcomes. Our point in reviewing these nine factors is to examine the degree to which principals can influence the effects of these factors. As you review each factor, think about whether each is within the principal's sphere of instructional leadership influence.

Nine Educational Productivity Factors

Student Aptitude

1. Ability, or preferably, prior achievement as measured by the usual learning tests
2. Development as indexed by chronological age or stage of maturation
3. Motivation or self-concept as indicated by personality tests or the student's willingness to persevere intensively on learning tasks

Instruction

4. Amount of time students engage in learning
5. Quality of the instructional experience, including method (psychological) and curricular (content) aspects

6. Curriculum of the home
7. Morale or climate of the classroom social group
8. Peer group outside school
9. Minimum leisure-time television viewing

Together these nine factors interact and influence one another, and they are themselves affected as students learn and thus bring new knowledge into interaction with these factors. Walberg acknowledges that

> other social factors influence learning in school but are less directly linked to academic learning. For example, class size, financial expenditures per student, and private governance (independent or sectarian in contrast to public control of schools) correlate weakly with learning, especially if the initial abilities of students are considered. Thus, improvements in the more direct and more alterable factors hold the best hope for increasing educational productivity. (p. 281)

Some factors are much more amenable to influence by principals than are others; nevertheless, all are important and thus must be considered as principals make choices and set priorities in their daily work. Principals must invest their expertise and energy where they most count. The research indicates that the greatest impact and most significant effects of principals' influence on student learning are the result of their efforts to create and nurture positive learning climates and high-quality instructional organization.

Throughout this chapter we have described how effective principals habitually think in terms of student and school outcomes while they work under the press of sometimes paradoxical, and other times distracting, pressures of personal, professional, organizational, and political forces. Recognizing how to get the biggest payoff from spending instructional leadership money might tempt you to think that principals need to "stick to their professional knitting" (focusing only on within-school factors), with little regard for educational productivity factors beyond their immediate spheres of influence. Most educators who have dedicated their professional careers to education immediately see the naiveté of such insular thinking. Each of the nine factors, whether within one's direct control or not, or inside or outside classrooms and schools, has the potential of minimizing student learning if ignored and left completely unattended. If, for example, we translate this theory into a simple mathematical equation, the effect that a large negative value or a zero has on the product is immediately obvious.

In actual social settings some educational productivity factors have such a diffuse impact on learning that their overall effect may be multiplicative rather than additive. For example, a well-fed child from a stable and highly educated home may respond very differently in a school with low morale and a marginal instructional program than a hungry child from a dysfunctional home. Similarly, a child who comes to school having been nurtured for five years in a highly verbal, experientially rich environment is likely to respond to language arts instruction somewhat differently from a child with limited life experiences, whose primary companions have been television sitcom characters.

Wehlage (1989) provides additional insight into the impact of principals' instructional leadership within and beyond the school. In a study of at-risk students and school drop-outs, Wehlage identified schools where educators were making a difference in the lives of at-risk students.

> The most fundamental belief among the professionals we studied was that teacher-student interactions should be governed by reciprocity. . . . Reciprocity requires both parties to engage in respectful relations, and in the education of at-risk students, it requires educators to take the initiative in helping students overcome impediments to social bonding and membership. (p. 135)

Based on their findings, Wehlage and colleagues proposed a theory of drop-out prevention positing that student academic and social learning outcomes were the products of educational engagement and school membership.

> The theory explains how educators can induce alienated students to become active in the educational process. Theory argues that students who are school members and engaged in school work are likely to be better achievers and to develop personal and social characteristics valued by the society. (p. 195)

Wehlage and colleagues identified a number of impediments to student engagement and membership—adjustment difficulty, incongruence, isolation, and lack of extrinsic and intrinsic rewards. They concluded that by working to minimize the deleterious effects of these obstacles practitioners have their greatest points of leverage within the school to influence two intermediate goals—engagement and membership, which help students achieve affective, behavioral, and cognitive outcomes. Drop-out prevention theory has implications for the impact of principals' leadership beyond the school and throughout the community. Working with parents, social service agencies, and community organizations is a logical extension of interagency collaboration that offers other points of leverage for principals and educational professionals.

CONCLUSION

In this chapter we discussed two dimensions of principals' instructional leadership behaviors and their impact on student and school outcomes—sources of influence (behaviors, beliefs, and symbols) and types of impact (direct and indirect). Principals influence student learning outcomes directly and indirectly by what they do, what they believe, and how they use symbols. The direct and indirect effects of these sources and types of influence are felt by students, in classrooms, throughout the school, and in the community.

SUGGESTED ACTIVITIES

1. Refer to Figure 9.1. Identify specific behaviors, beliefs, and symbols that your principal uses to influence desired student and school outcomes. Are there any inconsistencies or contradictions across the three sources of influence? What impact do they have on your school?

2. Using Figure 9.1 develop a plan, which is congruent with your personal and professional strengths, to influence student and school outcomes positively.

3. We would like you to identify examples from your own experiences that are illustrative of the interrelationships and interdependence of aptitude, instructional, and psychological factors.

4. Review your school's mission statement. Using Figure 9.1, identify specific examples in each source of influence your principal uses to accomplish the stated mission. Compare these with examples describing other principals.

5. In this chapter we described what principals do as instructional leaders to protect teaching and learning time in their schools. Do a systematic assessment of the use of time in your school. If time is a valuable resource, are there places within the day where this resource is being poorly used?

6. Organizational sagas and stories often illustrate important organizational values and beliefs. Identify an organizational story that expresses important values, characteristics, and/or beliefs in your school. Share this story with your colleagues. How does this story illustrate cultural norms that support the importance of high-quality instruction and school success?

Becoming a Principal

Socialization is the process of acquiring the knowledge, skills, attitudes, and values characteristic of a particular social role. Socialization processes occur in families, organizations, communities, and professional work cultures. The purpose of this chapter is to examine the socialization processes of becoming a principal. Through description and reflective interaction, we hope to stimulate your thinking about your own socialization experiences in becoming a principal and to guide you through them.

The model of professional socialization displayed in the section, "Becoming a Principal," provides a framework within which you can examine the multiple sources of influence that affect your preparation for the principalship. The five major process dimensions of this model of professional socialization for principals serve as the organizers for the central focus of this chapter, following the discussion of theory. They include antecedent conditions, anticipatory socialization, professional socialization, organizational socialization, and role making and visualization.

As with any two-dimensional model, one must take care to view it interpretively rather than literally. The linearity and sequentiality represented do not mean that principals' professional socialization is a rigid, prescriptive process. The model represents a useful way of framing our discussion on becoming a principal. While stages and sequenced processes are part of becoming a principal, many of the socialization processes we discuss occur concurrently, recurrently, and interactively rather than sequentially and independently. There are commonalities in the professional socialization process for principals, but differences in individual personalities and backgrounds, in work settings, and in historic and sociocultural factors will make your experiences and outcomes unique as you prepare for and enter the principalship.

The notion of *becoming*, in this chapter, implies learning and transition directed toward a new state of knowledge and being—that of school principal. The principal works in a social environment—the school. Consequently, before we turn to the specific dimensions of principal socialization laid out in the model, we review three conceptualizations that place the process of becoming in context. After a brief overview of social role theory, social and observational learning theory, and role transition theory, we discuss each dimension of the professional socialization model in detail. As you read the descriptions of each dimension, reflect on each and identify examples in your experiences of professional socialization and growth.

SOCIAL ROLE THEORY IN FICTION AND SCHOLARSHIP

Literature and scholarly inquiry provide numerous descriptions, explanations, and interpretations of the everyday social behavior of people. "Novelists, dramatists, and other astute observers of the human scene have noted that behavior often is determined less by characteristics of the person than by the part one is assigned to play" (Allen & van de Vliert, 1984, p. 4). Social role theory posits that people's behaviors are patterned and predictable, not random, disconnected, and meaningless. Fein (1990) describes these patterned behaviors as social role scripts, the rules and structures that guide people during their everyday conduct and interaction with others. Within patterned social scripts, people create meaning as they enact various social roles and interact with one another. (See also the works of Merton, 1957; Biddle, 1979; Sarbin, 1954; Turner & Colomy, 1988; and Van Maanen & Schein, 1979).

The concept of social role includes the related concept of position, "a designated location in the structure of a social system" (Biddle & Thomas, 1966, p. 11). In complex social systems, like schools, individuals may fill several positions and carry out multiple roles associated with various formal and informal positions. For example, a third grade teacher may also be the school's union representative, the PTA liaison, and the chair of the school-community site council. Think about the formal and informal roles you play in your school. To what degree are these parts socially scripted? As you reflect on particular roles you play, in what ways do you influence the role (role making)? How does the role shape your behavior (role taking)?

Two major perspectives, structuralism and social interactionism, have informed the work of social role theorists. These two perspectives illuminate very different aspects of your future work as a principal. Structuralists define social roles as sets of behavioral expectations associated with positions in particular social systems. From the structuralist perspective, a principal learns his role by enacting the part, role taking. He responds to expectations that exist in the normative system. He takes on and internalizes those expectations (Ebaugh, 1988, p. 18). Interactionists define the learning of social roles as dynamic and interactive. Individuals become "role makers" who negotiate meaning and shape the roles they assume. We have argued throughout this text that both role taking and role making are important dimensions of your professional socialization and growth as an educator.

The literature on the school principalship has long recognized that principals occupy many roles. (See, for example, accounts by Johann Sturm (1538),[1]

---

[1]See *Memoirs of Eminent Teachers and Educators with Contributions to the History of Education*, H. Barnard, ed. Republished from *The American Journal of Education*. Hartford: Brown & Gross, 1878.

Ensign (1923), Pierce (1934), and Button (1966)). Small (1974) described principals as organizational change agents who carry out ten roles as formal leaders in schools. He said principals may play various roles. For example, the principal can be an initiator (making changes); stimulator (encouraging and facilitating opportunities for others to make changes); reactor (responding to the ideas and initiatives of others); implementor (carrying out change initiatives); conduit (connecting those requesting change to resources and personnel to support the change); orchestrator-mediator (creating a supportive environment for managing change among affected parties); persuader-dissuader (providing feedback to influence initiatives of others); advocate (pushing for particular changes and supporting others); and ombudsman (listening to and voicing the concerns of others). The principal may choose to be a nonactor (rejecting the roles described above and playing only a minimal role in organizational change).

Another framework used to examine the roles of principals is Henry Mintzberg's taxonomy of managerial roles. In Chapter 6 we discussed the interpersonal roles (leader, liaison, figurehead), informational roles (monitor, disseminator, spokesperson), and decisional roles (entrepreneur, disturbance handler, resource allocator, negotiator) that principals play in schools. Other scholars and practitioners have described equally diverse and challenging roles for principals. The knowledge base organizers that we presented in Table 2.1 also provide a list of social roles commonly used to describe and categorize the roles and the work of principals. The roles described above and in previous chapters are roles that principals take on in their work; however, principals are also *role makers*. They actively choose to emphasize some roles while minimizing others. Context, culture, and situational demands influence the roles principals play. Becoming a principal is a process of role development.

Principals take on various roles as formal and symbolic leaders; they confront role ambiguity, role overload, and role conflict in their leadership role. Given the dizzying array of possible roles they could play, principals as instructional leaders are guided by their values, especially those focused on teaching and learning. In your journey to the principalship, you will encounter these same contradictions, conflicts, and dilemmas. The test of your effectiveness as an instructional leader will not be how deftly you avoid these obstacles—a fruitless endeavor. Rather, your leadership will be judged by the role(s) you play to influence others, to become committed to and engaged in professional work that makes a difference for the growth and development of children in your school.

SOCIAL-OBSERVATIONAL LEARNING THEORY

Social learning theory asserts that people acquire new knowledge and regulate their behavior by observing responses to and consequences of their actions and the actions and experiences of others. Social learning is a natural cognitive process according to Bandura (1977a).

> Cognitive processes play a prominent role in the acquisition and retention of
> new behavior patterns. Transitory experiences leave lasting effects being

coded and retained in symbols for memory representations. Because acquisition of response information is a major aspect of learning much human behavior is developed modeling. (p. 192)

Social modeling and learning can shape teachers' behaviors during your entry into the principal's position in a school. As teachers observe others' actions and reactions to events associated with the change in principals, for example, their reactions convey information about responses the group will view as appropriate.

When social learning has occurred, those who observe and learn can transfer the behavior to new situations and behave in ways in which the model might behave in similar circumstances, "even though subjects had never witnessed the model's behavior in these new situations" (Bandura, 1972, p. 37). This is a form of social mimicry in which people observe the interactions of others and learn from them. Although social learning theory relates directly to the feedback and consequences arising from the social environment, social learning theory takes a psychological view of learning that focuses on social behavior resulting from modeling rather than emerging social realities.

Based on observations and self-corrective adjustments each of us makes in our own behavior, we develop appropriate social-behavioral responses and patterns, and we construct meaning in various roles. Socially learned scripts provide us with information on how we can achieve our goals in a given setting, and thus help us avoid behaviors that result in negative outcomes. Social learning is the mental process we use to integrate experience in meaningful ways into our professional knowledge base. These sets of learned social responses become a constellation of aggregated experiences each of us brings to various social roles, including to professional roles such as the principalship.

ROLE TRANSITION THEORY

You will recall from our discussion in Chapter 4 that social role learning is a dynamic process. Implicit in this understanding is the notion that social roles and their defining dimensions are mutable. As changes occur in social settings and social roles and as individuals move from one role to another, the process of changing roles and trading one set of expected behaviors in a social system for another is referred to as *role transition* (Allen & van de Vliert, 1984). Role transitions are accompanied by significant changes in tasks, behaviors, norms, and values for individual role holders. Allen and van de Vliert provide a model that depicts six major dimensions of the social role transition process: antecedent conditions (the potential causes of the role transition); role transition (change events for individuals between two sets of role expectations); role strain (discomfort, anxiety, perplexity, and uneasiness) experienced by people as they go through role transitions); moderators (personal and environmental factors that intervene and modify role transition events and reactions to them); reactions (behaviors and activities that help role holders reduce the intensity of role strain); and consequences (the totality of effects and impact of role holders' reactions to role strain). To illustrate, Table 10.1 provides examples of the six dimensions of role transition that characterize the professional educator's move from classroom teacher to school principal.

Social role theory, social learning theory, and role transition theory provide the theoretical lenses we will use to examine more closely the personal and professional socialization processes that you will experience in preparation for the principalship. Table 10.2 portrays a framework that includes five major dimensions of professional socialization and growth.

BECOMING A PRINCIPAL: A PROCESS MODEL OF PROFESSIONAL SOCIALIZATION

The process model depicted in Table 10.2 is a framework that highlights major dimensions and their relationships to the professional socialization of school principals. The five major components of the model include antecedent conditions; anticipatory socialization; professional socialization; organizational socialization; and role making and professional visualization.

Antecedent Conditions

If we were to ask practicing principals how and why they became principals, each would share a story of early personal characteristics, environmental influences, professional biography, and prior experiences. Common themes and patterns would appear across these stories, but each principal's story would be unique. Your preparation for the principalship is also a shared, yet personal, journey. Antecedent conditions are those factors, personal and environmental, that form the substrate upon which more deliberate and personally directed socialization processes for becoming a principal are constructed. Personal factors include personality characteristics and traits, individual biographies, and work and life experiences. Environmental factors include historic, social, eco-

TABLE 10.1. Role Transition: Classroom Teacher to Principal

Role Transition Dimensions	Selected Examples
Antecedent Conditions	Career advancement; more money; greater impact on school
Role Transition	Teacher to Principal; sense of responsibility for my class to whole school
Role Strain	Role ambiguity; sense of isolation; lack of contact with children; new relationship with teachers, parents, and students
Moderators	Norms of collegiality, other school culture dimensions; interpersonal and role adjustment skills; tolerance for ambiguity
Reactions	Professional growth and development; adapt new indicators of success as an educator
Consequences	Successful role transition; embrace role changes; welcome opportunities leadership role permits

nomic, political, and organizational influences affecting individuals' socialization. All these factors contribute to the profile of a corps of principals. What do we currently know about people who become principals?

A Profile of Principals

The Digest of Education Statistics (1993) provides a composite profile of the 127,039 principals and assistant principals in public and private schools in the United States at this time. The average principal is a white male in his mid to late forties. He works in a public school and has over eleven years' experience as a principal. He taught nine years prior to his first administrative position. Principals are career educators with limited work experiences outside the field of education. The data in Table 10.3 provide a more detailed summary of selected characteristics of school principals in the United States.

This composite profile of school principals reveals that—even in this decade—greater attention should be paid to ethnicity, gender, and socioeconomic status (SES) characteristics of those we recruit to become principals to better reflect features of the general population. As dramatic changes occur in school-age populations, especially in large urban districts, the data in Table 10.3 suggest that schools would benefit tremendously from the leadership of educators who more closely represent the diversity of Americans.

There are many unique features in the overall profile of school principals. These are the result of years of cultural, historic, political, and ideological influences. For example, education remains a female-dominated profession, yet men occupy three times as many principalships as women. The 1987–1988 data reveal that 87 percent of teachers in elementary schools were women, yet they held only 30 percent of elementary school principalships. In addition to disparities in gender representation in administrative positions in schools, the data indicate very limited numbers of non-Anglo principals.

TABLE 10.2 Becoming a Principal: A Process Model of Socialization

Antecedent Conditions
   Personal Characteristics
   Biography
   Prior Experiences

Anticipatory Socialization
   Preservice Preparation and Training   Formal processes
                                              Informal processes

Professional Socialization
   Five Stages of Socialization   Technical
                                            Moral

Organizational-Situational Socialization
   Learning the ropes
   The way things are done around here

Role Making and Professional Visualization
   Translating ideas into action

Enrollment data from preparation programs for school administrators provide grounds for optimism about alleviating gender disparities in the principalship. The low proportion of non-Anglo students enrolled in principal certification programs, however, means that the pool of available candidates for future principalship vacancies will remain small, thus ensuring future underrepresentation of minorities in leadership positions in schools. The profile of administration candidates also greatly affects the recruitment and hiring of qualified educational leaders for our largest urban school districts. Many districts in the United States can no longer refer to their student population as minority because the majority of their students are non-Anglo. As we look at the current profile of school principals and combine these data with those describing incoming teachers and principals, the differences among educational professionals and the students with whom they will work become even more glaring and problematic than simple demographic profiles indicate. Beyond numbers, personal experience and background, personal biography, and individual experience also influence the socialization and role of school principals. Next we explore the ways in which each contributes to an individual's preparation for the principalship.

Survey data from the National Association of Elementary Principals and the National Association of Secondary Schools Principals provide descriptions of the general patterns of career advancement for school principals. For elementary and secondary principals, the gateway to the principalship is through the classroom. Ninety-nine percent of first-year principals reported having three or more years of classroom teaching experience. For all principals, only eight percent reported having fewer than three years of teaching experience. Women are more likely than men to have moved directly from the classroom into the principalship. In a survey of elementary school principals, Daud reported that, "men were twice as likely as women to have had secondary teaching experience, three times as likely to have been a secondary assistant principal, and about 23 times more likely to have been a coach (27.8%) than were women (1.2%)" (1989, pp. 39–40).

The experiences of first-year elementary principals vary considerably. Slightly over 15 percent have been assistant principals, 6 percent have counseling or college teaching experience, and 7.4 percent previously worked in

TABLE 10.3. Elementary and Secondary Principal Profile

Education	Master's degree 53%	Specialist/Doctorate 44%
Experience	Principal 10 years	Teacher 10 years
Gender	Female 25%	Male 75%
Ethnicity	White 89%	Minority/Nonwhite 11%
Age	Under 50 62%	Over 50 38%

Averages taken from 1987–1988 U.S. Department of Education

central office positions. Secondary principals reported having experiences as coaches (52%), department chairs (46%), counselors (22%), athletic directors (28%), and as deans of students/attendance (14%).

Elementary principals listed on-the-job experience in the principalship, experience as classroom teachers, and experience as assistant principals as the most valuable on-the-job contributors to their professional preparation (Doud, 1989). Though questioned slightly differently in their survey, secondary principals listed the amount and quality of their professional preparation, success in the job interview, the fact that the superintendent wanted them in the position, success as teachers, and success as assistant principals as *very important* or *important* factors influencing appointment to their first principalships (Pellicer et al., 1988).

Social Forces Influencing Role Learning

The social processes of becoming a principal are also influenced by historical, professional, personal, organizational, and cultural factors. Role theory argues that hierarchical relationships among various role holders in schools greatly affect our perception of formal roles. The principal's role is defined to a great extent by the expectations others have for principals. The expectations of students, teachers, other administrators, parents, and school board members shape the role of the principal and preparation for that role. Organizational cultures, community values, traditions, precedents and predecessors in the job also contribute to this professional role legacy.

All of these factors shape the principal's role as well as contribute to role ambiguity. In a study of elementary school principals, Foskett (1967) concluded,

> The evidence suggests that the position is not clearly defined. In part, the principal is identified as an administrator and as a member of the teaching staff. Similarly, principals sometimes see themselves as administrators and sometimes as members of the teaching staff. However, there is a tendency for the principals to see themselves as administrators more frequently than do the several populations of others. This ambiguity is heightened by a low level of agreement among principals themselves and among others for a number of norms that appear to be critical. (p. 95)

Earlier in the chapter we described how social learning helps people gain valuable information about social roles. Principals are under constant scrutiny by students, teachers, parents, and other community members. Each of us knows principals who—by both positive and negative example—taught us a great deal about the role of principals as formal leaders in schools. We watched and learned from their interpersonal interactions, work priorities, participation in public ceremonies and school rituals, and expressions of values, beliefs, and shared purposes in the school.

Our observations and subsequent perceptions of principals' behaviors were mediated by the social roles we occupied. One of the authors found this to be so. When I was a classroom teacher my interactions with my principal were more limited than they were when I was an administrative intern in the same school. When I was an assistant principal my opportunities to interact and discuss the nature of principal's work on a daily basis provided important information on leadership complexity, role ambiguity, and the indeterminacy of practice. An issue that may have seemed relatively simple and unambiguous from my perspective as a classroom teacher, seemed more complex and less clear from a different role perspective. Our perceptions of principal work are moderated by the roles we hold and by our proximity to and frequency of contact with principals. These recollections, combined with current observations, insights, and experiences with principals are important sources of experientially based job information. As you think about becoming a principal, the ways in which principals you know have carried out their leadership role contribute to your own learning and professional socialization.

> A cursory review of the role(s) of the principal can be summed up by simply saying the job is in the eye of the beholder. This ambiguity is compounded by both local edict and legislative mandates. Educators, legislators and lay-persons are all quite willing to add to the list of the principal's responsibilities without inquiring about the current ones. (Howell, 1981, p. 333)

Socialization to the Principal's Role: A Student Perspective

Because all educators have been students in schools and many now work in schools as teachers, counselors, support staff and administrators, social role theory and observational learning theory explain how educators gather a great deal of information about the principal's role. Think about your own experiences as a student. In what way have these experiences been influential forces in your perceptions of the principalship and your preparation for it?

These memories from our own school experience can be very vivid. Bredeson (1991) reported that 82.5 percent of 137 respondents (graduate students enrolled in the principalship class over a five-year period) could recall in vivid detail principals from their student days.

> In contrast to caricatures of low witted, hyper-managerial principals often portrayed in popular media, the principals these students recalled were noted for being caring, respectful, visible, active, and fair, even if they were strict disciplinarians. (p. 513)

Students help to shape principals' perception and enactment of their leadership role in schools. We recently asked students in several schools to describe what principals do. A listing of comments by students in grades 2 to 8 illustrates students' perceptions of the work of principals. Embedded in these perceptions are role expectations students have for building administrators.

What Principals Do Through Students' Eyes

They tell you not to run in the halls and throw balls in people's faces. They look at you if you're doing something bad. (2nd grader)

I think our principal runs the school by sending paper back and forth. (3rd grader)

His job may be talking to people . . . people that come to the school like parents or teachers. (3rd grader)

I think principals do a lot of things. They solve fights and help people who have problems. They also have ice cream socials and lunch at the Ritz. They also buy toilet paper, Kleenex, and paper towels. (3rd grader)

A principal is in charge of the whole school. (3rd grader)

Principals walk the hall asking if it takes two to go to the bathroom. (5th grader)

A principal's job is to make kids smarter. (5th grader)

I really don't know what principals do. I think that they discipline kids, set up school programs, and make decisions on how to spend school money—like to buy lockers. I think they get paid a lot because ours has lots of clothes and jewelry. (7th grader)

Principals in my book are the # 1 public enemy. Whenever I see a principal anywhere but the office, they're usually looking for someone to yell at. When she calls us into the music room, gym or comes around to our rooms, it's usually to give us a lecture. (7th grader)

A principal makes rules for us to follow to get ready for laws in the world. (8th grader)
(Hart & Bredeson, 1993, *Student Survey Data*)

The observations of these students, though less systematically gathered, resonate with the empirical findings from observational studies discussed in Chapter 5. In part these comments reflect students' general perception of the work of principals. They also reveal the hierarchical relationship that exists between principals and students in schools. For more than a century under the legal principle of in loco parentis, principals have been responsible for caring for and disciplining children in schools. Thus, it is not surprising that some students view principals as "super cops" and menacing disciplinarians. Other role expectations such as controller, monitor, communicator, consummate manager, jack-of-all-trades and bureaucrat can also be found in this sampling of student views on the principal's role.

Students' expectations, like teachers', are shaped by the portion of principals' work visible to them. Because principals work at the intersections between the community and the school, between teachers, between students and teachers, parents, counselors, and others, they are boundary spanners in the classic sense. Much of their work is invisible to each of these groups.

Socialization to the Principal's Role: A Teacher's Perspective

Experiences as a teacher, perceptions of the principal's role from the classroom, and teacher expectations of principals are important sources of role socialization information. Teachers work with principals on a daily basis. Given this close working relationship, it should not be surprising that teachers have particular role expectations of principals and that these expectations affect the principal's role. Since the pathway to the principalship is teaching, what teachers expect from the principal becomes a part of their own sense of role when they become principals. For example, when a teacher sends a misbehaving child to the principal's office, he expects 100 percent backing from her. When an angry parent calls the principal about a problem in a classroom, a teacher expects the principal to discuss the parent's concern with him before making any promises to correct the situation. If scheduling classes affects students in a teacher's classroom, he expects to have input before decisions are made. The expectations teachers hold for principals constitute an antecedent factor that contributes to their professional socialization to the principal's role.

Teachers have many expectations of principals. Giannangelo and Malone (1987) reported that the overwhelming majority of teachers define the principal's primary role as instructional leader. In addition, teachers want their principals to be responsible for building management and public relations with parents and the community at large, while nurturing a healthy school climate. Finally, these researchers found that teachers believe principals tend to be overly concerned with nonacademic matters and that principals need to be more visible in the school, to make more visits to classrooms, and to provide more support for instruction. Together the expectations, commonly expressed by teachers as "do's and don'ts," establish the normative structure shaping the principal's role. Foskett (1967), in addition, noted that the principal's role is shaped by a large number of conditional guidelines. Summarizing Foskett's findings, Blumberg and Greenfield (1980) conclude,

> Thus, while principals may appear to have some freedom of choice in acting out their role, depending on the actors and the characteristics of the situation at a particular time or place, certain penalties may accompany this fluidity. (p. 32)

This fluidity may be changing. As school become more complex, teachers' expectations appear to be rising. In 1992 Bredeson reported,

> Teachers expect principals to listen, be supportive, provide feedback, endorse their decisions, model appropriate leadership behaviors, be knowledgeable, promote professionalism, and create nurturing and supportive environments for professional work and development. (p. 17)

Teachers want their "principal's unequivocal support, especially in conflicts with students or parents" (p. 15). Similar findings of teachers' expectations for the unfailing support of their principal were reported by Bredeson, Fruth, and Kasten (1983). "The most frequently mentioned kind of support was help with discipline. Teachers and former teachers wanted 'back-up on discipline,' '100% backing,' and 'consistency in dealing with students' " (p. 55). A common theme is reported in these studies: Teachers have high expectations for their principals. On occasion these expectations are a source of role conflict for principals because they may be in conflict with the expectations of others. In addition, teacher expectations may put the principal in a bind when professional standards and practice may take a back seat to providing support to teachers.

Principals also describe teachers' expectations of them as heroic and larger than life. This perception of the role raises questions about anyone's ability to succeed, let alone excel. Gottfredson and Hybl (1987) reported selected responses from principals' self-descriptions of their leadership role in school. We chose a few examples from this report to illustrate principals' understanding of their roles and how they translate and express these understandings to others.

> The school administrator of today needs to be, not necessarily in this order: a lawyer, an accountant, an exorcist, a damn fool.
>
> There is a Hebrew word for what a principal does: me'afsher, 'make things possible.'
>
> One is called upon constantly to be a beacon of hope for students and faculty . . . an affirmer and believer in what can be. It requires the understanding of Solomon, the leadership of Moses, . . . the vision of John F. Kennedy, [the] patience of Job and the commitment and care of a teacher—one who loves and believes in kids and their future. (p. 115)

Given the demanding set of role expectations expressed in these insider accounts of the principalship, perhaps it is understandable that nobody has ever written the book, *I Want to Be a Principal,* for the children's series.

The expectations administrators, school board members, parents, and community influentials hold for principals also contribute to the antecedent conditions influencing principal role socialization. Individual characteristics, background, personal experience, and the expectations of others are antecedent conditions that both shape and provide insight into the work of principals. These factors also mediate individual professional socialization experiences. Next we examine the impact of antecedent conditions on the second dimension in our professional socialization model, anticipatory socialization.

Anticipatory Socialization

One of the authors vividly recalls an experience in this dimension of socialization. Our school accreditation team had just completed its review of a neighboring high school. I remember feeling excited about being a member of this evaluation team and about being able to tap into seldom-used professional skills. After six years of teaching, I had begun to look at teaching as my life's work. I watched and listened to my colleagues who had made various choices and trade-offs in their careers and lifestyles. I thought about thirty more years in a classroom. I began to question whether I could keep my enthusiasm going for five classes a day, "900 shows a year" (Palonsky, 1986) into the twenty-first century. At first my imagination ran wild—new fields, new occupations, and new work settings! I fantasized about a career change. Maybe I could go to dental school. All of these thoughts drifted through my mind as I drove back to my high school.

After some weeks of professional soul searching, I made up my mind. I decided that I was going to remain in education. I loved the work, and I was good at it. My experiences as a member of an external evaluation team had profoundly affected my thinking. I began to think about myself in a different professional role in education. Though I could not identify what was happening at the time, I had begun the process of anticipatory socialization.

Every educator's journey to the principalship is unique. The events that characterize this journey may be epiphanic, incremental, or perhaps not even recognized as they unfold. It is likely that you are reading this chapter as a requirement for a class in an administrator preparation program. Preservice administrator preparation and training are major components of anticipatory socialization. If this description fits your experience, reflect on your own set of anticipatory socialization processes and outcomes.

Robert Merton (1968) described anticipatory socialization as a pattern of behavior in which people begin to conform to the norms, values, and attitudes of a group they wish to join. For example, college students visit classrooms to observe teaching and learning. As they prepare to leave their undergraduate student group, these novices begin to have positive orientations toward the teacher group they are observing. Similarly, the experiences I gained as a member of a curriculum accreditation team triggered my own thoughts of leaving the classroom for a position with broader responsibilities and more freedom—perhaps the principalship.

Anticipatory socialization processes help aspiring administrators on the route to the principalship in several ways. First, mental rehearsing and social role fantasizing help nonadministrators gain entry into the principals' group. For instance, changes in a teacher's attitude toward administrators and their work in general may affect the relationship between the teacher and principal. Unwittingly, a teacher may begin to pay greater attention to the details of the principal's role. A teacher might become more aware of the principal's frustrations, or find that he is volunteering to participate in meetings and take on extra duties. For aspiring administrators, volunteering to chair meetings, participate on curriculum committees, and supervise students at special events provide greater opportunity to observe principals and to learn from them. The interaction also puts the aspiring administrator into closer contact with the principal. As a result the principal may begin to think about this teacher as a promising administrator. Within these activities the GAS (Getting the Attention of Superiors) phenomenon occurs. High visibility throughout the school and district greatly influences the impressions of key members of the educational community, especially those who select principals and their assistants. These activities often set the stage for subsequent formal and informal socialization processes.

A second purpose of anticipatory socialization is to ease adjustments required as one makes the transition from one role (a classroom teacher) to another (a building principal). As a teacher begins to think of himself as a principal, he becomes more positively oriented toward the norms of this administrator group. In addition, he begins to assess himself in terms of the characteristics and demands of membership in the administrator group. For a teacher thinking about the principalship, such a self-assessment might include thinking about differences in attitudes and behaviors between teachers and principals, in required professional credentials, in daily work, in the number of contract days per year, and in experience. As the teacher begins to size himself up in the role of principal, he may see gaps in his own experience and preparation. He might begin to make adjustments in how he thinks about curriculum issues, discipline concerns, and conflict resolution strategies.

Anticipating the changes that accompany the transition from teacher to principal is an important part of professional learning. This is a self-selecting process. If a person fails to find affinity with the norms and values of the group to which she aspires, she generally rejects the group in favor of her own, or she finds another. Nearing the end of a course on the principalship a graduate student reflected aloud about what she had learned in the class. "Perhaps the most valuable thing I've learned is that I don't want to be a principal." Though we hope this is not your reaction, her conclusion is illustrative of anticipatory socialization in action.

Affinity to group norms, however, does not mean complete surrender. The efforts of individuals to shape their role over time through personalization and role making change the norms and values of these groups. Anticipatory and professional socialization processes can not prepare novice administrators to face every eventuality in the principalship; however, these processes do help to moderate the effects and intensity of role strain resulting from very real changes in professional roles, responsibilities, and relationships.

From the aspiring principal's point of view, anticipatory socialization represents structured growth. From many teachers' point of view, these experiences represent a form of betrayal, rejection of the teaching role. "What is anticipatory socialization from the standpoint of the individual is construed as defection and nonconformity by the group of which he is a member" (Merton, 1968, p. 323). Anticipatory socialization is affected by the reaction of one's current social work group, as one of the authors found. For example, as a teacher, I remember clearly the reactions of my teacher colleagues when I told them I was taking an educational administration course at the university. Their remarks, though delivered in friendly, mostly humorous jabs, were meant to remind me of group loyalty and identification as well as to restrain my own positive orientations and enthusiasm for the administrator group. From their perspective, my colleagues saw that I would eventually leave their ranks and become "one of them" in the office. Interestingly, the reactions of my referent group, fellow teachers, accelerated my socialization to the principalship. My colleagues' reactions to my new career interests and their gentle reminders that were meant to bridle my interest and orientations to administration had just the opposite effect; their reactions tended to distance me further from the teacher group and its rewards. The cumulative effect over time was disassociation and disidentification—normal responses in the role socialization processes.

Leaving one role for another has its cost. For example, first-year principals often describe feelings of isolation in their administrative role (Hart, 1988; Weindling & Early, 1987; Davis, 1988). The censure of social groups to the deviant behaviors by a group member, beginning in anticipatory socialization processes for aspiring principals, provides a partial explanation for feelings of isolation frequently described by beginning principals. Bredeson describes role strain and stress that accompany changes in professional roles in schools.

> Understanding work role transitions and their outcomes is beneficial to principals and to other educators in schools. Awareness of potential negative consequences of role transitions is a fundamental step in planning for and acting to reduce role strain and to limit any deleterious effects on individual role holders and on organizational goals. Role holders who are aware and able to employ effective strategies to deal with multiple dimensions and implications

of work role transitions are more likely to grow professionally and to foster healthy modes of adjustment to change and organizational adaptations to it as opposed to being resistant and calculating professional survivors who intend to ride out yet another wave of educational reform. Relinquishing traditional mechanisms of control and letting go of outlived professional identities are never easy. Thus, understanding work role transitions can be helpful to individuals and to organizations as they think about and examine role exit and role transition as important psychological, social, and political dimensions in professional work life.

The perspectives of these principals also suggest that pre-service and ongoing professional development activities for principals could focus on helping administrators develop situationally appropriate responses and modes of adjustment to work role transitions in dynamic professional work environments. Training programs and activities would be designed to help individuals understand the processes of role transition and role evolution, both of which necessarily include letting go of particular residual role facets. However, the notion of loss might be framed as contributing to individual growth and role evolution and not as a threat to professional survival. (1993, pp. 62–63)

Dimensions and Processes of Role Socialization

In addition to the five stages of role socialization represented in Table 10.2, two dimensions cut across socialization stages and events. These include technical and moral socialization and formal and informal socialization. We begin with an overview of technical and moral socialization based on the work of William Greenfield (1985b).

Technical and Moral Socialization. The knowledge base that guides the daily work of effective principals is complex and by no means certain (National Policy Board for Educational Administration, 1993; University Council for Educational Administration Knowledge Base Project, 1993). Regardless of the learning venue, formal or informal, there is a massive amount of material to be learned by anyone wanting to become a successful principal. The traditional knowledge base for school administrators and preservice administrator preparation programs designed to transmit specified professional knowledge is often criticized because it relies heavily on disconnected technical knowledge (skills, proficiencies, and behaviors) (Bredeson, in press). While technical knowledge is critical to successful administrative practice, William Greenfield (1985b) would argue that the knowledge base for principals must include substantive moral components (values, attitudes, and beliefs). The moral dimension moves principals beyond simple reliance on technical knowledge "doing things right" to levels of reflection and action directed at "doing the right things."

> Completing formal preparation and certification requirements are necessary but not sufficient for appointment to an administrative position; one must also demonstrate adequate moral socialization to the values, attitudes, and beliefs central to members of the administrative group. (Greenfield, 1985, p. 100)

Greenfield refers to technical socialization outcomes as "knowledge and behavior reflecting technical, conceptual, and social skills and activities associated with role enactment. Moral socialization outcomes refer to the attitudes, values, and beliefs required for adequate performance in the role" (p. 100). Moral socialization outcomes tend to be peripheral to administrator preparation programs and in current knowledge base projects. Thus, the acquisition of the values, attitudes, and beliefs associated with being a successful principal becomes the cumulative, and often ambiguous, product of learning in informal settings. Whether learned in formal or informal settings, technical and moral socialization contribute to the development of role perspective, a coordinated set of ideas and actions a person uses in dealing with specific situations of practice. Greenfield (1985b) argues that role perspective is influenced by personal values and beliefs, the views and expectations of one's colleagues, the role orientation and beliefs of one's immediate supervisor, the dominant school culture, and the work priorities and activities associated with learning and carrying out the principal's role.

Administrative role perspective for students of the principalship means seeing situations of practice through the eyes and experiences of a principal. Without actually being a principal, how does one gain such a perspective? Field experiences and administrative internships are designed specifically to provide opportunities for aspiring administrators to understand the world of professional practice from the principal's role perspective. Case studies are often used in classes to help students of principalship acquire perspective, rehearse strategies, and gain insight into administrative problem solving. Design studios (Hart et al., 1989) simulations (Young & Norris, 1988), problem-based learning activities (Bridges, 1992), and research projects are other possibilities for students to acquire knowledge, skills, and to develop an administrative perspective. Each of these instructional modes is a valuable source of relevant information that contributes to students' acquisition of an administrative perspective; however, each has its limitations.

Simulations provided the earliest means through which administrator preparation programs sought to provide practice applying technical skills (Young & Norris, 1988). The NASSP assessment center exercises use simulations to assess aspiring school administrators' potential, and the Springfield Simulation provides administrators the opportunity to return to and reflect on their use of technical knowledge. In-basket exercises and other simulation media become dated and thus their relevance and focus is always an issue. A recent interactive simulation project sponsored by the University Council for Educational Administration (UCEA) focuses on the design of a comprehensive information-learning environment, IESLP (The Information Environment for School Leader Preparation), that brings to learners and instructors the complexity of contemporary schools. However, IESLP is conceptualized as much more than traditional simulations.

> While older style simulations based on "in-basket" exercises tended to define school administration in terms of dealing with problems that find administrators, the IELSP system is based on another idea, that the most critical skills administrators can develop are those having to do with problem finding and problem identification. The IESLP system contains five interrelated components:
>
> 1. the Problem Exercises (problem finding and problem presented),
> 2. the Information Environment (housing the information resources),

3. Tools and Templates (housing the computer-based tools for using and analyzing data),
4. the Navigational Engine (consisting of the interface for navigating the system, software and data management and reporting tools), and
5. the IESLP Student Handbook. (UCEA Document, May 5, 1994)

Case studies have a long and popular history in business education. Case studies used to teach educational administration, however, suffer from being data poor. While they provide an opportunity to view the problems of practice critically, they often require as much discovery of missing information as problem-finding and problem-structured analysis. Still, many educational administration faculty and educational administration practitioners rely on cases to convey and apply technical knowledge and moral components of professional practice (Ashbaugh & Kasten, 1991).

Problem-based learning (Bridges, 1992) and design studios (Hart, Sorenson & Naylor, 1993) provide a third method of professional-technical instruction. Based on problems or conditions of practice, these methods require the student to view and use professional knowledge in a problem-finding and problem-solving mode, designing potential action steps and solutions. As professional socialization, these instructional methods foster the habit and expectation that principals will apply this knowledge to what they do.

Since gaining perspective is an incremental and cumulative socialization process, it is not always easy to reconstruct how or what contributed to the acquisition of an administrative perspective. The following are selected examples of situations that contributed to the development of perspective during the administrative internship experiences of one of the authors.

As an administrative intern I watched and learned as my cooperating principal wrestled with the complexities of a high school class schedule; one that would meet the needs of students, teachers, coaches, parents, bus drivers, and many others. From the principal's desk I began to see the not-so-subtle effects that scheduling students into my foreign language classes had on ability groupings of students in other academic areas. On another occasion during my internship, I was given primary responsibility for planning and carrying out a series of five one-hour, after school, inservice programs titled "The Heart of Teaching." The faces of my high school colleagues looked different to me as I stood in front of them at 3:30 P.M., eager to begin the first session. Most of the faces had the same skeptical and captive look on them. No wonder my principal was so willing to include staff development activities in my internship responsibilities. These and many other experiences were instrumental in helping me gain an administrative perspective.

At this point we ask you to reflect on your anticipatory socialization experiences with specific attention to the concept of administrator perspective. What experiences or factors have contributed to your developing sense of an administrator perspective?

Formal and Informal Socialization. If you are a graduate student in an educational administration class, you are participating in a formal setting for professional role socialization. The setting is defined as formal or informal depending on whether the role of the learner and the material to be learned is explicitly specified. In formal socialization settings, such as a university class, the role of the learner and the material to be learned are specified. Let's examine your current learning setting. If you are a student registered in a class, your role as a learner and the material you need to learn to complete the course have already been specified. Your role as a learner is specified and institutionalized at many levels: in the requirements for entry into the university; in department-program requirements; in administrator certification standards; and, in student expectations and outcomes delineated in the course syllabus. The material to be learned has also been specified in the curriculum, in texts and other readings, in tests, and in performance criteria in particular domains of professional knowledge and competencies. Administrator preservice preparation programs, workshops, inservice programs, and meetings at conferences are all examples of formal professional socialization settings.

Professional role socialization processes also occur in informal settings. In fact, students often claim that these exchanges are where they gain *real* craft knowledge for successful professional practice (Bredeson, 1991a). Even in formal socialization settings, a great deal of informal social learning occurs. In contrast to formal social learning, informal socialization does not require that the role of the learner and the material to be learned are specified. Besides the intended and structured learning outcomes stipulated in formal socialization, students of the principalship learn from each other by observing, listening, and interacting. One example is learning from vicarious experiences often shared among students in hallways during a class break. A student may learn from the stories of fellow students what not to do in his first year as a principal. Other students may listen to an account of how a principal skillfully disarmed a knife-wielding student in her building and then add this tactic to their own repertoire of skills for handling disruptive students. Informal socialization may also be more subtle and symbolic. For example, you may observe that principals tend to dress more formally than do classroom teachers. This may affect your own choices for appropriate professional attire. In each case, learning occurs without explicitly stated roles for the learner and without clearly specified content to be learned. Informal learning is an important dimension of professional role socialization. As you continue your preparation for the principalship and begin your first formal assignment as an administrator, you will move through anticipatory socialization to a third stage of role socialization to the principalship—professional socialization.

Professional Socialization

Self-assessment and mental rehearsals for new social roles are key activities in anticipatory socialization. As social learning occurs, you may discover that more deliberate strategies for entry into a particular professional role are required. In our model, we refer to the decision to seek greater role knowledge through formal and informal sources as professional socialization. Professional socialization refers to the stage of role entry in which "one becomes a member of a profession and over time, develops an identity with that profession" (Parkay et al., 1992, p. 45). Professional socialization processes include intentional strategies as well as unplanned activities beyond preservice preparation and training that help people gain entry into a professional group. In this section we review briefly two interrelated dimensions of professional socialization: on-the-job role learning-socialization as described by novice principals and the five stages of professional socialization for principals described by Parkay et al. We discussed these in detail in Chapter 4.

On-the-Job Training: The First Year

There are rites of passage to the principalship. Earning the appropriate academic degree, completing a practicum, attaining an administrative license, and gaining experience as an assistant principal or department coordinator are predictable steps in preparation for the principalship. The formal and informal requirements to move successfully through these preparation stages serve an important gatekeeping function. Personal interests and goals, the investment of time and money to attain advanced degrees and professional licenses, changes in working conditions (number of hours per day and days per year), and opportunity for employment are major factors affecting entry into the principalship. Completion of one stage typically affirms earlier stages of professional socialization and strengthens one's commitment to becoming a principal.

Next, through the use of selected personal, narrative accounts and empirical research, we describe first-year experiences of principals. We began this chapter by pointing out disappointing trends in the racial and ethnic diversity among principals. The gatekeeping power of professional socialization steps, regretfully, contributes to this problem. Each formal or informal hurdle that a nontraditional school leader must overcome creates an opportunity for conscious and unconscious filtering bias to function.

Actual entry into a principal's position is another important stage of professional socialization. Principal induction is a process by which new or novice principals make their role transition from theoretical to operational leadership (Andrews, 1989). "The first year of the principalship is really made up of two jobs—'learning it and doing it'" (Roder & Pearlman, 1989, p. 70). Earlier socialization processes are the foundations of this stage of social role learning. The entry experiences for first-year principals range from survival tales measured by whether one "sinks or learns to swim," to professional socialization guided systematically by a personalized blueprint for entry into the job. Duke, Isaacson, Sagor and Schmuck (1984) reported that a typical on-the-job socialization experience for a new principal was intense, short-lived, and predominantly informal rather than planned and formal. As a result new principals commonly experience stress and anxieties arising from role overload, time constraints to accomplish all that needs to be done, feelings of loneliness, and perceived lack of skills to manage the demands of their job. Daresh (1986) identified three major concerns for first-year principals—role clarity, the limitations of technical expertise in dealing with daily problems, and learning how to pick up the important cultural and organizational cues of the school.

Stephen H. Davis (1988), a high school principal in California, characterized his first year as a principal as "life in a fishbowl." He describes on-the-job learning during his first year as highly public, with few places for him to hide. His reactions and behaviors were continually under scrutiny and they were often distorted or misconstrued from his point of view. Professional life under a public microscope raises individual anxiety because there is little chance for experimentation, risk-taking, and learning without relatively high public visibility. For Davis, survival required

> establishing positive relationships with members of the school-community, patience, maintaining a global perspective on the activities of the organization, and acquiring the resiliency to adapt quickly to the continual ebb and flow of people, ideas, and problems. (pp. 82–83)

Weindling and Earley (1987) also found that principals experienced frustrations and strains accompanying entry into the principalship. Studying first-year head teachers in the United Kingdom, they reported that during the entry stage principals experienced feelings of professional isolation and expressed a desire to have support and consultation in technical matters and to have a neutral listener outside the school available to them. Despite their initial concerns and anxieties, they found that headmasters believed the positive aspects of the principal's role far outweighed the negative factors related to entry. In another study of first-year principals, Parkay and colleagues (1992) suggest that first-year principals need a "tripod of support" (training, networking, and coaching), which would not only help them survive their first year, but would enable them to progress to higher stages of professional development in their leadership role.

From principal preparation program to actual appointment to a principalship, professional socialization processes help novices transform abstract ideas and aspirations into personalized definitions of their professional role. Mirroring the findings of other researchers and reports from first-year principals, Parkay and others (1992) identified five stages of professional socialization for first-year principals: survival, control, stability, educational leadership, and professional actualization. These researchers found that not all principals manage to move beyond survival and many remain focused on control and stability. The fact that principals go through similar stages of professional socialization is not meant to suggest that the process is invariant across individual experiences. The data indicate four general patterns: (1) principals begin their administrative careers at different stages of professional development; (2) they move through stages at different rates; (3) the staging of a principal's professional development depends on individual and situational characteristics; and (4) beginning principals tend to operate at more than one stage of professional socialization at a time.

Parkay and colleagues (1992) also found several patterns of professional socialization across the experiences of twelve high school principals in their first three years of the principalship. As beginning principals moving through five stages of professional socialization, they tended to move from reliance on positional power, often centered in controlling the behaviors of others, to personal power that promoted learning and growth in others. It is likely that each of us can identify individuals who remain locked into early stages of professional socialization and entry, unable to move to higher levels of professional behavior. As the principals in this study gained experience, however, their expectations for change, in magnitude and speed, also became more realistic. Finally, each principal's eventual level of professional socialization was strongly indicated by the stage he or she was in at the end of the first year. For these twelve principals, not much change in professional socialization was apparent after the first year on the job. This finding supports the conclusions of Bridges (1965) and Wiggins (1970) that over time the forces of socialization in bureaucratic organizations work to mold principals into roles that are congruent with school norms and role expectations.

Professional socialization is tightly linked to the next stage of role learning, organizational socialization. In our model of becoming a principal, organizational socialization locates the new administrator within a particular school context and its situational uniqueness.

Organizational Socialization

As you recall from Chapter 4, organizational roles help to define particular dimensions of an organization's culture. Various roles are also products of that particular culture. Organizational socialization is "[t]he fashion in which an individual is taught and learns what behaviors and perspectives are customary and desirable within the work setting as well as what ones are not" (Van Maanen and Schein, 1979, pp. 211–212). Unless a new principal is an insider and remains at the same school in which he was a teacher, the first year is the proverbial double whammy—new position and new organization. At the same time the new principal is learning what it means to be a principal, he is also a student of organizational culture, what Deal and Kennedy (1982) describe as the "way things work around here."

Since organizational culture is socially constructed over time by people who live and work in those settings, organizational socialization is a learning process that is "ubiquitous, persistent and forever problematic" throughout one's entire professional career (Van Maanen & Schein, 1979, p. 213). Organizational socialization "entails the learning of a cultural perspective that can be brought to bear on both commonplace and unusual matters going on in the work place" (p. 212). This learning is in dynamic tension with forces of personalization (what the individual brings to the role and work setting such as values, assumptions, needs, and questions) and organizational socialization in which "[m]ore experienced members must therefore find ways to insure that the newcomer does not disrupt the ongoing activity on the scene, embarrass or cast a disparaging light on others, or question too many of the established cultural solutions worked out previously" (p. 211).

As an individual moves from one position to another and from one organization to another, "the intensity, importance, and visibility on a given passage will vary across a person's career" (p. 213). Nicholson's theory of work role transition (1984) identifies four modes of individual adjustment to transitions and organizational socialization processes—replication, absorption, determination, and exploration. *Replication* requires only minimal adjustments for the individual or the role. *Absorption* requires an individual to invest substantial amounts of energy and effort to learn and adjust to a new role in an organization. *Determination* is an adjustment strategy in which the person remains relatively unaffected by organizational socialization processes and works to change the content and structure of the roles he is assuming. *Explo-*

ration is a two-way interactive process in which change is reciprocal and occurs simultaneously in the person and the role.

In our discussion of professional socialization, we described an entry plan for learning the principal's role. Stephen H. Davis (1988) provides the following advice for beginning principals coming into a new school:

> Schools, like most complex organizations, include an intricate tapestry of formal and informal norms, policies, and practices. For the new principal, knowing what to do and how to do it involves far more than a reservoir of experience in another school or an advanced degree. For the first few months, proceed slowly when making decisions that could affect the working conditions, routines, or tasks of staff members. Ask questions from a variety of people likely to be affected by your decisions, and, above all, get to know your staff, students and parents. (p. 78)

Earlier in the chapter we referred to the work of Jentz, (1982). They recommend that new administrators develop a plan of entry into an organization to increase the likelihood of a smooth transition into both the job and the organization, and to avoid the pitfalls of ill-advised strategies and activities while learning the ropes.

At this point in our discussion, it would be helpful to illustrate organizational socialization processes by describing several examples from our own experiences as building principals. In Chapter 8 we discussed school rituals, ceremonies, and traditions as important symbolic elements in schools. The tradition of a holiday banquet and the meanings attached to how it would be served to graduating seniors was an example of one principal's being socialized to the way things were done in that school. Other examples abound in schools; for instance, principals may or may not be welcomed in staff lounges. Typically the nonverbal behaviors of teachers will be your best clues. Teacher inservice days at the beginning and end of the school year may customarily have been time for teachers to work in their rooms, not for group development. If a new principal fills the time with outside speakers and activities, the norms of the existing culture may be violated and conflict will emerge. This does not mean that principals must passively accept all existing cultural norms. In fact, some aspects of existing school cultures are dysfunctional—harmful to teaching and learning—and they need to be changed. Your entry into a school may represent the district's decision to effect changes in the school. As leaders, principals are affected by organizational socialization forces, but they are also shapers of school cultures.

In Chapter 6 we described how effective principals use five primary mechanisms to create, nurture, and sustain positive learning climates. The consideration of principals as proactive culture builders provides the final component in our model of professional role socialization, role making and professional visualization.

Role Making and Professional Visualization

We described how principals move at different rates and with differing levels of growth through various stages of professional socialization. It is quite possible that an individual principal may never move beyond what Parkay and others (1992) described as "the stability stage." Our purpose in this section is to describe how you can move beyond one-sided professional socialization, dominated by role taking and the prescriptive fetters of professional leadership that are defined by sets of technical skills and functional tasks. Organizational and professional norms, technical expertise, and role preferences are important dimensions of a principal's professional competency. These dimensions are necessary, but not sufficient to highly successful leadership.

In Chapter 5, "Principals and Their Work," we reviewed a substantial body of literature on the professional work of school principals. These studies provide a detailed description of the daily work routines of principals. Principals' work is characterized by brevity, variety of daily activities, fragmentation, uncertainty, discontinuity of work routines, long hours, a preference for verbal media, high levels of interpersonal interactions, role overload, and limited control and authority in accomplishing professional work. Given these constraints it's reasonable to ask, Is there room for role innovation and personal growth in the school principalship? Our response to this query is unequivocal. Role making and professional visualization are the tools you will use as a principal to nurture and sustain your own personal and professional growth and the development of others. Professional visualization is your emerging theory of practice as a formal school leader.

Role Making

Social learning and role theories have been used throughout this text to describe the social-psychological processes of becoming a school principal. Each of us has had to negotiate a number of social roles on personal and professional levels. Depending on the situation, role-making opportunities contributed to the way each of us adjusted to social role transitions. Think back for a moment about social role changes you have experienced. What do you already know about the dynamics of role transition processes from your own experiences as a student? As a teacher? As a family member?

Let's examine a common role change for educators: the move from being a full-time student to being a teacher. Depending on job characteristics, situational variables, and individual patterns of socialization, each person employs one or more of the social role adjustment modes described by Nicholson (1984)—replication, absorption, determination, and exploration. In addition, role discretion (opportunities to alter such job facets as goals and interpersonal relationships) and job novelty (the degree to which the role permits reliance upon prior knowledge, skills and experiences) affect individual role-making processes. For example, as a new teacher you may have encountered very powerful school norms concerning student evaluation, curriculum emphasis, testing, and student discipline. Within strong cultural norms you may have had only limited opportunities for discretionary role adjustment. Work role transition theory posits that low discretion and low novelty typically yield replication of existing role behaviors and thus little opportunity for role making, according to Nicholson.

At the other end of the continuum are situations in which there is high discretion and high novelty. For instance, you may be hired as a learning coordinator in the school. If this is a newly created position, there will be significant leeway in role discretion and job novelty. For most of us, however, assuming the role of classroom teacher resembles most other occupational roles in that as newcomers we tend to encounter "bounded discretion" (Simon, 1957) with moderate levels of novelty. Thus, each person's separate, yet similar, transition experiences from full-time student to teacher, require that she or he utilize each of the various role-adjustment modes depending on the situation and the job or role facet involved.

Aspiring principals (primarily teachers) report expectations of significant work role adjustments in moving from the classroom to the principal's office. In a survey of graduate students in a principal preparation program Bredeson (1991a) reported that these certification candidates were attracted to the principalship because they perceived important differences between the work of teachers and the work of principals. Nearly one-third (32.3 percent) of the respondents believed that the principalship would provide greater power "to effect changes, to influence and lead others, to make important professional decisions, and to take action on one's ideas" (p. 513). Such expectations suggest that educators preparing for the principalship do not want a technocratic, managerial position in schools, but one that offers real possibilities for making a difference in the lives of children, in the lives of people with whom they work, and in their own professional lives. The tension between what principals want to make of themselves and their roles in the principalship and what the organization and others expect of them creates the dynamic interaction and tension between role making and role taking.

Reflection is critical to role making, turning learning back on itself to create active participation in learning and the creation of social roles (Schon, 1983). The social learning process of becoming a principal is not a tabula rasa on which new individual experiences and social learning are etched. Through reflection, principals transform what has been learned from prior experiences into opportunities for further learning, growth, and development in their personal and professional roles.

Professional Visualization

Throughout this chapter we have described various stages of socialization that characterize the growth and professional development of school principals. The professional socialization hierarchy described by Parkay and colleagues (1992) is a multistaged, personal and professional growth sequence in which beginning principals move from concerns about survival in a new position to desires to develop a personal vision in the school. The empirical research discussed in previous chapters supports the assertion that principals who have a vision for their school and purposefully act on that vision make a difference in their schools and in the lives of students and teachers in them. A vision suggests ethereal, unsubstantial idealization. When this notion of the ideal is combined with projected action, a school leader may visualize herself and the school in the desired state of performance. Like athletes who practice visualizing themselves completing the desired activity, the visualization of a school and the principal's part in it serves to extend vision into the realm of specific, high-performance leadership. What is vision? What part does vision play in becoming a principal? What is "purposing"? Finally, what does visualization add to vision?

Definitions of vision abound in current leadership literature. "Vision is a mental journey from the known to the unknown, creating the future from a montage of current facts, hopes, dreams, dangers, and opportunities" (Hickman & Silva, 1984, p. 151). "A vision articulates a view of a realistic, credible, attractive future for the organization, a condition that is better in some important ways than what now exists. . . . a target that beckons" (Bennis & Nanus, 1985, p. 89). Vision needs to "be viewed more as a compass that points the direction to be taken, that inspires enthusiasm, and that allows people to buy into and take part in the shaping of the way that will constitute the school's mission" (Bricker, 1985). "Vision is the signal to normal people, operating in normal organizations, that they can accomplish ends that are beyond those they thought they could accomplish" (Stout, 1993, p. 290). Each of these definitions suggests that vision is a critical link between what is and what might be; it is forged out of principals' experiences, their individual professional growth, and the school settings in which they work. These factors are common to all principals regardless of setting. Vision is a product of individual growth, professional maturity, and social learning accessible to all principals.

Shieve and Schoenheit (1987) describe a five-step process in which leaders move from value preferences that define personal vision to more publicly accepted and shared organizational visions. The five stages include (1) valuing, (2) reflection, (3) articulation, (4) planning, and (5) action. As one principal reported in a study by Bredeson (1994), "My school had to become our school" (p. 201). Personal vision offers promise. Shared vision has the power to move the school toward desired cognitive, affective, and behavioral goals.

Sergiovanni (1991) describes a vision as a "covenant" that binds teachers, principals, and others to a shared understanding and mission for their school. The role of the principal in moving from a personal vision to an organizational vision (covenant) is accomplished through "purposing." Purposing is

> what principals do to bring about a shared consensus tight enough and coherent enough to bond people together in a common cause and to define them as a community, but loose enough to allow for individual self-expression. (p. 180)

Bennis and Nanus (1985) also see a very proactive role for school leaders in vision building.

> If there is a spark of genius in the leadership function at all, it must lie in this transcending ability, a kind of magic, to assemble—out of all the variety of images, signals, forecasts, and alternatives—a clearly articulated vision of the future that is at once simple, easily understood, clearly desirable, and energizing. (p. 103)

This is a daunting, but nevertheless achievable task for school principals. Ordway Tead (1935) captured the essence of visioning in this general description of leadership:

> Leadership [vision] (bracketed words are ours) is known by the personalities it enriches. Leadership [vision] is not a matter of hypnosis, blandishment or

"salesmanship." It is a matter of leading out from within individuals those impulses, motives, and efforts which they discover to represent themselves most truly. (p. 81)

The truthful representation of desirable ends that vision creates must find its way into practice to be fulfilled. It must move from the abstraction of ideal to the actualization of the ideal in the real, with real people, in real time. By applying visualization techniques, you can deliberately picture the productive interactions among educators and students that promote the ideal captured in the vision. Over and over, each time striving to come closer to that ideal, the school leader can take action and analyze the discrepancy between the goal (the visualization) and real unfolding events. We emphasize the differences between vision, visualization, and action because in all human endeavor "the road to hell is paved with lofty ideas and good intentions." Only as you act, observe others' reactions, and interact toward the common ideal, does vision move through visualization to action.

CONCLUSION

The role socialization model described in this chapter provides a framework for understanding the social-psychological learning processes in becoming a principal. In your preparation for the principalship, there are common phases and stages of professional growth and learning, yet your biography of personal experiences, professional preparation, and situational factors will make your passage to the principalship a unique socialization experience. In Chapter 11 we move to a discussion of the building blocks of expert thinking and professional visualization.

SUGGESTED ACTIVITIES

1. Using Figure 10.1, a process model of socialization, list examples of each dimension of socialization from your own experiences. As you review your background and current level of preparation and/or socialization, what specific experiences would enhance your current level of socialization? Are there areas where you have had only limited experiences? What opportunities are there for you to gain these experiences? To what degree are socialization experiences transferable from one role to another? Are some socialization experiences unique to particular roles?
2. In this chapter we presented a descriptive profile of school administrators. Is this profile an accurate description of administrators in your district? What conditions and factors either enhance or hinder changes in the demographic profile of principals, assistant principals, and other administrators in your school district?
3. Examine the recruitment and selection procedures for principals in your district. What specific procedures are used to enlarge the pool of principalship applicants?

4. The personal interview is the primary personnel selection activity used to hire principals. In teams, develop questions that you would ask candidates for the principal's position in your school or district. Conduct simulated interviews with your colleagues. As an interviewee, which questions were easy to answer? Which were most difficult? Based on your responses to these questions, what do you need to do to prepare yourself for future interviews?

5. you are currently working in a school, what perspectives and insights do you have about the role of a principal based on your personal observations? Or, think back to your days as a student at any level. Do you remember your principal(s)? What do you remember about each? Project a few years into the future. You are a principal. What characteristics will your students most likely remember about you?

6. Can you identify when you first entertained the idea of becoming a principal? What do you recall about these initial thoughts? Was there a specific incident or event that encouraged you to think about becoming a principal?

7. As you think about a career as a principal, what are the major trade-offs (positive and negative) compared to your current position?

8. Since you began your studies in educational administration, how would you characterize the reactions of your colleagues at work to your decision to pursue graduate work in school administration? How have those reactions influenced your socialization?

9. We described processes of informal socialization to the principalship. If you were writing a book titled, "Things they don't teach you in principal preparation programs," what would the chapter titles be? Share your chapter titles with your colleagues in class. How might these areas be addressed individually? collectively?

10. You may want to refer to the work of Barry Jentz (1982) as you think about your own entry into an administrative position. In his book, *Entry*, Jentz provides a systematic plan for beginning administrators. Based on this work, develop a professional entry plan for the principalship.

11. Think about your first day as a classroom teacher. Do the five stages of professional socialization outlined by Parkay and others describe your experiences? What about other role transitions you have made?

12. One dimension of professional socialization is role exit. As you reflect on your past experiences with role transitions, which aspects of role exit will be most challenging for you personally and professionally? In what way do these challenges affect your career plans and thinking about the principalship?

Building Blocks of Expert Thinking and Leadership

INTRODUCTION

Aspiring architects and tour guides at Taliesin, home of Frank Lloyd Wright's design studio and prairie school of architecture in Spring Green, Wisconsin, inform visitors that as a child he received from his mother a set of geometric blocks (a circle, a square, and a triangle). From child's play to creative genius, he became familiar with these basic shapes and used them over and over again in new combinations and for different purposes as he designed new illusions of space. Later these same building blocks appeared as design themes and became distinctive signatures on some of his greatest architectural achievements: the Guggenheim, Fallingwater, the Robey House, and the Johnson Wax Headquarters. Principals are also designers; they too rely on basic building blocks and foundational knowledge of leadership as they work to create and nurture positive and highly productive environments for individual growth and learning in schools.

THE BUILDING BLOCKS OF LEADERSHIP, THINKING, AND EXPERTISE

In this chapter, we describe the four basic building blocks of principals' expert thinking—professional values, knowledge, processes and behaviors, and intent. Our discussion of these building blocks is based on the concept of professional theorizing and visualizing. We use selected examples we have found helpful as former principals, professors of educational administration, and university administrators to illustrate the contribution of each building block to principals' expert thinking, to the construction of situational maps of practice, and to the theory of professional visualization. In the examples we have chosen to illustrate the content of the building blocks, we make no claim to be all-inclusive, nor is it our intention through these examples to be prescriptive. Our theory of professional visualization posits that the building blocks of professional knowledge shape our thinking about leadership, contribute to our understanding of problems and ways of dealing with them, help to define our leadership roles, and inform the actions we take. Our primary purpose in this chapter is to introduce the building blocks of expert thinking as a prelude to a discussion of professional visualization theory. These foundational materials and the process of professional visualization can guide your preparation for the principalship. Once you are familiar with the basic building blocks of expert thinking, you can integrate your growing knowledge into professional theorizing and action.

We begin with a discussion of *leadership values and beliefs* that shape expert thinking and inform action. Next we describe principals' *professional knowledge* as an organic mix of experiential, empirical, and theoretical knowledge. The third building block is *leadership processes and behaviors*. We describe these processes and behaviors, grounded in values, professional knowledge, and intentions, as expressions of expert thinking in action. The fourth building block, *leader intent*, focuses on the principal's role as a communicator of organizational purpose and direction.

Leadership Values and Beliefs

That values and beliefs are essential to successful leadership seems self-evident. Underestimating their importance diminishes our understanding of what it takes to be an effective principal. Values shape and inform thinking while serving as guides to action. Values influence principals' expert thinking, and by extension their behavior, as lenses for viewing problems of practice and as substitutes for professional knowledge in the face of novel problems (Leithwood, 1994, p. 18).

At least two levels of values shape the thinking and behaviors of principals. The first level of values is preconscious. Values at this level are not articulated or expressed overtly. These deeply embedded values are basic to the way we view the world. They represent assumptions and beliefs we hold about such things as relationships, organizational structures, the purposes of education in a democracy, human growth and learning, equity, individual liberty, and autonomy. Scholars often examine core values to differentiate among various social and organizational cultures. In Chapter 9 we discussed examples of these unquestioned aspects of commonly held values, beliefs, and social norms at three different levels—the school, the school district, and the larger community.

A second level of values includes beliefs we talk about openly and use to guide choices and behaviors in our daily work and interactions. Fairness, support, appreciation for cultural diversity, honesty, and what's right and what's wrong are espoused publicly and expressed in actions. Although these values are expressed openly, perfect congruence does not exist between espoused values and beliefs and those values and beliefs by which we live. The challenge is to match "our walk with our talk." If you want to see what a principal values, watch what she does. Leadership behavior over time is a much more accurate measure of principals' actual values than are vision statements, slogans, and faculty pep talks.

In his recent text on the school principalship, Thomas Sergiovanni (1987), citing the work of Rosemary Stewart, argues that the work of principals is contingent upon demands (mandatory components of the job), constraints (internal and external factors that limit what principals do), and choices (the opportunities principals have to work differently from other principals in similar circumstances). In Sergiovanni's view, since all principals face similar demands and constraints, the choices principals make define their leadership. Throughout this book we have described these individual choices as role-making opportunities. Principals' choices of role, leader behavior and style, and relationships with others reflect different views of schools, their purposes, and their operations. These choices also are expressions of values and personal characteristics. We concur with Leithwood's and Sergiovanni's conclusion that the expression of these values through actions distinguishes ordinary principals from highly successful ones.

As formal leaders principals have many opportunities to express existing values through their leadership of their schools and communities as well as to introduce new values. Contrasting traditional leaders from highly successful leaders, Sergiovanni (1987) identified new leadership values articulated and expressed in the behaviors of leaders in highly successful schools. He argues that purposing is an example of an emerging leadership value. As an expressed leadership value, purposing provides a compelling view of organizational purpose to which others in the organization can commit their personal and professional energies and expertise.

Another leadership value is the empowerment of others. Successful principals recognize that leadership is not restricted to formal position holders in schools, but that it is vested in teachers and staff. Successful principals empower others and facilitate their accomplishments rather than control their behaviors. A third example of emerging leadership values among highly successful principals is patience. Principals who value patience are skeptical of quick-fix models and facile solutions to complex school problems and dilemmas. Patience as a leadership value recognizes that the education of children requires long-term commitment and time. Eclecticism and pragmatism are valued over faddish reform initiatives and one-shot inservice elixirs.

The findings of Bredeson (1994) provide empirical support for values and beliefs as a building block of principals' expert thinking. Bredeson describes new leadership values for principals in restructured schools and the impact of these emerging values on principals' understanding of their role as formal leaders. He reports that principals are moving from traditional leadership behaviors to group-centered behaviors and values reflecting their understanding of leadership in organizations with self-managing professionals.

As leadership responsibilities and control are shared among teachers and principals, the traditional role of the building principal continues to be redefined. In their descriptions of the evolution of the principalship, these respondents supported Bradford's prescriptions for group-centered leader behavior: careful attention to individual and group needs; emphasis on consulting and facilitating rather than directing and controlling; modeling and coaching appropriate leader behaviors; nurturing an accepting climate; encouraging teacher groups to be self-monitoring; and relinquishing control by allowing others to make final choices in appropriate kinds of decisions. (p. 219)

These findings suggest that shifts in leadership values and beliefs are more than internalized commitments. These emerging values affect leadership processes and principals' behavior.

Values are a basic building block of principals' expert thinking. The importance of their contribution to and relationship with the other building blocks becomes apparent when one tries to imagine professional knowledge, leadership processes and behaviors, and intent devoid of values.

Professional Knowledge and Expertise

A second critical building block is professional knowledge and expertise. In Chapters 1 and 2 we discussed sources of professional knowledge and professional knowledge in action. The quest for a professional knowledge base in educational administration is not a new endeavor (Culbertson, 1988). For example, in 1943 the Department of Supervisors and Directors of Instruction of the National Education Association (NEA) described the frustration of educators trying to grasp an elusive prey.

> To track down *instructional leadership* to its lair, and once having it firmly in hand to nail its hide to the side of the house so that all good educational pilgrims who came that way in search of this golden fleece could recognize it and benefit therefrom. (DSDI, 1943, p. 1., as cited in *Change and Continuity in Supervision and Leadership*. Pajak [1993])

Recent efforts by the National Commission for the Principalship (1990), the University Council for Educational Administration (1993), and the National Policy Board for Educational Administration (1993) are testimony to the enduring quest to capture and codify professional knowledge for school principals. The National Policy Board for Educational Administration, for example, published *Principals for our Changing Schools* (1993), specifying a knowledge and skill base for principals. This knowledge and skill base is organized around four domains (functional, programmatic, interpersonal, and contextual) and enumerated in twenty-one proficiencies across the four domains. The UCEA Knowledge Base Project (Hoy, 1994) resulted in the articulation of seven knowledge domains mapping the field of educational administration and suggesting curriculum organizers for preservice preparation programs for school administrators. The seven domains included (1) societal and cultural influences of schooling; (2) teaching and learning processes; (3) organizational studies; (4) leadership and management processes; (5) policy and political studies; (6) legal and ethical dimensions of schooling; and (7) economic and financial dimensions of schooling.

Our view is that while these projects are worthy efforts, they remain too narrow and too taxonomic, and they represent individual dimensions of knowledge rather than the "whole cloth" of comprehensive and integrated professional expertise. Lacking from these efforts in large part are the processes through which basic formal knowledge can be applied to professional action and choices—the absolutely necessary parts of this knowledge base that remain poorly developed. We argue throughout this text that multiple sources of knowledge inform professional expertise and thinking, and processes are part of this knowledge base.

Professional knowledge is an organic mix of theoretical, empirical, and experiential sources of knowledge. The professional knowledge base for principals continues to evolve through individual processes of reflection that provide novel and insightful ways of addressing problems of practice. Our view of the professional knowledge base for principals is not an argument for complete relativism nor for idiosyncratically constructed professional knowledge. Rather, it recognizes the active role you as an aspiring principal will take as you develop an internalized professional knowledge base informed by ongoing empirical research, theoretical propositions, personal and professional work experiences, and systematic reflection on them. Selected examples of sources of professional knowledge, discussed in earlier chapters, illustrate how each forms the substrate that supports and informs the expert thinking, situational mapping for practice, and actions of successful school leaders.

Experiential Knowledge

Each of us learns from our experiences. Some are personal experiences while other are vicarious, but nonetheless instructive. Because of their vividness, immediacy of access, and relevance to other experiences that enhance our ability to recall and utilize what we have learned, experiences are a valuable source of professional knowledge. Experiences represent unique biographical stores of knowledge that contribute to who we are, what we value, how we think, and how we act. Not all experiences, however, are equally valuable contributors to professional growth and learning. Dewey (1938) argued that some experiences may distort or diminish opportunities for further learning and individual growth. The potential to learn from experience has less to do with whether those experiences are positive or negative and more to do with our capacity to make sense of them, connect them to prior experiences, and integrate what we have learned from those experiences into our thinking and behavior in future situations. The ability to integrate current experiences with prior experiences and knowledge and then link what has been learned from those experiences to future situations is what distinguishes a principal with ten years of administrative experience from another principal who has one year of experience repeated ten times. The former grows and links his experiences to his professional knowledge while the latter continues to repeat past behaviors and responds predictably, failing to make the connections between past, present, and future situations of practice.

Boud, Keogh, and Walker (1985) describe a three-stage model of experiential learning that includes (1) returning to the experienced event, (2) attending to feeling, and (3) reevaluating the experience. In Chapter 2, in the section, "Hired in Haste," as a new principal I felt forced to start the school year with a full complement of teachers and recommended hiring a teacher, about whom I had a number of doubts, to the school board. In the classroom, the teacher's performance confirmed my earlier suspicions and clearly pointed out my error in judgment. New problems, more serious and troublesome than starting the school year with a limited-term employee, presented themselves. Now sixteen years later, I can replay this experience in vivid detail: the hasty personnel decision, the complications it created for me as a beginning principal, and the events that unfolded around it. The uncertainty and anxiety I felt sixteen years ago as a new principal, whose administrative performance was being judged by this one poor decision, also return in highly emotive waves. Hiring in haste remains vivid, immediately accessible, and highly relevant—especially when I find myself in decision-making situations in which artificial deadlines and the calendar become dominant in decision processes. This experience has been valuable to me over time because of its lessons on common problem-solving errors, including incorrect synthesis, inadequate synthesis, and premature closure.

As you begin the principalship, many of your experiences will prove to be equally valuable contributors to your developing a professional knowledge base and expert thinking. For instance, try to recall an incident in which you dealt with a serious conflict with another person. How has that experience helped you deal more effectively with interpersonal conflicts in subsequent situations? Both positive and negative experiences have the potential to further learning. For example, think about a serious interpersonal conflict you have dealt with in the past. As you think back on the conflict, there are interpersonal skills that helped you deal with the situation. In retrospect, there may also have been aspects of the situation—how you reacted and what you said—that you would change in a future conflict. Again, not all of your experiences with conflict will be relevant nor educative in the development of conflict management skills as a principal. Prior experience with conflict management is an example of one source of professional knowledge that informs expert thinking. These experiences provide opportunities to learn and to develop the ability to see recurrent patterns across experiences (generalization), to highlight salient aspects within various experiences and understand their relevance to new situations (selection), and to develop systematic ways of recording, organizing, and retrieving important information within diverse experiences (Cell, 1984; Hart, 1992; Bredeson, 1991a). As with any source of professional knowledge, the potential to inform principals' expert thinking is dependent on careful reflection and appropriate application, not simply the recounting of administrative "war stories" or passive replication.

Throughout this book we have drawn upon our personal experiences to illustrate particular ideas. We have done this quite deliberately because these *are* our experiences, with all of their unique aspects that contributed to who we are today. In addition, we acknowledge the importance of *place* (geographical location) and its influence on our personal and professional thinking. The states of Utah and Wisconsin have shaped our thinking, our values, our experiences, and the images we use to express them in this text. Our personal career paths likewise have shaped our choices and the trade-offs we have made.

In Chapter 12 we describe situational maps of practice that conform to the workscapes of professional educators. The idea of conformance and harmony of expert thinking with situation is an important point in the perspective we have maintained throughout this book. Reflecting on Wallace Stegner's essay, "Striking the Rock," we have come to understand and appreciate the important of harmony and conformance to effective educational leadership. Stegner writes about an encounter he and his wife had with a daring western architect. It seems this architect regaled the Stegners one evening with a slide show of multimillion dollar houses he had designed for construction in the California desert. The architect boasted that these creations represented imagination, technical know-how, the innovative use of modern building materials, and the endless possibilities that generous financial resources made available to the architect, builder, and resident regardless of climate or geographic location.

> In that waterless pale desert spotted with shad scale and creosote bush and backed by barren lion-colored mountains, another sort of architect, say, Frank Lloyd Wright, might have designed something contextual, something low, broad-eaved, thick-walled, something that would mitigate the hot light, something half-underground so that people could retire like the lizards and rattlesnakes from the intolerable daytime temperatures, something made of native stone or adobe or tamped earth in the colors and shapes of the country, something no more visually intrusive than an outcrop.
>
> Not our architect. He had built of cinderblock, in the form of Bauhaus cubes, the only right angles in that desert. . . .
>
> Studying that luxurious, ingenious, beautiful, sterile incongruity, I told its creator, sincerely, that I thought he could build a comfortable house in hell. That pleased him; he thought so too. What I didn't tell him, what he would not have understood, was that we thought his desert house immoral. It exceeded limits, it offended our sense not of the possible but of the desirable. There was no economic or social reason for anyone's living on a barren flat, however beautiful, where every form of life sought shelter during the unbearable daylight hours. . . . The house didn't fit the country, it challenged it. It asserted America's never-say-never spirit and America's ingenious know-how. It seemed to us an act of arrogance on the part of both owner and architect. . . .
>
> That desert house seemed to me, and still seems to me, a paradigm— hardly a paradigm, more a caricature—of what we have been doing to the West in my lifetime. Instead of adapting as we began to do, we have tried to make country and climate over to fit our existing habits and desires. Instead of listening to the silence, we have shouted into the void. (Stegner, 1992, *Where the Bluebird Sings to the Lemonade Springs*, pp. 77–78)

Lack of conformity and harmony with surroundings, insensitivity to unique features and characteristics of the setting, the hubris of technology and unlimited resources to confront any situation, and shouting into the void resonate with many of the experiences of educators. Stegner's view of this architect's failure to appreciate his natural environment and to work in harmony with it rather than rail against it with the arrogance of a distant technocrat speaks to us. Harmony and situational fit are characteristic of effective professional practice and principal leadership. The expert thinking of principals informed by values, knowledge, leadership processes and behaviors, and intent respond to the unique features within a school and to the specific needs of faculty and students. They do not deny their character and force them into an unnatural conformity within the boundaries of the educationist's model. Working in harmony, however, does not mean blind acceptance of impoverished conditions, poor performance, and unproductive cultures for individual growth and learning. It does mean that professional visualization and expert thinking interact with the realities of the school setting and are appropriate to its character. Stark right angles, railing against the local contours and culture, and insensitivity to long-term gains for the school reflect professional arrogance. Professional visualization is the process by which principals articulate harmony and conformance between values and beliefs, leadership behaviors, expert thinking, intent, and situations of practice. The challenging work of principals as educational designers is to remain focused on the development of lasting contributions to individual learning and growth that are morally defensible and consonant with the unique qualities of setting, student and community needs, and purposes desired.

Empirical Knowledge

A second major source of professional knowledge for principals is empirical knowledge. As discussed in Chapter 1, was empirical knowledge is formal knowledge based on systematic experimentation, observation, and analysis. We often refer to such knowledge as scientific or research-based professional knowledge. In the field of educational leadership, where tightly controlled experimental conditions are often difficult to attain, scholars and practitioners rely on systematic investigations conducted in field studies, case studies, and analyses of actuarial data sets—for example, statewide student achievement scores, financial expenditures, and tax revenue data. Despite assurances of methodological rigor provided by researchers, educational practitioners often eschew empirical research because the findings do not match their experiences or provide insight into circumstances in their everyday practice. In addition, empirical knowledge often fails to provide highly specific information that tells principals what to do in a given circumstance. For instance, a novice principal may want to know what to do if a gun-wielding student comes into the school. The empirical findings on conflict management and effective strategies for dealing with violence in schools may be generally very descriptive and would likely report the probabilities of success among alternative actions. As a result, new and experienced principals may consider the empirical findings from studies on violence and conflict in schools interesting, but not particularly useful. The legitimacy of empirical research is not based on a claim of particularized solutions to specific problems, such as foolproof strategies for disarming violent students; however, when these same findings are used as a basis for training and professional development experiences, principals often find them highly salient and valuable to their everyday practice.

Principals deal with specific problems requiring highly specific responses in particular contexts. Generalizability of findings and applicability beyond the school are less important to them than are specific ideas and strategies to deal effectively with the problem at hand. Thus, principals tend to rely heavily on their own experiences and those of their peers as primary sources of professional knowledge. Though not necessarily systematic, experiential knowledge and shared craft knowledge are viewed by educational practitioners as more helpful and accessible than empirical knowledge because they provide concrete information with immediate strategies for dealing with problems of practice and they are generally strengthened by testimonies of their peers. The challenge for researchers, then, is to provide methodologically rigorous findings that are accurate descriptions of the realities of schools, relevant to principal's work, accessible in terms of understanding and application, and insightful and enriching for the understanding of problems of practice and effective leadership. The primary benefit of empirical knowledge is that it provides valuable information to principals to move them beyond unexamined and unsystematic, anecdotal exchanges often characterized by facile bromides, canned responses, and managerial gimmicks.

Next we refer again to the work of Herbert J. Walberg (1990) as an illustration of the contributions of empirical knowledge to principals' professional knowledge. In Chapter 2 we reviewed Walberg's findings based on his analysis of results from 2,575 studies of educational outcomes, which included experimental studies, field studies, and actuarial analyses. Using meta-analytical techniques, Walberg proposed a theory of educational productivity identifying factors that demonstrably influenced students' cognitive, affective, and behavioral learning outcomes. Based on analyses of empirical findings, he argued that reinforcement and reward for correct performance, acceleration and other advanced learning opportunities, reading training, instructional cues, and feedback are among the most powerful factors (instructional behaviors) that influence student outcomes. These findings provide important cues to principals as they think about the relationships among their instructional leadership behaviors, teachers' work, the school's teaching and learning environment, and student outcomes.

Using field studies, researchers have contributed a great deal to principals' professional knowledge. In Chapter 5 we examined principals and their work. Citing findings from studies by Peterson (1978); Kmetz and Willower (1982); Martin and Willower (1981), Bredeson (1987; 1988a; 1988b; 1989; 1991a; 1993) Hart, (1986); Hart and Murphy 1989; and Leithwood (1994), we presented a description of the principal's role in schools as one characterized by brevity and variety of daily activities, fragmentation, uncertainty and discontinuity of work routines, long hours, a preference for verbal communication with high levels of interpersonal interaction, a high volume of activities, role overload, and limited control and authority. These empirical findings are useful to principals and to aspiring principals as they attempt to shape their leadership role in the school and to understand the constraints and opportunities accompanying role making and role taking. In addition, as educators work to restructure schools and to redefine the roles of educational professionals in them, descriptive empirical findings provide valuable information and insight into the complexities of role and its relationship to change initiatives at the school level.

Case studies, using a variety of research traditions, are also a valuable source of empirical knowledge for principals. An excellent example is a study reported by Reitzug and Reeves (1992). Their observations and analyses of the leadership behaviors of one elementary principal, Steve Sage, provide an excellent description of symbolic leadership in schools.

Symbolic leadership is the hidden dimension of principal's leadership. The tendency of principals (and, indeed, of all individuals) is to focus on the substance and intent of their actions. They are less likely to consider the multiple interpretations that followers construct of the meaning of these same actions. . . . The implication for principals has less to do with exchanging substance for symbol than it does with becoming sensitive to symbol in substance. (p. 217)

Systematic inquiry conducted under experimental conditions, in field studies and case studies, and through actuarial data analyses contributes to the professional knowledge base of principals. The central issue is how to put these findings into useful forms of professional knowledge. Huck, Cormier, and Bounds (1974) describe three types of individuals in the world. The first type includes individuals actively engaged in systematic inquiry in schools, districts, policy centers, and universities. Teachers and principals engaged in active research and in systematic analyses of learning outcomes in their schools are examples of this type. A second type includes those who are interested in research findings and their application to their professional practice, but are not researchers. The third type includes people who are not engaged in research, nor do they express any interest in the results of systematic inquiry. Principals in either of the first two types can tap into valuable sources of information to enhance their developing professional knowledge base. Anyone in the third category forfeits the benefits of empirical knowledge that informs the professional thinking and actions of successful educational leaders. Next we turn to the third source of professional knowledge, theoretical knowledge.

Theoretical Knowledge

Theories and the relationships they posit among variables of interest make up a third side to the building blocks of professional knowledge. We begin this discussion of theoretical knowledge with a caveat: In any narrative description of professional knowledge, there is the danger that sources of knowledge might be viewed as separate, distinct, and unrelated to one another. Viewing sources of knowledge as discrete and independent often results in creation of artificial dichotomies and trichotomies of professional knowledge. Such artificial categorizations are common in education. Some examples include theory versus practice, technical knowledge and craft knowledge, administration as an art or as a science, and the familiar trichotomy— theory, research, and practice.

In schools you may hear your colleagues say, "Oh, that's theoretical. Here's what you need to know. Just do this." "Research! Who's got time for research? I've got twenty-five kids to teach. Research is what they do at the university. Here we work with real problems and real kids." Statements such as these reflect two general problems. The first is the chasm between the work of professors of educational administration in colleges and universities and the everyday work of teachers and principals in schools. The second is a fundamental misunderstanding of the strengths and limitations of each source of knowledge—its contribution to principals' professional knowledge, and its relationship to practice.

Perhaps the most common dichotomy expressed in education circles is the one that separates the world of theory from that of practice. Practical, craft knowledge is the coin of the realm in schools while theory is the currency of the ivory tower. Perhaps you may have expressed similar sentiments as you have tried to reconcile your experiences and the demands of everyday practice with the world of graduate studies in education. We reject the idea that theory necessarily resides only with academics while practice belongs to the world of school administrators. The problematic nature of this dichotomy becomes immediately apparent if you reflect on your own experience as an educator. Consider for a moment the following question: What would a theoryless world be like for you as a teacher or as a principal? One of two possibilities exists: The first is that everything would be known and therefore theoretical frameworks used to help describe, examine, and explain events would be unnecessary; at the other extreme is a chaotic world in which behaviors, events, and other phenomena are completely idiosyncratic and unrelated. There would be no patterns of behavior, no systems for classifying information, no strategies for cognitively organizing the world you experience. Both possibilities would result in cognitive overload for professional educators. Since neither of these two extremes represents the real world of educators, theory and practice are naturally linked. Though each source of professional knowledge represents a distinct way of knowing, with particular rules of adequacy, the sources are complementary and interdependent—not antithetic and mutually exclusive.

The professional knowledge base of principals and their world of practice are greatly informed by theory. For purposes of illustration we highlight the following theories, some described in earlier chapters of this book, and others familiar to you as an educator. Social learning theory, role theory, and role transition theory provide frameworks that help describe the social processes of becoming a principal. Various change theories help scholars and practitioners understand the dynamics of change in schools, resistance to change, the effects of change and innovation on people and organizational structures, stages of change, and the relationship among visions, skills, resources, incentives, action plans, and change outcomes. The theory of school culture stresses the importance of the symbolic aspects of organization and leadership expressed in values, beliefs, and norms. Finally, the theory of self-managing work groups and leaderless groups suggests important implications for principals and for leadership in teacher empowered, restructured schools. Whether expressed in formal theoretical propositions, embedded in the way(s) we think about issues and problems, or contained in analogies or taxonomies, theory is a major contributor to professional knowledge. We turn next to the third building block of expert thinking, leadership processes and behaviors.

Leadership Processes and Behaviors

The third building block of expert thinking is leadership processes and behaviors. Leadership processes and leader behaviors are expert thinking in action. Values, professional knowledge, and intentions are building blocks of expert thinking that complement principals' behaviors and leadership processes. Various conceptualizations of leadership processes and behaviors from the literature have been described in earlier chapters of this book. In Chapter 5, "Principals and their Work," we discussed the influence of studies in business and industry on the conceptualization of administrators' work in schools. For example, *Administration Industriale and Generale,* by Henri Fayol (1916), provides an excellent description of leadership processes. The administrative processes of planning, organizing, commanding, coordinating, and controlling continue to be reflected in contemporary conceptualizations of the work of principals elaborated in textbooks, reform reports, and administrator preparation program curricula.

> To manage is to forecast and plan, to command, to co-ordinate, and to control. To foresee and provide means examining the future and drawing up the plan of action. To organize means building up the dual structure, material and human, of the undertaking. To command means maintaining activity among the personnel. To co-ordinate means binding together, unifying and harmonizing all activity and effort. To control means seeing that everything occurs in conformity with established rule and expressed command.[1]

In addition to these basic administrative processes, the work of principals has been systematically examined in literally hundreds of empirical studies. For example, the works of Peterson (1978), Kmetz and Willower (1982) and Martin and Willower (1981) provide detailed descriptions of principal work and on-the-job leader behaviors.

A person who is busy carrying out elemental administrative processes and behaving like a leader is not necessarily demonstrating expert thinking in action. Leadership processes and behaviors that express expert thinking in action are grounded in values, professional knowledge, and purpose. For example, students in principal preparation programs often express their frustration with the content and the quality of preservice experiences they encounter in the curriculum. Without being grounded in values, professional knowledge, and purpose, simply learning decontextualized technical skills, proficiencies, and processes would do little to provide opportunities for professional growth and the development of expert thinking in aspiring principals. At best, the focus on leadership behaviors and processes alone results in leadership by mimicry and recall rather than by expert thinking.

A common component in most principal preparation programs, the instructional supervision component, illustrates these dangers of recall and mimicry. Typically, students practice classroom observation skills and develop strategies for summative teacher evaluations. Classroom observation, conferencing, assessment, and teacher evaluation require a number of important technical skills. However, without guiding values (trustworthiness, fairness, and norms of professionalism), clear intents and goals (to provide support and recognition, and to enhance teacher growth and learning), and professional knowledge (an understanding of the structure and intent of the lessons observed, their relationship to other aspects of the curriculum, and knowledge of pedagogy), classroom observation, assessment, feedback, and evaluation skills remain perfunctory technical skills, not leadership expertise in action.

It is important to understand the links among the building blocks of pro-

---

[1]*General and Industrial Management* (1949). Translated by Constance Storrs.

fessional expertise because together they are much more than the sum of their parts. Leithwood (1994) states that overt administrative processes and leader behaviors

> are essentially uninterpretable in the absence of knowledge about their purposes and their effects. This explanation is consistent with earlier evidence reporting almost no difference between the tasks engaged in by highly effective and more typical school principals, including how their time distributed across these tasks (Leithwood & Montgomery, 1986). Indeed, most of the overt practices of transformational leaders look quite managerial. Transformational effects depend upon school leaders infusing day-to-day routines with meaning and purpose for themselves and their colleagues. (pp. 20–21)

In an era of reform, with constant pressures to initiate changes in schools, the danger exists of focusing on techniques and tactic rather than substance, meaning, purpose, and goals. Workshops, training seminars, and professional conferences are replete with neo-educational gurus hawking the latest line of leadership snake oils to grease the squeaky wheels demanding facile innovations and flashy educational reform initiatives. With demands for efficiency and innovation, educators have been Hunterized, restructured, Demmingized, and recultured across the nation. Many valuable ideas and practices are embedded in these initiatives, but they tend to be short-lived. Fullan & Miles (1992) refers to the attrition of pockets of educational successes. Thus, even good ideas become marginalized and are often doomed to failure because they remain fragmented in content, decontextualized in presentation, and decoupled from the other building blocks of professional expertise. We turn next to a discussion of the fourth building block of expert thinking, intent.

Leader Intent

Studying expert thinking and the relationships that exist among leader values, professional knowledge, and leadership processes and behaviors is a bit like trying to configure various shapes from the array of stars in the evening sky. The lines of leader intent provide the outline and reveal the connections that make the constellation of expert thinking visible to others. The literature on leadership abounds with synonyms for intent. *Purpose and purposing, aim, direction, vision, goal, meaning,* and *design* are commonly used to describe the importance of intent to successful leadership in organizations. We deliberately use the term *leader intent* because of its denotative and connotative meanings derived from the Latin word *intentus,* meaning *aim* or *purpose.* What leaders pay attention to is an expression of the other building blocks of expert thinking. Sergiovanni (1987) describes leader attention and intent as *purposing.* Purposing is a continuous stream of actions, substantive and symbolic, that help to provide clarity, consensus, and commitment to the organization's basic purposes. He concludes,

> The leader's behavioral style is less important in reflecting the value of leadership by purposing. Instead, what the leader stands for and communicates to others is emphasized. The object of purposing is the stirring of human consciousness, the enhancing of meaning, the spelling out of key cultural strands that provide both excitement and significance to one's work life. (p. 340)

The fact that principals pay attention to some things in their schools while ignoring or de-emphasizing others infuses the ordinary routines of faculty, staff, and students with meaning and purpose—intent.

You recall in Chapter 6 we described a framework that included ten managerial roles based on empirical studies of the work of managers (Mintzberg, 1973). Similar observational studies by Kmetz and Willower, 1982, and Martin and Willower, 1981, were conducted to examine the work of principals. While accurate in their descriptions of the role and task behaviors of elementary and secondary principals, these findings failed to differentiate observed tasks and behaviors by their purpose(s). Hundreds of written communications, verbal exchanges, and other managerial tasks were simply recorded as observed tasks. Leithwood (1994) noted that leadership practices and behaviors are contingent; thus, connecting specific behaviors and practices to measures of success or effectiveness was problematic. Without understanding the intent behind leader practices and behaviors, it is difficult to assess the efficacy of a particular leadership style or of a given cluster of leadership behaviors. To illustrate how intent influences leader behavior and thus expert thinking, we use the example of a principal's visit to a teacher's classroom.

If Gertrude Stein had been asked to describe differences among principals' visits to classrooms in their schools, she might have penned, "A classroom visit is a classroom visit is a classroom visit is a classroom visit. . . ." Are there meaningful differences in what appears to be a familiar principal instructional leadership behavior? Your response to such a query would be unequivocal: Of course there are differences! We would agree with you and argue that the differences are the result of leader intent. For example, principals' visits to classrooms may be intended to (1) demonstrate interest in the core technology of the school, teaching and learning; (2) monitor the curriculum; (3) evaluate teaching; 4) establish ties with students; (5) legitimate the principal's authority as formal leader in the school hierarchy; (6) support staff; (7) model professional collegiality; and (8) inspect the facilities. Leader intent makes all the difference as to the efficacy of a principal's visits to classrooms—the impact of those visits on students and teachers, on the school culture, and on the accomplishment of the school's goals. Leader intent as demonstrated through regular classroom visits can clarify the primary mission of the school (teaching and learning is why we are all here), validate this mission to others (students, teachers, and parents), engender excitement and high expectations for teaching and learning, and infuse the daily work routines of students, teachers, support staff, and the principal with meaning and significance. What leaders pay attention to—leader intent—is a building block of expert thinking and a powerful leadership mechanism for embedding cultural norms in schools.

CONCLUSION

In this chapter we described four primary building blocks of principals' expert thinking—values, professional knowledge, leader processes and behaviors, and intent. We have argued that the relative contribution of each building block to specific problems of practice varies depending on the situational demands and context. Thus, a principal may rely more heavily on professional

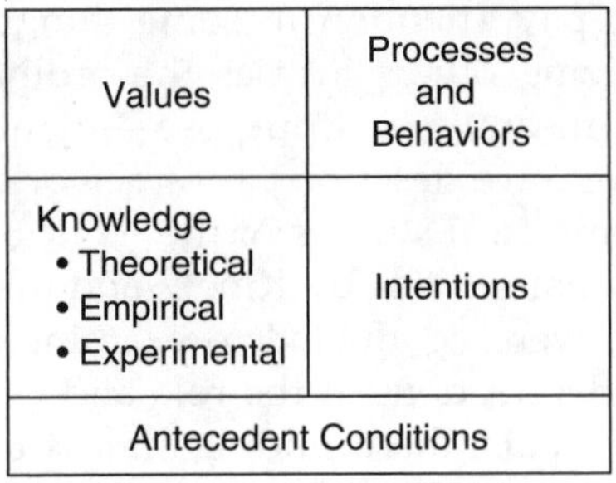

Values	Processes and Behaviors
Knowledge • Theoretical • Empirical • Experimental	Intentions
Antecedent Conditions	

FIGURE 11.1. Building blocks of principals' expert thinking and action.

knowledge, for example, direct experience in one case. In another problem situation a principal may find that leader values and intent are more useful as guides to administrative action. The dotted line in Figure 11.1 suggests permeability among the building blocks. The building blocks are complementary in their contribution to expert thinking.

We began the chapter comparing the work of an architect to that of a principal. A casual observer of activity in an architectural design studio may not be able to distinguish between the work of the draftsman and that of the architect. Both use the fundamental building blocks of their profession. The draftsman relies primarily on technical skills and knowledge to flesh out the details in spatial designs. The architect's work—informed by technical skills and professional knowledge, however—is characterized by expert thinking and creativity that go beyond repetitious technical processes to match the spatial designs to situational demands. Similarly, superficial observation of the work of principals in schools would do little to inform the observer of the meaningful differences between highly successful and ordinary principals. The work of successful principals more closely parallels the expert thinking and creativity of the architect than it does the routine and repetitive application of skills of the draftsman. The building blocks of expert thinking are the foundation of our theory of professional visualization. We turn next to expert thinking in action.

SUGGESTED ACTIVITIES

1. Figure 11.1 represents a framework for describing essential building blocks that support principals' expert thinking and practice. We described components within each of these building blocks. Assess the building blocks of expert thinking and practice that will support you as a principal. Specify the elements you consider to be most important in each building block. What would you identify as your primary strengths? What components or areas need strengthening?
2. Observe several principals in schools. Using the observational data, describe what you believe to be the basic building blocks that inform their thinking and leadership practices.

3. Harmony and situational fit are characteristic of effective professional practice and principal leadership. Identify several seemingly intractable problems in your school. How does the principal maintain balance, harmony, and respect for the school setting while at the same time exert significant influence to ameliorate the problems? Identify any "stark right angles" in the principal's leadership and practices.

4. In your next faculty meeting, listen for explicit or implicit references to theoretical knowledge and its use in your school. In what way(s) does theory inform professional discussions, problem solving, and practice in your school?

5. Principalship preparation programs are often criticized for failing to provide students with adequate opportunities to enhance critical leadership skills and behaviors. Using the list of leadership competencies in *Principals for our changing schools*, how would you assess your level of professional competence across the four performance domains? What will you do to enhance your skills in areas you have identified as weak or needing improvement?

A Theory of Professional Visualization

Schools are professional work groups requiring the application of professional knowledge to constantly shifting educational challenges. As we repeatedly have asserted, this professional work environment makes recipes for the right action in every contingency virtually useless. In Chapter 1, we introduced experiential, empirical, and theoretical forms of professional knowledge in educational administration and the induction process experienced by new school principals. Experiential knowledge develops from vivid personal and vicarious experiences; empirical knowledge comes from systematic qualitative and quantitative inquiry; and theoretical knowledge functions as a conceptual framework or map explaining and organizing the other forms of knowledge.

Research's aim is to find empirical evidence that can be developed into general theories or test existing theory. To accomplish this goal, research findings are generalized rather than being situated in a specific context. They sometimes may give the impression that schools are more homogenous than is actually the case and imply a uniformity of leadership roles that does not exist. Consequently, most prescriptive recipes for leadership behavior given to principals do not jibe with the reality in which they work. We have returned repeatedly to this theme throughout the book and now turn to a specific mechanism to assist you in bringing research to bear on practice.

In this final chapter, we describe a method through which you can make your professional practice more consistent with your knowledge, values, and principles. Visualizing or professional theorizing provides a means for constructing situational maps that guide you closer to approximations of superior professional possibilities. You may utilize an ideal or profile of the principal you would like to be within a context, visualizing that ideal and the "amount of change required . . . into incremental steps leading towards some ideal image of the role" (p. 20). You can also use this framework to visualize not only the amount of change but the processes suggested by the school's needs and steps that will reveal appropriate actions unfolding as part of the outcome of previous actions.

We pointed out that many new principals work within a "sink or swim" mentality that leaves them to their own devices to experience "surprise and sensemaking" on their own. Even if you find yourself in such a situation, you can develop the skills and opportunities for creating your own cycles of deliberate professional learning. This process will be even more powerful if you also have the support of deliberately structured and growth-promoting induction experiences from your district or school board. In response to the induction needs of new principals, some states have established formal support programs at local universities. University supervisors and experienced principals are matched with first-year principals to provide a valuable support network during their entry year. In states where formal requirements for mentors do not exist, many universities are establishing these programs on their own or in consortiums with other universities in the state.

The process we call *professional theorizing*, then, is a means for creating deliberate structures, theories, or maps for taking action—action that will lead toward successfully meeting educational leadership challenges and structuring your principal leadership career. It depends on your willingness and ability to systematically integrate new knowledge from experience, research, and theory as you grow and develop professionally. Your professional vision and the visualization that help you construct actions as a principal will change over time, but the process of reflection-on-action and reflection-in-action forms the core of your professional growth.

We begin the chapter with a brief overview of the interaction and social learning framework for school leadership built by the preceding chapters. We then describe what we mean by professional theorizing, lay out a process of professional theorizing and visualizing, and enumerate steps for professional visualization. In the third section of this chapter, we apply this framework to pressing current issues in education and illustrate how knowledge can be applied to action through this process. We also provide opportunities for you to frame your own theory-building and visualization process that will lay the groundwork for future professional growth and development as your knowledge expands and you become more systematic in the ways you add and integrate new knowledge with current knowledge. Finally, we return to the theories, norms, and practices that shape a pattern of professional growth in educational leadership. We review common problem-solving errors against which we must be constantly vigilant and methods for querying your own expert thinking and practice in schools.

OVERVIEW: EXERTING LEADERSHIP THROUGH INTERACTION

The educational administration profession is changing so rapidly, in content knowledge and the paradigms organizing that knowledge, that no principal can expect to live out her career relying only on the knowledge acquired in her early training. In Chapter 1, we laid out a framework of experiential, empirical, and theoretical knowledge that principals can learn to systematize and apply, maximizing their impact on schools. By interacting with and integrating this knowledge, we argued that principals can become more effective.

Chapter 2 introduced processes for connecting knowledge and action in the principalship. Expertise and expert thinking through which principals apply their knowledge to the unique situations of practice were discussed, and we emphasized that misapplied technical skills and competencies are no more effective than no skill at all and may be more harmful. Our conclusion, after reviewing the development and current state of a professional knowledge base for school leaders: Changing concepts of social science, norms of inquiry, and standards for validation of new knowledge in an environment in which the challenges of education are rapidly changing make it necessary for school leaders to adapt and integrate knowledge from many sources applied within the contexts of their work. The various typologies educational administrators and scholars have developed for school leadership likewise change with the sensibilities of their times. The shifting definitions of professional expertise and professional practice we visited—from the acquisition of technical skills and competencies to the application of theory—illustrate the broad menu from which you can choose to construct a framework for applying knowledge to action as a principal. You recall Schon's description of this process from Chapter 2: "When someone reflects-in-action, he becomes a researcher in the practice context. He is not dependent on the categories of established theory and technique, but constructs a new theory of the unique case" (1983, p. 68). In a sense, he is the ultimate participant observer who accepts the pitfalls of participant observation in order to reap the benefits for practice. Further, he then becomes a theoretician in the practice context. The end of the chapter illustrated that by avoiding or mitigating the effects of five common problem-solving errors—inappropriate scanning, incorrect synthesis, inadequate synthesis, premature closure, and anchoring—principals can improve the salutary effects of their action decisions.

The role of the researcher and theoretician in the practice context moves the principal beyond the function of the technician and into the work of the professional. She can then hold herself to an elevated standard of understanding and performance as a school leader. A simple analogy of the practical effect of this difference can be found in architecture. As naive observers, we might watch a group of architects working in a design studio and say that they are all doing the same thing. Their behaviors are similar, and we see little difference in their ability to use their technical skills. When their designs become buildings, however, dramatic differences are apparent to all of us. The built designs create dramatically different qualities in the physical environment. Leithwood (1994) observed similar patterns in studies attempting to distinguish the visible behaviors of effective from those of ineffective principals. He argued:

> Overt practices are essentially uninterpretable in the absence of knowledge about their purposes and their effects. This . . . is consistent with earlier evidence reporting almost no difference between the tasks engaged in by highly effective and more typical school principals, including how their time is distributed across these tasks. Indeed, most of the overt practices of transformational leaders look quite managerial. Transformational effects depend upon school leaders infusing day-to-day routines with meaning and purpose for themselves and their colleagues. (pp. 20–21)

Chapter 3 introduced the context of leadership within the social and technical systems of the school. Social structures, core technologies, goals, participants, and environments all combine to make up the contingency context in which principals work to apply their professional knowledge to action. We emphasized that the work of principals cannot be divorced from this context, that the knowledge and expert thinking on which the principal draws are not contingent but are applied to an individual problem or school context that is contingent and must be assessed and reassessed by the principal. In particular, the technology of schools and schooling, including all instructional processes and ways of organizing teachers' and students' work and ways of assessing outcomes, fall within the boundaries of context into which the principal must become integrated and productive.

Our discussion of the principal and the school in Chapter 4 extended this context to a proactive interaction in which principal and school function synergistically. The organizational socialization of the principal into a school was described as a means by which new principals can tap the power embedded in the school context and exercise leadership through interaction. We discussed the processes and stages found to characterize socialization and the "surprise and sensemaking" of the contact and integration time. With Firestone (in press), we argued the concept of leadership as an organizational characteristic in which formal leaders and others share in the combined functions of leadership.

Returning to the stories of principals in their work, we drew in Chapter 5 on experiences portrayed by principals that shaped their professional expectations and self-concepts, often resulting in the perception that "ordinary mortals need not apply" for the job. A brief conceptual and practical history of school administration was placed in the context of management and organizational theory, educational administration theory, empirical research on principals and their work, observational studies, survey research, and other sources of qualitative data such as survey interview, naturalistic, and autobiographical studies.

Chapter 6 extended this discussion to the role of principals as formally appointed leaders in schools. We introduced constructs shaping our understanding of this role such as social role theory and power, traditional leadership studies of traits, situation, behavior, and contingency, and functions of leadership (skills, processes, and responsibilities). Skills of leadership included the technical, human, and conceptual; processes included delegation, organization, coordination, and evaluation; and responsibilities included the wide-ranging conceptualizations of managers. Finally, we explored metaphors used to capture the roles of principal-leaders—designer, teacher of teachers, steward, and symbol.

The taking-charge experience formed the central focus of Chapter 7. We emphasized that a succession or taking-charge experience is a unique time in the career of a principal during which many opportunities that will not be repeated arise. We reviewed the literature on principal succession that looked for positive effects springing from the appointment of new school leaders, and for factors in the principal, school, and community that seem to moderate effects.

Chapter 8 focused on theories and processes of interaction that school leaders can apply to this taking-charge process. The motivation to interact, interaction processes, and interaction outcomes were discussed from a broad-based perspective of social sciences and applied management research.

The most valued effect sought from a principal succession is improved student and school performance, the topic of Chapter 9. We moved in this discussion to the potential of personal, social, and technical factors to shape school outcomes. These connections are indirect and guided by assumptions about principals' daily work activities, instructional leadership, mediating factors, and the additive and indirect influence of principals on student and school outcomes. Effective schools and effective principals frequently are tied together by the traditions of educational scholarship focusing on outcomes for students in schools. We reviewed a few of the many models, frameworks, and images of instructional leadership.

The process of becoming a principal through which you now are passing, discussed in Chapter 10, carries with it many opportunities and pitfalls. The role-taking and role-making experiences that are shaping your careers, the interaction that yields trust and validation, and the stages and processes of transition to the principalship you are experiencing and will experience in increasing intensity contribute to your professional learning and growth. Once you are appointed as a principal, all the preservice and prior socialization you bring to the position are further shaped in the new context by the social interactions you experience. Chapter 10 addresses this process of leadership as social and symbolic interaction between the principal and the school.

In Chapter 11, we introduced our theory of professional visualization. We argued that successful leadership is expert thinking constructed of specific building blocks applied to the construction of situational maps of practice. These maps of practice in turn guide professional actions and affect school-level factors that lead to student learning and growth. Chapter 11 focused on the building blocks of expert thinking; in the following sections of this chapter, we fill in the details of our theory in order to present a framework for your own professional theorizing in the practice context.

FRAMEWORK FOR PROFESSIONAL THEORIZING

One of the most frustrating realities all professional school students face is the transition from student to practicing professional. The systematic application of knowledge to action for the most expert professionals has become tacit and automatic, so practitioners find it difficult to convey the process to the novice (Schon, 1983, 1987). Figure 12.1 presents a framework for professional research and theorizing in the practice context in the form of a theory of professional visualization. It portrays the relationships among elements in a theory of professional visualization for principals. We propose that an input stimulus, opportunity, or problem triggers the principal to draw on her building blocks for expert thinking. These stimuli can either present themselves from the internal or external environment of the school, or be found and deliberately brought to the school by the principal or by others. The building blocks of expert thinking are laid on a foundation of the antecedent conditions we talked about in

Chapter 10. Knowledge includes the principal's strengths and weaknesses relative to the challenge at hand, and intentions include espoused theories and theories in action developed over the course of the principal's education career. The particular combination, emphasis, and role of building blocks used depends on the stimulus, and they are bonded together by the mortar of expert thinking.

With this resource of building blocks and processes, the principal constructs situational maps of practice or theories in the practice context and begins to construct a series of professional actions appropriate to the practice theory embodied in the situational map. He may move to establish a decision-making or *ad hoc* committee of teachers, draw on a particular governance struc-

FIGURE 12.1. A theory of professional visualization.

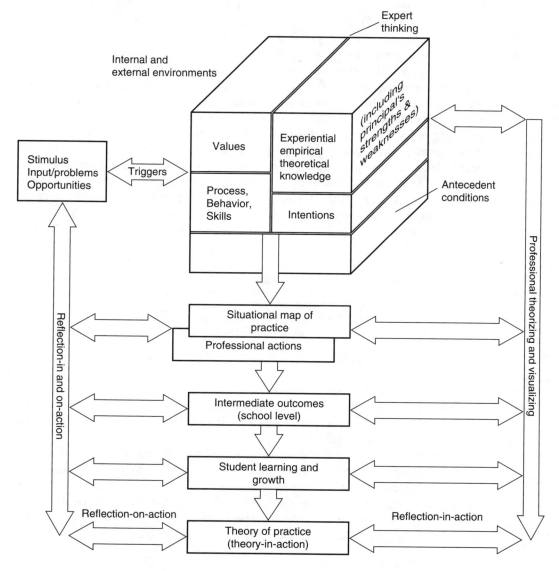

ture or repository of expertise among the professional staff or parents, or apply specific expert knowledge of his own about finance and budgeting, instruction, law, or any number of other sources of knowledge. He may turn to an experience related to earlier practice and contact a colleague, peer, or previous supervisor.

These options are as varied and numerous as education problems are complex. The result of this process is a visualization of actions, people, and resources fitted together toward desired ends. During principal professional visualizing, it produces intermediate outcomes at the school level focused on stimulating student learning and growth at the final level of performance. These school level outcomes may be such things as a professional norm of experimentation and instructional innovation in the faculty (Little, 1982); high and achievable expectations (effective schools literature); teacher professional efficacy (Ashton & Webb, 1986); reduced student alienation and drop-out rates (Wehlage, 1989); or a school culture that celebrates diversity, tolerance, and growth (Kozol, 1991). Throughout this process (professional visualization), the principal integrates feedback, incoming information, and the results of her expert thinking into the growing theory of practice she is developing. She also engages in reflection-in-action and reflection-on-action, feeding new interpretations and information into her theory development. The results produce ongoing stimulus for input into more theory building and visualization. Visualization permits principals to move from expert thinking and theorizing to concrete behaviors in the world of daily practice. Through this process, the expert professional brings her espoused theories and theories-in-action into greater congruence and raises her professional practice to higher levels of expertise. Like the architects in the design studio we referred to earlier, the professional principal turns ideas and conceptual building blocks into principles of design and action and then *takes* action. The elements of this framework are simple:

Knowledge from Experience, Research and Theory ⇒

Visualization ⇒ Professional Theorizing
Professional Theorizing ⇒ Situational Map Construction
Situational Map ⇒ Expert Thinking ⇒ Expert Practice Plan
Practice Plan ⇒ Action

Throughout this process, the expert practitioner visualizes the model of expert action she aspires to and visualizes herself performing the actions likely to bring about desired results.

The abstract theory building of scholarship and the theory building of practice are complementary. Each is more important in its particular environment, and each affects the other when professional practice advances. The standards of rigor by which we judge theorizing in practice and theorizing in scholarship are different, however. Theorizing in scholarship requires that the scholar design systematic, abstract, and discipline-based maps among the critical variables. These abstract maps are used to explain and predict outcomes in multiple settings and to design and conduct further inquiry and theory building. Theorizing in the practice context requires concrete and visible outcomes, emerging in a particular setting out of the use of appropriate situational maps of practice. Theories of practice require that the theorizer (the principal in this case) deal with particular problems in specific contexts, whether he is functioning as problem solver, facilitator, designer, teacher, steward, or coach.

The standards of adequacy for practice and scholarly theories are very different. While the scholar examines social phenomena and constructs comprehensive and inclusive maps for inquiry and prediction, practitioners look within settings and construct situational maps that guide appropriate and promising actions that in turn lead to desired outcomes. Motivation theory provides one example of these different standards of adequacy. A principal seeking to motivate teachers, students, and staff to work together and to improve the relationships, collaboration, and schoolwide efforts in a school measures successful motivation by whether people choose to interact, by the utility of emerging interactions, and by the outcomes of those interactions. A scholar measures success of motivation theory in interaction analyses by the statistical significance of the measured relationships among variables, or, in other paradigms, by the vivid rendering of social reality and the adequacy of description and goodness of fit to the setting studied. Theories built by scholars are among the many sources of inputs into the building blocks of expert thinking. Professional practice is grounded in expert theorizing *and* in expert practice, not in one or the other.

As a natural consequence of the field's development, educational administration moved from exclusive reliance on craft knowledge to a commitment to apply social science theory to educational leadership practice. The theory movement in educational administration may have become separated from its original purpose—the improvement of educational administration as a discipline—when it was interpreted as different from and isolated from the professional practice of school administration. The result is a theory-practice debate constructed as a set of false dichotomies.

Similarly, a reification of the "firefighter" view of management occurs when educational administrators rely on descriptions of uncritically chronicled activities, as in Mintzberg. Unexamined acceptance of observed behavior creates a picture of school principals and other managers careening through a chaotic world. Everything is viewed as idiosyncratic and new with no culture, no patterns, no definitions, no history, and no explanation. This view of the principalship becomes mired in a short-term memory syndrome in which the principal learns from neither experience nor scholarship.

Many thoughtful principals and writers seek alternatives to these extremes. Interest in the moral dimensions of leadership, strategy and politics, and contextualized thinking and learning (Prestine & LeGrand, 1991, Greenfield, 1985b, Sergiovanni, 1992), as well as the other thoughtful views of school leadership discussed in earlier chapters, abound as testimony to the desire of scholars and practitioners alike to respectfully and accurately portray the rich dimensions of leadership in schools.

The theory of professional visualization introduced in Chapter 11 and expanded on in this discussion grew out of our dissatisfaction with the artificially heroic implication of other attempts to capture principals' impacts on schools through images based on philosophy and vision. We have worked as school administrators and university professors during eras of professional platforms, principals' philosophies of education, and principal vision statements. Each of these movements captured a facet of the subtle relationship between leader and school and addressed a strongly felt need among practitioners, but each failed to provide a mechanism for including the knowledge, aspirations, and goals of other members of the school social group, and failed also to systematically move from abstract visioning to action in real schools.

Sports psychology provided us with the additional action and interaction components missing from these attempts to capture the spirit of idealism and commitment common to educators. Visualization provides athletes with three key components for enhancing performance: (1) detailed knowledge of the physiology, physics, and psychology of their sport and the contexts in which they compete; (2) a process for imaging their performance, for seeing themselves achieving their ideal action outcomes; and (3) procedures for assessing their performance and refining their skill. Other human endeavors requiring action also take advantage of the visualization process. For example, pilots preparing for their turn to compete in stunt flying competitions can be seen quietly walking through their maneuvers, often with their eyes closed, rehearsing their actions and planning the adjustments needed to wind and weather conditions and the condition and flying characteristics of their airplanes.

The press of problems in schools to which our framework for professional theorizing can be applied is so diverse that we hesitate to single out any particular examples. Many problems receive close scrutiny at the state or policy levels, but this book and our discussions throughout focus on the actions of principals as school-level leaders and your preparation for this important role. The following examples are, therefore, only illustrative and we confine the discussion to the way a school principal might approach his professional theorizing and visualizing toward actions to address these problems at the level where teachers and students work to teach and learn. Our examples include problems that require multiagency collaboration: the need for community involvement versus a tidal wave of competing pressures in turbulent times ("pluribus" vs. "unum"); school choice, vouchers, and privatization; cultural pluralism; access and excellence (who gets what and why). From your own immediate experience, you probably are thinking of many more situations in which the framework can be applied. Our hope is that these five examples of current, pressing issues will illustrate the processes of professional theorizing.

Collaboration

The American Educational Research Association chose collaboration as its conference theme for 1995. In its call for paper proposals, the association stated that its call was based on a

growing acceptance of the need for interdependence among the human service professions (e.g., education, social work, school psychology, public health
administration) in order to effectively serve children, adults, and families in
America. It is apparent that partnerships of this nature will transform schools
and their relationships with families and community agencies. . . . [The annual
meeting] will focus on pioneering research and scholarly efforts associated
with interdisciplinary partnerships and the resulting interprofessional collaboration. (*Educational Researcher,* May, 1994, p. 36)

This year's theme is grounded in growing acceptance of the need for interdependence among the human service professions (e.g., education, social work,
school psychology, public health) in order to effectively serve children, adults,
and families in America. It is apparent that partnerships of this nature will
transform schools and their relationships with families and community agencies.

The problems of youth, children, and families—increasingly complex—
stimulate increasingly serious attempts by social service agencies, government,
and education to find ways to provide children and youth the health, nutri-
tion, emotional and psychological support, and learning resources they need
in a single setting—the school. The Readers' Digest-DeWitt Wallace Foundation is supporting a major consortium of social work and educational agencies
and colleges aimed at finding ways to address the combination of social and
intellectual problems that currently limit the educational and personal achievement of so many young people. Other initiatives abound, yet principals, teachers, parents, children, university and college students and faculty, and social
agency professionals face daunting challenges when they apply this commitment to collaboration to the everyday work in schools. Figure 12.2 illustrates
how a school principal might go about orchestrating the collaboration of social
work and educational professionals to serve children and families in a school
setting. The specific individual and contextual examples we use in this figure
are fictional and illustrative, but they are in harmony with our personal experiences and with experiences shared with us by our students (as are all descriptive factors used in subsequent illustrations). They also are highly abbreviated
and include only a sampling of the factors you would actually use in such a
process.

Much of the dialogue surrounding collaborative arrangements emerges
from accounts of school drop-out rates, violence at school, and poor academic
achievement attributed to the interaction of social, economic, and educational
factors. As stimuli or problems, these conditions have already triggered a great
deal of talk about the need for interventions. A collaboration opportunity
arises when various agencies, including schools, see a chance to achieve shared
goals by pooling their resources in a single setting in which children can be
served.

The building blocks held together by expert thinking in this collaboration
case would include values, processes, knowledge, and intentions related to the
stimuli. *Values* could include a commitment to democracy in the workplace
and sharing. Process, skills, and behaviors could include diverse professional
processes such as counseling, reading instruction, and group conflict-manage-
ment processes. Knowledge about decision-making techniques and theories,

the time-consuming nature of collaborative agreements, and diverse knowledge about the social, emotional, and physical development of children and instructional techniques, cognitive psychology and development, and content acquisition could be used as those involved examine their situation and problem. A complex set of intentions, some of which are conflicting, would be included in the mix of factors to be considered. A social worker would be charged as part of his professional obligation to intend improvements in fam-

FIGURE 12.2. Collaboration.

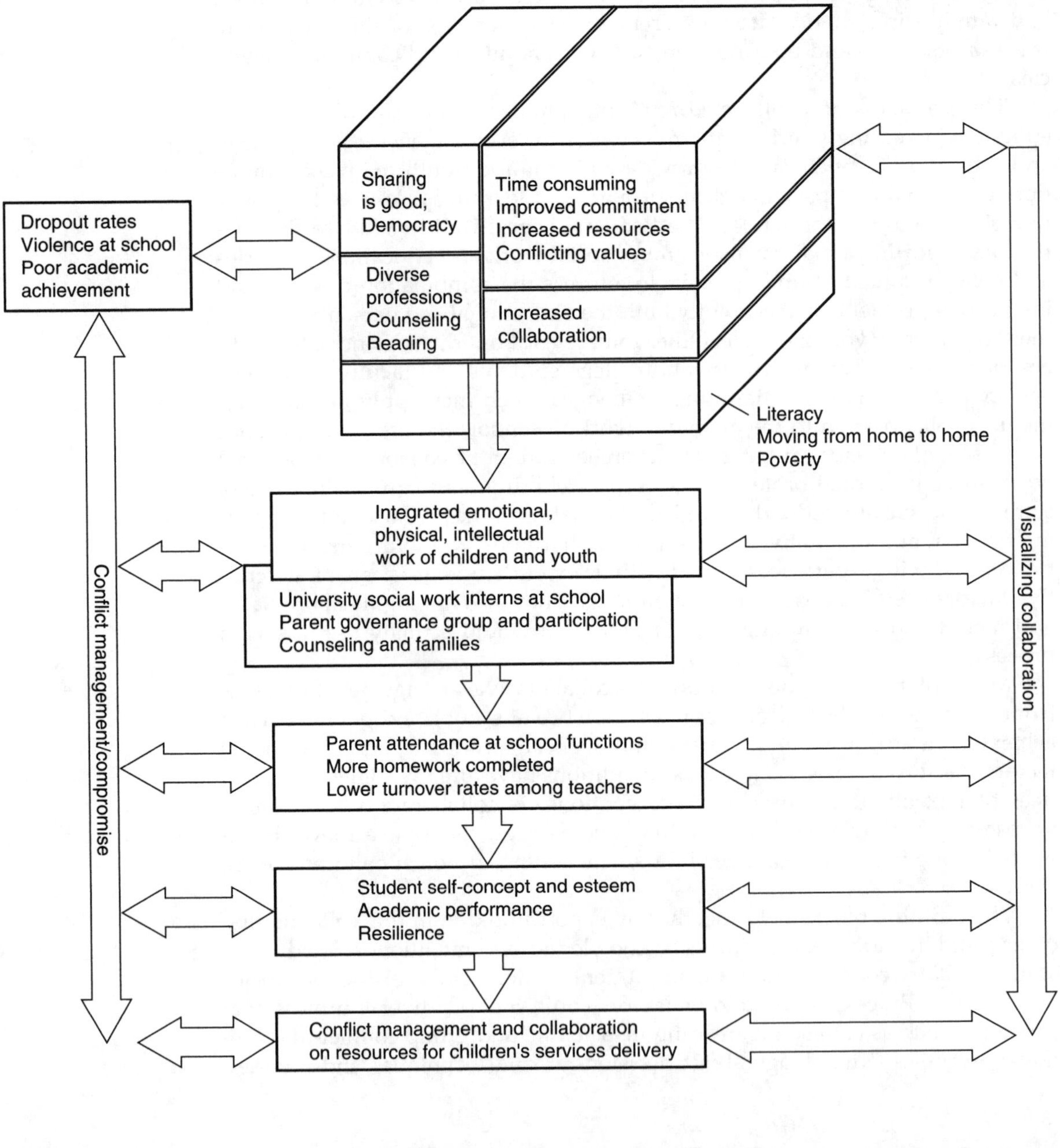

ily relationships and emotional health while a teacher would be obligated to focus on the child's acquisition of knowledge. (This conflict can play out as competition for the child's time during the day—a counseling session on family processes versus the reading group.) Antecedent conditions might range from past cooperation among agencies (or competition for resources), to the number of families with telephones in their homes and the proportion of children who move in and out of the school each year, to the availability of conference rooms and office space for social workers and counselors in the school.

The situational map of practice constructed from these inputs would present a rendering of the integrated emotional, physical, and intellectual work of these children and youth in this neighborhood, family, and school context. Even at this stage, the map takes on the abstract qualities of a scholarly theory, because it generalizes characteristics in order to convey a systemic view of the school-level challenges. Although this theorizing in the practice context does not necessarily represent the actual reality of any child's, teacher's, or family's life, it provides a general framework of the group members' shared experiences and challenges.

As the map of practice emerges, the principal and other professionals, family members, and community members begin to develop actions in harmony with the knowledge, values, intentions, antecedent conditions, and other factors included in the visualizing process. At all stages of this process, the visualizing or theorizing changes and evolves; it is not static.

Actions taken as a result of professional visualizing begin to yield outcomes (or, less linearly, are associated with the interventions), observations interact with the visualizing process, and new stimuli also emerge. For example, if teachers and social workers discover that neither their counseling nor their instruction sessions function well when some children miss portions of each, a new stimulus challenges them to use their knowledge informed by their values and goals to reorganize a portion of the situational map and revise an action. Conversely, those involved may see a conflict arise, but judge other alternatives as less desirable than the observed effects of the designed actions, so they choose deliberately to retain practices—even when they have some negative trade-offs as side effects. Other intermediate school-level outcomes might include such things as absentee rates, student arrests, school vandalism, or lack of attendance at parent-teacher meetings. Eventually, student learning and growth measures that affirm positive effects on individual student's lives should be observable, but they may take time.

Through this process, the principal develops a theory of practice related to interagency collaboration and the purposes of schools and schooling that becomes part of the building block array she brings to future experiences. As years of experience, characterized by careful and deliberate professional theorizing, accumulate—shaped by reflection-in-action and reflection-on-action—a strong and complex system of professional expertise results. The process is never static; it continually contributes to a dynamic professional career of increased knowledge and prowess for the educational leader.

In the following examples, we provide more abbreviated illustrations of several current educational problems. Again, we caution that these illustrations are incomplete portrayals of the real problems they represent.

Involvement versus Competition between Factions

Another issue, closely related to social agency collaboration and forming the subject of intense debate—even ideological fervor—is parent involvement in schools. Both of our states, Wisconsin and Utah, have governors or legislators who believe that parent involvement in site-based decision-making councils will improve schools, schooling, and student achievement. In 1994, Utah's Legislative Strategic Plan for Education and Governor Michael Leavitt's Centennial School Program, as well as projects funded through the Utah

FIGURE 12.3. Parental Involvement.

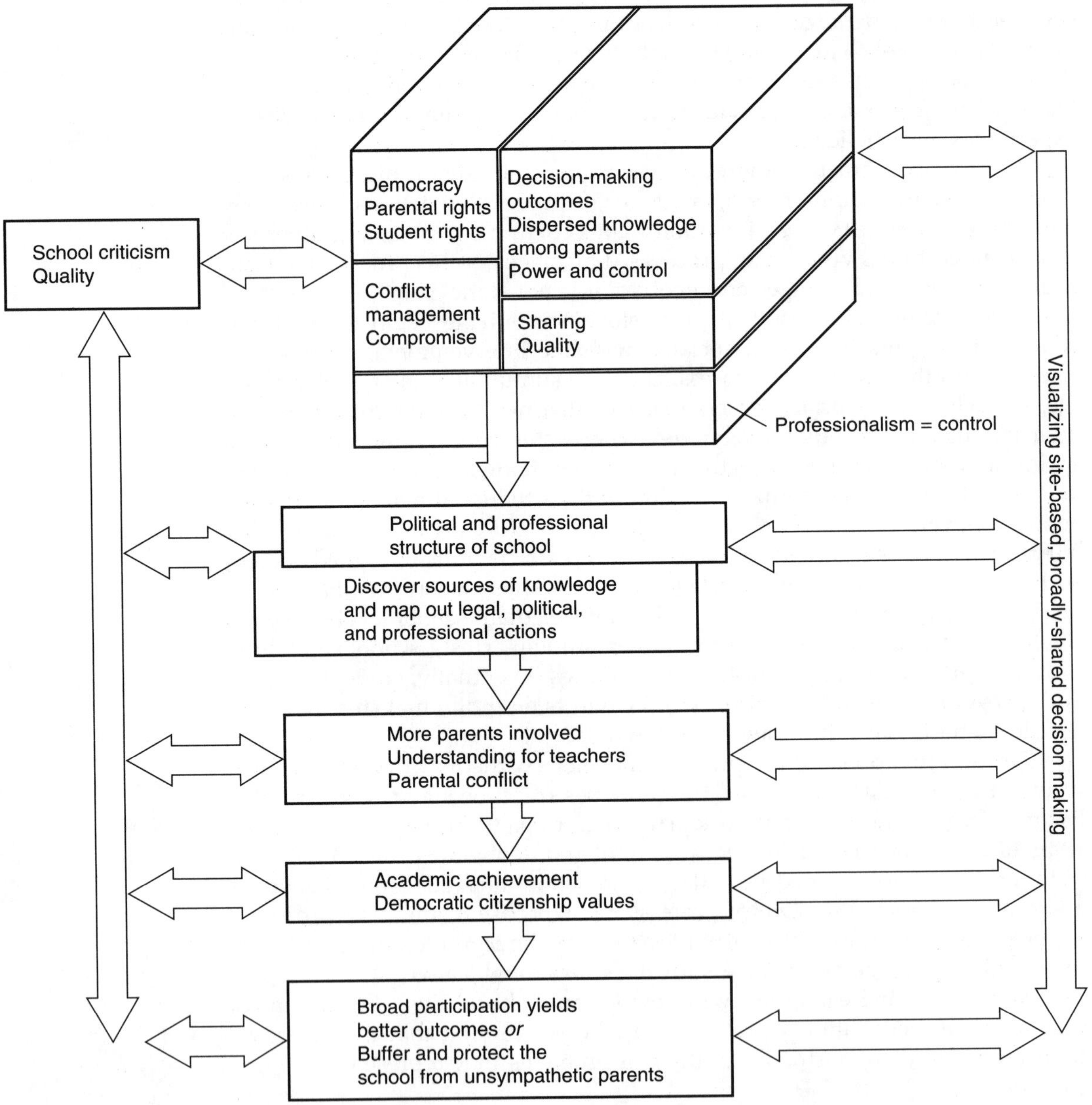

State Office of Education and the ten-year-old Teacher Career Ladder Program, all rely on the participation of parents in decision making in schools as a core feature of school improvement initiatives. Such initiatives as the Wisconsin Educational Standards, A Blueprint for Excellence, A New Design for Education in Wisconsin (Capper, 1993), and the School Tech-Prep Initiative in the 1990s enlist the support and involvement of parents in planning, implementing, and evaluating programs to meet new educational challenges for individuals and their communities across the state. Other states have similar programs.

We use Wisconsin and Utah as illustrations only. Other examples that have received more national publicity abound. These include the Dade County, Florida, schools, the Chicago school system, and the Kentucky schools. The person most responsible for facilitating, nurturing, and building on these parent involvement initiatives—the school principal—faces many challenges. Figure 12.3, using the professional visualization model, illustrates some of these challenges.

Stimuli for parent involvement currently spring from academic, vocational, and moral-ethical criticisms of schools. Students are failing to meet performance expectations; disagreements over the nature of work young people will face in the twenty-first century divide beliefs about the appropriate structure of "vocational" education; or parents disagree over prayer in the schools, AIDS education, sex education, or the moral lessons conveyed by fairy tales or literature. Values related to democracy; parental and student rights; processes of conflict management and compromise; decision-making theories, dispersed knowledge among parents; power and control; and intentions may include increased empowerment, sharing, or "quality." Antecedent conditions in the school, such as equating professionalism with control over the school, also come into play.

The situational map constructed would include, among other things, the political and professional structure of the school, the nature of the content students were expected to master, and prevailing mores and values. Professional actions could include new governance structures, new legal arrangements and contracts, and revised curriculum. Intermediate outcomes would by necessity focus on the ideology of participation and include things like more parent involvement, the function of the new governance structure, and parent and teacher agreement (or conflict). Eventually, the professionals and parents involved should ask questions about the democratic citizenship values of students, academic achievement, vocational achievement, and other factors related to the issues at hand. A theory of practice resulting from this process might be "broad participation yields better outcomes" or "buffer and protect the school from unsympathetic and uninformed parents." Through the processes of professional visualization, principals connect the purposes and structures (bureaucratic and altered) of the schools to the aspirations and energies of parents to enhance teaching and learning outcomes. The image of an orchestra director suggests the professional skills that successful educational leaders use to transform a cacophony of seemingly discordant opportunities and obstacles into educational compositions that are in harmony with their context and achieve their greatest potential. The conductor knows what to exclude as well as what to include!

Choice, Vouchers, and Privatization

Like issues of parent involvement, the questions surrounding school choice, vouchers, and privatization challenge long-established practices in American schooling. Unlike European parents, who have long been free to select from among private and public schools that receive state support, Americans have subscribed to the egalitarian philosophy that all children who live within the boundaries of a neighborhood school should attend that school. When parents and children reject that value, the stimuli of opportunities and problems involve issues such as desire to improve through quality schooling, government subsidy for religious or racially based schools, or failing support for public schools.

These inputs trigger value conflicts; they require political and group process skills. They depend on social and behavioral science knowledge about groups and group processes and academic knowledge about the canon of Western learning. They draw from memories of exclusive or public education experiences and challenge the access and excellence intentions (individually illustrated in Figure 12.6) of participants.[1] Antecedent conditions from the earliest era of American common schools to the present shape commitments to conflicting values, and the deterioration of inner-city public schools that many argue are becoming racial enclaves of deprivation contributes to antecedent conditions—as do parents' fears for the academic future and physical safety of their own children.

The situational maps of practice developed from these inputs can represent several different levels, even for the individual school principal. A map can involve state finance formulas, district policy, and individual school commitments, and it can have major implications for the way the principal's work is shaped. Kerchner (1990), for example, argues that principals will become fund raisers and entrepreneurs in an era of choice, garnering resources and recruiting students much as the presidents and officials of exclusive private colleges do now. The professional actions warranted by these maps differ dramatically. Fund raising, school closures, specialized schools, and new transportation systems could result. Intermediate outcomes—redistribution of children across communities and exacerbated divisions among schools on economic bases—could be intermediate outcomes. Average achievement on standardized tests, specialized rather than generalized education for young people, budgets for all-public schools, and learning opportunities for the least advantaged might be measured as student learning outcomes. The results could be greatly modified theories of practice for American education. As in the previous examples, modifications of the visualization and professional theory based on cycles of input throughout the process will occur.

The effects of choice, market mechanisms, and privatization would also affect the dynamics and social interactions within schools. Principals would have to balance competing values of choice, equity, the needs of individual

---

[1]The presence of access versus excellence within this debate—and illustrated later with its own professional theorizing figure—illustrates the complexity and interactivity of professional theorizing in the practice context and the importance of attending to this process for professionals seeking to expand their expertise.

children and groups of children (which often conflict), and the concerns and needs of the professional staff. This would be especially important in providing access and inclusion to children with disabilities. Choice and privatization operationalized through the currency of vouchers may serve parents' rights and political goals more than they do the needs of some children. A principal's professional visualization provides a mechanism for assessing and choosing among competing values and good within the school in service of children and youth (see Figure 12.4).

FIGURE 12.4. Choice, vouchers, privatization.

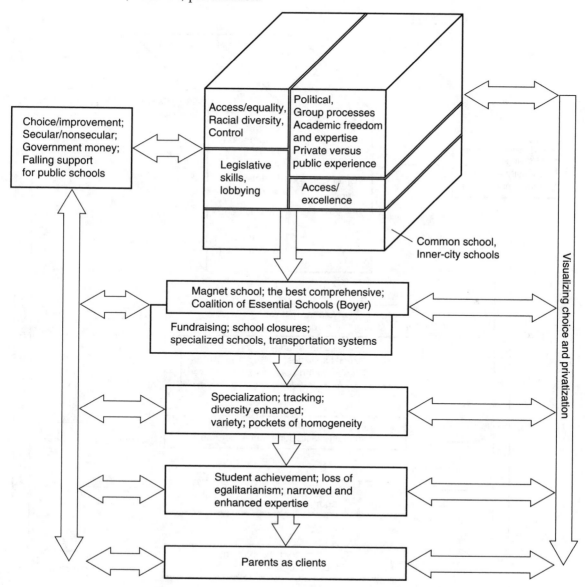

Cultural Pluralism

Diversity of students, faculty, administrators, neighborhoods, curriculum, and instructional methods dominates much current debate in education (see Figure 12.5). Cultural pluralism raises educational issues grounded deeply within cultures and values. Unlike the previous examples, values play a central part in the stimulus, building blocks, and choice of intermediate and student-level outcomes sought and measured. Differential valuing of different forms of knowledge, citizenship principles, appropriate roles for men and women, academic freedom and norms of expertise, and secular-moral dimensions of education illustrate the complexity of cultural pluralism pressures on principals

FIGURE 12.5. Cultural pluralism.

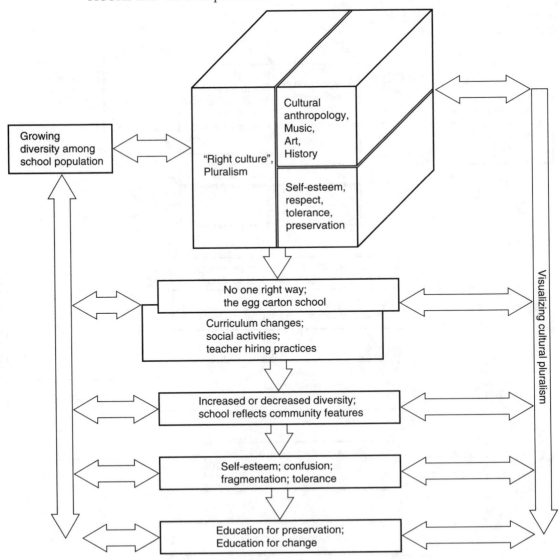

and schools. An intervention to rectify the lack of cultural reinforcement for one ethnic or racial group in a school may be seen to create problems for other groups. Pluralism versus the "best" or "right" culture dominates many of the diversity debates (even in state legislatures). When William Jennings Bryan asserted, during the Scopes evolution trial in Tennessee, that the people who pay for the schools should have the right to determine what is taught in them, he foreshadowed many of the educational debates currently faced by principals. Decisions about the intermediate school-level and student-learning and growth outcomes chosen for measurement flow directly from the maps of practice developed.

The principal's roles as celebrant and mediator suggest the potential for pluralism and diversity to either divide or unify in schools. As a celebrant, the principal focuses on legitimating the value of differences to enrich educational experiences of all learners. However, the principal also is a mediator who reconciles sources of conflict embedded in coexisting values, traditions, and mores. Through processes of professional visualization, principals work to nurture a positive teaching and learning environment that balances the "pluribus" of unreasoned diversity with the "unum" for a unified service to children and youth.

Access and Excellence

Like the divisions over cultural pluralism, access and excellence debates highlight our beliefs about the purpose of education. The back-to-basics movement, the school improvement initiatives springing out of the *Nation at Risk* report in 1983, and work redesign and school restructuring plans seeking to redefine and reshape teachers' careers and school structures all reflect a general dissatisfaction and disagreement over excellence in schooling and the relative success and failure of the public schools as the great levelers of American society.[2]

The stimulus-triggering questions of access and excellence immediately draw building blocks of knowledge about issues such as social and economic inequality, access to educational opportunities, and definitions of excellence. Western philosophy, commitment to individualism, and political ideology also come into play (Hodgkinson, 1983).

Equality of access and equality of outcomes as competing values shape the economic policies and school finance formulas developed as part of the general policy, but these issues also emerge at the school level. Drawing on available building blocks, for example, a principal might construct a map of practice that completely restructures her system for allocating funds to support different programs in a school, as one of the authors found. For example, when I examined the budget and expenditure records of one school to which I was assigned, I found that the department chairs traditionally met and allocated the materials, supplies, and textbook budgets, and snack bar and vending machine profits were supposedly set aside for student activities. In reality,

[2]See *The Great School Legend* (Cremin), *Anti-intellectualism in American Life* (Hofstadter), and *Schooling in Capitalist America* (Bowles and Gintis) for interpretations of the American school tradition.

however, the wood and metal shop teachers had routinely overspent their budget by thousands of dollars every year, and the principal had simply covered the deficit from instructional funds, thus limiting the resources available to other academic programs. While adequate wood and metal supplies were available to the shop classes, the mathematics and English departments were unable to replace outdated textbooks and supplemental materials. An outcome of a situational map that allowed one group of teachers to quietly limit the resources available to others had major intermediate and student learning outcomes.

The principal's theory of practice in the above example could be described as "principal as matriarch" (see Figure 12.6). Regardless of planning and symbolic access to decision making, the principal knew best and wanted to con-

FIGURE 12.6. Access and excellence.

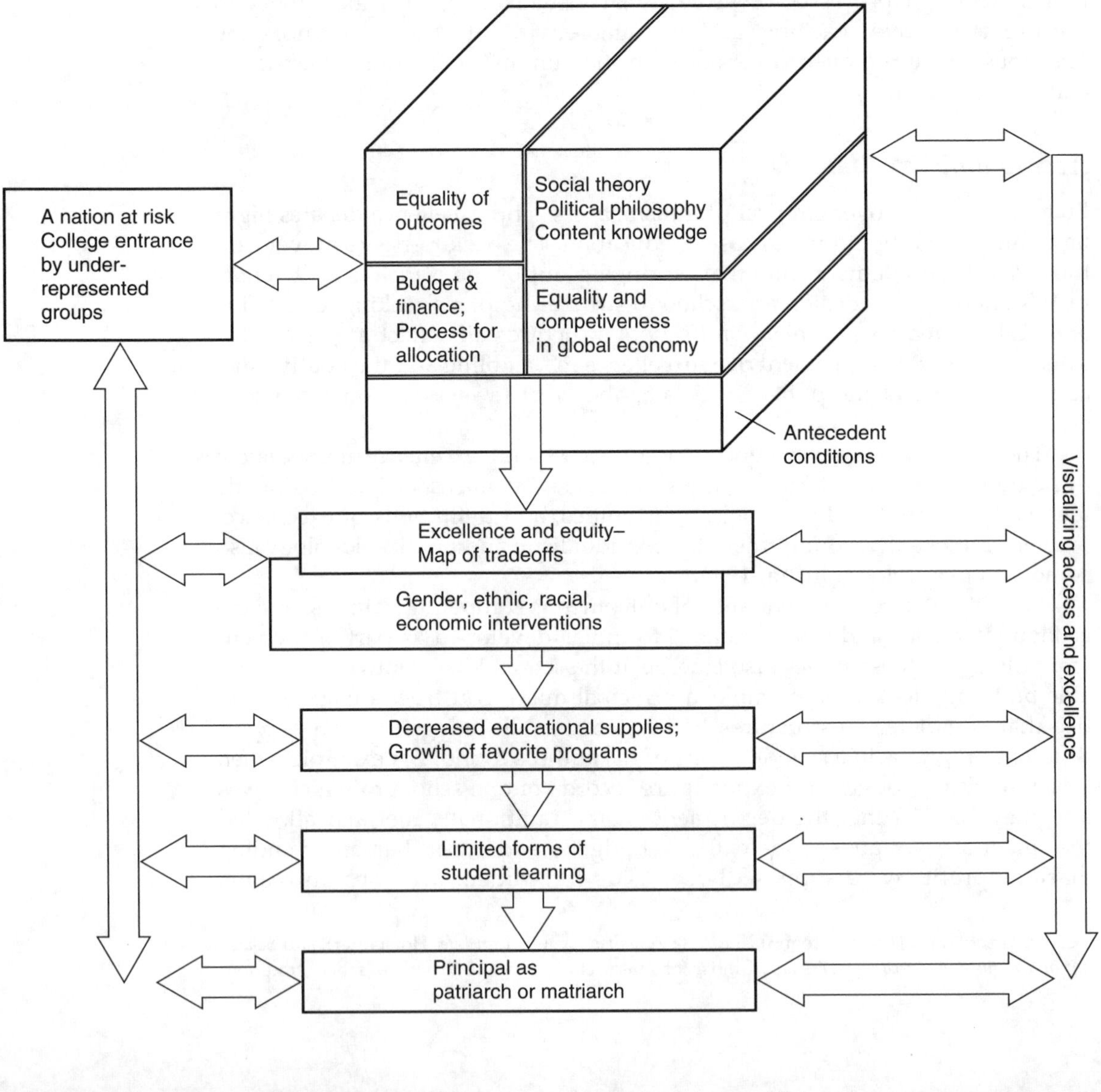

trol outcomes. This particular principal sometimes described her interactions with students as motherly and recounted her successes in giving motherly advice to students when they had problems in school. However, she would be shocked that a systematic examination of the theory of practice emerging from this chain of events led me to describe a visualization of this school as one that bordered on patronizing.

INTEGRATING THEORIES, RESEARCH, AND PRACTICES: A FRAMEWORK FOR THE FUTURE

The preceding illustrations demonstrate how new principals can use visualizing and professional theorizing to develop their own professional theories in action and rely on professional action structures that purposively apply what they know to what they do. Experienced principals build on and expand this process as their knowledge from experience, research, and theory grows.

We caution that this systematic framework for applying knowledge to action does not guarantee that a principal will develop a repertoire of simple, repeatable solutions to educational problems. However experienced a principal becomes, critical incidents are unpredictable, and the mix of contextual, personal, and professional factors is fundamentally unique. Any model such as ours also tends to overrationalize the world and make it seem more dependable than it ever will be. Part of the knowledge feeding into this process comes from phenomenological traditions that assert and describe the unique and perceptual nature of human experience; each principal draws on personal values and a paradigm of the social world of the school as part of his building blocks for expert thinking. The professional visualization model provides a means through which you can apply your own values and paradigms and your experiential, empirical, and theoretical knowledge more consciously—capitalizing on their strengths and compensating for their weaknesses or gaps.

The unique combination of factors in each problem faced by professionals includes the gaps and missteps that are an inevitable feature of human life and imperfect human knowledge. Consequently, we return to our discussion of the common problem-solving errors revealed by research in the professions—inappropriate scanning, incorrect synthesis, inadequate synthesis, premature closure, and anchoring—all of which can come into play at different stages of professional visualizing and threaten the quality of actions taken and results achieved.

The earliest threats to a principal's professional visualizing come from inappropriate scanning and premature closure. As a stimulus of problems or opportunities arises and triggers the need for expert thinking and knowledge application, a principal may be tempted to take a parent survey, hold endless public meetings, assign a fact-finding committee, or engage in endless questions and queries in inappropriate directions. Not only is cognitive overload from too much information a problem, but the information may be completely inappropriate to the stimulus at hand. Careful self-query and thought should go into the information-gathering and knowledge-application steps long before a situation map of practice is developed for a stimulus.

If the principal too quickly seeks a method for gathering information with which he is familiar (e.g., a parent survey), the data may be useless. If he recognizes some features from his experiences and jumps to a map of practice that inaccurately represents the present situation, he risks premature closure and possible frustration and failure. (Researchers also are vulnerable to these problems—using research methods they prefer rather than methods appropriate to the research question.)

In Chapter 2, we warned that pressure on principals to be decisive leaders sometimes leads to a third problem-solving error—incorrect synthesis. Premature closure often springs from incorrect synthesis, when the press of a school problem and demands for action lead the principal to distill disparate facts from the environment that are poorly related or unrelated to the problem at hand into an inaccurate situational map of practice. Conversely, inadequate synthesis or failure to reach warranted conclusions also threatens the viability of the map you work to create. The chain of logic from appropriate and reliable information may escape decision makers when the logical conclusion is unfamiliar or distasteful, or appears to be too difficult to achieve.

The final problem-solving error that threatens the construction of vivid and accurate situational maps of practice and theories in practice is anchoring or selective inattending. Schon (1983) emphasizes that this error remains a threat to professional work throughout a career and may even become more of a problem for experienced professionals than it was in their early careers. Most of you already fall into the category of experienced educational professional because of your work as teachers and educators in other professional roles. The threat of this error arises when a principal fails to attend to information or feedback inconsistent with her experience, ways of thinking, or previously developed situational maps of practice. She fails to notice events or innuendo in a conversation, or actions in a classroom, or she thinks, "This can't be right; I must have misunderstood."

A quick check of your professional theorizing and visualizing processes will help mitigate and guard against this last common problem-solving error, especially if you carefully attend to intermediate outcomes of professional actions and chains of effects on student learning and growth. Too often, because of the indeterminacy of educational work, we evaluate our performance by taking a snapshot look at professional actions without seriously examining the antecedent situational maps of practice and the building blocks of professional practice (values; processes, behaviors, and skills; intentions; and experiential, empirical, and theoretical knowledge) and the subsequent intermediate and student-level outcomes that make up the whole of professional practice. Your challenge as a professional theoretist is to rectify this shortsightedness and apply the full range of knowledge and analysis at your disposal as a growing and constantly improving school leader.

CONCLUSION

Theoretical scholars and theorizing principals are equally uninformed if they eschew and see as unconnected the contributions of one another's work. In a theoryless world every event and stimulus would be idiosyncratic and would demand a unique response structure—with no previous information. We would be paralyzed by cognitive overload. Professionals must check their own selective inattention, because this filtering by past experiences is characteristic of all human thinking. We may construct theories that are situationally inappropriate because we define the problems based on past experience, using the wrong building blocks and without systematic checks on our own theory building. Interagency collaboration arises from understanding problems that were previously labeled school problems as problems requiring interagency collaboration—societal problems. Our past reliance on the school may have prevented us from seeing solutions that do not depend entirely on the school.

The Theory of Professional Visualization reconciles the unnatural separation of practice from theory. Just as the family physician is more significant to her patients' immediate health than is the medical researcher, so is the principal more critical to the immediate health of his school than is the educational researcher. Were medicine, however, to have developed independent of research—unappreciative of the contributions of the medical researcher—we would still be treating gravely ill patients with camomile tea and leeches.

SUGGESTED ACTIVITIES

1. Apply the theory of professional visualization to a major issue affecting education in your community, district, or school. Lay out on a blank copy of the figures for professional visualization in Chapter 12 the stimulus input, problem, or opportunity you plan to analyze, building blocks of expert thinking on which you can rely, antecedent conditions, a situational map of practice, proposed professional actions, expected intermediate outcomes, student learning and growth outcomes, and ways in which reflection in and on action can enhance your analysis. Apply your analysis to a personal experience and discuss possible forms a theory of practice or theory-in-action that might explain and illuminate your experience, remembering that a theory of practice is always evolving and grounded in emerging and developing practice.
2. Pair off with another administration student in your seminar or class. Question each other about the professional, cultural, and educational situations and events that led to your conclusions. Test alternative explanations. Make revisions.
3. An expert practitioner may be more or less vulnerable to different kinds of problem-solving errors at different stages in her or his professional visualizing. Analyze the professional visualization process you laid out in the first activity using the five common problem-solving errors. When might you be most vulnerable to these common errors? Why? How might you guard against these errors in reference to the specific educational problem or opportunity you analyzed?

References

ALDRICH, BRYCE H. (1984). All decisions great and small. In John J. Lane (Ed.), *The making of a principal*. Springfield, IL: Charles C. Thomas Publisher.

ALLEN, M. P. (1981). Power and privilege in the large corporation: Corporate control and managerial compensation. *American Journal of Sociology* 86: 1112–1123.

ALLEN, M. P., and PANIAN, S. K. (1982). Power, performance, and succession in the large corporation. *Administrative Science Quarterly* 27: 538–547.

ALLEN, M. P., PANIAN, S. K., and LOTZ, R. E. (1979). Managerial succession and organizational performance: A recalcitrant problem revisited. *Administrative Science Quarterly* 24: 167–180.

ALLEN, V. L., and VAN DE VLIERT, E. (1984). *Role transitions: Explorations and explanations*. New York: Plenum Press.

ALVEY, H. B. (1983). The problems of new principals. Doctoral dissertation, University of Montana. *Dissertation Abstracts International* 44: 1979-A.

ANDERSON, R.C. (1984). Some reflections on the acquisition of knowledge. *Educational Researcher* 13: 5–10.

ANDERSON, R.C., and PEARSON, P.O. (1984). A schematic theory view of basic processes in reading. In P.O. Pearson (Ed.), *Handbook of reading research*. New York: Longman.

ANDREWS, C. (1989). Inducting principals. *Research Roundup* 6(1): 1–6.

ARGYRIS, C., & SCHON, D. A. (1974). *Theory in practice: Increasing professional effectiveness*. San Francisco: Jossey-Bass.

ARGYRIS, C., and SCHON, D.A. (1978). *Organizational Learning: A theory of action perspective*. Reading, MA: Addison-Wesley.

ARTIS, JOHN B. (1984). New principal/Old community. In John J. Lane (Ed.), *The making of a principal*. Springfield, IL: Charles C. Thomas Publisher.

ASHBAUGH, C.R., and KASTEN, K.L. (1991). *Educational leadership: Case studies for reflective practice*. New York: Longman.

ASHFORD, S. J. (1989). Self-assessment in organizations: A literature review and integrative model. In L. L. Cummings and B. Staw (Eds.), *Research in organizational behavior*. Vol. 2: 133–174. Greenwich, CT: JAI Press.

ASHTON, P., and WEBB, R. (1986). *Making a difference: Teachers' sense of efficacy and student achievement*. New York: Longman.

AUSUBEL, D.P. (1977). The facilitation of meaningful verbal learning in the classroom. *Educational Psychologist* 12: 162–178.

AUSUBEL, D.P. (1978). In defense of advance organizers: A reply to the virtue. *Review of Educational Research* 48: 251–257.

BACHARACH, S. B., Ed. (1990). *Education reform: Making sense of it all*. Needham Heights, MA: Allyn and Bacon.

BACHARACH, S. B., BAMBERGER, P., and MITCHELL, S. M. (1990). Work design, role conflict, and role ambiguity: The case of elementary and secondary schools. *Educational Evaluation and Policy Analysis* 12: 415–433.

BACHARACH, S. B., CONLEY, and SHEDD, (1986). Beyond career ladders: Structuring teacher career development systems. *Teachers College Record,* 87: 563–574.

BALES, ROBERT F. (1954). In conference. *Harvard Business Review* 32: 41–49.

BALTZELL, D.C., and DENTLER, R. A. (1983). *Selecting American school principals: A sourcebook for educators.* Washington, DC: U.S. Department of Education, National Institute of Education.

BANDURA, A. (1972). Modeling theory: Some traditions, trends, and disputes. In R. D. Drake (Ed.), *Recent trends in social learning theory,* 35–61. New York: Academic Press.

BANDURA, A. (1977a). *Social learning theory.* Englewood Cliffs, NJ: Prentice-Hall.

BANDURA, A. (1977b). Self-efficacy: Toward a unifying theory of behavioral change. *Psychological Review,* 84(2): 191–215.

BARNARD, CHESTER I. (1938). *Functions of the executive.* Cambridge, MA: Harvard University Press.

BARNETT, B. (1985). Peer-assisted leadership: A stimulus for professional growth. *Urban Review* 17: 47–64.

BARR, R., and DREEBEN, R. (1983). *How schools work.* Chicago: University of Chicago Press.

BARROWS, H. S. (1988). *The tutorial process.* Springfield, IL: Southern Illinois University School of Medicine.

BARTH, R.S. (1988). *Improving schools from within: Teachers, parents, and principals can make the difference.* San Francisco: Jossey-Bass

BASS, B. M. (1981). *Handbook of leadership: A survey of theory and research.* New York: Free Press.

BECKER, H. S. (1963). *Outsiders: Studies in the sociology of deviance.* New York: Free Press.

BEISCHEL, K. (1994). Predicting organizational commitment of superintendents. Dissertation. University of Wisconsin-Madison.

BENNIS, W. G., and NANUS, B. (1985). *Leaders: Strategies for taking charge.* New York: Harper & Row.

BERLEW, D. E., and HALL, D. T. (1966–67). The socialization of managers: Effects of expectations of performance. *Administrative Science Quarterly* 11: 207–223.

BERMAN, P., and McLAUGHLIN, M. W. (1978). *Federal programs supporting educational changes, IV.* Santa Monica, CA: Rand.

BIDDLE, B. J. (1979). *Role theory: Expectations, identities, and behaviors.* New York: Academic Press, Inc.

BIDDLE, B. J., and THOMAS, E. J. (1966). *Role theory: Concepts and research.* New York: Wiley.

BIDWELL, C.E. (1965). The school as a formal organization. In J.G. March (Ed.), *Handbook of organization,* 972–1022. Chicago: Rand McNally.

BIRD, T.D., and LITTLE, J.W. (1983). Finding and founding peer coaching. Paper presented at the annual meeting of the American Educational Research Association, Montreal.

BLAKE, R. R., and MOUTON, J. S. (1964). *The managerial grid.* Houston: Gulf.

BLAKE, R. R., and MOUTON, J. S. (1985). *The managerial grid.* Houston: Gulf.

BLANCH, M. C. (1989). Culture as a control mechanism in schools. Dissertation. Salt Lake City: Department of Educational Administration, University of Utah.

BLASE, J. J. (1989). The micropolitics of the school: The everyday political orientation of teachers toward open school principals. *Educational Administration Quarterly* 25: 377–407.

BLAU, P. M. (1964). *Exchange and power in social life.* New York: Wiley.

BLAU, P. M. (1967). *Exchange and power in social life.* New York: Wiley.

BLUMBERG, A., and GREENFIELD, W. (1980). *The effective principal: Perspectives on school leadership.* Boston: Allyn and Bacon.

BLUMBERG, A., and GREENFIELD, W. (1986). *The effective principal: Perspectives on school leadership.* Boston: Allyn and Bacon.

BOLDT, E. D. (1978). Leadership succession among the Hutterites: Ascription or achievement? *Canadian Review of Sociology and Anthropology* 15: 395–396.

BORG, W.R., and GALL, M.D. (1989). *Educational research: An introduction.* New York: Longman.

BOSSERT, S. T. (1988). School effects. In Norman J. Boyan (Ed.), *Handbook of research on educational administration,* 341–354. New York: Longman.

BOSSERT, S. T., DWYER, D. C., ROWAN, B., and LEE, G. V. (1982). The instructional management role of the principal. *Educational Administration Quarterly* 18: 34–64.

BOUD, D., KEOGH, R., and WALKER, D. (1985). *Reflection: Turning experience into learning.* New York: Nichols Publishing.

BOWER, G. H., BLACK, J. B., and TURNER, T. J. (1979). Scripts in memory for text. *Cognitive Psychology* 11: 177–220.

BOWERS, D. G., and SEASHORE, S. E. (1966). Predicting organizational effectiveness with a four-factor theory of leadership. *Administrative Science Quarterly* 11: 238–264.

BRADY, G. F., and HELMICH, D. L. (1985). *Executive succession: Toward excellence in corporate leadership.* Englewood Cliffs, NJ: Prentice Hall.

BRASS, I.D. (1953). *Design for decision.* New York: MacMillan.

BREDESON, P. V. (1985). An analysis of the metaphorical perspectives of school principals. *Educational Administration Quarterly* 21 (1): 29–50.

BREDESON, P.V. (1987). Principally speaking: An analysis of the interpersonal communications of school principals. *The Journal of Educational Administration* 25(1): 55–72.

BREDESON, P.V. (1988a). Languages of leadership: Metaphor making in educational administration. *Administrators' Notebook* 22(6): 1–6.

BREDESON, P.V. (1988b). Communications as a measure of leadership in schools: A portraiture of school principals. *The High School Journal* 71(4): 178–186.

BREDESON, P.V. (1989). Redefining leadership and the roles of school principals: Responses to changes in the professional worklife of teachers. *The High School Journal* 73(1): 9–20.

BREDESON, P.V. (1991a). Reappraising personal experience in the preparation of administrators. *Journal of School Leadership* 1(2):176–189.

BREDESON, P.V. (1991b). A profile of prospective principals: School leaders for the next century. *Education* 111(4): 510–515.

BREDESON, P.V. (1992). Responding to illegal inquiries on job application blanks: The effects of information management strategy, gender and position type on applicant ratings. *Journal of Personnel Evaluation in Education* 5: 245–256.

BREDESON, P.V. (1993). Letting go of outlived professional identities: A study of role transition and role strain for principals in restructured schools. *Educational Administration Quarterly* 29(1): 34–68.

BREDESON, P.V. (1994). Empowered teachers-empowered principals: Principals' perceptions of leadership in schools. In P. Thurston and N. Prestine (Eds.), *Advances in educational administration.* Vol. 3.

BREDESON, P.V., (in press). Building a professional knowledge base in educational administration: Opportunities and obstacles. In Donmoyer, R., Scheurich, J., and Imber, M. (Eds.), *The knowledge base in educational administration: Multiple perspectives.* Albany, NY: SUNY Press.

BREDESON, P.V., and FABER, R.Z. (1994). What superintendents mean when they say they are involved in curriculum and instruction. Paper presented at the annual meeting of the AERA in New Orleans, LA.

BREDESON, P.V., FRUTH, M.J., and KASTEN, K.L. (1983). Organizational incentives and secondary school teaching. *Journal of Research and Development in Education* 16(14): 53–58.

BRIDGES, E.M. (1965). Bureaucratic role and socialization: The influence of experience on the elementary principal. *Educational Administration Quarterly* 1:19–28.

BRIDGES, E.M. (1992). *Problem based learning for administrators.* Eugene, OR: ERIC Clearinghouse on Educational Management, University of Oregon.

BROOKOVER, W. B., BEADY, C., FLOOD, P., SCHWEITZER, J., and WISENBAKER, J. (1979). *School social systems and student achievement: Schools can make a difference.* New York: Holt, Rinehart & Winston.

BROUSSEAU, K. R. (1983). Toward a dynamic model of job-person relationships: Findings, research questions, and implications for work system design. *Academy of Management Review* 8: 33–45.

BROWN, M. C. (1982). Administrative succession and organizational performance: The succession effect. *Administrative Science Quarterly* 29: 245–273.

BUCHANAN, D. (1979). *The development of job design theories and techniques.* Farborough, England: Saxon House.

BUCHANAN, F. (in press). *A century of culture conflict and accommodation: Public schooling in Salt Lake City, 1890-1990. Salt Lake City: Signature Books.*

BUCHER, R., and STELLING, J. G. (1977). *Becoming professional.* Beverly Hills, CA: Sage.

BURNS, J. M. (1978). *Leadership.* New York: Harper & Row.

BUTTON, H.W. (1966). Doctrines of administration: A brief history. *Educational Administration Quarterly* 2(3): 216–24.

BYRNE, D.R., HINES, S.A., and McCLEARY, L.E. (1978). *The senior high school principalship.* Vol. 1: *The National Survey.* Reston, VA: Association of Secondary School Principals.

CALLAHAN, R.E. (1962). *Education and the cult of efficiency.* Chicago: University of Chicago Press.

CAMPBELL, J. P. (1977). On the nature of organizational effectiveness. In P. S. Goodman and J. M. Pennings (Eds.), *New perspectives on organizational effectiveness,* 13–55. San Francisco: Jossey-Bass.

CAMPBELL, J. P., DUNNETTE, M. D., LAWLER, E. E., III, and WEICK, K. E., JR. (1970). *Managerial behavior, performance, and effectiveness.* New York: McGraw-Hill.

CAMPBELL, R., FLEMING, T., BENNION, J., and NEWELL, J. T. (1987). *A history of thought and practice in educational administration.* New York: Teachers College Press.

CAPPER, C.A. (Ed.) (1993). *Educational administration in a pluralistic society.* Albany: SUNY Press.

CARLSON, R. O. (1962). *Executive succession and organizational change.* Chicago: University of Chicago, Midwestern Administration Center.

CARLSON, R. O. (1972). *School superintendents: Careers and performance.* Columbus, OH: Charles E. Merrill.

CARNEGIE FORUM ON EDUCATION AND THE ECONOMY. (1986). *A nation prepared: Teachers for the 21st century.* Hyattsville, MD: Author.

CARROLL, G. R. (1984). The dynamics of publisher succession in newspaper organizations. *Administrative Science Quarterly* 29: 93–113.

CARTWRIGHT, D., and ZANDER, A. (1953). *Group dynamics: Research and theory* (3d ed.). New York: Harper & Row.

CARTWRIGHT, D., and ZANDER, A. (1968). *Group dynamics: Research and theory.* New York: Harper & Row.

CELL, E. (1984). *Learning to learn from experience.* Albany, NY: SUNY Press.

CERVERO, R.M. (1988). *Effective continuing education for professionals.* San Francisco: Jossey-Bass.

CICOUREL, A. V., JENNINGS, K. H., JENNINGS, S. H. M., LEITER, K. C. W., MACKAY, R., MEHAN, H., and ROTH, D. R. (1974). *Language use and school performance.* New York: Academic Press.

COLLINS, R. (1985). *Three sociological traditions.* New York: Oxford University Press.

COMMITTEE FOR ECONOMIC DEVELOPMENT (1985). *Investing in our children.* New York: Committee for Economic Development.

CONNELL, M. L., and PECK, D. M. (1993). Report of a conceptual change intervention in elementary mathematics. *Journal of Mathematical Behavior* 12(4): 329–350.

CORBETT, H.D. (1990). *On the meaning of restructuring.* Philadelphia: Research for Better Schools.

CORBETT, H. D., FIRESTONE, W. A., and ROSSMAN, G. B. (1987). Resistance to planned change and the sacred in school cultures. *Educational Administration Quarterly* 23: 36–59.

COSGROVE, D. (1986). *The effects of principal succession on elementary schools.* Doctoral dissertation. Salt Lake City: Department of Educational Administration, University of Utah,

COVEY, S.R. (1989). *The 7 habits of highly effective people.* New York: Simon & Schuster.

CREMIN, L. (1990). *Popular education and its discontents.* New York: Harper & Row.

CROW, G. M. (1990a). Career incentives of elementary school principals. *Journal of Educational Administration* 28: 38–52.

CROW, G. M. (1990b). Conceptions of the principalship: A career history perspective. Paper presented at the annual meeting of the American Educational Research Association, Boston.

CROW, G. M. (1993). Reconceptualizing the school administrator's role: Socialization at mid-career. *School Effectiveness and School Improvement* 4(2): 131–152.

CUBAN, L. (1988). *The managerial imperative and the practice of leadership in schools.* Albany, NY: SUNY Press.

CULBERTSON, J. A. (1988). A century's quest for a knowledge base. In N. J. Boyan (Ed.), *Handbook on research of educational administration.* New York: Longman.

CURCIO, J. L., and GREENE, E. (1989). *Crises of integrity of the first-time high school principal.* Paper presented at the annual meeting of the American Educational Research Association, San Francisco.

DACHLER, H. P. (1984). On refocussing leadership from a social systems perspective of management. In J. G. Hunt, D. M. Hosking, C. A. Schriesheim, and R. Steward (Eds.), *Leaders and managers: International perspectives on managerial behavior and leadership,* 100–108. Oxford: Pergamon.

DALTON, D. R., and KESNER, I. F. (1983). Inside/outside succession and organization size: The pragmatics of executive succession. *Academy of Management Journal* 26: 736–742.

DANSEREAU, F., GRAEN, G., and HAGA, W. (1975). A vertical dyad linkage approach to leadership in formal organizations. *Organization Behavior and Human Performance* 13: 46–78.

DARESH, J. C. (1986). Support for beginning principals: First hurdles are highest. *Theory into Practice* 23: 169–173.

DARESH, J. C., and PLAYKO, M. A. (1989). *The administrative entry year: A resource guide.* Westerville, OH: Ohio LEAD Center.

DAUM, J. (1975). Internal promotion—a psychological asset or debit. *Organizational Behavior and Human Performance* 13: 404–473.

DAVIS, S.H. (1988). Life in the fishbowl: Revelations and reflections of the first year. *NASSP Bulletin* 72(512): 74–83.

DAWIS, R. V., and LOFQUIST, L. H. (1984). *A psychological theory of work adjustment.* Minneapolis: University of Minnesota Press.

DEAL, T.E., and KENNEDY, A.A. (1982). *Corporate Cultures: The rites and rituals of corporate life.* Reading, MA: Addison-Wesley.

DEAL, T. E., and PETERSON, K. D. (1990). *The principal's role in shaping school culture.* Washington, DC: U.S. Department of Education, Office of Educational Research and Improvement.

DEAL, T.E., and PETERSON, K.D. (1994). *The leadership paradox: Balancing logic and artistry in schools.* San Francisco: Jossey-Bass.

DEBEVOISE, W. (1984). Synthesis of research on the principal as instructional leader. *Educational Leadership* 41(5): 14–20.

DEWEY, J. (1933). *How we think.* Chicago: Henry Regnery Company.

DEWEY, J. (1938). Experience and Education. New York: Macmillan.

DIAMOND, M.A., and ALLCORN, S. (1985). Psychological dimensions of role use in bureaucratic organizations. *Organizational Dynamics,* 14: 35–59.

Digest of Education Statistics. (1991,1992,1993). Washington, DC: U.S. Department of Education, National Center for Education Statistics.

DIENESCH, R., and LIDEN, R. (1986). Leader-member exchange model of leadership: A critique and further development. *Academy of Management Review* 11: 618–634.

DORNBUSCH, S. M., and SCOTT, W. R. (1975). *Evaluation and the exercise of authority.* San Francisco: Jossey-Bass.

DOUD, J.L. (1989). The K–8 principal in 1988: A ten year study. Alexandria, VA: National Association of Elementary School Principals.

DOUGLASS, H.R. (1932). *Organization and Administration of Secondary Schools.* Boston: Ginn and Company.

DRAKE, T.L., and ROE, WM.H. (1986). *The Principalship.* New York: Macmillan.

DRAKE, T.L., and WAGNER, I. (1984). Paper presented at the annual NASSP conference, Las Vegas, Nevada.

DREW, C. J., HARDMAN, M., and HART, A.W. (in press). *Designing and conducting research: Education and social science.* Boston: Allyn & Bacon.

DUBOSE, E. (1986). A study of the task specific assistance and information needs of incoming elementary school principals in South Carolina. Doctoral dissertation. Columbia, SC: University of South Carolina.

DUBINSKY, A. J., and YAMMARINO, F. J. (1984). Differential impact of role conflict and ambiguity on selected correlates: A two-sample test. *Psychological Reports,* 55: 699–707.

DUCKWORTH, K. (1983). Specifying determinants of teacher and principal work. Eugene, OR: Center for Educational Policy and Management, University of Oregon.

DUKE, D. L. (1987). *School leadership and instructional improvement.* New York: Random House.

DUKE, D. L., and IMBER, M. (1985). Should principals be required to be effective? *School Organization,* 5(2): 125–146.

DUKE, D. L., ISAACSON, N. S., SAGOR, R., and SCHMUCK, P. A. (1984). *Transition to leadership: An investigation of the first year of the principalship.* Portland, OR: Lewis and Clark College, Transition to Leadership Project.

DUNLAP, D., and SCHMUCK, P.A., Eds. (1994). *Womens' leadership in education: An agenda for a new century.* Albany, NY: SUNY Press.

DWYER, D.C., LEE, G.V., ROWAN, B., and BOSSERT, S.T. (1983). *Five Principals in Action: Perspectives on Instructional Management.* San Francisco: Far West Laboratory for Educational Research and Development, 1983.

EARLEY, P., BAKER, L., and WEINDLING, D. (1990). *Keeping the raft afloat: Secondary headship five years on.* London, England: National Foundation for Educational Research in England and Wales (ISBN 0 7005 0975 5).

EBAUGH, H.R. (1988). *Becoming an ex: The process of role exit.* Chicago: The University of Chicago Press.

EDMONDS, R. (1979). Some schools work and more can. *Social Policy* 9: 32–36.

Educational Researcher, May, 1994: 36.

EDWARDS, A. L., and KLACKARS, A. J. (1981). Significant others and self-evaluation: Relationships between perceived and actual evaluations. *Personality and Social Psychology Bulletin* 7: 244–251.

EITZEN, D. S., and YETMAN, N. R. (1972). Managerial change. *Science Quarterly* 17: 110–116.

ELLETT, C.D., and WALBERG, H.J. (1979). Principal competency, environment, and outcomes. In H.J. Walberg (Ed.), *Educational environments and effects,* 140–167. Berkeley: McCutchan.

ENSIGN, F.C. (1923). Evolution of the high school principalship. *School Review,* March: 179–190.

ETZIONI, A. (1964). *Modern organizations.* Englewood Cliffs, NJ: Prentice-Hall.

ETZIONI, A. (1975). *A comparative analysis of complex organizations: On power, involvement, and their correlates.* New York: Free Press.

FAUSKE, J. R., and OGAWA, R. T. (1987). Detachment, fear, and expectation: A faculty's response to the impending succession of its principal. *Educational Administration Quarterly* 23: 23–44.

FAYOL, H. (1949). *General and Industrial Administration.* New York: Pitman.

FELDMAN, D. C. (1976). A contingency theory of socialization. *Administrative Science Quarterly* 21: 433–452.

FESTINGER, L. (1957). *A theory of cognitive dissonance.* Evanston, IL: Row, Peterson.

FIEDLER, F. E. (1957). *A theory of leadership effectiveness.* New York: McGraw-Hill.

FIEDLER, F. E., and GARCIA, J. E. (1987). *New approaches to effective leadership: Cognitive resources and organizational performance.* New York: Wiley.

FEIN, M.L. (1990). *Role change: A resocialization perspective.* New York: Praeger.

FIRESTONE, W.A. (November 1989). Cultural politics and executive succession in a modernizing school district. Paper prepared under a grant by the U.S. Department of Education (Grant no. OERI-G00860011) to the Center for Policy Research in Education (CPRE). New Brunswick, NJ: Rutgers University.

FIRESTONE, W. A. (1990). Succession and bureaucracy: Gouldner revisited. *Educational Administration Quarterly* 26 (4): 345–375.

FIRESTONE, W.A. (in press). Leadership—roles or functions. In K. Leithwood (Ed.), *International handbook of educational administration and leadership.* London: Kluwer.

FIRESTONE, W. A., and BADER, B. D. (1992). *The redesign of teaching: Professionalism or bureaucracy?* New York: SUNY Press.

FIRESTONE, W.A., and WILSON, B.L. (1985). Using bureaucratic and cultural linkages to improve instruction: The principal's contribution. *Educational Administration Quarterly* 21(2): 7–30.

FITZPATRICK, R.W. (1992). Socialization of beginning public school superintendents. Dissertation. University of Wisconsin-Madison.

FLEISHMAN, E. A. (1953). The measurement of leadership attitudes in industry. *Journal of Applied Psychology* 37: 153–158.

FLEISHMAN, E. A. (1957). A leader behavior description for industry. In R. M. Stogdill and A. E. Coons (Eds.), *Leadership behavior: Its description and measurement.* Columbus: Ohio State University, Bureau of Business Research.

FOLLETT, M.P. (1924). *Creative experience.* New York: Longmans Green & Co.

FOSKETT, J.M. (1967). *The normative world of the elementary school principal.* Eugene, OR: Center for the Advanced Study of Educational Administration, University of Oregon.

FOSTER, W. (1986). *Paradigms and promises: New approaches to educational administration.* Buffalo: Prometheus Books.

FREDRICKSON, J. W., HAMBRICK, D. C., and BAUMRIN, S. (1988). A model of CEO dismissal. *Academy of Management Review* 13: 255–270.

FRENCH, J. R. P., JR., and RAVEN, B. H. (1959). The bases of social power. In D. Cartwright (Ed.), *Studies in social power*, 150–167. Ann Arbor, MI: Institute for Social Research, University of Michigan.

FRIEDMAN, S. D. (1986). Succession systems in large corporations: Characteristics and correlates of performance. *Human Resource Management* 25: 191–213.

FRIESEN, J.W., CARSON, R. B., and JOHNSON, F.T. (1983). *The teacher's voice.* Lanham, MD: University Press of America.

FROMM, E. (1941). *Escape from freedom.* NY: Rinehart.

FULK, J., and CUMMINGS, T. G. (1984). Refocusing leadership: A modest proposal. In J. C. Hunt, D. M. Hosking, C. A. Schriescheim, and R. STEWART (Eds.), *Leaders and managers: International perspectives on managerial behavior and leadership*, Oxford: Pergamon.

FULLAN, M.G. (1991). *The new meaning of educational change* (2d ed.). New York: Teachers College Press.

FULLAN, M.G., and MILES, M.B. (1992). Getting reform right: What works and what doesn't. *Phi Delta Kappan*, June: 745–752.

GABARRO, J. J. (1987). *The dynamics of taking charge.* Boston: Harvard Business School Press.

GAMSON, W. A., and SCOTCH, N. A. (1964). Scapegoating in baseball. *American Journal of Sociology* 69: 21–31.

GANZ, H. G., and HOY, W. K. (1977). Patterns of succession of elementary principals and organizational change. *Planning on Changing* 8: 185–196.

GARFINKEL, H. (1967). *Studies in ethnomethodology.* Englewood Cliffs, NJ: Prentice-Hall.

GARLAND, H., and PRICE, K. H. (1977). Attitudes toward women in management and attribution for their success and failure in managerial positions. *Journal of Applied Psychology* 62: 29–33.

GARRISON, J. W. (1986). Some principles of post-positivistic philosophy of science, *Educational Researcher* 15: 12–18.

GECAS, V. (1981). Contexts of socialization. In M. Rosenberg and R. Turner (Eds.), *Social psychology: Sociological perspectives.* New York: Basic Books.

GEPHART, R. (1978). Status degradation and organization succession. *Administrative Science Quarterly* 23: 23–44.

GETZELS, J. W., and GUBA, E. G. (1957). Social behavior and the administrative process. *School Review* 65: 423–441.

GETZELS, J.W., LIPHAM, J.M., and CAMPBELL, R.F. (1968). *Educational administration as a social process: Theory, research, and practice.* New York: Harper & Row.

GIANNANGELO, D.M., and MALONE M.G. (1987). Teacher perceptions of the principal's role. Unpublished ERIC document, ED299672.

GIPS, C.J., and BREDESON, P.V. (1986). The selection of teachers and principals: A model for faculty participation in personnel selection decisions in public schools. *The High School Journal* 69(2): 81–90.

GIROUX, H., Ed. (1991). *Postmodernism, feminism, and cultural politics: Redrawing educational boundaries.* Albany, NY: SUNY Press.

GOFFMAN, E. (1959). *The presentation of self in everyday life.* New York: Doubleday.

GOLDHAMMER, R. (1980). *Clinical supervision: Special methods for the supervision of teachers* (2d ed.). New York: Holt, Rinehart & Winston.

GOLDHAMMER, K, BECKER, G., WITHYCOMBE, F.D., MILLER, E., MORGAN, C., DELORETTO, L., and ALDRIGDE, B. (1971). *Elementary principals and their schools: Beacons of brilliance and potholes of pestilence.* Eugene, OR: Center for Advanced Study of Educational Administration.

GORDON, G. E., and ROSEN, N. (1981). Critical factors in leadership succession. *Organizational Behavior and Human Performance* 27: 227–254.

GOTTFREDESON, G.D., and HYBL, L.G. (1987). *An analytical description of the school principal's job.* Washington, DC: Office of Educational Research and Improvement.

GOULDNER, A. (1954). *Patterns of industrial democracy.* Glencoe, IL: Free Press.

GREEN, G., and NOVAK, M. A. (1982). The effects of leader exchange and job design on productivity and satisfaction: Testing a dual attachment model. *Organizational Behavior and Human Performance,* 30: 109–134.

GREENFIELD, T. B. (1975). Theory about organizations: A new perspective and its implications for schools. In Hughes (Ed.), *Administering education: International challenge,* 77–79. London: Athlone.

GREENFIELD, W. D., JR. (1977a). Administrative candidacy: A process of new-role learning—Part I. *Journal of Educational Administration* 15(1): 30–48.

GREENFIELD, W. D., JR. (1977b). Administrative candidacy: A process of new-role learning—Part II. *Journal of Educational Administration* 15(2): 179–193.

GREENFIELD, W. D., JR. (1985a). Being and becoming a principal: Responses to work contexts and socialization processes. Paper presented at the annual meeting of the American Educational Research Association, Chicago.

GREENFIELD, W. D., JR. (1985b). The moral socialization of school administrators: Informal role learning outcomes. *Educational Administration Quarterly* 21: 99–119.

GREENFIELD, W. D., JR. (1991). Toward a theory of *school* leadership. Paper presented at the annual meeting of the American Educational Research Association, Chicago.

GRIFFIN, R. W. (1983). Objective and social sources of information in task redesign: A field experiment. *Administrative Science Quarterly* 28: 184–200.

GRONN, P. C. (1982). Neo-Taylorism in educational administration. *Educational Administration Quarterly* 18: 17–35.

GRONN, P.C. (1983). Talk as work: The accomplishment of school administration. *Administrative Science Quarterly* 28: 1–21.

GRUSKY, O. (1963). Managerial succession and organizational effectiveness. *American Journal of Sociology* 69: 21–31, 72–76.

GRUSKY, O. (1969). Succession with an ally. *Administrative Science Quarterly* 14: 155–170.

GUBA, E.G., and LINCOLN, E.S. (1981). *Effective evaluation.* San Francisco: Jossey-Bass, Inc., Publishers.

GUEST, R. H. (1962). Managerial succession in complex organizations. *American Journal of Sociology* 68: 47–54.

GUSKEY, T. R. (1986). Staff development and the process of teacher change. *Educational Researcher* 5: 5–12.

GUY, M. E. (1985). *Professionals in organizations: Debunking a myth.* New York: Praeger.

HACKMAN, J.R., and OLDHAM, G.R. (1980). *Work Redesign.* Reading: MA: Addison-Wesley.

HALL, D. T. (1986). Dilemmas in linking succession planning to individual executive learning. *Human Resource Management* 25: 235–265.

HALL, D. T. (1987). Careers and socialization. *Journal of management* 13: 301–321.

HALL, G., and HORD, S. (1987). *Change in schools: Facilitating the process.* New York: SUNY Press.

HALLER, E.J., and KNAPP, T.R. (1985). Problems and methodology in educational administration. *Educational Administration Quarterly* 21(3): 157–168.

HALLINGER, P., and MURPHY, J. (1987). The social context of effective schools. *American Journal of Education* 94(5): 328–355.

HALLINGER, P., LEITHWOOD, K., and MURPHY, J., Eds. (1993). *Cognitive perspectives on school leadership.* New York: Teachers College Press.

HALPIN, A.W. (1966). *Theory and research in administration.* New York: Macmillan.

HALPIN, A. W., and WINER, B. J. (1957). A factorial study of the leader behavior descriptions. In R. M. Stogdill and A. E. Coons (Eds.), *Leader behavior: Its descriptions and measurement.* Columbus: Ohio State University, Bureau of Business Research.

HAMBLIN, R. (1958). Leadership and crises. *Sociometry* 21: 322–335.

HAMBRICK, D. C., and MASON, P. A. (1984). Upper echelons: The organization as a reflection of its top managers. *Academy of Management Review* 9: 193–206.

HANNAN, M. T., and FREEMAN, J. H. (1984a). The population ecology of organizations. *American Journal of Sociology* 82: 929–964.

HANNAN, M. T., and FREEMAN, J. H. (1984b). Structural inertia and organizational change. *American Sociological Review* 49: 149–164.

HARRISBERGER, L. (1985). Curricula and teaching methods in engineering education. In S. Goodlad (Ed.), *Education for the professions: Quis custodiet . . . ?* Guildford, Surrey, England: NFER-NELSON.

HART, A.W. (1983). The challenge of academic freedom in the secondary schools. *The High School Journal* Dec/Jan: 91–99.

HART, A. W. (1986). The reflective principal. In Ducharme, E., and Fleming, D. S. (Eds.), *The rural and small school principalship,* 133–134 Chelmsford, MA: Northeast Regional Exchange, Inc., National Institute of Education.

HART, A. W. (1987a). A career ladder's effect on teacher career and work attitudes. *American Educational Research Journal* 24: 479–504.

HART, A. W. (1987b). Leadership succession: Reflections of a new principal. *Journal of Research and Development in Education* 20 (4): 1–11.

HART, A. W. (1988). Attribution as effect: An outsider principal's succession. *Journal of Educational Administration* 26 (3): 331–352.

HART, A. W. (1990a). Effective administration through reflective practice. *Education and Urban Society* 22 (2): 153–169.

HART, A. W. (1990b). Impacts of the school social unit on teacher authority during work redesign. *American Educational Research Journal* 27 (3): 503–532.

HART, A. W. (1991). Leader succession and socialization: A synthesis. *Review of Educational Research* 61: 451–474.

HART, A.W. (1992). Reflection—A learning technique in preservice education for school administrators. In P. Hallinger, K. Leithwood, and J. Murphy (Eds.), *Cognitive perspectives on educational leadership,* 231–230. New York: Teachers College Press.

HART, A. W. (1993). *Principal succession: Establishing leadership in schools.* New York: SUNY Press.

HART, A.W. (1994). Women ascending to leadership. In D.M. Dunlap and P.A. Schmuck (Eds.), *Womens' leadership in education: An agenda for a new century.* Albany, New York: SUNY Press.

HART, A. W. A design studio for reflective action. In P. Hallinger, K. Leithwood, and J. Murphy (Eds.), *Cognitive perspectives on school leadership.* New York: Teachers College Press.

HART, A. W., and MURPHY, M. J. (1989). Work redesign where it happens: Five comparative case studies of schools. In J. Murphy (Ed.), *The educational reform movement of the 1980s,* 215–242. Berkeley, CA: McCutchan.

HART, A. W., and MURPHY, M. J. (1990a). Career ladders and work in schools. In Joseph Murphy (Ed.), *The educational reform movement of the 1980s: Themes and cases,* 215–242. Berkeley, CA: McCutchan.

HART, A. W., and MURPHY, M. J. (1990b). New teachers react to redesigned teacher work. *American Journal of Education* 98: 224–250.

HART, A. W., and MURPHY, M. J. (1994). Preparing principals to lead in restructured schools. In P. Thurston and N. Prestine (Eds.), *Advances in Educational Administration,* Vol. 2. Greenwich, CT: JAI Press.

HART, A.W., and NAYLOR, K. (1992). *A meeting of the minds, so to speak: The organizational socialization of clinical faculty.* Paper presented at the annual meeting of the American Educational Research Association, April, San Francisco, CA.

HART, A. W., and SORENSEN, N. B. (October 1989). The conceptualization and development of a design studio for educational leadership. Paper presented at the annual meeting of the University Council on Educational Administration, Scottsdale, AZ.

HART, A. W., SORENSEN, N. B., and NAYLOR, K. (1993). Learning to lead: Reflective practice in preservice preparation. In F. Wendel (Ed.), *Leadership in the profession,* 5–22. University Park, PA: University Council for Educational Administration.

HAYES, R.H. (1985). Strategic planning: Forward in Reverse? *Harvard Business Review* 63, N-D, 111–119.

HECK, R. H., LARSEN, T. J., and MARCOULIDES, G. A. (1990). Instructional leadership and school achievement: Validation of a causal model. *Educational Administration Quarterly* 26(2): 94–125.

HELMICH, D. L. (1974). Organizational growth and succession patterns. *Academy of Management Journal* 17: 771–775.

HELMICH, D. L. (1977). Executive succession in the corporate organization: A current integration. *American Management Review* 2: 252–266.

HELMICH, D. L., and BROWN, W. B. (1972). Successor type and organizational change in the corporate enterprise. *Administrative Science Quarterly* 17: 371–381.

HEMPHILL, J. K. (1964). Personal variables and administrative styles. In D. E. Griffiths (Ed.), *Behavioral science and educational administration,* Part II, 178–198. Chicago: University of Chicago Press.

HEMPHILL, J. K., and COONS, A. E. (1950). *Leader behavior description.* Columbus: Personnel Research Board, Ohio State University.

HERITAGE, J. (1984). *Garfinkel and ethnomethodology.* Cambridge, England: Polity Press.

HERSEY, P., and BLANCHARD, K. (1977). *Management of organizational behavior: Utilizing human resources.* Englewood Cliffs, NJ: Prentice-Hall.

HICKMAN, C.R., and SILVA, M.A. (1984). *Creating excellence: Managing corporate culture, strategy, and change in the new age.* New York: New American Library.

HITT, M. A., and IRELAND, R. D. (1987). Peters and Waterman revisited: The unended quest for excellence. *Academy of Management Executive* 1: 91–98.

HODGKINSON, C. (1983). *The philosophy of leadership.* New York: St. Martin's Press.

HOLLANDER, E. P. (1978). *Leadership dynamics: A practical guide to effective relationships.* New York: Free Press.

HOLLANDER, E. P., and JULIAN, J. W. (1978). A further look at leader legitimacy, influence, and innovation. In L. Berkowitz (Ed.), *Group processes,* 153–165. New York: Academic Press.

HOLLANDER, E. P., FALLON, B. J., and EDWARD, M. T. (1977). Some aspects of influence and acceptability for appointed and elected group leaders. *Journal of Psychology* 95: 289–296.

HOPSON, B., and ADAMS, J. (1976). Towards an understanding of transition: Defining some boundaries of transition dynamics. In J. Adams, J. Hyes, and B. Hopson (Eds.), *Transition,* 3–25. London: Martin Robertson.

HOWELL, B. (1981). Profile of the principalship. *Educational Leadership* 38(4): 333–336.

HOY, W.H. (1994). Foundations of educational administration: Traditional and emerging perspectives. *Educational Administration Quarterly* 30(2): 178–198.

HOY, W. K., and MISKEL, C. G. (1991). *Educational administration: Theory, research, and practice* (4th ed.). New York: McGraw-Hill.

HUCK, S.W., CORMIER, W.H., and BOUNDS, JR., W.G. (1974). *Reading statistics and research.* New York: Harper & Row.

HUGHES, L. W., and UBBEN, G. C. (1989). *The elementary principal's handbook.* Boston: Allyn and Bacon.

HUNT, D., and MICHAEL, C. (1983). Mentorship: A career training and development tool. *Academy of Management Review* 8: 475–485.

IANNACCONE, L. (1962). Informal Organization of school systems. In D. Griffiths et al. (Eds.), *Organizing schools for effective education*. Danville, IL: Interstate.

IANNACCONE, L. (1993). Politics in Education, Keynote address presented at the Educational Administration Conference, Madison, WI.

IMMEGART, G. L. (1988). Leadership and leader behavior. In N. J. Boyan (Ed.), *Handbook of research on educational administration*, 259–278, New York: Longman.

JACQUES, E. (1989). *Requisite organizations*. Arlington, VA: Casson Hall.

JAMES, D. R., and SOREF, M. (1981). Profit constraints on managerial autonomy: Managerial theory and the unmaking of the corporation president. *American Sociological Review* 46: 1–18.

JENTZ, B., (1982). *Entry: The hiring, start-up, and supervision of administrators*. New York: McGraw-Hill.

JOHNSON, D.W., and JOHNSON, R.T. (1987). *Learning together and alone: Cooperative, competitive, and individualistic learning*. Englewood Cliffs, NJ: Prentice Hall.

JONES, G. R. (1986). Socialization tactics, self-efficacy, and newcomers' adjustments to organizations. *Academy of Management Journal* 29: 262–279.

JOYCE, B.R., and SHOWERS, B. (1980). Improving inservice training: The message of research. *Educational Leadership* 37(5): 379–385.

KAGAN, J. (1978). *The growth of the child: Reflections on human development*. New York: Norton.

KATZ, D., and KAHN, R. L. (1978). *The social psychology of organizations* (2d ed.) New York: Wiley.

KAYON, D.R. (1993). Job commitment and turnover of school superintendents. Dissertation, University of Wisconsin-Madison.

KELLY, B.E. (1987). Measures of meaning in public and parochial schools: Principals as symbol managers. Dissertation, State College, PA: Pennsylvania State University.

KELLEY, B., and BREDESON, P.V. (1991). Measures of meaning in a public and in a parochial school: Principals as symbol managers. *Journal of Educational Administration* 29(3): 6–22.

KENNEDY, M.M. (1987). Inexact sciences: Professional education and the development of expertise. In E.Z. Rothkopf (Ed.), *Review of research in education*, 133–167. Washington, DC: American Educational Research Association.

KERCHNER, C. T. (1990). Educational administration: Choice as a reflection of today's *social* values. In S. B. Bacharach (Ed.), *Education reform: Making sense of it all*, 270–281. Needham Heights, MA: Allyn and Bacon.

KIMBROUGH, R.B., and BURKETT, C.W. (1990). *The principalship: Concepts and practices*. Englewood Cliffs, NJ: Prentice Hall.

KLEINE-KRACHT, SISTER PAULA. (1993). Indirect instructional leadership: An administrator's choice. *Educational Administration Quarterly* 29(2): 187–212.

KMETZ, J. T., and WILLOWER, D. J. (1982). Elementary school principals' work behavior. *Educational Administration Quarterly* 18: 62–78.

KNIGHT, P. A., and WEISS, H. M. (1980). Effects of selection agent and leader origin on leader influence and group member perceptions. *Organizational Behavior and Human Performance* 26: 7–21.

KOCH, J. L. (1978). Managerial succession in a factory and changes in supervisory leadership patterns: A field study. *Human Relations* 31: 49–58.

KOHN, M. L., and SCHOOLER, C. (1983). *Work and personality*. Norwood, NJ: Ablex.

KOZOL, J. (1991). *Savage inequalities: Children in America's schools*. New York: Crown Publishers.

KRIESBURG, L. (1962). Careers, organizational size, and succession. *American Journal of Sociology* 68: 355–359.

KUNZ, D., and HOY, W. L. (1976). Leader behavior of principals and the professional zone of acceptance of teachers. *Educational Administration Quarterly* 12: 49–64.

LAMOREAUX, D. (1990). *New shoes: An educational criticism of a new principal's first quarter*. Paper presented at the annual meeting of the American Educational Research Association, Boston.

LEAVITT, H. J. (1965). Applied organizational change in industry: Structural, technological, and humanistic approaches. In J.G. March (Ed.), *Handbook of organizations*. Chicago: Rand McNally, 1144–1170.

LEITHWOOD, K. (1994). Leadership for school restructuring. Invited address to the International Congress for School Effectiveness and Improvement, Melbourne, Australia.

LEITHWOOD, K.A., and HALLINGER, P. (1993). Cognitive perspectives on educational administration: An introduction. *Educational Administration Quarterly* 24(3): 296–301.

LEITHWOOD, K. A., and MONTGOMERY, D.G. (1986). *Improving principal effectiveness: The principal profile*. Toronto: OISE Press.

LEITHWOOD, K. A., STEINBACH, R., and BEGLEY, P. (in press). The nature and contribution of socialization experiences to becoming a principal in Canada. In F. W. Parkay and G. E. Hall (Eds.), *Becoming a principal: The challenges of beginning leadership*. Boston: Allyn and Bacon.

LIDEN, R. C., and GRAEN, G. (1980). Generalizability of the vertical dyad linkage model of leadership. *Academy of Management Journal* 25: 451–465.

LIEBERMAN, A., Ed. (1988). *Building a professional culture in schools*. New York: Teachers College Press.

LIEBERMAN, A., SAXL, E.R., and MILES, M.B. (1988). Teacher Leadership: Ideology and practice. In A. Lieberman (Ed.), *Building a professional culture in schools*. New York: Teachers College Press.

LIEBERSON, S., and O'CONNOR, J. F. (1972). Leadership and organization performance: A study of large corporations. *American Sociological Review* 37: 117–130.

LIPHAM, J.A. (1981). *Effective principal, effective school*. Reston, VA: National Association of Secondary School Principals.

LIPHAM, J.A., and HOEH, J.A. (1974). *The principalship: Foundations and functions*. New York: Harper & Row.

LIPHAM, J.M., RANKIN, R.E., and HOEH, J.A. JR. (1985). *The principalship: Concepts, competencies, and cases*. New York: Longman.

LITTLE, J. W. (1982). Norms of collegiality and experimentation: Workplace conditions of school success. *American Educational Research Journal* 19(3): 325–340.

LITTLE, J. W. (1990a). The mentor phenomenon and the social organization of teaching. In C. B. Cazden (Ed.), *Review of research in education*, Vol. 16: 297–352. Washington, DC: American Educational Research Association.

LITTLE, J. W. (1990b). The persistence of privacy: Autonomy and initiative in teachers' professional relations. *Teachers College Record* 91: 509–536.

LORTIE, D.C. (1975). *Schoolteacher: A sociological study*. Chicago: University of Chicago Press.

LOUIS, M. R. (1980). Surprise and sense making: What newcomers experience in entering unfamiliar organizational settings. *Administrative Science Quarterly* 25(2): 226–251.

LOUIS, M. R., POSNER, B. Z., and POWELL, G. N. (1983). The availability and helpfulness of socialization practices. *Personnel Psychology* 36: 857–866.

MACPHERSON, R. J. (1984). On being and becoming an educational administrator: Some methodological issues. *Educational Administration Quarterly* 20(4): 58–75.

MANNING, P. K. (1977). Talking and becoming: A view of organizational socialization. In R. L. Blankenship (Ed.), *Colleagues in organizations*, 181–201. New York: Wiley.

MANZ, C. C., ADSIT, D., CAMPBELL, S., and MATHISON-HANCE, M. (1988). Managerial thought patterns and performance: A study of perceptual patterns of performance hindrances for higher and lower performing managers. *Human Relations* 41: 447–465.

MANZ, C. C., and SIMS, H. P., JR. (1987). Leading workers to lead themselves: The external leadership of self-managing work teams. *Administrative Science Quarterly* 32: 106–128.

MARCH, J.G. (1976). The technology of foolishness. In J. G. March and J. P. Olsen (Eds.), *Ambiguity and choice in organizations*, 69–81.

MARRION, B. (1983). A rationalistic study of the experiences of first-year elementary school principals. Doctoral dissertation. University of Colorado at Boulder, 1983. *Dissertation Abstracts International*, 44: 939-A.

MARTIN, W. J., and WILLOWER, D. J. (1981). The managerial behavior of high school principals. *Educational Administration Quarterly* 17: 69–90.

McCLEARY, L. E., and OGAWA, R. (1989). The assessment center process for selecting school leaders. *School Organisation* 9(1): 103–113.

McEACHERN, A. (1975). *Managerial control and performance.* Lexington, MA; Heath.

McENRUE, M.P. (1984). Perceived competence as a moderator of the relationship between role clarity and job performance: A test of two hypotheses. *Organizational Behavior and Human Performance*, 34: 479–486.

McGIVERN, C. (1978). The dynamics of management succession. *Management Decision* (U.K.) 16: 32–42.

McNEIL, E. B. (1969). *Human socialization.* Belmont, CA: Brooks/Cole.

McPHEE, J.H. (1966). *The Headmaster.* New York: Farrar, Straus and Giroux.

MEAD, G. H. (1934, 1962). *Mind, self, and society: From the standpoint of a social behaviorist.* Edited and with introduction by Charles W. Morris. Chicago: University of Chicago Press.

MERTON, R.K., (1957). *Social theory and social structure.* Glencoe, IL: Free Press.

MERTON, R.K. (1968). *Social theory and social structure* (ENL. ED) New York: Free Press.

MERTON, R. K., READER, G. G., and KENDALL, P. L. (1957). *The student physician.* Cambridge, MA: Harvard University Press.

METZ, M.H. (1978). *Classrooms and corridors: The crisis of authority in desegregated secondary schools.* Berkeley: University of California Press.

MEYER, P. S. (1979, July 18). The ITT coup: Why Harold Geneen got the board to strip power from Hamilton. *Wall Street Journal:* 1, 27.

MIKLOS, E. (1988). Administrator selection, career patterns, succession, and socialization. In N. J. Boyan (Ed.), *Handbook of research on educational administration*, 53–76. New York: Longman.

MINER, J.B., and MINER, M.G. (1977). *Personnel and industrial relations: A managerial approach.* New York: Macmillan.

MINTZBERG, H. (1973). *The nature of managerial work.* New York: Harper & Row.

MINTZBERG, H. (1983) *Power in and around organizations.* Englewood Cliffs, NJ: Prentice-Hall.

MISKEL, C., and COSGROVE, D. (1985). Leader succession in school settings. *Review of Educational Research* 55: 87–105.

MISKEL, C. G., and OWENS, M. (1983). Principal succession and changes in school coupling and effectiveness. Paper presented at the annual meeting of the American Educational Research Association, Montreal.

MONANE, J. H. (1967). *A sociology of human systems.* New York: Appleton-Century-Crofts.

MORELAND, R. L., and LEVINE, J. M. (1983). Socialization in small groups: Temporal changes in individual-group relations. *Advances in Experimental Social Psychology* 15: 137–192.

MORGAN, G. (1986). *Images of organization.* Thousand Oaks, CA: Sage.

MORTIMER, J. T., and LORENCE, J. (1979). Work experience and occupational value socialization: A longitudinal study. *American Journal of Sociology* 84: 1361–1385.

MURPHY, J. (1990). *The educational reform movement of the 1980s: Perspectives and cases.* Berkeley, CA: McCutchan.

MURPHY, J., and HALLINGER, P. (1988). Characteristics of instructionally effective school districts. *Journal of educational research* 81: 175–180.

MURPHY, M. J., HART, A. W., and WALTERS, L. C. (1989). *Satisfaction and intent to leave responses of new teachers in target populations under redesigned teacher work.* A paper presented at the annual meeting of the American Educational Research Association, San Francisco.

NATIONAL ASSOCIATION OF ELEMENTARY SCHOOL PRINCIPALS (1990). *Principals for twenty-first century schools.* Alexandria, VA: National Association of Elementary School Principals.

NATIONAL ASSOCIATION OF SECONDARY SCHOOL PRINCIPALS (1982). *The Effective Principal.* Reston, VA: National Association of Secondary School Principals.

NATIONAL COMMISSION FOR THE PRINCIPALSHIP (1990). *Principals for our changing schools: Preparation and certification.* Fairfax, VA: National Commission for the Principalship.

NATIONAL COMMISSION ON EXCELLENCE IN EDUCATION (1983). *A nation at risk.* Washington, DC: Government Printing Office.

NATIONAL COMMISSION ON EXCELLENCE IN EDUCATIONAL ADMINISTRATION (1987). *Leaders for America's schools.* Tempe, AZ: University Council for Educational Administration.

NATIONAL EDUCATION ASSOCIATION (1988). *Employee participation programs: Considerations for the school site.* Washington, DC: National Education Association.

NATIONAL GOVERNORS' ASSOCIATION, CENTER FOR POLICY RESEARCH AND ANALYSIS. (1986). *Time for results: The governor's 1991 report on education.* Washington, DC: National Governor's Association.

NATIONAL POLICY BOARD FOR EDUCATIONAL ADMINISTRATION (1989). *Improving the preparation of school administrators: An agenda for reform.* (May 1989). A report of the National Policy Board for Educational Administration, Charlottesville, VA: National Policy Board for Educational Administration.

NATIONAL POLICY BOARD FOR EDUCATIONAL ADMINISTRATION (1993). *Principals for our changing schools: The knowledge and skill base.* Fairfax, VA: National Policy Board of Educational Administration.

NICHOLSON, N. (1984). A theory of work role transitions. *Administrative Science Quarterly* 29: 172–191.

NICHOLSON, N., and WEST, M. A. (1988). *Managerial job change: Men and women in transition.* Cambridge: Cambridge University Press.

NICKOLSON, T., and IMLACK, R. (1981). Where do their answers come from? A study of the inferences which children make when answering questions about narrative stories. *Journal of Reading Behavior* 13: 111–129.

NOTA, B. (1988, August). The socialization process at high-commitment organizations. *Personnel:* 20–23.

O'CONNOR, E. J., and BARRETT, G. V. (1980). Informational cues and individual differences as determinants of subjective perceptions of task enrichment. *Academy of Management Journal* 22: 697–716.

OGAWA, R. T. (1991). Enchantment, disenchantment, and accommodation. How a faculty made sense of the succession of its principal. *Educational Administration Quarterly* 27: 30–60.

OGAWA, R. T., and POUNDER, D. G. (1991). The University of Utah's field-based doctoral program: A multi-dimensional approach to advanced administrative preparation. Paper presented at the 1991 University Council for Educational Administration Conference, Baltimore, MD.

OGAWA, R. T., and BOSSERT, S. T. (1990). Leadership as an organizational characteristic. Paper presented at the annual meeting of the American Educational Research Association, Boston, MA.

OGAWA, R. T., and HART, A. W. (1985). The effect of principals on the instructional performance of schools. *Journal of Educational Administration* 23(1): 59–72.

OGAWA, R. T., and SMITH, J. (1985). How a faculty made sense of the succession of its principal. Paper presented at the annual meeting of the American Educational Research Association, Chicago.

OLIVER, J. (forthcoming). *The professional socialization of principals.* Dissertation, Department of Educational Administration, University of Utah.

ORTIZ, F. I., and MARSHALL, C. (1988). Women in educational administration. In N. J. Boyan (Ed.), *Handbook of research on educational administration,* 123–142. New York: Longman.

ORTONY, A. (1975). Why metaphors are necessary, not just nice. *Education Theory* 25(1): 45–53.

OSKARSSON, H., and KLEIN, R. H. (1982). Leadership change and organizational regression. *International Journal of Group Psychotherapy* 32: 145–162.

OSTERMAN, K. F. (1989). Building a knowledge base from experience: An analysis of administrative problem-solving strategies. Paper presented at the annual meeting of the University Council for Educational Administration, Phoenix, AZ.

OWENS, R.G. (1987). *Organizational behavior in education.* Englewood Cliffs, NJ: Prentice Hall.

PAJAK, E. (1993). Change in continuity in supervision and leadership. In G. Cawelti (Ed.), *Challenges and achievements in American education.* The 1993 ASCD Yearbook.

PALONSKY, S.B. (1986). *900 shows a year: A look at teaching from a teacher's side of the desk.* New York: Random House.

PARKAY, F. W., and HALL, G. E., Eds. (1993). *Becoming a principal: The challenges of beginning leadership.* Boston: Allyn and Bacon.

PARKAY, F. W., CURRIE, G., and RHODES, J. W. (1992). Professional socialization: A longitudinal study of twelve high school principals. *Educational Administration Quarterly* 28(1): 43–75.

PARKAY, F. W., RHODES, J., CURRIE, G., and RAO, M. (1989). First time high school principals: Their characteristics and professional concerns. Paper presented at the annual meeting of the American Educational Research Association, San Francisco.

PATTERSON, J.P. A descriptive analysis of the instructional leadership activities of elementary principals. Doctoral dissertation, University of Oregon.

PEARSON, P. D., HANSEN, J., and GORDON, C. (1979). The effect of background knowledge on young children's comprehension of explicit and implicit information. *Journal of Reading Behavior* 11: 201–209.

PELLICER, L. O., ANDERSON, L. W., KEEFE, J. W., KELLEY, E. A., and McCLEARY, L. E. (1988). *High school leaders and their schools,* Vol. 2: *Profiles of effectiveness.* Reston, VA: National Association of Secondary School Principals.

PERSELL, C.H., COOKSON, P., and LYONS, H. (1982). *Effective principals: What do we know from various educational literatures?* Washington, DC: National Institute of Education.

PETERS, T.J., and WATERMAN, R.H., JR. (1982). *In search of excellence*. New York: Harper & Row.

PETERSON, K.D. (1978). The principal's tasks. *Administrator's Notebook* 26(8): 1–4.

PETERSON, K.D. (1989). *Secondary principals and instructional leadership: Complexities in a diverse role*. National Center for Effective Secondary Schools, University of Wisconsin—Madison.

PETERSON, M. F. (1985). Experienced acceptability: Measuring perceptions of dysfunctional leadership. *Group and Organization Studies* 10: 447–477.

PETTIGREW, A. (1979). On studying organizational cultures. *Administrative Science Quarterly* 24: 570–581.

PFEFFER, J. (1978). The micropolitics of organizations. In M. W. Meyer (Ed.), *Environments and organizations*, 29–50. San Francisco: Jossey-Bass.

PFEFFER, J. (1981). Management as symbolic action: The creation and maintenance of organizational paradigms. In L. L. Cummings and B. Staw (Eds.), *Research in organizational behavior*. Vol. 3: 1–52. Greenwich, CT: JAI Press.

PFEFFER, J., and DAVIS-BLAKE, A. (1986). Administrative succession and organizational performance; How administrator experience mediates the succession effect. *Academy of Management Journal* 29: 72–83.

PHILLIPS, J. S. (1984). The accuracy of leadership ratings: A cognitive categorization analysis. *Organizational Behavior and Human Performance* 33: 125–138.

PIERCE, P.R. (1934). The origin and development of the public school principals. Doctoral dissertation, University of Chicago.

PIERSON, P.R. (1989). *Analysis of elementary principals' use of humor in their interpersonal communications with teachers*. Doctoral dissertation, The Pennsylvania State University-University Park-Pa.

PITNER, N.J. (1988). The study of administrator effects and effectiveness. In N.J. Boyan (Ed.), *Handbook of research on educational administration*, 99–122. New York: Longman.

PITNER, N.J., and OGAWA, R. T. (1981). Organizational leadership: The case of the school superintendent. *Educational Administration Quarterly* 17: 45–66.

PLAYKO, M. A., and DARESH, J. C. (1989). Beginning principals: Entry year programs and principal development. Paper presented at the annual meeting of the University Council for Educational Administration, Phoenix, AZ.

POLANYI, M. (1966). *The tacit dimension*. New York: Doubleday.

PONDY, L. R., FROST, P. J., MORGAN, G., and DANDRIDGE, T. C., Eds. (1983). *Organizational symbolism*. Greenwich, CT: JAI Press.

PORTER, L. W., LAWLER, E. E., III, and HACKMAN, J. R. (1975). *Behavior in organizations*. New York: McGraw-Hill.

POUNDER, D. G. (1988). The male/female salary differential for school administrators: Implications for career patterns and placement of women. *Educational Administration Quarterly* 24: 5–20.

POUNDER, D. G. (1989). The gender gap in salaries of educational administration professors. *Educational Administration Quarterly* 25: 181–201.

PRESTINE, N. A., and LEGRAND, B. F. (1991). Cognitive learning theory and the preparation of educational administrators: Implications for practice and policy. *Educational Administratihon Quarterly* 27(1): 61–89.

PURKEY, S. C., and SMITH, M. S. (1983). Effective schools: A review. *Elementary School Journal* 83: 427–453.

RAMSAY, R., and WHITMAN, N. (1989). *A problem-based, student-centered approach to teaching geriatrics in the classroom: Guidelines and sample cases*. Cleveland, OH: The Western Reserve Geriatric Education Center.

REINGANUM, J. R. (1985). The effect of executive succession on stockholder wealth. *Administrative Science Quarterly* 30: 46–60.

REITZUG, U.C. (1994). A case study of empowering principal behavior. *American Educational Research Journal* 31(2): 283–307.

REITZUG, U.C., and REEVES, J.E. (1992). Miss Lincoln doesn't teach here: A descriptive narrative and conceptual analysis of a principal's symbolic leadership behavior. *Educational Administration Quarterly* 28(2): 185–219.

REYES, P. (1994). UCEA presidential address: 1993. *UCEA Review for Educational Administration* 35(1): 1, 11–13.

RICE, R.W., BENDER, L.R., and VITTERS, A.G. (1980). Leader sex, follower attitudes toward women, and leadership effectiveness: A laboratory experiment. *Organizational Behavior and Human Performance* 25: 46–78.

RICHARDS, E. W. (1984). Undergraduate preparation and early career outcomes: A study of recent college graduates. *Journal of Vocational Behavior* 24: 279–304.

RILEY, P. (1983). A structuralist account of political culture. *Administrative Science Quarterly* 28: 414–437.

ROBERTS, J. (1989a). Cultural orientations of first-time high school principals during selection and entry. Paper presented at the annual meeting of the American Educational Research Association, San Francisco.

ROBERTS, J. (1989b). Principal preparation: The school culture component. Paper presented at the annual meeting of the University Council for Educational Administration, Phoenix, AZ.

ROBERTS, J. (in press). Building the school culture. In F. W. Parkay and G. E. Hall (Eds.) *Becoming a principal: The challenges of beginning leadership.* Boston: Allyn and Bacon.

ROBERTS, J., and WRIGHT, L. V. (1989). A study of the change efforts among first-time high school principals. Paper presented at the annual meeting of the American Educational Research Association, San Francisco.

RODER, L., and PEARLMAN, D. (1989). Starting on the right foot: A blueprint for incoming principals. *NASSP Bulletin* 73 (519): 69–77.

ROSENBERG, M. (1979). *Conceiving the self.* New York: Basic Books.

ROSSMILLER, R.A., BREDESON, P.V., and FRUTH, M.J. (1993). *Implementing the effective schools process in the Chicago Public Schools: A report of findings of a feasibility study.* Report prepared for the Chicago Community Trust. Madison, WI: National Center for Effective Schools, Wisconsin Center for Education Research.

ROWAN, B., and DENK, C. E. (1984). Management succession, school socio-economic context, and basic skills attainment. *American Educational Research Journal* 21; 517–537.

SALAMAN, G. (1977). An historical discontinuity: From charisma to routinization. *Human Relations* 30: 373–388.

SALANCIK, G. R., and PFEFFER, J. (1978). A social information processing approach to job attitudes and task design. *Administrative Science Quarterly* 23: 224–253.

SALANCIK, G. R., and PFEFFER, J. (1980). Effects of ownership and performance on executive tenure in U.S. corporations. *Academy of Management Journal* 23: 653–664.

SAMUELSON, B. A., GALBRAITH, C. S., and McGUIRE, J. W. (1985). Organizational performance and top-management turnover. *Organization Studies* 6: 275–291.

SARBIN, T.R. (1954). Role theory. In G. Lindzey (Ed.), *Handbook of social psychology.* Cambridge, MA: Addison-Wesley.

SCHEIN, E. H. (1971). Occupational socialization in the professions: The case of the role innovator. *Journal of Psychiatric Research* 8: 521–530.

SCHEIN, E. H. (1985). *Organizational culture and leadership.* San Francisco: Jossey-Bass.

SCHEIN, E. H. (1986). A critical look at current career development theory and research.

In D. T. Hall and Associates (Eds.), *Career development in organizations,* 310–331. San Francisco: Jossey-Bass.

SCHON, D. A. (1983). *The reflective practitioner: How professionals think in action.* San Francisco: Jossey-Bass.

SCHON, D. A. (1987). *Educating the reflective practitioner.* San Francisco: Jossey-Bass.

SCHLECHTY, P. C., and VANCE, V. (1983). Recruitment, selection, and retention: The shape of the teaching force. *Elementary School Journal,* 83: 469–487.

SCOTT, W. R. (1982). Managing professional work: Three models of control for health organizations. *Health Services Research* 17: 213–240.

SCOTT, W. R. (1987). *Organizations: Rational, natural, and open systems,* (2d ed.) Englewood Cliffs, NJ: Prentice Hall.

SENGE, P.M. (1990). The leader's new work: Building learning organizations. *Sloan Management Review* Fall: 7–23.

SERGIOVANNI, T. (1987). *The principalship: A reflective practice perspective.* Boston: Allyn and Bacon.

SERGIOVANNI, T. J. (1991). *Value-added leadership: How to get extraordinary performance in schools.* San Diego: Harcourt, Brace, Jovanovich.

SERGIOVANNI, T.J. (1992). *Moral leadership.* San Francisco: Jossey-Bass.

SHAKESHAFT, C. (1989). *Women in educational administration* (2d ed.) Newbury Park, CA: Sage.

SHERMAN, J., SMITH, D., HOWARD, L., and MANSFIELD, E. R. (1986). The impact of emergent network structure on organizational socialization. *Journal of Applied Behavior Science* 22: 53–63.

SHIEVE, L.T., and SCHOENHEIT, M.B. (1987). Vision and the worklife of educational leaders. In 1987 ASCD Yearbook. *Leadership: Examining the elusive.* Virginia: ASCD.

SHORT, E.C. (1985). The concept of competence: Its use and misuse in education. *Journal of Teacher Education* 36(2): 2–6.

SIMON, H.A. (1957). *Administrative Behavior.* New York: Macmillan.

SIMON, H.A. (1993). Decision-making: Rational, non-rational, and irrational. *Educational Administration Quarterly* 29(3): 392–411.

SLAVIN, R.E. (1983). *Cooperative learning.* New York: Longman.

SMALL, J.F. (1974). Initiating and responding to social change. In J.A. Culbertson, C. Henson, and R. Marrison (Eds.), *Performance objectives for school principals: Concepts and instruments,* 18–53. Berkeley: McCutchan.

SMIRCICH, L. (1983). Concepts of culture and organizational analysis. *Administrative Science Quarterly* 28: 339–358.

SMIRCICH, L., and MORGAN, G. (1983). Leadership: The management of meaning. *Journal of Applied Behavioral Science* 18: 257–273.

SMITH, K. K., and SIMMONS, V. M. (1983). A Rumpelstiltskin organization: Metaphors on metaphors in field research. *Administrative Science Quarterly* 28: 377–392.

SMITH, M., and WHITE, M. C. (1987). Strategy, CEO specialization and succession. *Administrative Science Quarterly* 32: 263–280.

SMITH, P. B., and PETERSON, M. F. (1988). *Leadership, organizations and culture: An event management model.* London: Sage.

SMYLIE, M.A. (1992). Teacher participation in school decision making. EEPA.

SOLOMON, M. (1980). The role of products as social stimuli: A symbolic interactionism perspective. *Journal of Consumer Research* 10: 319–329.

SONNENFELD, J. (1986). Heroes in collision: Chief executive retirement and the parade of future leaders. *Human Resource Management,* Summer: 303–333.

SORENSEN, N. B. (1991). *Participative decision making in public schools: The effects of structural and process properties on the decision equilibrium in four decision content domains.*

Unpublished dissertation, The Department of Educational Administration, University of Utah.

STARBUCK, W. H., HEDBOERG, B. L. T., and GREVE, A. (1977). Responding to crises. In C. F. Smart and W. T. Stanbury (Eds.), *Studies on crisis management*, 111–137. Toronto: Institute for Research on Public Policy.

STEGNER, W.E. (1992). *Where the bluebird sings to the lemonade springs: Living and writing in the West.* New York: Random House.

STOGDILL, R.M. (1948). Personal factors associated with leadership: A survey of the literature. *Journal of Psychology* 25: 35–71.

STOGDILL, R.M. (1963). *Manual for the leader behavior description questionnaire—form XII.* Columbus, OH: Ohio State University, Bureau of Business Research.

STOGDILL, R. M. (1974). *Handbook of leadership: A survey of the literature.* New York: Free Press.

STOUT, R.T. (1993). Establishing the mission, vision and goals. In P.B. Forsyth, and M. Tallerico (Eds.), *City schools: Leading the way.* Newbury Park, CA: Corwin Press.

TAYLOR, F.W. (1911). *The principles of scientific management.* New York: Harper & Brothers.

TEAD, ORDWAY. (1935). *The Art of Leadership.* New York: McGraw-Hill.

TERBORG, J. R. (1977). Women in management: A research review. *Journal of Applied Psychology* 62: 647–664.

THOMPSON, J.D. (1967). *Organizations in action.* New York: McGraw-Hill.

THORUM, C.W. (1994). *Leadership and culture: A participant leader's perspective.* Unpublished dissertation, University of Utah, Department of Educational Administration.

TOFFLER, ALVIN. (1970). *Future Shock.* New York: Random House.

TURNER, J. (1988). *A theory of social interaction.* Stanford, CA: Stanford University Press.

TURNER, R. H., and COLOMY, P. (1988). Role differentiation: Orienting principles. In Lawler, E.J. (Ed.), *Advances in group processes.* Greenwich, CT: JAI Press.

TYACK, D., and HANSOT, E. (1982). *Managers of virtue: Public school leadership in America, 1820–1980.* New York: Basic Books.

UCEA KNOWLEDGE BASE PROJECT (1993). University Park, PA: University Council for Educational Administration.

UNIVERSITY COUNCIL FOR EDUCATIONAL ADMINISTRATION (1994). *IESLP student handbook.* University Park, PA: UCEA.

U.S. SENATE RESOLUTION 359. Washington, DC: U.S. Government Printing Office 1979.

VALENTINE, J. et al. (1981). *The middle level principalship*, Vol. 1. Reston, VA: NASSP.

VALVERDE, L. A. (1980). Promotion socialization: The informal process in large urban districts and its adverse effects on non-whites and women. *Journal of Educational Equity and Leadership* 1: 36–46.

VAN MAANEN, J. (1976). Breaking in: Socialization to work. In R. Dubin (Ed.), *Handbook of work, organization, and society*, 67–130. Chicago: Rand McNally.

VAN MAANEN, J. (1977). Experiencing organization: Notes on the meaning of careers and socialization. In J. Van Maanen (Ed.), *Organizational careers: Some new perspectives*, 15–45. New York: Wiley.

VAN MAANEN, J. (1978). People processing. *Organizational Dynamics* 7: 18–36.

VAN MAANEN, J., and SCHEIN, E. H. (1979). Toward a theory of organization socialization. In B. Staw (Ed.), *Research in organizational behavior*, Vol. 1: 209–264. Greenwich, CT: JAI Press.

VROOM, V. (1976). Leadership. In M. D. Dunnette (Ed.), *Handbook of industrial and organizational psychology*, 1527–1551. Chicago: Rand McNally.

WALBERG, H.J. (1990). Enhancing school productivity: The research bias. In P. Reyes (Ed.), *Teachers and their workplace: Commitment, performance, and productivity*, 277–296. Newbury Park, CA: Sage.

WANOUS, J. P. (1980). *Organizational entry: Recruitment, selection, and socialization of new-comers.* Reading, MA: Addison-Wesley.

WASLEY, P.A. (1991). *Teachers who lead: The rhetoric of reform and the realities of practice.* New York: Teachers College Press.

WATTS, W. D., SHORT, A. P., and WELL, C. B. (1987). Fitting the professional to the job: Idealism and realism. *The Journal of Student Financial Aid* 17: 22–30.

WEHLAGE, G.C. (1989). *Reducing the risk: Schools as communities of support.* London: Falmer Press.

WEICK, K. E. (1976). Educational organizations as loosely coupled systems. *Administrative Science Quarterly* 21: 1–19.

WEICK, K. E. (1978). The spines of leaders. In M. W. McCall, Jr., and M. M. Lombardo (Eds.), *Leadership: Where else can we go?*, 37–61. Durham, NC: Duke University Press.

WEIGEL, R., WISER, P., and COOKS, S. (1975). The impact of cooperative learning experiences on cross ethnic relations and attitudes. *Journal of Social Issues* 31: 218–245.

WEINDLING, D. (1991). Evolving leadership styles: A longitudinal study of headteachers in England and Wales. Paper presented at the annual meeting of the American Educational Research Association, Chicago, IL.

WEINDLING, D., and EARLEY, P. (1987). *Secondary headship: The first years.* Philadelphia, PA: NFER-Nelson.

WEISS, H. W. (1978). Social learning of work values in organizations. *Journal of Applied Psychology,* 63: 711–718.

WENTWORTH, W. M. (1980). *Context and understanding: An inquiry into socialization theory.* New York: Elsevier.

WEST, M. A., FARR, J. L., and KING, N. (1986). Innovation at work: Definitional and theoretical issues. Paper presented at the annual convention of the American Psychological Association, Washington, DC.

WHITE, J. K. (1978). Individual differences and the job quality-worker response relationship: Review, integration, and comments. *Academy of Management Journal,* 21: 36–43.

WIGGINS, T. (1970). Why our urban schools are leaderless. *Education and Urban Society* 2: 169–177.

WILSON, W. (1887). The study of administration. *Political Science Quarterly* 2: 197–222.

WITTROCK, M.C., Ed. (1986). *The handbook on research and teaching.* New York: Macmillan.

WOLCOTT, H.F. (1973). *The man in the principal's office: An Ethnography.* New York: Holt, Rinehart & Winston.

WORRELL, D. L., and DAVIDSON, W. N., III. (1987). The effect of CEO succession on stockholder wealth in large firms following the death of the predecessor. *Journal of Management* 13: 509–515.

WRIGHT, L. V. (1992). A study of supervisory priorities of first-time high school principals. In F. W. Parkay and G. E. Hall (Eds.), *Becoming a principal: The challenges of beginning leadership.* Boston: Allyn and Bacon.

YIN, R. K. (1985). *Case study research: Design and methods.* Beverly Hills, CA: Sage.

YOUNG, F. E., and NORRIS, J. A. (1988). Leadership change and action planning: A case study. *Public Administration Review* 48: 564–570.

YUKL, G. A. (1989). *Leadership in organizations* (2d ed.). Englewood Cliffs, NJ: Prentice Hall.

Name Index

Subject Index

313